Polish Pioneers in Illinois 1818–1850

5-6-2010

Polish Pioneers in Illinois

1818–1850

James D Lodesky

James D. Lodesky

Library of Congress Control Number:		2009906452
ISBN:	Hardcover	978-1-4415-5046-0
	Softcover	978-1-4415-5045-3

Cover Illustration by Richard Sperry

This book was printed in the United States of America.

To order additional copies of this book, contact:
Xlibris Corporation
1-888-795-4274
www.Xlibris.com
Orders@Xlibris.com
52829

Contents

Acknowledgments

Research assistants Mike Kozuch, Chicago, Illinois; Joseph Lodesky, Gurnee, Illinois; Zibigniew Wlodecki, Krakow, Poland.

Polish-Ukrainian guide and interpreter Marek Koblanski, Salt Lake City, Utah.

Computer aides Predrag and Tatjana Simic, Naperville, Illinois; Christine, Emma, and Lisa Lodesky, Naperville, Illinois.

Computer reclaimer Gerry Witt, Downers Grove, Illinois.

Typing assistants Crissy; Jennifer Kasheimer Puzzo, Lake Zurich, Illinois; John and Carol Kozuch, Gurnee, Illinois; Dan and Jean Klinesmith, Waukegan, Illinois.

These people gave me a place to stay while researching: Walt and Marie Dawson, Glen Carbon, Illinois; Roman and Marta Wolny, Olesno, Poland. Roman also helped me interpret Polish documents. Marinan, Anna, and Wiesia Koluz, Wadowice, Poland, Bill Bailey, Springfield IL.

Thanks to Al Westerman of Zion, Illinois, for his help with the Polish emigrants of Lake County.

Also the many helpful people at the Lisle Library, Lisle, Illinois, and the Fremont Public Library, Genealogical Society, especially Carol Knigge and Allen Ellis, the County Historical Societies throughout Illinois, the Polish Museum and Library of Chicago, and the Polish Genealogical Society of Chicago.

Foreword

The idea behind this book is to find out exactly how many Poles or people of Polish descent lived in Illinois before 1850, who they were, and when they came to the state. It is not intended to trace anyone's genealogy even though there are many in the book. I have added some people's genealogies which I found while researching, but the main focus is the amount of Polish emigration to Illinois before 1850.

The early Polish emigrants were called Polanders by their neighbors. The Polish "ski" name is used a lot, but a number of names end in "ske" or "sky" too. I have also found some names that I was sure were Polish but turned out to be Irish names ending in "ski" or "sky" like Comminski or Comisky. These types of Irish names have an "e" added to them nowadays which is located between the "k" and "y." Comisky is spelled Comiskey now, but in the eighteenth century the "e" was left out. A few German names also end in "ske," but they always seem to be much shorter names as compared to Polish names.

How I Became Polish

Now that I have your attention, let me explain. I have the blood of at least seven and probably eight different nationalities. My father's side considered themselves Polish in name only. The last Lodesky who was all Polish was my great-great-grandfather Franciszek Wlodecki. There were few Poles in America when he came here in 1834. Polish women were basically nonexistent in America. Franciszek was Catholic of course, and many of the Catholic churches in America were Irish Catholic churches. Franciszek married Ellen O'Sullivan in New York in 1835, and we fell in with the Irish for the next hundred years. Franciszek and Ellen moved to Warren Township in Lake County, Illinois, in 1844. The nearest Catholic church was St. Mary's (now Immaculate Conception), in Waukegan. My great-grandfather Frank Lodesky married Bridget McCarthy, a parishioner of Immaculate Conception. Their son, my grandfather Gene, married Calista Hoye, also of Irish descent and a parishioner of Immaculate Conception. This made my father seven-eighths Irish and one-eighth Polish. No wonder he considered himself Irish.

My father was the first person not to marry an Irish girl in three generations. My mother was half German and Dutch and half New England Yankee who definitely had Scottish, English, and Welch blood in her. This makes your author one-sixteenth Polish. So what nationally do I call myself? Why Polish of course. Here's why. I grew up during the heyday of Polak jokes. Having a "ski" last name made me instantly Polish, and I was routinely told Polak jokes and called a Polak by just about everyone. I have to confess that most people meant no harm by it and much of it was just good-natured kidding. There were some problems with the hillbillies at work, some of whom were downright hurtful. After finding out I was a Polak, I immediately started reading Polish history. This is natural for me since I love history. I found Polish history so interesting that I knew right away that I was going to like being Polish.

Years ago I began researching the Lodesky side of the family. The only book on early Polish history was "Polish Exiles in Illinois" by Mrs. Isaac Rawlings and written in 1927. Most Illinois historians thought that there were only a few Poles living in Illinois in the 1830s and 1840s, but Mrs. Isaac Rawlings changed history by finding more. I was disappointed to find nothing in her book about my ancestor Franciszek. While checking other sources, I kept finding other Poles not mentioned in the book either and soon realized there were a lot more Poles in Illinois than anyone thought. I have much more information available to me now than Mrs. Rawlings did in 1927. My book is more like an updated version of her book and begins were she left off. Mrs. Rawlings contains information on fifteen different Poles living in Illinois before 1850. These fifteen were the parents of forty children, which means Mrs. Rawlings found about fifty-five people with ties to Poland in Illinois before 1850. Most but not all their children were born before 1850. I have added to their stories when possible.

List of Poles in the book "Polish Exiles in Illinois" by Mrs. Isaac Rawlings:

Alexander Bielaski
Ludwik Chlopicki
Joseph Colclonzhh
Antoni Guyoski
Dr. Alfonso Xavier Illinski
Napoleon Koscialowski
Edward Mlodianowski
Pavel Sobelewski
Isaac Sandusky
Charles Sominski

George Suprunowski
Ludwik Turowski
Longin Joseph Wronowski
Dr. Christian Zabriskie
Elias Zabriskie

You will see a lot of mentions in this book about the 234 Polish exiles from Trieste. The exiles were all soldiers in the 1830 Polish uprising against Russia and were the first large emigration of Poles to America. The first two shiploads of exiles containing 234 men and one woman arrived in New York on March 28, 1834. More exiles followed on other ships until about 425 exiles made the trip here. My ancestor Franciszek was a passenger on one of the first two ships.

The exiles came from a number of different Polish armies. The Polish rebellion against Russia started November 29, 1830, and ended October 18, 1831. During and after the war, a number of Polish armies crossed the Russian-Austrian border into the former Polish province of Galicia to escape the large Russian armies. Much of the population of Galicia were Poles, so the soldiers felt right at home there. The Austrians did not know what to do with all the Polish soldiers and had no set policy to handle them all. Sometimes the Austrians arrested all the officers but at other times they let everyone go back to Poland and continue to fight in the war. Some soldiers like Franciszek spent two years in Austrian prisons. After the rebellion, many Polish soldiers remained in Austria. The Austrians ordered them all to leave and go back to either Russia or France. Some did go to France, but a number of Poles ignored the order.

Even though the last rebellion had failed, a Pole named Zalivski was soon trying to organize another rebellion. Zalivski was instrumental in starting the 1830 rebellion as well. His second attempt was a complete fiasco. The Polish soldiers still in Austria took part and again the Austrians ordered them to leave the country. This time those who refused to leave were arrested and sent to prison near the city of Brno, Moravia, in the present Czech Republic. Austria ruled the region at the time. Those Poles arrested two years earlier were already imprisoned in or on their way to Brno. At first the Austrians told the Poles they were sending them all to France. The French would not take them. No other European country would take them either except Russia. On August 1, 1833, the Austrians began interviewing the Poles. This time they were given the option of either going back to Russia or going to America. Going back to Russia was suicide, so the only choice was America. The Poles did not want to go to America either because it was too far away and they wanted to stay in Europe and continue the fight against Russia.

On August 14, 1833, the Austrians sent about three hundred Poles to the sea port of Trieste, Italy. Although Trieste is in Italy, it was ruled by Austria at the time. The first two shiploads, carrying the worst of the Polish insurrectionists left Trieste on November 22, 1833. The 234 exiles arrived in New York on March 28, 1834. They all wished to stay together in America and create a Polish settlement. The exiles petitioned the United States government for a tract of land soon after landing, and President Andrew Jackson signed the bill "Donation of Lands to Polish Patriots" on June 30, 1834. I write a more in-depth story of the Polish land grant in my stories about Winnebago and Woodford counties. To make a long story short, the exiles never got the land tract for a variety of reasons. They all dispersed in different directions and made new lives for themselves.

I found records of 35 Polish exiles from Trieste in Illinois before 1850. Thirty-one were passengers on the first two ships of 234 exiles. The other four came from Trieste on later ships. In addition, the Polish exiles from Trieste were the fathers of 102 children in Illinois.

List of 234 Polish exiles from Trieste who left a record of themselves in Illinois before 1850:

Felix Boczkiewiez (Marion County)
Alexander Bilinski (Lake County)
Ludwik Chlopicki (Tazewell, Peoria, and Woodford counties)
Theodore Dombski (Lake County)
Vincent Dziewanowski (Joe Daviess County)
Francis Jasinski (Winnebago and De Kalb counties)
Stefan Gasiorowski (Lake County)
Antoni Gajkowski (Fayette County)
Julian Hulanicki (city of Chicago and Iroquois counties)
Dr. Alfonso Xavier Illinski (St. Clair County)
Joseph Jablonski (St. Clair County)
Nicholas Jaworski (Lee County)
Thomas Jaworski (cook and city of Chicago)
Napoleon Kosialowski (Morgan County)
Joseph Krakowski (Joe Daviess County)
Kurlowicz (city of Chicago)
Marcin Lewkowicz (Alexander County)
Stanislaus Lisiecki (Lake County)
Alexander Materski (St. Clair County)
Edward Mlodzianowski (Morgan County)
Pawlinski (city of Chicago)
Maximilian Pendzinski (Marion and Madison counties)

Edward Polkowski (Peoria County)
Anton Poniatowski (St. Clair County)
Teofil L. Rutkowski (St. Clair County)
Jan Rychlicki (Woodford County)
Pavel Sobelewski (Boone County)
Michael Sodowski (city of Chicago)
Franciszek Wlodecki (Lake County)
Longin Joseph Wnorowski (Marion County)
Alexander Zakezewski (city of Chicago)

Polish exiles from Trieste who came on later ships:

Joseph Baranowski (Randolph County)
Basil Jaroshinski (Lake County)
George Suprunowski (St. Clair and Shelby counties)
Stefan Wyszomirski (Madison County)

I had to divide the rest of the Poles in this book into a number of different categories. Twenty Polish emigrants settled in Illinois before 1850. Nineteen men and one woman who were the parents of twenty children.

Louis Annet (St. Clair County)
Alexander Bielaski (Effingham County)
M. Cattinsky (city of Chicago)
Christina Cronkosky (city of Chicago)
William Hall (Randolph County)
Andrew Johnson (Morgan County)
Otto Kaminski (Randolph County)
Kukkosky (city of Chicago)
John J. Lehmanowski (Montgomery County)
Captain Joseph Napieralski (city of Chicago)
Alexander Niewiardowski (Madison County)
Stephen Owaska (city of Chicago)
S. Poniatowski (Will County)
Jean Powlowiez (Hancock County)
John Seick (Logan County)
John Sieawski (city of Chicago)
Rudolf Soloski (Joe Daviess County)
Captain Bernard Stempoffski (city of Chicago)
Charles Szirkowski (St. Clair and Randolph counties)
Edward Wodetsky (Logan County)

Polish Jews in Illinois before 1850 numbered twenty-three men and four women who were the parents of eight children.

John Bauman (city of Chicago)
J. Isaac Cohen (city of Chicago)
Michael Cohen (Green County)
N. Cohen and wife (city of Chicago)
Gabriel Goldburgh (Wabash Country)
M. Goodman (city of Chicago)
Solomon and Hanna Harris (Adams County and city of Chicago)
Maurice Jacobs (Adams County)
J. Kenny (city of Chicago)
William Laniden (Adams County)
Isaac Levi (Adams County and city of Chicago)
E. Long (city of Chicago)
James Marks (city of Chicago)
Samuel and Sarah Marks (Adams County and city of Chicago)
Maxwell (Hancock County)
John Morris (La Salle County)
Aaron Neustadt (La Salle County)
J. and Eutrine Nithorowsky (city of Chicago)
Oppenheim (La Salle County)
Louis Reubin (Adams County)
Casper Sommerfield (Adams County and city of Chicago)
David Witkowski (city of Chicago)
J. Conrad Wovlbiske (city of Chicago; Conrad might be David Witkowski's brother)

Illinois had 7 different groups of families of Polish descent which numbered 22 people. These were people who had a parent, grandparent, etc., from Poland. Between them all, there were 110 children for a total population of 132 before 1850. By groups I mean a number of related families using the same last name. Most people of Polish descent were members of the Sandusky family.

Mary Jane Aversky (Hancock County)
Abigail Awadawski (Hancock County)
Samuel Baum (Vermilion)
Margaret Everdiska (Hancock County)
Hanson Minsky (Lake County)

Robert Minsky (Lake County)
Elijah Probasco (Tazewell County)
Jacob Probasco (Tazewell County)
Peter Probasco (Tazewell County)
Samuel Probasco (Tazewell County)
Samuel Probasco (Tazewell County)
Samuel Probasco (Tazewell County)
James Reed (Sangamon County)
Abraham Sandusky (Vermilion County)
Abraham Sandusky Jr. (Vermilion County)
Elizabeth Sandusky (Tazewell County)
Isaac Sandusky (Vermilion County)
Jacob Sandusky (Green and Morgan counties)
James Sandusky (Vermilion County)
John Sandusky (Franklin County)
Josiah Sandusky (Vermilion County)
Josiah Sandusky (Vermilion County)
Killion Sandusky (Franklin County
William Sandusky (Vermilion County)
William H. Sandusky (Tazewell County)
William T. Sandusky (Shelby and Vermilion counties)
Harvey Sodowsky (Vermilion County)
Dr. Christian Zabriskie (Morgan County)
Elias Zabriskie (Morgan County)
Jacob Zabriskie (Morgan County)
Lewis Curtiss Zabriskie (Hancock County)

Six emigrants with German last names claimed to be born in Poland. They were the fathers and mother of five children.

Julius Bamberger (Jackson County)
Andrew and Mary Hohn (St. Clair County)
Adolph Kettz (Adams County)
Harris Leib (Adams County)
William Steine (Adams County)

The last category is those persons with Polish-looking last names. I cannot determine if they are Polish, but from the looks of their names there is good reason to believe they are. There were twenty-five men and five women in this category. Also three children.

Jacob Artenbuski or Froscoboski (city of Chicago)
Stanislaus Bielansky (Winnebago County)
William Blocki (city of Chicago)
Michael Collinski (city of Chicago)
Nicholas Darsula (Tazewell County)
August Duda (Monroe County)
Basil Ignatius Joursky (city of Chicago)
Thomas Giawaski (city of Chicago)
Stefan Jankiewicz (Shelby County)
Charles Kalowsky (Monroe County)
Ferdinand Krizoski (city of Chicago)
John Kulozjcky (city of Chicago)
John Latzky (city of Chicago)
Michriski (city of Chicago)
Matthew Mileusky (Alexander County)
Francis Muliski (Green and Jersey counties)
A. Panakaske (city of Chicago)
John Polaski (Green and Jersey counties)
Anthony Polenski (city of Chicago)
Matthieu Maximilian Potocki (Hancock County)
Charles Pznosovsky (city of Chicago)
Ferdinand Sebisky (city of Chicago)
Snyseski (city of Chicago; this might be a poor spelling of Sodowski)
Alexander Vandebesky (Joe Daviess County)
J. Zoliski (city of Chicago)

Women

Nancy Annosky (city of Chicago)
Cynthia Ann Labieskei (Adams County)
Barbara Levanbrske (city of Chicago
Sarah Ann Meskie (Alexander County)
Paulina Silcosky (St. Clair County)
Brazila Weiska (city of Chicago)

Adding up all the categories and their offspring just mentioned comes to 387 people in Illinois with some type of connections with Poland before 1850. These people lived in thirty-five different counties or about a third of the counties in Illinois before 1850. Most but not all their children were born before 1850. A reasonable figure of 325 Poles and their descendants lived in Illinois before 1850.

Map of Illinois

Poles pioneers lived in shaded areas

Zabriskie

Illinois had some members of the well-known Olbracht Zabriskie family living in the state before 1850. The Zabriskies are one of the oldest Polish families in the country, emigrating here in 1662. They have a two-volume book containing the genealogies of 18,280 Zabriskies who were born or died in America since coming to this country. Most of my information about them comes from this book. Originally, the name was spelled Zaborowski, but records from the state of New Jersey contain over one hundred spellings for the name. Two different groups of Zabriskies lived in Illinois, one in Morgan County, and the other in Hancock County. You will find their stories in those two counties. The Morgan County Zabriskies were the descendants of Olbracht's son Jan, his grandson Christian, and his great-grandson Jacob C. The Hancock County Zabriskies were descendants of Olbracht's son Christian, his grandson Hendrick, and great-grandson Christian. I wrote down their family tree as accurate as possible but good luck understanding it.

Olbracht, also called Albrecht, was born around 1638 in the present country of Kaliningrad, Russia. Kaliningrad is a small territory located on the Baltic Sea between Poland and Lithuania. At the time of Olbracht's birth, the German state of Prussia ruled the territory around Kaliningrad. Olbracht might have had some German blood in him. He was not Catholic like most Poles but rather a member of the Lutheran Church. He was probably Polish nobility and might have been highly educated. As a young man, Olbracht attended a Lutheran college in Amsterdam, Holland, but dropped out after a short time for lack of interest. He went back home and either enlisted or was drafted into the Prussian Army. There are two stories about what happened next. The first story claims that Olbracht deserted the Prussian Army when Prussia allied itself with Sweden and invaded Poland in 1655. He went back to Amsterdam and finally to America. The second story writes that Olbracht was a member of a band of nonconformists who chose to leave Poland in 1658 with a group of heretics known as Arians. They went to Amsterdam for a short time and then to America.

The Dutch East India Company first came to America in 1609. The Dutch founded New Amsterdam in 1624, but lost the region to the British in 1664. Soon after, the British renamed New Amsterdam New York. By this time, the Dutch had already settled all along the Hudson River as well as parts of New Jersey. In May of 1662, Olbracht left Amsterdam for America on board the ship *D' Vos* (*Fox*). After a short stay-over in England, D' Vos set sail for America in the middle of June. They arrived at New Amsterdam on August 31, 1662.

Olbracht settled down among the Dutch and spent the next ten years moving around their settlements. He settled down for good when he married a Dutch girl named Machtelt Vanderlinde on December 17, 1676. Olbracht was thirty-eight years old, while his bride was sixteen, a twenty-two-year difference, nothing! The marriage produced five sons: Jacob, born April 12, 1679; Jan and Joost, dates of birth unknown; Christian, born June 2, 1694; and Hendrick, born November 1, 1696. The Zabriskies continued to marry in with the Dutch and over time considered themselves Dutch.

After marrying, Olbracht bought up lands between the Hudson and Hackensack rivers and became a farmer/planter. He bought and sold land a number of times before settling down for good around Hackensack, New Jersey. Once in Hackensack, Olbracht bartered with an Indian tribe in 1702 for ownership of 2,100 acres of land located next to some land he already owned. Olbracht might have lived with an Indian tribe for a time. He could speak an Indian language and was an interpreter in the years 1679 and 1709. His oldest son Jacob also lived with the tribe for some time. Jacob might have been kidnapped by them so might have been living there against his will.

Olbracht died September 1, 1711. The date of Machtelt's death is not known, but is thought to be sometime after 1725. The summary in The Zabriskie family writes,

> Albert, though not the first of the Polish settlers in the United States, will always be an important figure in the Polish immigration. He was humane toward the Indians, loyal to the white settlers; he helped build communities with his spirit and hard work, never marring the good name of Poland by a bad deed. He beat the path for succeeding generations, and fathered a Polish American family that became one of the most prominent in the United States.[1]

Olbracht's son Jan, the progenitor of the Morgan County Zabriskies, was born in Hackensack, Bergen County, New Jersey. He was a farmer and

---

[1] George Olin Zabriskie, The Zabriskie Family: [Copyright, 1963 by George Olin Zabriskie] p. 9.

owned land all over Bergen County, New Jersey, and Rockland County, New York. Jan was married twice; his first wife died after six years of marriage. His first marriage was to Elizabeth Romeyn on September 20, 1706. Four children were born from the marriage: Albert J. baptized August 24, 1707; Christina, born March 3, 1709; Machtelt, baptized November 9, 1710; and Claes, baptized May 4, 1712. Elizabeth died in 1712 in Hackensack, New Jersey.

Jan's second marriage occurred December 6, 1712, to Margrietje Durie. Nine children were born from this marriage: Elizabeth, baptized June 27, 1714; Jan J., baptized August 5, 1716; Jacob J., baptized November 29, 1718; Peter, baptized November 5, 1721; Joost, baptized September 22, 1723, but died soon after; Joost, baptized September 14, 1727; Rachel, baptized September 7, 1729; Cornelius, baptized April 10, 1732; and Christian J., baptized May 5, 1734. Jan died around 1765. The Morgan County Zabriskies' line came from Jan's youngest son Christian J., born from his second marriage.

The Revolutionary War split Jan's family. His son Peter sided with the American colonists. General Washington used Peter's home in Hackensack as headquarters for one night during the American withdrawal from New York. Peter continued to help the American cause until the British arrested him in 1780. He was imprisoned in New York City at Sugar House Prison for an undetermined amount of time. Jan's brother John and son Christian J. were both loyalists. Christian J. was the progenitor of the Morgan County Zabriskies' line. Both had their property seized for their support of Britain. John's house was handed over to the famous Baron Von Steuben and from then on known as the Von Steuben house.

Christian J. was born in Hackensack, Bergen County, New Jersey, but moved to New Barbados Township as an adult. He married Lena Van Voorhees on February 18, 1753. The marriage produced five children: Albert C., born July 9, 1755; Margrietje, born July 13, 1758, died four years later; John C., born January 18, 1764; Jacob C., born December 4, 1767; and Margrietje, born February 19, 1775. Christian only lived to be forty-four years old. The loyalist Christian died on of all days July 4, 1778, a year before his property was seized by the United States on November 5, 1779.

Next on the Morgan County, line is Christian's son Jacob C. Jacob, was born in Hackensack, Bergen County, New Jersey. He married Maria Brevoort on December 28, 1797. Eleven children were born from this marriage: Elias, born April 5, 1799, but died September 29, 1800; Christian, born June 29, 1801; James, born January 22, 1804; John, born March 20, 1806; Henry, born December 5, 1808; Jacob Brinkerhofff, born May 24, 1811; Maria, born July 2, 1813; Jacob Westervelt, born April 11, 1817, and his twin brother Albert, born April 11, 1817; Helen, born October 10, 1819; and Catherine, born

June 14, 1822. Two of Jacob's children came to Morgan County, Christian and Jacob Westervelt. Christian became a doctor and served in the Mexican War. Jacob Westervelt was a captain during the Mexican War and died at the Battle of Buena Vista. The rest of their stories are in my article about Morgan County.

Olbracht's son Christian was the progenitor of the Hancock County Zabriskies. He lived in Paramus, New Jersey, all his life and was a farmer by trade. Christian married Leah Hopper May 28, 1715, in Hackensack, New Jersey. Five children were born from the marriage: Albert C., born September 2, 1716; Hendrick C., born April 1718; Jacob, born January 22, 1721, but died soon after; Jacob C., born December 22, 1724; and Andries, born December 22, 1724. Christian was a religious man and served as a church elder a number of years. He died June 7, 1774. The Hancock County Zabriskies are the descendants of his son Hendrick C.

Hendrick C. was born in Paramus, New Jersey. His occupation was farmer. Hendrick was married twice, first to Neesje van Horn and second to Maria Haring. He married Neesie Van Horn May 12, 1743. They were the parents of three children: Leah, born June 7, 1744; Dirck, born September 2, 1745; and Geertje, born November 5, 1750. There is no information about what happened to Neesje.

His second marriage to Maria Haring occurred August 31, 1753. Their marriage produced eight children: Christian, born September 19, 1754; Martyntje, born May 27, 1756; Neesje, born January 7, 1759; Margrietje, born March 3, 1762; Maria, born August 13, 1765; Sarah, born June 19, 1768; Abraham, born December 22, 1771; and Elizabeth, born August 8, 1774. The Hancock Zabriskies trace their line to Christian, the oldest son from Hendrick's second marriage to Maria.

History of the Zabriskie family considers Hendrick a neutral in the Revolutionary War. The war had to have really messed Hendrick up. His nephew Albert was a loyalist zealot who joined the British Army and became a spy. The State of New Jersey fixed Albert; they seized his property June 10, 1779. Hendricks brother Jacob C. was the complete opposite of Albert. He was so enthusiastic for the American cause that he was known as "King Jacob." Jacob was the owner of a Mill on the Saddle River in New Jersey known as Zabriskie mills. During the Revolutionary War, his nephew Albert, the spy, urged the British to confiscate it. Lucky for Jacob the British left it alone. However, he was arrested by the British on May 11, 1778, and sent to Provost Prison in New York City. While in Prison, a mob of British loyalists broke in and stabbed Jacob fifteen times. Jacob survived and lived until April 14, 1804. Hendricks brother Albert C. had his property seized by the British in November 1776. What the British could not take, they razed.

Hendricks son Christian was born in Paramus, New Jersey. Christian was the restless type and moved frequently. While still young, he moved to Pennsylvania. During the Revolutionary War, he was a member of the Pennsylvania Militia. Christian stayed in Pennsylvania when the war ended and bought a farm in Monroe County. He met Elizabeth Morgan while serving in the militia and married her on October 17, 1784. Christian and Elizabeth were the parents of five children: Sarah, born June 6, 1786; Henry, born August 11, 1788 (Henry was the ancestor of the Hancock County, Illinois, Zabriskie's) Maria, born April 11, 1792; Lewis, born March 8, 1796; and Abraham, born November 21, 1799.

Christian resided in Pennsylvania until 1799, and then bought a farm in Cayuga County, New York. He lived there until 1814, and then moved west to Anderson Township, Ohio. A couple years later, he moved west to Lawrence County, Indiana. By 1823, he was on the move again, this time west to Vermilion County, Indiana. Christian died in Vermilion County on September 26, 1830. Elizabeth died December 6, 1823, in Lawrence County, Indiana.

Christian's son Henry was born in Northampton County, Pennsylvania. His father Christian moved the family to Cayuga County, New York, in 1799. Henry enlisted in the New York State Militia during the War of 1812 and held the rank of private. He married Eleanor Galpin in New York, but the date of their marriage is unknown. Five children were born: twin sisters Cynthia and Matilda, born May 11, 1811; Sarah Elizabeth, born August 8, 1814; Lewis Curtis, born September 17, 1817; and Huldah, date of birth unknown. Henry was married twice. Something must have happened to Eleanor, but there is no information about what it was.

Henry's second marriage was to Nancy Newgin, date unknown. Their marriage produced seven more children: Zeno, born October 23, 1825; Jerome, born January 24, 1828; Charles, born November 9, 1829; Napoleon Bonaparte, born December 19, 1831; Abraham, born September 8, 1833; Alma, born August 19, 1835; and Susanne, born April 3, 1840.

Henry was restless just like his dad. Not only did he move a number of times, he set his family on a new course by converting to the Mormon faith. Henry moved to Hamilton County, Ohio, in 1814. A couple of years later, he was living in Lawrence County, Indiana. In 1823, they moved to Vermilion County, Indiana. His father Christian moved to Vermilion County the same year. While in Vermilion County, Henry and Nancy made a major lifestyle change; they converted to the Mormon faith on August 11, 1832. The family moved to the Mormon settlement at Clay County, Missouri, in 1836. Two years later during the winter of 1838-39, the Mormons were expelled from Missouri and fled to Illinois. Henry did not leave Missouri at this time. He was imprisoned for a time with some of the heads of the Mormon Church, including Joseph Smith, before leaving the state.

Most Mormons settled in Illinois after leaving Missouri, but Henry settled in Lee County, Iowa, across the Mississippi River from Nauvoo. Nauvoo was the de facto capital of the Mormons in Illinois. Two of Henry's sons also lived in the area near him, Lewis Curtis and Zeno. On August 10, 1845, Henry was appointed a high priest of the Mormon Church. The Mormon Church was run out of Illinois in 1846. Most Mormons left the state at that time and made the journey west to Utah. Henry left Lee County, Iowa, in 1846 and moved to the town of Council Bluffs on the western side of Iowa. He lived there three years, and then moved west to Provo, Utah. Henry died December 13, 1857. Nancy died March 17, 1879.

In some ways, the Zabriskies remind me of my own family. The Zabriskies married in with the Dutch and over time became Dutch. My family married in with the Irish and by the third generation considered themselves Irish. Both of our last names underwent a number of different spellings before settling on their permanent spelling. When it comes to reproducing though, the Zabriskies have us beat by a mile.

Sandusky and Baum

The Sanduskys and the Zabriskies are two of oldest and most well-known families of Polish descent in America. The Sanduskys are the first family of Polish descent in Illinois, and the most numerous before 1850. I have found them living all over the state, but Vermillion County had the largest and most influential number of them. Polish history books and magazines have written about the Sanduskys for years. The first Illinois census in 1818 contains the name of John Sandusky, and every Illinois census since then has had someone of Polish descent listed on it. The Baums claimed to be the descendants of Polish nobility and were early settlers in Vermilion County. The Baums and Sanduskys intermarried with each other a number of times.

According to Sue E. Watkins, Antoni Sadowski was the first Sandusky in America and the progenitor of the Sandusky family. His family was minor nobility, and he was born in Gostyl, Poland, in 1669. Antoni and his brother were in the Polish Army when the Great Northern War started in 1700. Both were stationed at Riga when the Swedish Army attacked. Antoni's brother was killed during the assault, and Antoni was captured by a "press-gang," which tried to force him to join the Swedish Army. Antoni declined to enlist in the Swedish Army. or tell the Swedes any information about the Polish Army. The Swedes were supposed to have tortured him on the rack, but he still refused to cooperate with them. They sent him to a prison ship where he managed to escape.

No one is sure when Antoni first came to America. He married Marya Bordt in New Jersey sometime between 1704 and 1706. The marriage produced five children. Only three lived past their youth: Andrew, Sofia, and Ann. The first record of Antoni in America is May 21, 1709. On that date, he testified for the will of Benjamin Cook in Freehold, New Jersey. Antoni might have worked as a farmer in New Jersey. He did not stay in New Jersey long, and in 1712, he bought four hundred acres of land along the banks of the Schuylkill River in the Pennsylvania wilderness.

In Pennsylvania, Antoni established a farm and took up a different occupation. He became an Indian trader, starting a trading post at Shamokin, Pennsylvania. Antoni also learned the ways of the local Indian tribes and became fluent in the Delaware and Iroquois languages. He assisted the local colonial government as a go-between in their dealings with the Indians. In 1734, Antoni became a naturalized British citizen. Antoni died in 1736, but he was not forgotten. On April 20, 1969, the governor of Pennsylvania established "Anthony Sadowski day." Five hundred people attended the ceremony at St. Gabriel's cemetery in Douglassville, Pennsylvania. Part of the ceremony included the unveiling of a statue of Anthony Sadowski. A speaker at the ceremony also read a letter sent by President Richard Nixon to the proceedings. Written on Antoni's monument are the words "Here lies the greatest Polish frontiersman of colonial times, an organizer of Amity Township in 1719, and founder of the Sandusky family in America."[2]

Antoni's son, Andrew, does not have nearly as much written about him as his father. Andrew was a surveyor by trade. His wife's name was Catherine, last name unknown. Seven children were born from their marriage: Samuel, born in 1746; Emanuel, born in 1747; Jacob, born in 1750; James, born in 1751; Jonathan, born in 1756; Anthony, born in 1758; and Hannah, born in 1763. Andrew inherited all of Antoni's land, which had grown to five hundred acres at the time of Antoni's death. In 1748, Andrew sold all his land to George Boone, the grandfather of Daniel Boone, and relocated to the Shenandoah Valley in Virginia. Andrew's grandson Ephraim claimed that Andrew was murdered in 1774.

> Andrew Sowdusky, my grandfather, was watching a lick to catch their horses that were running at large in the mountains. Another man was with him. When the Indians came on them he saw a white man, whom he knew, and thought he would be safe with. That very man tomahawked and killed him, probably fearing he would make disclosures on him.[3]

Over the years, all of Andrew's children would leave Virginia and settle in Kentucky. James and Jacob left for Kentucky first. James was a member of the first group of surveyors to claim land in Kentucky in 1773. In 1774, James and Jacob were working as surveyors in Kentucky for the Fincastle Surveying Company. The company had worked their way to the mouth of the Kentucky River by May 13, 1774. At this point, eleven members of the group

---

2 Sue E. Watkins, The Sandusky Story: [Polish Museum and Library: Chicago, Illinois 1983] p. 12.

3 Sue E. Watkins, p. 15.

parted company with the main body and left for Harrodsburg, Kentucky, James being one of them. Harrodsburg was the first settlement in Kentucky and was under construction at the time.

The main group kept on working with the intension of surveying up to the Falls of the Ohio River. The work was almost completed when a war party of Shawnee Indians showed up. The surveyors divided into three groups and left the area. The group in which Jacob belonged was under the direction of John Floyd. The governor of Virginia, Lord Dunmore, got wind of a possible Indian war and dispatched Daniel Boone and Michael Stoner to forewarn the surveyors. Boone arrived too late. The surveyors had already found out for themselves about the Indians and were gone.

Jacob's group went to Harrodsburg but found the settlement destroyed. They found evidence that Indians were still in the area and decided to leave as fast as possible. The group made their way to the Ohio River and found some canoes there. It was too dangerous to go east, so they went west. They went all the way to the Mississippi River, turned south, and sailed downriver to New Orleans. In New Orleans, a ship captain chanced to hear their story and offered them passage on his ship, which was leaving for New York. After arriving in New York, Jacob made his way back to Virginia. The whole time this event was unfolding, Jacob's family did not know if he was dead or alive. According to his grandson, Jacob caused quite a stir when he came home with a beard and wearing buckskins.

James Sandusky returned to Kentucky in March 1775 with a party under the direction of Captain James Harrod. They rebuilt Harrodsburg, this time with much stronger fortifications. For a time, there was a dispute as to which settlement was older, Boonesboro or Harrodsburg. Daniel Boone established Boonesboro. The dispute was resolved after researchers found that the rebuilding of Herrodsburg began twenty days before the construction of Boonesboro started. Jacob did not stay home long; he was back in Kentucky by 1775.

The population of Harrodsburg must have grown extremely fast. By 1776, James Sandusky already considered it too confining for him. He set out from Harrodsburg with the idea of building his own fort and found the perfect spot in a valley alongside a creek, which he named Pleasant Run Creek. The location was a little farther from the fort than he had planned, but he liked the site. James went back to Harrodsburg and recruited Jacob and some friends to help construct the fort. Jacob decided to settle there as well, and the fort became known as Sandusky Station. Baylor wrote a description of James Sandusky in early times in Washington County, Kentucky. "He was dressed in the usual pioneer style of the day. James wore a hunting shirt, overalls, leggins and moccasins, with a handkerchief tied around his head.

Besides his rifle he carried a knife which he used for scalping purposes as well as any Indian."[4]

Baylor also goes on to say that Sandusky Station was widely known to the early settlers of Nelson, Washington, and Marion Counties. Most stayed at the fort on the way to their future homes and farms. The station was also a refuge from Indians. The period between 1774 and 1790 was a particularly perilous time because of Indian incursions. The stations all had bad reputations. Most people on the frontier were decent folks, but the frontier regions always had a lot of misfits and criminal types. Their petty squabbles sometimes escalated into knife fights or gun battles.[5] In 1963, the Marion County, Kentucky, Historical Highway Marker Program erected a sign where Sandusky Station stood. It reads,

Sandusky Station, 1776

> James and Jacob Sandusky came from Va., 1774, in Hite's Company. They helped lay out Harrodstown. James was first explorer in this area, 1775. In 1776, Fort Harrod men assisted in building station around Pleasant Run spring, 150 feet SE. James and Jacob moved, 1785, to region now Jessamine Co. Anthony Sandusky left in charge. Family long identified with area.[6]

Anthony was James's son. James eventuality moved to Bourbon County where he built himself another fort known as Cane Ridge Station. Jacob spent the rest of his life in Jessamine County. In 1785, Patrick Henry, governor of Virginia, gave him a one-thousand-acre land grant.

In 1777, Jacob married Jemima Vose in Virginia. She had some interesting experiences with Indians during her youth. Indians captured her when she was seven or eight years old. She ran away from the tribe seven years later and made her way back home. Jemima brought back a reminder of her time with the Indians. One day during her captivity, she was crying too much. An Indian got mad and hit her over the head with his tomahawk. The blow was so hard; the wound disfigured her head for the rest of her life. The injury must have really been bad because she kept a dressing on her head her entire life.

---

4 Orval W. Baylor, Pioneer History of Washington County, Kentucky: [Owensboro, Kentucky: McDowell Publications 1980] p. 83.

5 Orval W. Baylor, p. 83.

6 Sue E. Watkins, p. 25.

Anthony, brother of James and Jacob, also had his own adventures in Kentucky. He came to Kentucky in 1782, just in time to take part in the battle of Blue Licks. A band of fifty British soldiers and five hundred Indians were besieging Bryan Station, a fort near present-day Lexington, Kentucky. During the siege, a few of the settlers had escaped and were coming back with reinforcements. When the British heard the Kentuckian force was approaching, they decided to retreat. The British fled north and crossed the Ohio River with the Kentuckians on their heels. The Kentuckians stopped at the river and held a council to decide what to do. Daniel Boone thought it best to wait for more troops to arrive, while the officers wanted to cross over and attack the enemy. The officers would not listen to Boone and ordered the men to cross the Ohio River. The Kentucky force crossed over to the other side and walked right into an ambush. Sixty Kentuckians were killed and seven captured in fifteen minutes of fighting. Among the dead was Israel Boone, Daniel's son. Anthony's horse was stolen by Indians during the battle, but he managed to get away on Israel Boone's horse. He also picked up another soldier and carried him to safety.

John and Killion Sandusky

John Sandusky was the first person of Polish descent to settle in Illinois. John's on the first Federal Census of Illinois in 1818, the year Illinois became a state.[7] Because of John, there has been someone of Polish descent on every Illinois census since statehood. John's brother Killion settled in Illinois a short time later and is on the 1820 Federal Census of Illinois.[8] Both of them settled in Franklin County, which is about seventy-five miles southeast of St. Louis, Missouri.

Franklin County was organized on January 2, 1818, from parts of White and Gallatin counties. Franklin County was itself divided in 1839 to create Williamson County. The county is located in Southern Illinois, in the central part of the state. Frankfort is the county seat. Franklin County was a favorite hunting ground of the local Indian tribes. There was a large amount of wooded land and the gradually sloping prairies teemed with wildlife. The Big Muddy

---

7 Illinois Census Returns 1810, 1818. [Edited by Margaret Cross Norton] [Published by the Trustees of the Illinois State Historical Library, Springfield, Illinois] p. 81.

8 Illinois Census Returns 1820: [Edited by Margaret Cross Norton] [Published by the Trustees of the Illinois State Historical Library Springfield, Illinois 1934] [Reprinted by Genealogical Company, Baltimore 1969], p. 65.

River ran through the county, and its floodplains created numerous swamps for part of the year. Franklin County was a beautiful but dangerous place. The county was covered with wildflowers, but the many swamps always produced large swarms of flies and malaria-carrying mosquitoes. Joseph F. Jurich wrote, "Franklin County in the early 1800's was a paradise for men and dogs, but hell for women and oxen. Social life was limited, but hunting and fishing were excellent."[9]

Being close to the south, the first settlers of the county were from the southern states of Kentucky, Tennessee, and North Carolina. Settlers from the Northeast came later as did German and Irish emigrants. The seven Jordan brothers from Tennessee were the first white people to come to the county, settling in 1804. The Jordans also built the first fort for protection from Indians. Southern culture predominated here until about 1900. The county also had a few slave owners. In 1818, Franklin County had fifteen black slaves and fifty-two black indentured servants. Franklin County was proslavery in 1822, when 170 citizens voted for and 113 against the slavery question at the Illinois Slave Convention. Some of the citizens of Franklin County fought for the south during the Civil war.

John was born in Kentucky in 1795. His father's name was Andrew, and I think his grandfather's name was Samuel. I am not completely certain. There were a lot of Sanduskys, and each new generation always seems to have the same names as the previous one. Samuel was the oldest son of Andrew Sandusky, the son of Antoni Sadowski. This would make John one-sixteenth Polish, the same as the author of this book. I am sure John would agree better to have a little Polish than none at all.

The best source I have found about John Sandusky is a story written by Edward Pinkowski and printed in the *St. Louis Hejnal.* According to Edward, Indians murdered John's father when he was four years old. His grandfather on his mother's side was a German emigrant named Killion Krieg who taught John the trade of stonemason. John enlisted in the Kentucky cavalry when he was seventeen years old. The war of 1812 was just starting and John's stepfather loaned him a horse to use during the war.[10]

After the war, John married Elizabeth Hutson. The marriage produced four children: John, William, Mary Amelia, and Parmelia Ann. They moved to Barron Township, Franklin County, Illinois, in 1818. There John bought 160

---

9 Joseph F. Jurich, This is Franklin County: [Benton Evening News Print, 1954] p. 5.

10 Edward Pinkowski, Hejnal: [Polish American Cultural Society of St. Louis, Summer, 2001] p. 7.

acres of land beside the Big Muddy River.[11] Besides farming, John supported his family by hunting and fishing. John was a charter member of the Mount Pleasant Missionary Baptist Church, organized in July 11, 1829.[12] The 1850 Federal Census of Franklin County, Illinois, shows that John is a fifty-five-year-old farmer. Wife Elizabeth is forty-seven years old. Only one son, William, sixteen years old, lives there. His occupation is farmer.[13] According to Aiken, John Sandusky is supposed to be the first person to settle in Barron Township. Aiken claims that John and the other early settlers were all squatters and did not have title to their land until the government first surveyed it. John did not have his title until 1831.[14] John's mother and stepfather moved to Franklin County soon after him, settling there by at least 1820.[15] Barron Township got the name Barron because a considerable amount of the land there was unsuitable for agriculture. The township was sparsely populated as a result. Any land that could be used for farming was very productive.[16] John died sometime in the 1870s.

Barron Township was a great place for someone like John who farmed and was a hunter/fisherman. In 1965, the Army Corps of Engineers dammed up the Big Muddy River. This brought into existence the 18,900-acre Rend Lake. The Sanduskys have two campgrounds named after them on Rend Lake. In addition, a hiking and bike path named South Sandusky Recreation Area is located on the lake.[17]

Killion Sandusky

Killion settled in Franklin County not long after John. He was born in 1796 in Bourbon County, Kentucky.[18] Killion might have also been in the war of 1812.[19] He is on the 1820 Federal Census for Franklin County.[20] Killion

11 Facts & Findings, Frankfort Area Genealogical Society, West Frankfort, Illinois [Volume 19 #4 Winter 1994] p. 13.

12 Edward Pinkowski, p. 7.

13 1850 Federal Census of Franklin County, Illinois [National Archives, Box M432, Roll 106, Page 56]

14 H. M. Aiken, Franklin County History Centennial Edition: [Evansville, Indiana: Unigraphic, Inc. 1975.] p. 36.

15 Facts & Findings, p. 14.

16 H. M. Aiken, p. 73.

17 Edward Pinkowski, p. 7.

18 WWWFamilySearch.Org [Family History Library]

19 Facts & Findings, p. 14.

20 Facts & Findings, p. 14.

seems to have been part gypsy and moved frequently. In 1829, the Killion Sandusky family was living near his grandparents in Gibson County, Indiana. By 1830, they were living at the border of Shelby and Clark Counties, Illinois. In 1835, the family was living in Fayette County, Illinois. The year 1840 saw them back in Franklin County where they settled for good.[21] The 1850 Federal Census of Franklin County shows that Killion is fifty-four years old and a farmer. His wife, Elizabeth, is fifty-two years old. Daughters Lucinda, twenty-four; E. J., seventeen years old; and A. M., thirteen years old. Sons W. R., twelve, and Jackson, eight.[22] Killion died in 1852.[23] Killion claims to have thirty improved acres and eighty unimproved acres in 1850. He owned one horse, three milk cows, five sheep and twenty-six pigs. The farm produced three hundred bushels of corn, four pounds of wool, twenty-five bushels of peas, thirty-five bushels of potatoes, and two hundred pounds of butter.[24]

Two other Sandusky families were also living in Franklin County. I am not sure if they were John's or Killion's sons. John Sandusky, twenty-one years old, farmer and born in Illinois. His wife Nancy is nineteen years old.[25] Living next door to John was Andrew Sandusky. He was a twenty-eight-year-old farmer and born in Illinois. His wife Elenor is twenty-seven years old. Their daughters Lusorna, seven, and Maria, one, and son Killion, eight years old.[26]

William T. Sandusky

William was one of three children born to William and Julia (Earp) Sandusky. William was the middle child and was born March 1, 1829, in Bourbon County, Kentucky. William was a relative, probably a cousin of John and Killion Sandusky. When he was only six months old, his parents moved to Shelby County, Illinois, arriving in the fall of 1829. They made the trip by covered wagon. Killion Sandusky was living in Shelby County when they first arrived. William's father died in March of 1830, only six months

21 Facts & Findings, p. 14.

22 1850 Federal Census for Franklin County: [National Archives, Box M432, Roll 106, Page 5]

23 Edward Pinkowski, p. 7.

24 1850 Franklin County, Illinois Agriculture Census: [Illinois State Archives, Roll 31-2]

25 1850 Federal Census of Franklin County, Illinois: [National Archives, Box M432, Roll 106, Page 11]

26 1850 Federal Census of Franklin County, Illinois: [National Archives, Box M432, Roll 106, Page 11]

after the family settled in Illinois. His mother died ten years later in 1840, leaving William and his two sisters orphans. There is no record of anyone adopting William or his sisters.

When the going gets tough, the tough gets going, and it looks like William did just that. He writes that he fended for himself at an early age working as a farm laborer for twenty-five cents an hour or splitting fence rails for twenty-five cents a hundred. Chapman wrote that William "was bred to a farmer's life in Shelby County, and amid the pioneer influences that surrounded his early life, became strong, manly, self-reliant and energetic."[27] William stayed in Shelby County for the next eight years. In 1848, he moved to Vermilion County and got himself a job looking after a herd of cattle. There was a number of Sanduskys already living in Vermilion County when William came on the scene. He lived in Vermilion County the next five years and engaged in a number of cattle drives to the east as well as managing cattle ranches.

William longed to own his own farm and soon realized that working as a farm laborer would take too long. In 1853, he set off for the California goldfields. William left Vermilion County with three or four hundred dollars in his pocket and went to New York. There he boarded a ship headed for California, passing through the Isthmus of Panama on the way there. William spent the next three years mining gold. He also managed a large cattle ranch for a time. His time out west was for the most part successful, and he decided to return to Vermilion County.

Once back, William went back to the cattle business, this time becoming a cattle trader. In the back of his mind, he toyed with the idea of returning to California. William always talked himself out of it and kept on trading cattle. He frequently went out west on cattle-buying trips, and the thought of going back to California persisted in his head. In the spring of 1859, he tried to make the trip again but only made it as far as Greencastle, Putnam County, Indiana. There William became a partner in a hotel. The year 1859 brought another important event in William's life. He married Emily Clements of Shelbyville, Illinois on November 11. Their marriage produced two daughters, Maggie and Katie. Three years later, William bought out his partner and ran the business himself. William also built a hotel in Greencastle named the "Junction House." He conducted that hotel until 1866, then sold out and came back to Vermilion County.

The first thing William did in Vermilion County was to buy a 160-acre farm, paying for it with six thousand dollars in cash. Four months later, he

[27] Portrait and Biographical Album of Vermilion County, Illinois: [Chicago: Chapman Brothers, 1889] [Reprinted Owensboro, Kentucky: McDowell Publications 1981] p. 378.

bought a 190-acre farm for eight thousand dollars. William was not done buying yet and bought another farm for four thousand dollars. William aimed to stay in Vermilion County for good this time and became a prosperous and well-known farmer in Catlin Township.

William went on to become vice president of the Vermilion County Agricultural and Mechanical Association. He was also the school director for a number of years. William was a passionate Republican and donated money to the Republican Party on a regular basis. He continued to expand his land holdings and eventually owned six hundred acres. William also built and rented four houses. His wife Emily died January 13, 1899.

William H. Sandusky

I only know a small amount about William H. Sandusky. He might have lived in Shelby County for a time. History of Shelby and Moultrie Counties, Illinois, wrote that William Sandusky was one of the first settlers in Okaw Township. He came from Kentucky around 1830 but soon left.[28] There is no middle initial H, so it is impossible to tell if this is the same person.

William H. Sandusky definitely lived in the town of Havana. The town was located in Tazewell County when William first came there, but became a part of Mason County when Mason County was created on January 20, 1841. Havana is situated in west-central Illinois, about thirty-five miles southwest of Peoria. William was elected to the office of notary public in Havana's first election on August 7, 1837.[29] He was elected clerk on August 8, 1838.[30] William must have come to Havana at an early date, for he was already selling a lot to Joshua C. Morgan on July 20, 1835.[31] Tazewell County Land Records show William buying a number of lots in town after 1835. One land transaction records William buying a lot from James M. Sandusky

28 Portrait Biographical Record of Shelby and Moultrie Counties, Illinois: [Chicago: Biographical Publishing Co. 1891] [Reprinted by Shelby County Historical and Genealogical Society, Utica, Kentucky: McDowell Publications] p. 298.

29 The History of Menard and Mason Counties, Illinois: [Chicago: O. L. Baskin & Co. 1879] [Reprinted by Whipporwill Publications, Evansville, Indiana 1985] p. 521.

30 The History of Menard and Mason Counties, Illinois, p. 567.

31 David C. Perkins, Tazewell County Illinois Land Records Index: [Published by Tazewell County Genealogical Society, Pekin, Illinois 1980] p. 46.

on April 19, 1837.[32] William moved out of state by at least December 1838, and William H. Holmes was designated clerk to replace William.[33]

Jacob Sandusky

The Morgan County Directory writes that Jacob was born in Kentucky about 1804. Jacob and his wife Melinda left Kentucky sometime between the year 1830 and 1832. Jacob was supposed to be somewhat well-off in Kentucky, but gave it all up to become a pioneer farmer in Morgan County, Illinois. He spent weeks wandering around the Illinois prairie looking for a good location to live before choosing to settle in Morgan County. Once there, he purchased eighty acres from the government and built a log cabin.[34] Jacob is on the 1840 Federal Census of Morgan County.[35] Jacob and his family moved to Green County sometime between 1840 and 1850, and are on the 1850 Federal Census of Green County. The 1850 census shows Jacob's age is forty-six, occupation farmer and born in Kentucky. Wife Melinda is forty-four years old and born in Kentucky. Son Wyley is twenty years old, born in Kentucky and farmer. Daughters Nancy, eighteen; Elizabeth, fifteen; Matilda, ten; and Melvina four, all born in Illinois. Sons Alexander, twelve, and James, eight, born in Illinois.[36] Jacob resided in Green County for a number of years before moving to Nebraska.[37] Morgan County marriage records show another Sandusky living in the county about the time Jacob arrived. On September 30, 1830, Maria Sadusky married Joshua Steward.[38]

Vermilion County

Vermilion County was the main area of settlement for the Sanduskys in Illinois. It is located in central Illinois, with its eastern boundary the

32 David C. Perkins, p. 46.

33 The History of Menard and Mason Counties, Illinois, p. 567.

34 History of Morgan County, Illinois: [Chicago: Donnelley, Loyd & Co. 1878] [Reproduction by Unigraphic, Inc. Evansville, Indiana 1975] p. 625 & 626.

35 1840 Federal Census of Morgan County, Illinois: [National Archives, Box 704, Roll 66, Page 440]

36 1850 Federal Census of Greene County, Illinois: [National Archives, Box M432, Roll 108, Page 121]

37 History of Morgan County, Illinois, p. 626.

38 Liahona Research, Illinois Marriages 1826 to 1850: [Bountiful, Utah: Heritage Quest 1999] p. 715.

Indiana state line. The county was organized on January 18, 1826, from Edger County. Danville is the county seat. Most of Vermilion County was prairie, Georgetown Township being the exception. Chicago is around 135 miles to the north.

Isaac Sandusky

Isaac was born in Bourban County, Kentucky about 1790.[39] I think, but am not completely certain, that Isaac was the son of James Sandusky, of whom I wrote about earlier in this story. The Sanduskys all seem to give each other the same names each generation. Isaac married Euphemma McDowell, who was also born in Kentucky. He went off to war not long afterwards and took part in the battle of Tippecanoe in 1811. Isaac also took part in Hull's surrender, one of the worst incidents in American military history. The British managed to bluff General Hull into surrendering Fort Detroit in the War of 1812. The American Army surrendered twenty-five hundred soldiers to the British without ever putting up a fight. The soldiers in the American Army were taken to Canada as prisoners of war. The militias were sent home, but were on parole. Vermilion County histories state that Isaac escaped from the British and went back to Kentucky. Part of the way back took him through Vermilion County where he was so impressed with the prairie that he swore to come back there someday and buy some land.

Thirteen years passed before Isaac returned in 1827. Isaac's family settled on the virgin prairie at Brooks Point, the future site of the village of Catlin. The whole family worked hard to establish the farm from the wilds and coped with all the rigors that go along with pioneer life. According to history of Vermilion County 1879,

> Isaac made his home at Catlin, and with his sons, a portion of whom lived there, became possessed of large landed property, buying up all the farms that were for sale around the mound. They are a remarkable family. In the history of Vermilion County no family has cut so important a figure in its business, social and agricultural concerns.[40]

---

39 1850 Federal Census of Vermilion County, Illinois: [National Archives, Box M432 Roll 130 Page 263]

40 W. H. Beckwith, History of Vermilion County: [Chicago: H. H. Hill and Company 1879] p. 974.

Isaac and Euphemma were the parents of eleven children: Sarah E., Mary A., Julia A., Josiah, James, Henry Clay, Ann Eliza, Stephen A. Douglas, Thomas, Susan A., and Laura. Most of the children were already born when the family made the decision to move to Illinois. Before they left, Isaac bought large herds of horses, sheep, and cattle to take with them. The whole family helped drive the herds, sleeping in tents along the way. The Sanduskys must have looked like a band of nomads on their move to Illinois. Isaac is supposed to have been the first person to bring sheep into Vermilion County. His herd of cattle contained a number of prizewinners, and some of his horses came from stock raised by the Sanduskys for the last hundred years. Isaac's farm was valued at $30,000 on the 1850 Federal Census of Vermilion County.[41] He claimed to own 2,500 improved and 500 unimproved acres on the 1850 Agriculture Census.[42]

The Sanduskys also encountered a new contraption while traveling to Illinois, a cooking stove. They were much taken in by it, so Isaac bought it. The stove was hauled the rest of the way to Illinois and was the first stove in the county. Isaac and Euphemma lived on the farm until their deaths. Isaac died August 6, 1852, and Euphemma died June 15, 1864.[43]

Josiah Sandusky

Two of Isaac's sons have write-ups in Vermilion County histories, Josiah and James. Josiah was born in Kentucky about 1815. He came to Vermilion County with his father Isaac in 1827. In 1837, Josiah went back to Kentucky and married Elizabeth Sandusky. I am not sure if she was a relative or married to another Sandusky in a previous marriage. They came back to Vermilion County the same year and settled at Brooks Point. A few years later they moved near the village of Catlin, which became their permanent home.[44]

History of Vermilion County, Illinois, wrote an interesting story about Josiah. There was a very desirable piece of land in the county located south of the village of Fairmount. Out in the middle of the prairie were limestone springs that everyone in the county wished to own. "Big Spring Farm" already owned the land though. Josiah yearned for the springs too and hoped to

---

41 1850 Federal Census of Vermilion County, Illinois: [National Archives, Box M432 Roll 130 Page 263]

42 1850 Agriculture Census of Vermilion County, Illinois: [Illinois State Archives, Roll 31-4.

43 W. H. Beckwith, p. 772.

44 Chapman 1889 p. 367.

buy it for his son Jacob. Josiah came up with a plan. He bought up all the surrounding land around Big Spring Farm until it was completely encircled. Josiah would go on to own Big Spring Farm as well; it made no sense to sell it to anyone else anyways.

After Josiah purchased Big Spring Farm, he bought one of the most well-known houses in the county and moved it there. Known as the Butler House, it was built by James Butler, one of the first settlers in the county. The house was built out of black walnut and is now enclosed within another house.[45] It's now called "the Sandusky Cabin" and is a popular tourist attraction in Catlin. I have seen it myself. Eight children were born from the marriage of Josiah and Elizabeth, but only four lived past childhood.[46] Josiah's occupation is listed as farmer, and his farm is valued at $110,000 on the 1860 census. His son Jacob was born in 1843. Daughter Mourning, born in 1850. Sons Guy, born in 1854, and Sy, born in 1857.[47] History of Vermilion County states that Josiah was "a prosperous and driving man."[48] Josiah died September 15, 1868, and Elizabeth died January 10, 1884.

James Sandusky

Isaac's son James was born July 17, 1817, in Bourbon County, Kentucky. James was ten years old when the family moved to Illinois. James lived on several different farms in or around Catlin, Vermilion County. He raised livestock and farmed all of his adult life. He was married on December 6, 1847, to Mary Ann Green. Their marriage produced eleven children: Sarah E., Josiah, James S., Henry C., Eliza, Stephen A. D., Thomas, Susan A., and Lora. According to my sources, two died sometime before 1879.[49] James owned a three-hundred-acre farm and raised horses from the same herd that his father brought from Kentucky.[50] James claims to own 500 improved acres and 248 unimproved acres worth $7,000 on the 1850 Agriculture Census. He owned two horses, three milk cows, two other cattle, two sheep, and thirty pigs. The farm produced two thousand bushels of corn, one hundred

---

45 W. H. Beckwith, p. 974.

46 Chapman 1889, p. 367.

47 1860 Federal Census of Vermilion County, Illinois: [National Archives, Box 653, Roll 233, Page 639]

48 W. H. Beckwith, p. 974.

49 Rev. Frank Gilroy, Obituary Records from the scrapbooks kept by Rev. Frank Gilroy of Sidell, Illinois: p. 133.

50 Chapman 1889, p. 495.

bushels of oats, ten tons of hay, a small orchard, and one hundred pounds of butter.[51]

Abraham Sandusky

Abraham was born March 29, 1793, in Bourbon County, Kentucky, and was the younger brother of Isaac Sandusky. Abe married Jane McDowell, a local girl from Bourbon County. Eight children were born from the marriage: Harvey, Elizabeth, Polly, Agnes, William, Abraham Jr., Euphemia Jane, and Josiah. Abraham left Kentucky in 1831, moving first to Indiana. Besides his family, he brought ten head of shorthorn cattle with him. Abraham's herd might have been the first herd of shorthorns in the state of Indiana. Abraham moved to Carroll Township, Vermilion County, in 1834, bringing his herd of shorthorns with him. The herd had grown to twenty-seven heads in Indiana. Some sources I have state that Abraham actually came to Vermilion County in 1831. Abraham bought three farms in Vermilion County upon his arrival. His family had grown to five children by this time, with the last three born in Illinois. Abraham became a wealthy farmer and stock raiser and

> is spoken of by the old residents as a man of strong convictions, of untiring energy, good judgment, and an excellent manager, strictly honest in all his dealings. One of the best things that can be said of him is that he brought up his boys to work. He was a Presbyterian in his religious views. He gave his children as good education as the opportunities of the times permitted.[52]

Abraham obviously believed in the Anglo-Saxon work ethic, which he passed down to his sons. Four of Abraham's sons have mug shots in Vermilion County histories. I will write about all of them shortly. There is one more item of note worth mentioning about Abraham. He was a slave owner in Kentucky.

The 1830 Federal Census for Bourbon County, Kentucky shows Abraham owning seven slaves.[53] He was not the only Sandusky to own slaves either. A

---

51 1850 Agriculture Census of Vermilion County, Illinois: [Illinois State Archives, Roll 31-4]

52 W. H. Beckwith, 772.

53 1830 Federal Census of Bourban County, Kentucky: [National Archives Box 19 Roll 33 Page 332]

number, but not all of the Sanduskys in Bourbon and Jessamine Counties, Kentucky, were slave owners. Jacob Sandusky of Jessamine County owned twenty slaves.[54] The rest of the Sanduskys owned less then ten slaves each. The Sanduskys were southerners and were living in a different era. My own ancestors probably owned serfs at one time or another, and at times, serfdom was not much different from slavery. The Illinois Sanduskys became prominent and successful people in the state without slaves. In fact, they became much wealthier in Illinois than Kentucky.

When Abe left Kentucky, he told his slaves they could either go with him or be sold to someone else. Only Polly Neal chose to go. She was known as "Aunt Polly," and Abe had to pay a two-thousand-dollar bond to bring her into Illinois. Illinois law required paying bond on any Negro brought into the state. This was done to guarantee that someone would look after them.[55] Aunt Polly was pregnant when the Sanduskys first came to Vermilion County. She bore a son named Gabriel, who became the first black born in the county. Gabriel became a very wealthy and educated man. In 1836, Aunt Polly petitioned circuit court judge John Pearson for a certificate stating she was free. Abraham had already freed her, and she carried a letter from him stating the fact.[56] Aunt Polly lived with the Sanduskys until at least the 1850s. Coffeen writes, "The Neals were highly respected as citizens of the community."[57]

Abraham owned a 770-acre farm. His farmhouse was one of the best houses in Vermilion County. Besides raising livestock, he also grew a large amount of field crops. Jane died February 2, 1865, and Abraham died April 17, 1866. They are buried in the "Old Sodowsky Cemetery," which is currently on the Stine farm. Mrs. Stine was a Sandusky.[58]

Harvey Sodowsky

Harvey was the oldest son of Abraham and Jane. He was born May 17, 1817, in Bourbon County, Kentucky. Harvey preferred to use the old spelling of

54 1830 Federal Census of Jessimine County, Kentucky: [National Archives Box 19 Roll 38 Page 212]

55 W. H. Beckwith, p. 775 & 776.

56 The Illiana Genealogist: [Published by: Illiana Genealogical & Historical Society, Danville, Illinois, Volume 22 1986] p. 116 & 117.

57 H. A. Coffeen, Vermilion County, Historical, Statistical, and Descriptive: [Published by H. A. Coffeen, Danville, Illinois] p.20.

58 Vermilion County, Illinois Cemetery Locater: [Vermilion County, Illinois Genealogical Society, 1997] p. 53.

the Sandusky name, "Sodowsky." His friends and neighbors called him "Uncle Harvey." Bowman put a picture of Harvey's house in his book.[59] Harvey took up the usual Sandusky occupation of raising livestock and named his farm "Woodlawn Stock Farm." His herd of shorthorn cattle was probably the best in the county. Some say the state. He exhibited cattle at fairs for fifty years and won a number of awards during that time. Harvey claimed to own 320 improved and 460 unimproved acres in 1850. His farm was worth $8,000 dollars. He owned seven horses, twelve milk cows, twenty-eight other cattle, fifteen sheep, and eighteen pigs. His farm produced fifty bushels of wheat, four thousand bushels of corn, four hundred bushels of oats, fifteen pounds of wool, twenty bushels of potatoes, a small orchard, and three hundred pounds of butter.[60]

Harvey married Susan Baum of Vermilion County on May 20, 1840. The Baum family claimed to be descended from Polish nobility. I will write more about them later. Harvey and Susan were the parents of three children, a small family by Sandusky standards. The firstborn died while still a baby. Emma was the second child. She became one of the wealthiest Sanduskys, inheriting land from both her mother and father. At one time, she owned 3,600 acres in Vermilion County. Son Gilbert was the baby of the family, but he died when only twenty-three years old.

Susan Baum was supposed to have been a very religious woman. She was a member of the Methodist Episcopal Church and was highly involved in church affairs. It appears that Harvey was not nearly as religious as his wife was, but over time, it rubbed off on him. An entry in his Bible states, "Harvey Sodowsky this day found peace with God. March 15, 1858."[61] Harvey was generous to the needy, a good businessman, and involved in community affairs. He also laid out and developed the southern part of the village of Catlin.[62] Harvey died December 18, 1886, and Susan died March 21, 1888.[63]

William Sandusky

William was another son of Abraham. He was born in Bourbon County, Kentucky, on November 19, 1827. William was three years old when the family moved to Vermilion County and settled alongside the Little Vermilion

59 A. Bowman, Vermilion County, Illinois 1867. [Published by A. Bowman] p. 4

60 1850 Agriculture Census of Vermilion County, Illinois: [Illinois State Archives, Roll 31-4]

61 Portrait and Biographical Album of Vermilion County, Illinois, p.193.

62 W. H. Beckwith, p. 624.

63 Rev. Frank Gilroy, p. 134.

River. The county's population was very small when the Sanduskys first arrived, and William grew up living the life of a pioneer. When he was not plowing up prairie or planting corn on the farm, he was hunting deer and wild fowl to supplement his family's diet. Wolf hunting was always necessary and practiced on a regular basis. William also liked to take his horse out for rides on the prairie.

William only went to school for three months of the year, all during the winter. He spent the rest of the year working on his father's farm. The school was a log cabin with a fireplace so big an eight-foot-long piece of wood could fit in it. He educated himself in this manner until he was eighteen years old. William continued to work on his father's farm until he was twenty-one years old, then went into farming for himself. He bought a 240-acre farm to start with. His father helped him get started by building a small house for him.

Soon after establishing his own farm, William married Mary Elizabeth Baum on April 19, 1849.[64] Mary's sister Susan was married to William's brother Harvey. Five children were born to William and Mary Elizabeth: Mary, Caroline, Adeline, Belle, and Rochester. Mary, the oldest daughter, died when she was a baby. Rochester would become a well-known farmer in the county.

William was a very successful farmer and stock raiser. He specialized in shorthorn cattle, owning a large herd. William also bought and fed large numbers of cattle. Throughout his farming career, he expanded his operation and by the early 1900s owned 1,520 acres. William was also interested in racehorses and over the years owned a number of famous horses.

Abraham Jr.

Abe Jr. was the sixth child of Abraham and Jane and was born March 24, 1833, in Bourbon County, Kentucky. He was only six months old when the family left Kentucky for Illinois. Abe Jr. had the same type of education as his brother William, but always claimed he learned more from his parents. He began buying land in 1862 and continued to buy land at regular intervals. Abe also made a lot of money during the Civil War by speculating on horses and cattle. Abe, however, continued to live at his father's farm until he married Ellen Baird on December 16, 1869.

After marrying, Abe became part owner of the Exchange Bank. After four or five years, the bank saw an opportunity to finance the Paris to Danville

64 Liahona Research, Illinois Marriages 1826 to 1850: [Bountiful, Utah: Heritage Quest 1999] p. 769.

Railroad. Unfortunately, the railroad was a bust and the bank had to sell it. The bank failed as well and Abe lost his shirt. Before buying into the bank, Abe was worth three hundred thousand dollars. After the bank went under in 1873, he lost every penny he owned and was bankrupt. Abe rolled with the punches and with help from his family got back on his feet. His brother William bought his farm and leased it back to him with the option to buy it back when possible. By 1889, Abe had already bought back six hundred acres. Abe stayed away from investing in banks after that and stuck to the old Sandusky specialty of raising shorthorn cattle.

Abe was a staunch Republican, frequently donating to the party. He was a Presbyterian by faith. Chapman wrote that Abe was "a public-spirited and generous citizen. Nearly every church, and all other enterprises designed for the public good, have felt the strength of his liberality."[65]

Josiah Sandusky

Josiah was the eighth child of Abraham and Jane Sandusky. He was born September 11, 1837, in Vermilion County. Like his brothers, he was a very successful businessman, probably the most successful member of the family. When Josiah was six years old, he had the misfortune to come down with a sickness known as the "white swelling." The result was a lame left leg for the rest of his life. Being a cripple must have slowed him down a bit, but he made up for it by cultivating a great memory. Josiah went to the same schools as his brothers and while there developed a great love of reading and became knowledgeable in many subjects. He amassed an extensive library over his lifetime where he spent all his free time.

Josiah was also interested in farming and raising livestock and spent his entire working career in agriculture. He lived at home working on his father's farm until his father died in 1865. Josiah was twenty-five years old at the time and inherited five hundred acres from his father. After his father died, Josiah and his brother Abraham became partners for a number of years. Josiah raised duchess cattle. I have never heard of this breed before. Josiah's herd of duchess cattle was one of the biggest and best in the country. So good, in fact, that he sold cattle to buyers from all over the country and Canada. Josiah also raised racehorses. He was a familiar sight at local fairs where he showed cattle and horses, usually winning. Over time, Josiah expanded the size of his farm and owned one thousand acres when he died in 1901. It was one of the most valuable farms in the area.

65 Portrait and Biographical Album of Vermilion County, Illinois, p. 473.

Josiah married Margaret Moreland on December 18, 1873. She happened to be born in Bourbon County, Kentucky, the old stomping grounds of the Sandusky clan. Her family settled in Vermilion County in 1857. Before they were married, Josiah built her a mansion at the cost of twenty thousand dollars. Josiah and Margaret were the parents of five children. Two died in early childhood. The other three were Pearl, William, and Abraham. Josiah considered himself a family man, and spending time with his family always brought him much joy.

Josiah helped build the village of Catlin when he platted out the western part of town in 1858.[66] Like the rest of the family, he was a member of the Republican Party. He died on February 13, 1901. The *Past and Present of Vermilion County, Illinois* writes that Josiah was an "upright, honorable man who always lived at peace with his neighbors and was trustworthy in all life's relations."[67] It also goes on to say that his "name was untarnished by any unworthy act."[68]

Baum

The Baum family claimed to be Polish nobility but could be German nobility. There are two versions of their story. Chapman wrote that Carl (Charles) Baum was Polish nobility and "was banished from his birth-place during the troubles of that unhappy country."[69] He escaped to Germany and lived there for a short time, then immigrated to America. Carl arrived in America while the Revolutionary War was in progress and enlisted in the militia. He was assigned to a reserve unit guarding the American border. While in the militia, he married Barbara McDonald. They moved to Ohio when that state first opened for settlement and settled along the Ohio River at Bullskin Creek. Carl's grandson Samuel left Bullskin Creek on October 12, 1827, and made it to Vermilion County November 12, 1827. Another grandson Charles came to Vermilion County in 1836.[70]

History of Vermilion County 1836-1986 has a little different story. Carl and his brother Heinrich were German nobility from Wurtenberg, Germany. They came to the aid of Poland about the time of the first partition of Poland

---

66 W. H. Beckwith, p. 624.

67 The Past and Present of Vermilion County, Illinois: [Chicago: S. J. Clarke Publishing Co. 1903] p. 260.

68 The Past and Present of Vermilion County, Illinois, p. 260.

69 Portrait and Biographical Album of Vermilion County, Illinois, p. 456.

70 Portrait and Biographical Album of Vermilion County, Illinois. P. 456 & 457.

in 1772. For siding with Poland, Carl and Heinrich were exiled from Germany. This story does not seem right to me. The German state of Prussia participated in the partitions, but the city of Wurtenburg was in West Germany and not a part of Prussia as far as I know. Why would Wurtenberg exile Carl and Heinrich for fighting on the side of Poland? The two brothers immigrated to America in 1775 on board the ship *Hero.* At least a third of the passengers on the *Hero* were supposed to have died from dysentery on the journey to America.[71]

The Baums and Sanduskys must have found each other attractive, for on three different occasions members of the two families were married to each other. Samuel Baum's second marriage was to Mary Sandusky, Watkin. Mary's first husband William died at twenty-seven years of age. She brought two children from her first marriage with her. Sam and Mary had four more children together. Samuel Baum's sister Susan was married to Harvey Sodowsky. Samuel's daughter from his first marriage, Mary Elizabeth, married William Sandusky, Harvey's brother. I am not sure who the parents of Mary Sandusky, Watkin were. I suspect she could have been one of Isaac Sandusky's daughters. Vermilion County Historical Society has an interesting piece of information about Samuel Baum. One of his descendants, Bob Jones, wrote a small article about him titled

A Man of Yesterday Samuel Baum

> He came to Vermilion County in 1828, bringing with him one dusty wagon and two strong oxen. Samuel had a way with him and quickly became one of the most popular and respected men in all of Vermilion County. His friends gave him the nickname of "Uncle Sam." Sam was a large man and reared a large family. He carried 350 pounds in his 6'2" frame. He raised nine children. At the first Vermilion County Fair, Sam was there to show off his cattle. And when he died in 1861, he owned 1,500 acres of Illinois' finest farmland.[72]

The article goes on to list thirteen descendants of Samuel Baum. Samuel's brother Charles, who settled in Vermilion County in 1836, had a family of

71 The History of Carroll Township [Vermilion County, Illinois] [in honor of Indianola's Sesquicentennial 1836-1986] [Danville, Illinois: The Interstate Printers & Publishers, Inc. Copyright by Indianola History Book Committee 1986] p.168.

72 Bob Jones, A Man of Yesterday, Sam Baum: [Baum file at the Vermilion County, Illinois Historical and Genealogical Society, Danville, Illinois]

twelve children. His occupation was farmer. The descendants of Samuel and Charles became well-known and influential citizens of Vermilion County for a long time.

I could have written even more about the Sanduskys, but I think that by now you probably understand how important the family was in Vermilion County. Some of the grandsons of the people I just wrote about also have their profiles in *Vermilion County Histories.* There were other Sanduskys in Green, Tazewell, and Morgan counties as well. I wrote a small amount about them in those counties. Fifty-four people in Illinois currently have the last name of Sandusky; one of them still lives in Catlin. Three hundred fifty-eight people in Illinois have the last name of Baum.

There is also a small village in far Southern Illinois named Sandusky. I drove past it and the residents all seem to be black people. No one I asked at the library in Cairo knew how it came to get its name. The state of Iowa also has a small village named Sandusky located in southeastern Iowa along the Mississippi River. No one knew how it got its name either, but one librarian in Keokuk thought possibly Sandusky, Ohio. Julian Hulanicki, one of the Polish exiles from Trieste, lived in Sandusky, Iowa, for a time.

Adams County

Adams County had a good-size community of Polish Jews living in Quincy before 1850. Only Chicago had more. There are too many names to list here but I will write about them later in the story. There was also a few Polish Germans living in Adams County before 1850. I also found the marriage of Cynthia Ann Labieskei to Phillip Curtis.

Adams County was organized January 13, 1825, from Pike County. The county is located in central Illinois with its western boundary the Mississippi River. The county seat is Quincy, which was named after President John Quincy Adams's middle name. Adams County was almost equal parts prairie and forest when it was first settled. The wooded areas were alongside or near the streams. The prairie land was slightly rolling with the exception of the northeastern part of the county where the land is mostly level. The residents of the county claim that Adams County is second to none in agricultural production.

The town of Quincy is located on a bluff overlooking the Mississippi River. Before white settlement, there was an Indian village on the site of Quincy. The early French fur traders called it "Sauk Village," after the Sauk Indian tribe. The first European settler was a French trader named Bouvet. John Wood is considered the founder of Quincy. He first came to the area in February 1821 and built the first cabin there in 1822. John later became the governor of Illinois. Quincy did not experience much growth until 1834. The population in 1834 was about 700. By 1840, the population had increased to 1,850 people and by 1849, 5,500.The present population is 42,342.

Quincy had a number of calamities in its early days. There was a serious cholera outbreak on the usually cheerful day of July 4, 1833. Many of the victims were supposed to have died on just one day between midnight and dawn. One out of ten people in town died that year from cholera. The year 1844 brought a monumental flooding of the Mississippi River. Smallpox visited the area during the winter and early spring of 1849. Just as smallpox was subsiding in the spring, cholera showed up again when a boatload of travelers on the Mississippi River stopped in Quincy and infected the town. The Mississippi River was also higher then usual that year and many people living in the Bottomlands along the river had to go to higher ground. The flood of 1851 washed away "buildings, fences, bridges and roads; the loss to crops was very great."[73] Our Polish emigrants settled in Quincy in the late 1840s. They managed to arrive just in time for smallpox, cholera, and an historic flood. As Jan Rychlicki said in a letter to Napoleon Felix Zaba, "You have to be a Pole to have such luck."[74]

In Quincy's early days, most of its citizens were from New England, Kentucky, and Virginia. A large number of Irish settled there during the years 1836 through 1840. From 1838 onward, German settlers flooded into town. By the Civil War, half of Quincy was German. The Reverend Landry Genosky's book contains a story about these German settlers.

> It was an odd, though it had become a common sight, a few years before, to find in the early morning, the entire public landing covered by these families, with their multifarious household goods of every description, many of them cumbrous articles, whose bulk and weight made the cost of transportation, to infinitely exceed their value, and perhaps among the score of newcomers not a single person was able to speak or understand the language of the land where they had come to make their home.[75]

Michael Mast, a tailor, was the first German settler arriving in 1829. A letter he wrote to Germany inspired the German emigration to Quincy. Many of the German emigrants were skilled tradesman and were responsible for building much of Quincy. A quote by Wilcox in Rev. Genosky's book states,

> A little thought will prove the importance of the German pioneers in the development of Quincy. In the churches, schools

[73] The History of Adams County, Illinois: [Chicago: Murray, Williamson & Phelps,1879] [Reproduction by Windmill Publications, Inc. Mt. Vernon, Indiana 1995] [Sponsored by the Great River Genealogical Society, Quincy, Illinois] p. 424.

[74] Adolph Pazik, A Polish American Letter: [Polish American Studies, Volume iii Number 3-4 July-December 1946] [The Polish American Historical Association of the Polish Institute of arts and sciences in America, St. Mary's College, Orchard Lake, Michigan] p. 108.

[75] General John Tillson, History of the City of Quincy, Illinois: [Chicago: S. J. Clark Publishing 1900] [Reproduced by the Great River Genealogical Society, Quincy, Illinois 1992] p. 124.

> and colleges; in the banks and commerce; in the factories and industrial life, we see the results of German thrift, energy and patience.[76]

I have one more thing about Quincy worth noting. It was famous for its beer. The large German population needed their beer, and the result was that many breweries sprouted up in town. By 1860, Quincy was producing two hundred thousand kegs of beer a year. Landrum wrote, "Quincy was the goal of many emigrants who heard of the city through its beer,"[77] So far, my story about Adams County contains more information about Germans than Poles. My intent is to show just what was happening in Quincy at the time. In this part of Illinois, Germans contributed much to the local culture.

Polish Jews

For most of these people, the only information I have about them is from the census records. The 1850 Federal Census for Adams County shows the following Polish Jews living in the Quincy's South Ward.

Solomon Harris, twenty-two years old and born in Poland. His occupation is peddler. His wife Hannah, eighteen years old and born in Poland.[78] Solomon moved to Chicago and is listed as a charter member of Kehila B'nai Shalom Synagogue in May 1852.[79] He was also the first president of the same synagogue which first "met in rooms above the clothing store of Solomon Harris.[80]

Samuel Marks, twenty-six years old and born in Poland. His occupation is peddler. Wife Sarah is twenty-eight years old and born in Poland. Daughter Eliza is seven years old and born in Poland. Son Ephram is five years old and born in Poland.[81] Samuel was one of the first Polish Jews in Chicago. He is

---

76 David F. Wilcox, Quincy and Adams County: [Volume 1] [Chicago: The Lewis Publishing Company 1919] p. 268.

77 Carl A. Landrum, Historical Sketches of Quincy the first 100 years: [The Historical Society of Quincy and Adams County: Quincy, Illinois 1886] p123.

78 1850 Federal Census Adams County, Illinois: [National Archives, M432, Roll 97, Page 481]

79 Hyman L. Meites, History of the Jews of Chicago: [Chicago, Illinois: Chicago Jewish Historical Society, Wellington Publishers 1990] p. 53.

80 Hyman L. Meites, p. 53.

81 1850 Federal Census of Adams County, Illinois: [National Archives, M432, Roll 97, Page 481]

listed in the 1846 Chicago Directory.[82] Samuel lived next door to Solomon Harris on the 1850 Adams County Census and rented a room to Casper Sommerfield whom I write about next.

Casper Sommerfield, twenty-one years old and born in Poland. His occupation is peddler.[83] Casper moved to Chicago in the 1850s and was a charter member of Kehila B'nai Shalom Synagogue in May 1852.[84] He was also president of the synagogue in 1857.[85]

William Laniden, twenty-five years old and born in Poland. Under occupation, he lists fruitary.[86]

Living in the City of Quincy's Middle Ward

Isaac Levi, forty years old and born in Poland. His occupation is merchant. His wife Henretta is thirty-two years old but lists Germany as place of birth.[87] Isaac moved to Chicago and was one of the founders of Chevra Kaddisha Cholim. This was a charitable organization that helped poorer Jews pay their medical bills and burial costs.[88]

Lewis Reubin, twenty years old and born in Poland. His occupation appears to be clothier. Lewis was living in the house of Albert Goldstein. Albert is twenty-nine years old and born in Prussia. His occupation is clothier.[89]

Living in the City of Quincy's North Ward

Maurice Jacobs, twenty-four years old and born in Poland on the 1850 census. His occupation is merchant/tailor, and he was living in the house of Lewis Ward. Lewis is thirty-seven years old and born in New York. His

---

82 Hyman L. Meites, p. 53.

83 1850 Federal Census of Adams County, Illinois: [National Archives, M432, Roll 97, Page 482]

84 Hyman L. Meites, p. 53.

85 Hyman L. Meites, p. 66.

86 1850 Federal Census of Adams County, Illinois: [National Archives, M432, Roll 97, Page 482]

87 1850 Federal Census of Adams County, Illinois: [National Archives, M432, Roll 97, Page 463]

88 Hyman L. Meites, p. 87.

89 1850 Federal Census of Adams County, Illinois: [National Archives, M432, Roll 97, Page 469]

occupation is grocer.[90] I believe this to be the same person who calls himself Moses Jacobs on the 1860 census. He was thirty-four years old in 1860 and born in Poland. Moses now lives in the Second Ward and his occupation is merchant.[91] Moses left us a portrait of himself in *History of Quincy and Its Men of Mark*. I will write the complete portrait below.

M. Jacobs, Merchant

> Among the Hebrew population of our city are many who aided largely in the development and progress of Quincy. Many of our leading and most enterprising business men come from their ranks, and of this number is the subject of this sketch.
>
> M. Jacobs, Esq., was born in Prussia, in 1828, and emigrated to America in 1844. He at once embarked in business in New York, commencing in the manufacture of hats and caps. He remained in New York but one year, when he proceeded to St. Louis, and there followed the same line of manufacturing. He soon gave this up and opened a dry goods house, which he conducted until 1847, when he came to Quincy and opened a clothing house. From then until now he has continued successfully in this department of trade in our city, his career having been an honorable and upright one throughout. In 1864, the citizens of the Second Ward recognizing his value as a man, and appreciating his integrity, elected Mr. Jacobs to represent them in the City Council, where he served them ably and efficiently.
>
> A man possessed of thorough business qualifications, and full of enterprise, Mr. Jacobs is both a valuable and influential citizen.[92]

The first Jews in Quincy were supposed to have arrived in 1848. As we just saw, Moses Jacobs was there a year earlier. These first Jews came to Quincy by way of the Ohio River Valley. They created the first synagogue in town on December 12, 1856. A grand total of twenty-three people belonged

---

90 1850 Federal Census of Adams County, Illinois: [National Archives, M432, Roll 97, Page 429]

91 1860 Census Adams County, Illinois City of Quincy: [Volume 5] [Compiled by the Great River Genealogical Society 1982] p. 45.

92 History of Quincy and its Men of Mark: [Quincy: Hairs & Russell, Book and Job Printers, 1869] p. 128.

to the temple, which was named "B'nai Avraham" (children of Abraham). Moses Jacobs was warden and Louis Reuben trustee. The synagogue split October 20, 1864. The splinter group named their temple "B'nai Shalom" (children of peace). *Adams County Sesquicentennial* writes, "They were very small in number but very dedicated Jews. It was a difficult decision to detach themselves from the old and established Synagogue."[93] Moses Jacobs was one of the founders of the new synagogue.

Polish Germans

Listed on the 1850 Federal Census as living in the North Ward of Quincy

William Steine, sixty-one years old and born in Poland. His occupation is rectifier. A rectifier mixes whiskey to obtain the desired proof. William was living in the house of John A. Brauner, thirty-seven years old and born in Virginia. Brauner's occupation is hotelkeeper.[94]

Listed on the 1850 Federal Census as living in the South Ward of Quincy

Adolph Kettz, thirty-nine years old and born in Poland. His occupation is carpenter. His wife Julia is twenty-eight years old and born in Germany. Son Charles is two years old, born in Illinois. Also living in the Kettz home is Charles Nodle, eighteen years old, born in Germany. His occupation is carpenter. Matilda Spicer, nine years old and born in Illinois, was also living with the Kettzes'.[95] Adolph is listed on the 1848 Quincy City Directory as a carpenter.[96] He is also on the 1855-66 Quincy City Directory.[97] Adolph's name shows up quite a bit in books at the Adams County Recorder of Deeds. He bought a number of lots in Quincy starting March 16, 1837.[98]

---

93 Peoples History of Quincy and Adams County Sesquicentennial: [Editor: Rev. Landry Genosky, O.F.M.] [Quincy, Illinois: Jost & Kiefer Printing Co.] p. 88.

94 1850 Federal Census of Adams County, Illinois: [National Archives, M432, Roll 97 Page 428]

95 1850 Federal Census of Adams County, Illinois: [National Archives, M432, Roll 97, Page 502]

96 Dr. J. S. Ware, A Directory for the City of Quincy: [Quincy: 1848]

97 J. F. Everhart, Quincy City Directory for 1855-1856: [Quincy, Illinois: Gibson & Morrison, 1855]

98 Adams County Recorder of Deeds, Quincy, Illinois: [Book H, p. 92-93]

Listed on the 1850 Federal Census as living in Columbus Township, Adams County

Harris Leib, twenty-five years old and born in Poland. His occupation is farmer. His wife Dena is twenty-one years old and born in Poland. Son William is one year old and born in Illinois.[99] Harris Leib seems like a Jewish name, but most Jews that I see in the census records are usually in occupations like merchant, etc. There was one Polish Jew living in Green County named Cohen who was a farmer.

There is also the marriage of Phillip Curtis to Cynthia Ann Labieskei on December 20, 1839.[100] This is the only record of her in the county. Cynthia's last name looks like it could be Polish. It does not have the "ski" that you find in Polish names now, but during this period, the Polish names have a variety of endings. Her first name does not look Polish, so she could be of Polish descent.

Moses Jacobs became a pillar of the community during his time in Quincy. At least four of the first Polish Jews in Quincy left town and moved to Chicago. You can read about them again in my story about Chicago. Adolph Kettz seems to have been well-known around Quincy. We will probably never know if Cynthia Ann Labieskei was Polish. I would like to thank Jean M. Kay for her help with this story.

99 1850 Federal Census of Adams County, Illinois: [M432, Roll 97, Page 94]

100 Liahona Research, Illinois Marriages: 1825 through 1850: [Bountiful, Utah: Heritage Quest, 1998] p. 469.

Alexander County

Alexander County had one Pole living there by 1850 and possibly more. Martin Leftcovitch moved to the city of Cairo by at least 1843 and possibly as early as 1841. Martin is likely Marcin Lewkowicz, whose name is listed as one of the 234 Polish exiles from Trieste. More about the exiles from Trieste in the forward.

The area where Alexander County is located on was first a part of Johnson and later Union counties. Alexander County was created from Union County March 4, 1819, and was divided itself March 3, 1843, when Pulaski County was created. Alexander County is located at the very bottom of the state and lies on a peninsula at the junction of the Mississippi and Ohio rivers.

The city of Cairo is located at the far southern tip of Alexander County at the river junction. You would think that Cairo's great position at the junction of two rivers would be one of the first places to build a city, but it didn't happen that way. The whole area was impenetrable forest and situated on low ground. Most of the peninsula flooded in the spring when the rivers were high from melted snow. The early settlers considered low ground to be an unhealthy place to live. Despite all these drawbacks, a small number of pioneers settled in the area in 1795. Most were hunters and trappers. They grew a small crop for themselves on a couple of acres, but hunting was their main occupation. Most left the area by the mid-1830s when the second city of Cairo was under construction. They also left something to be remembered by, a large number of dogs which turned wild, multiplied, and became a real nuisance for a long time.

Three different land companies attempted to build the city of Cairo. The first attempt in 1817 failed after a short time. The second attempt began March 4, 1837, when the Illinois legislature chartered the Cairo City and Canal Company to build the city. The third attempt started June 13, 1846, when the trusties of the Cairo City property obtained control of Cairo. The second attempt by the Cairo City and Canal Company did the most to build the city.

Darius B. Holbrook had complete control of the second project. Holbrook was a well-known and influential man in New York City before taking on the project. From January 16, 1836, to February 10, 1851, Holbrook poured his heart and soul into the project. John M. Lansden wrote that Holbrook was a "force of character, strong will, ceaseless activity and enterprise, initiative, ability to bring others to see things as he saw them, were only some of his remarkable endowments."[101] It seems he had one drawback: he spent money like there was no end to it when building the city.

The first thing Holbrook did was travel to London, England, to procure loans to build the new city. On his return, Holbrook bought most of the peninsula on credit with the company buying some of the land at exorbitant sums. The first priority was building a levee to hold back the annual floods. Work started immediately, and when completed, the levee stretched for 12,320 feet along the Ohio River and 4,780 feet along the Mississippi River. The levee never was completed during Holbrook's time in Cairo. The northern levee was not finished until 1844.

Next, Holbrook went about hiring contractors to build the city. The contractor's employees and their families soon arrived. At the same time members of the Illinois Central Railroad arrived in town to start building a railroad. Cairo's population swelled to almost two thousand overnight. The first building built was—guess what—a tavern. A store and all kinds of huts and shanties followed. Construction was also started on mills, foundries, manufacturing plants, and a shipyard. New roads built through the forest increased airflow, with the result being a better climate to live in. Living in a hut or shanty wasn't for everyone and soon people were living in boats tied to the levee. Businessmen took notice and soon opened shops on boats as well. Cairo had become a boomtown.

In the nine years that the Cairo City and Canal Company spent building the city, no land or lots were ever sold to anyone. Only long-term leases were used. Holbrook's policy was to wait till the city was established, and then sell to the inhabitants on the company's terms. The company owned every house and business in the city and nothing was built unless the company gave their approval. The company made all the rules and all the penalties for breaking the rules. It owned all the land between both rivers and no one could set foot on any of it without being charged with trespassing.

The city had been under construction from 1837 to 1841 when all hell broke loose. Holbrook had spent too much money. Wright and Company of London went bankrupt, so funds from the sale of bonds dried up. The State

---

101 John M. Lansden, A History of the City of Cairo Illinois, [Carbondale, Illinois: Southern Illinois University Press 1910] [Reproduced by Duopage Process, Cleveland, Ohio: Beel & Howell] p. 190.

of Illinois was also having money problems and stopped work on the railroad and public works. Holbrook knew Cairo was a sinking ship and left town before work stopped. He felt that he would be blamed for the downfall of the city, and was probably right. It didn't take much to get yourself lynched in those days, and I'm sure Holbrook took that into consideration. Holbrook didn't give up on Cairo after leaving. In fact he worked ten more years trying to save the city but without success.

Soon after Holbrook left, all work on the city stopped. Not only did everyone lose their jobs, but their backwages as well. The city went up for grabs. History of Randolph, Union, and Pulaski counties wrote about what happened next.

> Recklessness and mob law reigned supreme—idleness, rioting, demoralization and drunkenness held sway, and the seething, roaring mob were as a den of mixed wild beasts, where only the fierce and bloodthirsty passions were manifested or to be met. Here was the rapidly gathered together young city, of about two thousand people, plain laborers mostly, many skilled mechanics, boarding-house keepers, engineers, merchants, traders, contractors, and the women and children.[102]

Anthony Olney, the superintendent of the Cairo City and Coal Company, tried to hold down the fort but soon gave up. The city was being ransacked by just about everyone, including the women and children. The company gave up at this point and withdrew all its agents. The workmen they left behind were soon auctioning off much of the company's property for only a pittance of what it was really worth and then leaving town. The population rapidly plunged to about fifty people. Those who stayed had the whole city at their disposal. They soon began moving into the best abandoned houses, including Holbrook's. No one bothered to pay rent or taxes. The huts and shanties became a source of firewood. There was absolutely no law or order there either.

The floating city of boats tied to the levee still remained and became the hub of all business activity in the city. How they managed to stay in business with only fifty people living there is probably due to of all the river traffic landing there. The levee became the place to be as *History of Alexander, Union*

[102] History of Alexander, Union and Pulaski Counties, Illinois. Ed. William Henry Perrin., [Chicago, Illinois: O.L.Baskin & Co. 1883] [Evansville, Indiana: Unigraphic, Inc.1969] p. 91.

and Pulaski Counties notes," Here were the gathering places, eating places, drinking places and the center of all fun or excitement. People wanted to see the steamboats land; they wanted to go on board, look around and by examining the passengers, recall recollections of when they were innocent members of the civilized world."[103]

The Cairo City and Canal Company returned in 1843. The company sent Judge Miles A. Gilbert to reclaim the city in April of that year. Gilbert was no stranger to Cairo. He'd been highly involved with building the city since 1835. He was a stockholder in the company with influence on par with Holbrook. Judge Gilbert managed to take control of the city after first convincing one mob to leave, and then fighting off another mob. The company also managed to scrape together enough money and workers to complete the north levee in 1844. The north levee was completed just in the nick of time. The Mississippi River was so high in 1844 that the whole area from Saint Louis to New Orleans was flooded, Cairo being the only exception.

I realize I haven't written a thing about Leftcovitch but the history of Cairo is too good, plus it's my book and I can write whatever I want. I will start by stating that Martin filed his declaration of intension to become a citizen April 30, 1844, in Alexander County. He became a citizen in April, 1846.[104] According to the 1850 Federal Census of Alexander County, Leftcovitch's oldest son Robert was born in Alabama in 1841.The other son Matthew was born in Illinois in 1843, so it looks like the Leftcovitch family came to Cairo shortly after the cities collapsed. The 1850 census also shows Martin's age as forty-one, occupation grocer, and born in Poland. His wife Lucy is forty-two, born in North Carolina.

It also appears that the Leftcovitch family was running a boarding house at the time. The 1850 census shows the following people living with the Leftcovitches:

> James Dally, 35, Laborer, born in Ireland.
> Edmond Greenland, 34, Laborer, born in Ireland.
> Thomas Carrigan, 32, Laborer, born in Ireland.
> James Brown, 26, born in Missouri.
> John C. Walker, 24, Brewer, born in Ireland.[105]

---

103 History of Alexander, Union and Pulaski Counties, Illinois: p. 36.

104 Massac County Genealogical Society, Naturalization Records from the Illinois Court House of Alexander County, Transcribed by Darrel Dexter. [Melber, Kentucky: Simmons Historical Publications 2000] p. 32.

105 Maxine E. Wormer, Alexander County, Illinois 1850 census p. 3.

With this number of boarders, the Leftcovitches might have moved into a house. In 1848 they were living in a houseboat named *Cradle of Liberty*. The Leftcovitches suffered a tragic accident while living on their houseboat. Death notices for Cairo newspaper's 1848-1859 describes this sad story.

May 25, 1848

> On Friday morning at 8:00 Martin Leftcovitch's only daughter Josephine fell from the boat and drowned. She was two years old and one of the prettiest and most intelligent children we ever met, and a general favorite. She was missed a few minutes after the accident and her body found floating three fourths of an hour later. Efforts were made in vain to resuscitate her.[106]

The Leftcovitch family might have lost another daughter. Church records for Saint Patrick's Catholic Church shows Mary Ann Leftcovitch baptized on Christmas day 1844.[107] The 1850 census shows no daughter at all. I think the Catholic Church records must have their dates mixed up. The 1860 census contains the name Anna Leftcovitch, who is seven years old.[108]

Saint Patrick's Catholic Church was first created in 1838 and was the first church in the city of Cairo. *History of Alexander, Union and Pulaski Counties* has a very interesting description of the early church.

> The Catholic element, mindful of their religious obligations, set about the preparation of a place for the public worship of God. As they were limited alike in means and building materials, and as they desired to sub serve only a temporary purpose, they satisfied themselves with a rough, board roofed shanty in the depths of the convenient woods. In the forks of one of the trees overshadowing their unpretending church building, they suspended a bell, and this, every Sunday morning and evening, rang out through the deep woods and over the face of the surrounding waters the call of "Come, and let us worship."[109]

---

106 Darrel Dexter, [Death Notices from Cairo Newspapers 1848-1859 Alexander County, Illinois 1998] p. 5.

107 John M. Lansden, p. 138.

108 Darrel Dexter, Louise Ogg and Russell Ogg, Alexander County, Illinois 1860 Federal Census. [Published by The Genealogy Society of Southern Illinois C/O John A. Logan College] [Utica, Kentucky: McDowell Publications 1993] p. 42.

109 History of Alexander, Union and Pulaski Counties, Illinois. p. 27.

On the 1855 census, occupations are not listed. The 1855 census was a state, not federal, census, which means only the name of the head of household is written. Everyone else living there is broken down by male or female. Ages are between zero and ten, ten and twenty, etc. With the number of people still living in the house, it looks like Martin was still operating a boarding house. In 1855 there were one male and one female between the ages of zero and ten living there. One male between ten and twenty. Four men between thirty and forty and one man and one woman between forty and fifty. In addition, one black male lived with the family, age unknown.[110]

On the 1860 federal census, Martin is fifty-one, his occupation landlord. There's only one tenant listed though. John Turner, thirty-five, carpenter, born Philadelphia. Lucy is forty-nine and a housekeeper. Sons Robert, seventeen; Matthew, fifteen; and daughter Anna, seven, all attend school.[111]

The last record I have of Martin is in the 1865 Cairo City Directory under the listing "Martin Leftcovitch boarding house."[112] The 1870 federal census lists Lucy sixty-two, as the head of household.[113] Martin must have died. I've never been able to find the date of Martin's death, but we can assume it was sometime in the late 1860s.

I have one more thing worth mentioning about Cairo. It concerns the bad reputation the city had. It was common knowledge everywhere that Cairo was one of the worst, most dangerous river towns around. Cairo was a frequent stop for riverboats from both rivers. Many of their crews were comprised of tough-looking characters that spent most of their time hanging around the dock. The locals in town contributed to the city's bad reputation by making up grim stories to tell visitors as well. In reality Cairo was probably no worse than other river towns.

There might have been other Poles in Alexander County by 1850. Alexander County marriage records have a couple names that could be Polish. On June 12, 1842, Matthew Mileusky married Mrs. Mary McCormack.[114] On

---

110 Darrel Dexter, 1855 Alexander County, Illinois Census Records: [Published by The Genealogy Society of Southern Illinois C/O John A. Logan College] [Utica, Kentucky: McDowell Publications 1991] 1855: p. 46.

111 Darrel Dexter, Louise Ogg and Russell Ogg, 1860 Federal Census of Alexander County, Illinois p. 42.

112 1865 Cairo City Directory p. 101.

113 1870 Federal Census of Alexander County, Illinois: [National Archives, Box 593, Roll 188, Page 26]

114 Saga of Southern Illinois: [Volume 18] Alexander County, Illinois Marriages 1840-1850: P. 5.

June 13, 1843, George W. Barnes married Sarah Ann Meskie.[115] There's no way to determine if either of these people were Polish, or of Polish descent.

History of Alexander, Union and Pulaski Counties contains a record of once-thriving towns in the 1800s that are gone now. One town was known as "Poletown." It's worth noting that it didn't take much to become a town in those days, just two qualifications. The first was a cabin at a crossroad. The second was that a resident of the cabin could read and write. This person was then made postmaster, at which point the pony express would start to deliver mail there once a month.[116] Of course there's no way to know if Poletown actually had Poles living there, but it's worth mentioning.

Then there's this story in death botices from Cairo newspapers 1848-1859. This article takes place a year after the time frame of this book. I'm including it anyways.

20 November, 1851

> By telegraph from Caledonia we learn that on Friday night a traveling Polander stopped at a certain man's house named Bass in the Hazelwood Settlement, which is in this, and Pulaski County and requested to stay all night. He was told he could sleep in the schoolhouse across the road if he would pay .50 for the privilege. The next morning he started off without paying and the man to whom he made application followed him a short distance with a gun and shot him. He proceeded to the next house and was kindly allowed to stop. When last heard from he was in a critical condition and his life despaired of. One of Bass's tales is that the Polander was rapidly making off with one of his horses, but this statement is contradicted by some of the neighbors who saw the Polander between Bass's and the next house where he was taken in. Bass has fled the country.[117]

The Hazelwood Settlement no longer exists. What's the moral to this story? Pay your bills no matter how small or learn to control your temper. The traveling Polander was a victim of a senseless killing. We'll see another Pole involved in a senseless killing in Fayette County.

---

115 Liahona Research, Illinois Marriages: 1826-1850. [Bountiful, Utah: Heritage Quest, 1999] P. 41.

116 History of Alexander, Union and Pulaski Counties, Illinois: p. 471.

117 Darrel Dexter, [Death Notices from Cairo Newspapers 1848-1859 Alexander County, Illinois. 1998] p. 18-19.

Other people with Polish-looking names came to Alexander County in the 1850s. The 1855 Illinois State census contains two possible Poles. The first name is John Cinduska and wife. Both are between the ages of twenty and thirty years old. There's also a son between zero and ten years old.[118] The Bohemians began to settle in Illinois after 1850, so Cinduska could also be Bohemian. The second name is Nicholas Daruski. His age was between twenty and thirty. His wife is between ten and twenty years old.[119] Nicholas lived in Tazewell County before moving to Alexander County.

By the 1860 federal census, new Polish-looking names appear.

Valentine Malinski, 26, shoemaker, born Germany.[120]

Henry Malinski, 36, shoemaker, born Germany. They were both living in a boarding house owned by Fred Bross who was also born in Germany. Other tradesmen from Germany and England were also living there.[121]

Felix Malinski, 37, shoemaker, born in Poland. His wife Susanna, 21, born in France. Daughter Anna, 2, born in Illinois. Son Constantine, 4 months old, born in Illinois.[122]

Joseph Osthuski, 27, shoemaker, born Poland. Joe was living in a boarding house owned by Louis Weil, born in Germany. Irish tradesmen were also living there.[123]

The Leftcovitches and Malinskis continued to live in Cairo for a number of years. Telegram's 1895 Cairo City Directory has the last record of any Leftcovitches residing there.[124] The last record of a Malinski is the 1942 Cairo City Directory.[125] I'd like to thank Louise Ogg and Darrel Dexter for their help with this story.

---

118 Darrel Dexter, 1855 Alexander County, Illinois Census Records, p. 40.

119 Darrel Dexter, 1855 Alexander County, Illinois Census Records, p. 44.

120 Darrel Dexter, Louise & Russell Ogg, 1860 Federal Census of Alexander County, Illinois, p. 35.

121 Darrel Dexter, Louise & Russell Ogg, 1860 Federal Census of Alexander County, Illinois, p. 35.

122 Darrel Dexter, Louise & Russell Ogg, 1860 Federal Census of Alexander County, Illinois, p. 35.

123 Darrel Dexter, Louise & Russell Ogg, 1860 Federal Census of Alexander County, Illinois, p. 11.

124 Telegram's Cairo Directory, 1895. P116.

125 Cairo City Directory, 1942. P. 91.

Boone County

Boone County had one very famous Pole named Pavel Sobelewski. Boone County was created from Winnebago County on March 4, 1837. The county is located in northeastern Illinois with its northern border the Wisconsin state line. Belvidere is the county seat. In its primitive state, Boone County was almost all prairie. The countryside is level to rolling hills.

Pavel was one of the 234 Polish exiles from Trieste. He created the first Polish magazine in the country and was a newspaper editor, musician, translator, author, and poet. Pavel is most famous for translating the works of the Polish poets Slowacki, Mickiewicz, and Krasinski into the book *Poets and Poetry of Poland*. In his old age, he helped Polish emigrants get a start in Chicago. I can say with absolute certainty that my ancestor knew Pavel very well. They were both from Lower Podolia, probably in the same army, and most likely spent two years in prison together. They are both mentioned as "outstanding conspirators" in the Polish rebellion in Lower Podolia.[126] I doubt they hung out much together since Pavel was seventeen when he came to America, while my ancestor was almost forty.

Pavel was born June 16, 1816, in the town of Hajsyn. Hajsyn was located in Lower Podolia at the time but is currently a part of western Ukraine, being southwest of Kiev. Lower Podolia came under Russian domination after the second partition of Poland in 1793. Pavel's parents were Martin and Endoxa Sobelewski. The Sobelewskis were nobility, and Pavel had a good education at the Basilian Fathers Academy in the town of Uman. The Basilian fathers had administrated the highly esteemed academy in eastern Poland since the 1600s. Uman was a little east of Hajsyn and located in what was then the province of Kiev. Foreign language must have been very important at the Basilian Fathers Academy. Pavel's obituary writes, "He spoke fluently English, German, French, Polish, and Russian, besides a good Greek and

[126] Jozef Bialynia Cholodecki, General Kolyszko and his subordinates in the area of Galicia: [Lwow: Ossolinskich 16 1912] p. 3.

Latin scholar."[127] Pavel dropped out of the academy in the eighth grade to join the Polish uprising in the spring of 1831. He was only fourteen years old.

Pavel's daughter Ada wrote a biography of her father and claimed Pavel was the only son and not obligated to serve in the military. One day Pavel observed a group of soldiers marching past the Sobelewski house. One soldier saw him and urged him to join the rebellion, but Pavel declined. Cries of coward rang out from the other soldiers. Being called a coward was too much for Pavel, and he mounted a white horse owned by one of the soldiers and went off to war. It was the last time he would ever see his home.[128]

I am not convinced Ada got the whole story right. Sometimes details get lost in interpretation. Mieczylaw Haiman claimed Pavel was a cadet.[129] I have a document which lists Pavel as an outstanding conspirator of the rebellion in Lower Podolia. This indicates that Pavel was involved in the rebellion before it started.[130] At fourteen years old, you would think Pavel too young to help start a rebellion. I do not think age mattered as much then as now. That goes for old age as well. The commanding general of my ancestor's army was eighty-one-year-old General Benedykt Kolyszko.[131] Pavel might have been involved with the Jelowicki family of Haysyn who organized the local uprising. The Jelowickis joined forces with insurgents from the Olhopol region of Lower Podolia and another group from the province of Kiev. Benedykt Kolyszko was elected commander of the force.[132] In all fairness, their army was more of a militia than a professional army.

The rebellion in Lower Podolia was pretty much of a disaster. It started May 13, 1831, and was disorganized from the start. Despite all their problems, they did come close to winning the first battle with the Russians. If they had won, more men would have joined their cause. The rebellion only lasted ten days ending on May 23. I write more about the rebellion in Lower Podolia in the story about my ancestor Franciczek Wlodecki. On May 23, 1831,

127 The Standerd Newspaper, Belvidere, Illinois: [June 3, 1884]

128 Paul Sobolewski file, Illinois State Historical Library: Springfield, Illinois: [Biography copied from handwritten "biography" sent by Mrs. Shane to Mrs. Rawlings] P.1.

129 Mieczyslaw Haiman, Slady Polskie W. Ameryce: [Chicago, Illinois: Drukiem Dziennika Zjednoczenia 1938] p.120.

130 Josef Bialynia Cholodecki, p. 3.

131 Josef Bialynia Cholodecki, p. 3.

132 R. F. Leslie, Polish Politics and the Revolution of November 1830: [University of London, The Athlone Press 1956] [Westport, Connecticut: Greenwood Press Publishers 1969] p. 200 &201.

Kolyszko's army crossed the border into Austria to escape a large Russian Army. The Austrians arrested the whole army and interred them in a large castle in Chortkov, which is located in the present country of Ukraine. The army was never large to begin with. The force was a little over two thousand men strong at the beginning of the uprising. By the time they crossed the border, only four to five hundred men remained. At Chortkov, the Austrians put the officers and ringleaders under heavy guard, but looked the other way when the lower-ranking soldiers escaped.

After five and one-half weeks in confinement, those soldiers left were transferred under heavy guard by foot to the interior of the Austrian empire. Soldiers with means were allowed to use wagons. They were marched south through Ukraine into the Carpathian Mountains of present Romania, to the plains of Hungary.[133] Their final destination was a prison near Brno, in the present Czech Republic. Some insurgents write about spending time in a number of different prisons before ending up in Brno. Pavel's obituary claims he spent two years in prison.[134]

In 1833, the Austrians arrested another group of Poles who attempted to start a new rebellion under the leadership of Zaliwski. This group was sent to Brno as well. After four months in prison, the Austrians gave them the choice of going back to Russia or deportation to America. Going back to Russia was out of the question. The Poles all wanted to go to England or France, where they could continue the struggle for Poland's independence. Going to another European country was not an option, and the Poles were marched on foot from Brno to Trieste, Italy. The first group left Trieste on two ships on November 22, 1833, Pavel among them. The two ships arrived in New York on March 28, 1834.

Pavel was one of the youngest Polish exiles at seventeen years of age. Pavel and another one of the Polish exiles named August A. Jakubowski were about the same ages and best of friends. In 1835, August wrote and published one of the first Polish\American books in America called *Remembrances of a Polish Exile*. August was also a Podolian, growing up along the banks of the Dniester River. My family also lived along the Dniester River. Part of the book recounts the history of Podolia, and I use quite a bit of it in the story about my ancestor. After publishing his book, life went downhill for August, and he committed suicide in 1837.

Pavel moved to Philadelphia in 1834 and remained there until 1840. His first job was at a publication called "Portrait Gallery of Distinguished

133 Josef Bialynia Cholodecki, p. 2 & 3.

134 The Standard Newspaper, Belvidere, Illinois: [June 3, 1884]

Americans." He was supposed to have worked there a few years, but the 1836 Philadelphia City Directory lists his occupation as a "confectioner."[135] Pavel's first published work in America appeared in 1835-36 when he translated two Polish national hymns, "Jeszcze Polska" and "Warszawianka." These two hymns were the favorite songs of the late Polish rebellion. He paid for the publishing out of his own pocket. Pavel occasionally published some articles for a magazine named *The Lady's Amaranth.* The magazine published seven of his poems and one article during the years 1838 and 1839.

Pavel moved to New York in 1841 and in 1842 began publishing his own magazine called *Poland.* He felt the American public knew too little about Poland and developed his magazine to inform them about the music, history, folklore, literature, and architecture of Poland. It was the first Polish magazine in the country and the first Slavic magazine published in America. The first issue included stories about Copernicus, Jan Sobieski, Castle of Ostrog, Queen Hedwiga, Prince Joseph Poniatowski, and the Temple of Sybil. On May 28, 1842, the *New World* literary magazine wrote,

> Three numbers of this popular and interesting work have already appeared. Each number is well embellished with engravings, and contains well written and authentic articles on various subjects, relating to unfortunate Poland. The work is worthy of patronage, and we hope the American public will extend to it a liberal support. It is published at the low price of fifty cents a number.[136]

Pavel targeted his magazine to socialites and the middle class. He intended it to be "an addition and ornament to the Parlor.[137] Unfortunately, the magazine folded before the end of the year. Only four issues of Poland are now in existence.

Besides starting his own magazine in New York, Pavel found himself a wife there as well. After moving to New York, he had become friends with Charles van Zandt. Van Zandt was very well-off and invited Pavel to live in his house. There Pavel met and fell in love with Van Zandt's daughter Marie Louise. They were married sometime in the 1840s in a Lutheran church on Long Island. Marie was in poor health, and their marriage never produced any children. Pavel's daughter

---

135 The Polish Review: The Polish American Historical Association of the Polish institute of Arts and Sciences in America [St. Mary's College, Orchard Lake, Michigan, Volume xix Number 3-4 1974] p. 86.

136 The Polish Review, p. 91.

137 The Polish Review, p. 87.

Ada claimed Marie Louise was an invalid and told to move west by her doctor with the hope that her health might improve.[138] Pavel took her to Madison, Wisconsin, but her health never improved, and she died there in 1848.[139]

Pavel stayed in Wisconsin after his wife died. His daughter Ada thought he remained in Madison after his first wife's death and remained single until he married her mother Julia M. Beckwith. Pavel, however, had left Madison and was living to the east in Racine County, Wisconsin. Records from Racine County, Wisconsin, show that Pavel sold 80 acres to a Mr. Strong for $275 on October 18, 1844.[140] On the same day, Pavel paid Mr. and Mrs. Strong seven hundred dollars for 110 acres near the town of Bristol.[141] Bristol is located in southeast Wisconsin near the Illinois-Wisconsin state line. My ancestor Franciczek and five other Polish exiles from Trieste were all living a short distance south in Lake County, Illinois. Lake County is located in the far northeast corner of Illinois and borders the current Kenoska County, Wisconsin. It was still Racine County when Pavel bought his land there.

One of the 234 Polish exiles from Trieste was already living near Bristol. Thaddeus Pienkowski had moved to the area in the spring of 1843.[142] A manuscript written by two of Thaddeus's daughters claims that one of their father's fellow exiles proposed starting a farming partnership in the fall of 1843. Thaddeus wanted no part of any partnerships. He had been in partnerships before and got burned. Thaddeus did consent to manage the farm on shares. The Pienkowski family soon moved into the farm's large log cabin and managed the farm for four years.[143] The name of the exile offering the partnership is not mentioned, but it must have been Pavel Sobolewski.

Pavel bought another farm near Bristol on May 13, 1846,[144] and paid $800 dollars for 160 acres. On December 14, 1847, Pavel sold ten acres for

---

138 Paul Sobolewski file at the Illinois State Historical Library, p. 2.

139 The Polish Review, p. 89.

140 Racine County, Wisconsin, Mortgages: [Racine County Register of Deeds Office, Racine, Wisconsin Book D.] p. 325 & 326.

141 Racine County, Wisconsin, Deeds: [Racine County Register of deeds Office, Racine, Wisconsin: Book K.] p. 215.

142 Mrs. Sarah Norton Lockhart Young & Mrs. Minnie Eliza Pienkowsky Buckley, A Brief Sketch of the Late History of our Father and Mother: [Sent to me by Mr. Robert L. Pienkowski of Blackburg, Va.] p. 9.

143 Mrs. Sarah Norton Lockhart Young & Mrs. Minnie Eliza Pienkowsky Buckley, p. 10.

144 Racine County, Wisconsin, Deeds: [Racine County Register of Deeds Office, Racine, Wisconsin: Book O.] p. 407.

$120.[145] This last transaction was signed by Pavel and his wife Elizabeth. Now comes the confusing part. He was supposed to have been married to Marie Louise van Zandt until she died in 1848. Registration of marriages, Racine County, Wisconsin, shows that Pavel married Elizabeth Udall on December 17, 1847.[146] Elizabeth had signed the December 14, 1847, land transaction as Pavel's wife. Maybe the date of Marie Louise's death is wrong or else they were divorced?

The 1850 Federal Census for Bristol, Wisconsin, only adds to the confusion. The census shows Pavel living on the farm of Salmon Clark and family. Salmon is listed as head of household, sixty-three years old, occupation farmer and born in New York. His wife Polly is fifty-three years old and born in New York. Sons George, twenty, and William, twelve, were both born in New York. Daughter Elizabeth is seventeen years old born in New York. Pavel's wife Elizabeth Udall is not on the census.[147] What happened to her?

Pavel's oldest daughter Paulina was born in 1851 in Wisconsin, so Pavel and Julia M. Beckwith must have married right after the 1850 census was taken. Pavel's daughter Ada wrote that her dad was teaching languages in Madison when he married her mother. Julia M. Beckwith was born in Cazenovia, New York. She had much more education than most women of her time, having attended the University of Cazenovia. Julia traveled west for the same reason as Pavel. Her sister was sickly and advised to move west for her health where Julia became her nurse.

The Sobolewski family moved to Spring Township, Boone County, Illinois, sometime around 1851-53. Boone County is located in northeastern Illinois, and its northern boundary is the Wisconsin state line. Spring Township is located in the southeast part of Boone County. The 1860 Federal Census for Boone County, Illinois, shows Pavel's age is forty-three and his occupation farmer. Julia is thirty-one years old. Daughters Paulina, nine, and Ada, seven, both born in Illinois. Daughter Elizabeth is five years old and son James is four months old.[148]

A eulogy by Henry Archacki titled "Paul Sobolewski—the Pole Incarnate" contains some information about Pavel's time in Boone County. The local

145 Kenosha County, Wisconsin Recorder Office, Kenosha, Wisconsin: [Volume J] p. 347 & 348.

146 Racine County, Wisconsin Registration of Marriages: [Book 1] p. 78.

147 1850 Federal Census of Kenosha County, Wisconsin: [National Archives, Box 432 Roll 1000, Page 210]

148 1860 Federal Census of Boone County, Illinois: [At the Nation Archives, Roll 157, p. 408]

farmers considered him a "Latin farmer." A Latin farmer is a farmer who can speak Latin better than he can farm. Archacki goes on to write, "His personality and interest made him a local Diogenes and Plutarch rolled into one! He became a champion of many causes and a faddist of sorts. He strongly objected to men shaving, claiming it was injurious to the health and the cause of tuberculosis and other ailments. He became a phrenolgist and lectured widely on this subject turning over the proceeds to the Civil War widows and orphans."[149] A phrenologist believes the shape of the skull influences a person's characteristics. Pavel tried to join the Union army during the Civil War but was turned down because his left eye was almost blind.

I found a story about Pavel in the April 21, 1866, Waukegan Gazette. Pavel was lecturing about physiology and phrenology when he got off his subject and went into a diatribe about supporting the local newspapers. This story actually fits in with what is going on now with newspapers going out of business and reminds me of those people who read their paper on the Internet.

> The lecturer was trying hard to impress upon his audience the importance of supporting their county newspapers, adducing many good reasons why they should do so. While this argument was going on, some of the audience looked upon him with a peculiarly pleasing expression of countenance, as to say, "every word is true." Those were the individuals who patronized the printer, and always paid for their paper. Another part of the audience, as the plea was going on, seemed to look on the floor of the schoolhouse never raising their eyes. These were the gents who didn't take papers, and felt a little ashamed. But the third part of that assemblage presented the most painfully interesting sight-they neither looked on the floor nor on the lecturer, but had their faces turned sidewise looking towards the windows and the walls of the room, seemingly disliking the lecturer's meddling with what they thought was none of his business. And who do you suppose they were? Our reporter found out to a certainty, that they were all delinquent subscribers, who take their county paper, but never find it convenient to pay for

149 Henry Archacki, Eulogy delivered by Henry Archacki, National Chairman American Polish Civil War Centennial Committee-at the unveiling of the Sobolewski Memorial Stone in Graceland Cemetery, Chicago, Illinois on September 24, 1966. [Article found in the Paul Sobolewski file at the Illinois State Historical Library, Springfield, Illinois]

> it, and are in arrears from one to two years on their subscription. They are the gentlemen who indulge in the pleasing idea that publishers of county papers can live on the little end of nothing whittled to a point.[150]

Pavel was a real stickler about paying for your newspaper. He chastised the residents of Spring Township about it during one of his lectures on February 17, 1863.[151] Pavel got sidetracked another time on one of his lectures on March 3, 1863.

> Lecture>-Mr. Paul Soboleski, of the town of Spring, gave a lecture last Tuesday evening, at Phoenix Hall. It was Physiology brought down to every day life. The lecturer came down heavy upon the defective ventilation of our school-houses, public halls, etc. Children and audiences sat for hours inspiring a poisoned atmosphere, unconscious that they were violating physiological laws and breeding disease in the system. He went in for forming discussion clubs in every school district—the mind exercise produced thereby was beneficial. He came down on tight lacing, thin shoes, late hours, hurried eating, shaving, etc. pretty heavy. His remarks upon these points consumed so much time that but little was said on the subject of Phrenology. It was a common sense lecture by a plain farmer, adapted to benefit the masses of the people, especially the females, who go on unthinkingly, year after year, violate the plainest laws of health, become prematurely old and worn out, and drop into an untimely grave. But, as is usually the case, when any thing really practical and useful is to be offered, nobody wants to hear it. The audieance was quite a thin one, partly owing, we support, to the fact that the proceedings at the Court House engrossed so much attention.[152]

In 1867, Pavel moved to Chicago. His marriage to Julia was not going well.[153] The 1870 Federal Census for Boone County shows Julia as head of household, forty years old, keeps house and widow of Paul. Pavel was not dead yet. Paulina is eighteen years old, and her occupation is teacher. She

150 The Waukegan Gazette, [Waukegan, Illinois April 21, 1866]

151 The Belvidere Standard Newspaper, [Belvidere, Illinois February 17, 1863]

152 The Belvidere Standard Newspaper, [Belvidere, Illinois March 3, 1863]

153 Henry Archacki, Eulogy:

married James Rice in 1871. Ada is seventeen and lives at home. She married Dan Shane in 1871. Elizabeth is fifteen and James is ten. Also living at the farm is Oscar and John Whitney. Oscar is twenty-three years old and his occupation farmer. John is eighteen years old and a farm helper.[154]

In Chicago, Pavel lived in a neighborhood of Polish emigrants in a one-room apartment on Randolph Street. The population of the Polish community in Chicago at the time was around two thousand. His small apartment became a meeting place for Poles of all ages. Over the next ten years, Pavel helped many Poles adapt to their new country. He was also instrumental in forming the first Polish Theatre in Chicago. The Chicago Fire in 1871 was a complete disaster for Pavel. The fire destroyed his personal library, and all his years of work translating Polish poetry was ruined as well. Pavel went right back to work and in 1881 published his most famous book, *Poets and Poetry of Poland.* The book was five hundred pages long, complete with steal engraved pictures. He used his own money to publish it and almost went broke in the process. Pavel would go on to publish one more book about the famous Polish king John Sobieski.

While living in Chicago, Pavel met the famous Polish actress Helena Modjeska in April 1879. Pavel either gave her or sent her a copy of his book *Poets and Poetry of Poland.* Modjeska described him as a poor Ukrainian.[155] I mentioned earlier that Pavel came from an area that is now in Ukraine. Pavel's father was a Roman Catholic while his mother was a Greek Catholic.[156] The Greek Catholic Church or Uniates were originally Orthodox Ukrainians who converted to a form of Roman Catholicism. I think they retained much of the Orthodox practices but the pope is the head of the church. The Uniates in Russia probably endured more persecution than any other religion in Russia.

Pavel died on May 30, 1884, of stomach cancer. His third wife Julia died February 12, 1875. The American Polish Civil War Centennial Committee had Pavel's remains reburied among the graves of other Polish exiles in Chicago's Graceland Cemetery on September 24, 1966.[157] I went to the Belvidere Public Library hoping to find out more about Pavel. The Sobolewskis still have a file in the genealogy room, but there is no information about Pavel in it. It does contain the obituary of Pavel's son James.

---

154 1870 Federal Census of Boone County, Illinois, town of Spring: [At the National Archives, Roll 189, Page 462]

155 Marion Moore Coleman, Modjeska and Sobolewski: [Paul Sobolewski file, State of Illinois Historical Library, Springfield, Illinois] p. 6.

156 Marion Moore Coleman, p. 14.

157 Henry Archacki, Eulogy:

Obituary

Died at the residence of his brother-in-law, A. E. Gardiner, Chicago, April 3rd, 1895, of peritonitis, James B. Soboleski. He was born in Belvidere Ill., February 25, 1860, and was the only son of Paul and Julia Soboleski, and was well known to all the old settlers of Boone Co. His home was in Belvidere until his mother's death in 1875, where he will be remembered as a bright, manly boy, the pride of his mother's heart. In 1878 he learned telegraphy at Janesville, Wis., and ever since has been in the employ of the C. & N. W. road up to the time of his death, at Mankato, and St. Charles, Minn., as operator, then as agent, at Lewiston and Plainview, Minn, respectively. Two years ago he was given the responsible position of Traveling Auditor of the road, which place he held at the time of his decease. In January 1884, he married Miss Ella Gardiner, the only daughter of a prominent citizen of St. Charles, Minn., who survives him, as also a little daughter ten years of age.

His remains were taken to St. Charles, Minn., for burial, the road furnishing transportation for all who wished to attend the funeral. The Auditors and railway associates attended in a body. The funeral was conducted under the auspices of the "Knight Templars" of which he was a loved member. He was a young man of marked ability, gentlemanly and courteous, beloved and respected by all with whom he came in contact. In his position he will be sadly missed. His wife, daughter, and three sisters have the sympathy of their numerous Belvidere friends, who mourn his untimely death.

"Leaves have their time to fall,
And flowers their time to Bloom;
But thou oh death! Thou
Hast all seasons for thine own."[158]

Pavel is described as tall and having vivid blue eyes. I noticed some people in Poland and Ukraine had big brilliantly colored eyes when I was in both countries on a research trip years ago. Pavel was also known for his good manners. He was right at home with American socialites, being a frequent visitor in their homes. Pavel was also an accomplished guitar player and singer who loved to entertain.

158 Sobolewski file, [Belvidere Public Library, Belvidere, Illinois.]

Chicago

Chicago, as would be expected, had many Poles, Polish Jews, and people with Polish-looking names before 1850. There are too many names to list now, so I will write about them later. For some reason, the 1850 census missed many Poles living in Chicago. The Polish Jews are the exception. I managed to find a number of Poles living in Chicago from other sources. *Early Chicago* has a tremendous amount of history, so I will try to give a brief description of life there up to 1850.

Chicago is located in Cook County. Cook was established from Putnam County on January 15, 1831, and was divided into Mc Henry and Will counties in 1836 and Du Page County in 1839. It is located in northeastern Illinois with its eastern boundary Lake Michigan and the state of Indiana. The county is large and encompasses nine hundred forty square miles. Cook is forty-eight miles long and twenty-five miles wide at its northern tip.

The best source I have found for Chicago history is *Early Chicago* by Ulrich Danckers and Jane Meredith, and most of the following story was taken from that book. Chicago got its name from the Illinois and Miami Indians who called the site where the future city was located, "Chicagoua." Chicagoua means "wild garlic," which grew there in profusion. The site of Chicago was low, wet, and mainly flat prairie mixed with woods. In the spring, the entire area from the Chicago River to the Des Plaines River, about nine to ten miles wide, was underwater. The site was home to a great number of wildlife including waterfowl, deer, wolves, bears, and at one time buffalo. The Buffalo in Illinois were all killed off by 1830. The last bear seen near Chicago was in 1837. Wolf hunts were common in the city limits well into the mid-1830s. Andreas published a description of Cook County from Beck's *Gazetteer* of Illinois in 1823.

> The country around Chicago is the most fertile and beautiful that can be imagined. It consists of an intermixture of woods and prairies, diversified with gentle slopes, sometimes attaining the elevation of hills, and irrigated with a number of clear streams and rivers, which throw their waters partly into the Mississippi River.

> As a farming country, it unites the fertile soil of the finest lowland prairies with an elevation which exempts it from the influence of stagnant waters, and a summer climate of delightful serenity; while its natural meadows present all the advantages of raising stock of the most favored part of the valley of the Mississippi.[159]

The Chicago River led to the portage between Lake Michigan and the Illinois River, then to the Mississippi River. Indians used the portage long before Europeans came. Frenchmen Louis Joliet and Father Jacques Marquette were the first Europeans to use the portage in 1673. The Chicago River was described in 1830 as about forty feet wide and more like a creek than a river where it flowed into Lake Michigan. Farther inland, the river got deeper and wider depending on the time of year. In late summer, the river was only two feet deep where it entered Lake Michigan. The north and south branches were from ten to twenty-six feet deep. About a mile west of Lake Michigan, the Chicago River split, one branch flowing north and the other south. The most popular portage took the south branch four miles south to Mud Lake, then west to the Des Plains River. There was also a lesser-used portage on the north branch.

Indians tribes inhabited the Chicago area until 1835. French missionaries, soldiers, and traders came to the region in 1690 and found two tribes of Miami Indians living on both branches of the Chicago River. In 1700, French trader De Liette counted about three hundred families in each village with a population of three to four thousand. The Miami moved from the area in 1718. The Potawatomi tribe came down from Green Bay, Wisconsin, in 1750 and resided in the Chicago area until removed by the government in 1835. The Potawatomi were involved in two of Chicago's most memorable events of which I will write about later.

Jean Baptiste Point De Sable, a free black, is considered the founder of Chicago. Before coming to Chicago, De Sable conducted a trading post in Michigan City, Indiana, with his partner Pierre Durand. De Sable moved to the future site of Chicago in 1775 and took up farming at the mouth of the Chicago River. He became a very successful farmer and had the advantage of having the only farm in the area. De Sable sold his farm to Jean B. La Lime in 1800 and moved to Missouri.

The United States government built Fort Dearborn in 1803-04. The fort was located on the Chicago River about one hundred yards west of

159 A. T. Andreas, [Chicago: A. T. Andreas Publisher 1884] [Reproduction by South Suburban Genealogical and Historical Society, South Holland, Illinois, Evansville, Indiana: Unigrafic, Inc. 1976] p. 339.

Lake Michigan. Fort Dearborn got orders to evacuate on August 9, 1812, and all inhabitants of the fort were supposed to go to Fort Wayne, Indiana. Two army officers and twenty-seven Miami Indians showed up to help evacuate the fort on August 13. About five hundred Potawatomi Indians were nearby and promised not to interfere with the evacuation. Inside Fort Dearborn were sixty-nine soldiers, twelve militiamen, twenty women, and twenty children. The group left the fort on the morning of August 15. After going about a mile and a half south, they walked right into a trap set by the five hundred Potawatomi Indians hiding behind sand dunes. The recently arrived Miami Indians had been warned about the attack earlier and left the field. Eighty-eight soldiers and settlers were killed before the fighting stopped. A few settlers managed to escape. The family of John Kinzie was saved by a friendly Potawatomi Indian named "Black Partridge." The fort was burned down the next day. One of the Miamis, who also happened to be half Potawatomi, rode up to the massacre when it first started and said,

> Potawatomi I am much astonished at your conduct—You have been treacherous with these people. You promised to conduct them safely thro. You have deceived them and are about to murder them in cold blood—let me advise you to beware—you know not what evil the dead shall bring upon you—you may by and by hear your wives & children cry & you will not be able to assist them. Potawatomi beware—so saying he rode on.[160]

The bones of the massacre victims were still lying around when Captain Hezekiah Bradley and 112 troopers arrived on June 30, 1816. They went right to work rebuilding the fort on the site of the old one. Part of Fort Dearborn was decimated by lightning in July 1827. Luckily, no one was in it at the time. The army did not use the fort much after that, and in 1834, it was sold to Jean B. Beaubien for $94. The United States Supreme Court decided it was the wrong time to sell the fort and gave Beaubien back his money. Stephen S. Wright bought a part of the fort in 1856 and used the lumber to build souvenir furniture. The Chicago Fire razed what was left of Fort Dearborn in 1871.

---

[160] Ulrich Danckers and Jane Meredith, A Compendium of the Early History of Chicago to the year 1835 when the Indians left: [Published by Early Chicago, Incorporated, River Forest, Illinois, 2000] [Menomonee Falls, Wisconsin: Inland Press 1999] p. 157.

The other Potawatomi incident took place on August 1, 1835. Five thousand Indians had gathered in Chicago to collect their last annuities before leaving for the west. Annuities were money, cloth, utensils, etc., paid by the government for ceding their lands. Usually annuities were given once a year, for a set number of years. John D. Caton claims that on the last day of August, about eight hundred Potawatomi performed a war dance through the streets of Chicago. The war dance started on the north branch of the Chicago River. The Indians wore only loincloths, painting the rest of their bodies with brightly colored paint. Caton writes, "On their faces, particularly, they seemed to have exhausted their art of hideous decoration. Foreheads, cheeks, and noses were covered with curved stripes of red or vermillion, which were edged with black paints, and gave the appearance of a horrid grin over the entire countenance."[161]

Starting on the north branch of the Chicago River, the Potawatomi slowly danced along the river carrying their tomahawks and war clubs. They were led by a band of Indians beating together sticks, clubs, and drums. Stopping in front of every house, the Indians carried out all types of crazed dances and acrobatic feats. The war dance crossed the bridge and continued along the south branch of the river. The more they danced, the more excited they became. Their shrieks grew louder and their dances wilder. They no longer just carried their tomahawks and war clubs but were swinging them around like madmen. They managed to scare the hell out of everyone in town and there was a real worry that the Indians might get carried away and start massacring everyone. The dancing ended at Fort Dearborn, and the residents of Chicago were real happy when it did. Captain Joseph Napieralski might have been living in Chicago when the war dance occurred.

Chicago's population grew slowly at first. Only four families lived there in 1803. By 1820, the city had ten to twelve houses with a total population of sixty people. It barely grew at all the next ten years and by 1830 only had twelve to twenty houses and up to one hundred people. Real growth began in 1832 when there were thirty houses and a population of about six hundred. In 1834 when the first Poles came to town, the population was close to two thousand with 180 buildings. Even in 1840, the population was still small with not quite five thousand people living there. By 1850, the city had a population of over twenty-seven thousand.

Until the 1830s, Chicago's ethnic makeup was mainly native-born Americans of British or Pennsylvania Dutch descent. They came from a cross section of states. Foreign-born settlers arrived in the 1830s, most from Ireland

---

161 Ulrich Danckers and Jane Meredith, [John Dean Caton] p. 46 & 47.

or Germany.[162] In 1843, Chicago had a population of 7,580 of which 2,256 were foreign born; 816 of those foreigners were from Germany or Norway and 773 from Ireland. By 1850, 15,682 people out of the 27,375 residents of Chicago were foreign born, 6,096 from Ireland and 5,035 from Germany.[163] Long John Wentworth, mayor of Chicago in 1857-58 and 1860-61, wrote,

> We had Jews and Christians, Protestants, Catholics, and infidels; among Protestants, there were Calvinists and Armenians. Nearly every language was represented here. Some people had seen much of the world, and some very little. Some were quite learned, and some very ignorant. We had every variety of people, and out of these we had to construct what is called society. The winters were long; no railroads, no telegraphs, no canal, and all we had to rely upon for news were our weekly newspapers. We had no libraries, no lectures, no theatres or other places of amusement. If a stranger attended a gathering of any kind, the mass of attendants were equally strangers with himself; and the gentlemen outnumbered the ladies by about four or five to one.[164]

Long John went on to add that finding a wife usually meant a trip back east. He also claimed that Yankees and Southerners were at odds with each other in Chicago. This was pretty much the case throughout the state. Pease claims, "Even in a moderately well-to-do settlement of southern men, the Yankee's insistence on writings, mortgages, bonds, and the like, and his superstitious observance of days and times contributed to render him unpopular as being unneighborly."[165] Pease later wrote, "In spite of the prejudice against Yankee's, they were repeatedly placed in situations of importance, often probably because their education and disciplined attention to business rendered them indispensable for many duties."[166]

---

162 Theodore Calvin Pease, The Frontier State: [Chicago: A. C. McClure & Co. 1922] p. 390 & 391.

163 The People of Chicago, who we are and who we have been: [City of Chicago Department of Development and Planning, Lewis W. Hill, Commissioner 1976] p. 10.

164 Reminiscences of Early Chicago: [Introduction by Mabel McIlvane] [The Lakeside Press, Chicago] [R. R. Donnelley & Sons Company 1912] p. 104 & 105.

165 Pease, p. 18.

166 Pease, p. 18.

Long John Wentworth also wrote about a wolf hunt which took place one winter within the city limits. This story will probably get me in hot water with animal rights people, but I like the story. Two bands of horsemen started out from two different locations and planned to rendezvous near Blue Island. One band rode south along the lakeshore while the other band started from the Chicago River. Their goal was to scare up as many wolves as possible and chase them onto the ice of Lake Michigan. No shooting was allowed until the wolves were on the lake, and all shoots had to be directed east over Lake Michigan. A number of wolves ran out onto the ice, and the horsemen gave pursuit. The weight of the horses was too much for the ice and soon the ice cracked and separated from the shore. The sheet of ice, along with the wolves, started to float away in a northeastern direction. I will let Long John finish the story.

> Men, women, and children lined the bank of the lake, expecting to see the ice break in pieces and the wolves swim to shore. But it did not do so. Our people watched the ice, and could see the wolves running from side to side, until they faded away from view. When I took my last look, they appeared about the size of mice.
>
> About two weeks afterwards, a letter appeared in a Detroit paper containing an account of some farm settlements, on the eastern shore of Lake Michigan, being attacked by a large body of hungry wolves. They destroyed fowls and cattle, and for several days spread terror through the neighborhood. We always supposed that those were our wolves, but our hunters never laid any claim to them, as the news of their arrival was so long in reaching here.[167]

The year 1835 saw the start of an out-of-control land speculation set off by plans to build the Illinois and Michigan Canal. The price of land in Chicago and the areas along the proposed canal route appreciated wildly. In 1832, a lot in Chicago sold for $35. In 1834, the same lot cost $3,500. By 1837, lots were rising in value 20 percent a day.[168] The bottom fell out in 1837, and the event is known as the Panic of 1837. Andreas writes that when the land office opened in 1835, large numbers of land speculators came to town. The rest of the country was going through a depression at the time. By 1837,

---

[167] Reminiscences of Early Chicago, p. 94 & 95.

[168] Howard B. Furer, Chicago A Chronological & Documentary History 1784-1970: [Dobbs Ferry, New York: Oceana Publications, Inc. 1974] p. 3.

the land speculation had run its course and East Coast banks refused to lend any more money. Land prices plummeted, and many Chicago speculators and businessmen went broke.[169]

Chicago's harbor was a work in progress for years. In order to get supplies to Fort Dearborn, the soldiers had to repeatedly cut a channel through the sandbar at the mouth of the Chicago River. Work on the channel was initiated in the years 1816, 1818, 1823, and 1829. As soon as they stopped work, the channel would fill up with sand again. Congress finally stepped in and gave the city twenty-five thousand dollars to help develop a harbor in March 1833. First, a bigger channel was dug out. Then a seven-hundred-foot pier was constructed on the north end of the river's mouth. Next, a two-hundred-foot pier was constructed south of the river's mouth. The two piers solved the problem, and the sandbar soon eroded away. Chicago's new harbor saw 456 ships dock there in the year 1836.

Almost every visitor to Chicago during this time describes it as either wet or muddy. During the spring and fall, the roads were impossible to use. John H. Thurston wrote, "There are two things very plentiful in and about the city, especially after a rain-ducks and mud."[170] Pulling people and wagons out of the mud was also a common occurrence. Early Chicago claims that in 1835, fifteen-year-old Fernando Jones pulled out a drunken Frenchman sunk waist deep in the mud. He was too late to help though; the Frenchman was lying facedown in the mud and already dead.[171] *Chicago: Growth of a Metropolis* writes,

> The streets were dust traps in summer and a quagmire the rest of the year. "They were begot in mud, born in mud, and bred in mud," an early Chicagoan remembered. Residents placed signs reading "No Bottom," "Team Underneath," and "Stage Dropped Through" to warn the unsuspecting of particularly treacherous spots. At one place a hat was dropped on the mud with the marking "Man Lost."[172]

---

169 A. T. Andreas, p. 134 & 135.

170 John H. Thurston, Reminscences, Sporting and Otherwise, of the Early Days in Rockford, Illinois: [Rockford, Illinois: Press of the Daily Republican 1891] Reprinted by "The North Central Illinois Genealogical Society of Rockford, Illinois [Dixon, Illinois: The Print Shop] p. 20.

171 Ulrich Danckers & Jane Meredith, p. 206 & 207.

172 Chicago: Growth of a Metropolis, [Harold M. Mayer, Richard C. Wade, Glen E. Holt] [The University of Chicago Press, Chicago, Illinois 1969] p. 24.

Chicago's commerce in its early days was mainly lumber, grain, and meatpacking. Farmers from the surrounding areas drove their herds of livestock through town to the packing plants. Wagon trains carrying wheat, some up to eighty wagons long, rumbled through town. April 21, 1843, saw the passage of one of Chicago's most misguided laws. It became illegal to let hogs roam free in town. I think they should still be able to roam free in town.

I could go on and on, never touching on the building of the Illinois and Michigan Canal, railroads, sanitation, disease, etc. My story about LaSalle County contains some information about the Illinois and Michigan Canal. I have written a book about early Polish settlers but have scarcely wrote a word about any of them. Captain Joseph Napieralski is supposed to be the first Polish settler in Chicago, arriving in 1834. I am not convinced he was and will explain later. There might have been someone of Polish descent in Chicago as early as 1826.

Early Chicago lists the marriage of Theotis Arnwaiskie to Daniel Bourassa on May 20, 1823. John Kinzie performed the marriage.[173] Their marriage certificate shows the date was 1826 and the last name spelled Avanwaisky.[174] There was a family with a similar last name living in Vermillion County, Indiana, at the time. The 1830 Vermillion County, Indiana, Federal Census contains the name John Awnvdonski. He was between the ages of forty and fifty years old. A woman twenty to thirty years old was also living there.[175] The 1830 census only contains head of household and approximate age. The marriage of Abigail Awadawski to Samuel (Solomon) Davis occurred in Hancock County, Illinois, on March 28, 1839. Abigail was born in Ohio.[176] Living near Abigail was Mary Jane Aversky and Margaret Everdiska.[177] I believe both are either sisters or relatives of Abigail. Both Mary Jane and Margaret were born in Indiana. I write more about the Awadawskis in my story about Hancock County.

Captain Joseph Napieralski is regarded as the first Polish settler in Chicago, arriving in 1834. According to Early Chicago, Joseph was born in Kaliszy, Poland, in 1800 and fought in the 1830 Polish uprising. He left

173 Ulrich Danckers & Jane Meredith, p. 60.

174 Peoria County Clerk, Peoria, Illinois: [Marriage Certificate]

175 The 1830 Federal Census of Vermillion County, Indiana: [National Archives Roll 26, p. 211]

176 Wilma Bruenn, Pioneers of the Prairie: p. 320.

177 The 1850 Federal Census of Hancock County, Illinois: [National Archives Roll 109, p. 348]

Poland after the war going first to Prussia, then to Norway, and finally to America. Some of the soldiers who served under him in the rebellion also came to America with him.[178] Joseph's daughter, A. Emily Napieralski, was a very well-known and influential woman in Chicago's Polish community. She claimed her father helped establish six Polish parishes in Chicago, one being St. Adalbert's.[179] Poles in Chicago 1837-1937 writes that Emily was the vice president of the Civil Service Commission of Cook County and served as either president or secretary of the Polish Women's Alliance for twenty-five years. She was selected by Mayor Kelly to participate in the Chicago Safety Commission. Emily was a celebrated public speaker and is responsible for urging Chicago's Polish community to buy Liberty Bonds (U.S. savings bonds). The sale of bonds raised over a million dollars for the United States government. According to Poles of Chicago 1837-1937, "Miss A. Emily Napieralski inspired and originated many worth-while movements for the Polish women of Chicago; the history of her achievements would fill a book and would be most interesting reading."[180]

Captain Napieralski might be the first Polish settler in Chicago, but I have some problems with the story. I cannot find any census records for him, but this is not a serious problem because there are no census records for many Poles in Chicago in 1850. The Chicago City Council Proceedings 1833-1871 has no mention of him voting. The captain is not mentioned in the book *The First Chicago Church Records 1833-44* either. Maryellen Tobiasiewicz has no record of him in her 1871 directory of Poles in Chicago. Maybe he was already dead by then. Lerski also has a problem with a part of Napieralski's story and wrote, "A Captain Napieralski is the authority for the statement that between 130 and 140 exiles were disembarked from a Norwegian ship in the early 1830's. It is hard to believe that a large group of Poles should leave no trace behind, nor even contact other exiles who reached the United States in the spring of 1834."[181] A John Napieralski, possibly Joe's son, was supposed to have been in the Second Illinois Light Infantry during the Civil War. I checked the second Illinois roster but could not find any Napieralski listed. The Napieralskis are a mystery to me.

---

178 Ulrich Danckers & Jane Meredith, p. 269.

179 Miecislaus Haiman, Poles of Chicago 1837-1937: [Chicago, Illinois: American Catalogue Printing Co. Polish Pageant, Inc. 1937] p. 203.

180 Poles of Chicago 1837-1937, p. 203.

181 Jerzy Jan Lerski, A Polish Chapter in Jacksonian America: [Madison, Wisconsin: The University of Wisconsin Press 1958] p. 85.

Three more Poles came to town in September 1834. The identities of only two are known, Baron Ludwik Chlopicki and Jan Prehal. Jan Prehal was not Polish but Czech and was hired by the Polish Committee to assist Chlopicki. Chlopicki only knew a limited amount of English while Prehal was fluent. The September 20, 1834, *Sangamo Journal* carried this story.

> Three of the exiled Poles, to whom Congress at its last session granted a township of land, arrived at Chicago on the 7th inst. On an excursion in quest of a location. A public meeting was held in Chicago immediately on their arrival, at which it was resolved that the hospitality of the town of Chicago be respectfully tendered through the president of the board of Trustees, to the Polish exiles in said town. Committees were appointed to receive donations for the benefit of the Poles, to invite those remaining in New York to visit Chicago, and to address a circular to the citizens of this state, soliciting for the unforunate exiles, their civilities and attentions.[182]

Michael Sadowski, one of the 234 exiles from Trieste, left more records of himself in the city than any Pole before 1850. He signed a petition on an undetermined date (possibly 1835) urging the mayor to create the job of "inspector of lumber." The petition noted that "such an office is very necessary and important and will meet the approbation of a large majority of our community."[183] The petition is located in the first roll of the Chicago City Council Proceedings, which are the earliest records of the city. Sadowski is recorded as voting in Chicago's first election on March 31, 1837. He and A. Panakaske voted in the Second Ward and J. Zoliski in the Sixth Ward.[184] Michael was living in the Fourth Ward when he voted in the March 6, 1838, Chicago Municipal elections.[185] He was back voting in the Second Ward for the May 4, 1843, Chicago Municipal elections.[186] Michael signed another petition on May 10, 1843. This one petitioned His Honor, the mayor, to build a sidewalk on Randolph Street between Wells and Madison Streets.[187] The 1844 City of Chicago Directory lists Michael's occupation as chair maker and living

182 Sangamo Journal Newspaper, September 20, 1834.

183 Chicago City Council Proceedings 1833-1871: [At Northeastern Illinois University Irad, Chicago, Illinois] [Roll 1, Document 141]

184 A. T. Andreas, p. 362.

185 Chicago City Council Proceedings 1833-1871, Document 590.

186 Chicago City Council Proceedings 1833-1871, Roll 8, Document 1566.

187 Chicago City Council Proceedings 1833-1871, Document 1676.

at the corners of Washington, Wells, and Frank streets.[188] Michael left Chicago sometime after this and settled in Fairfield, Iowa. The 1850 Federal Census for Jones County, Iowa, shows Michael's occupation as painter and chair maker.[189]

Andreas claims that the first Chicago election occurred in 1837. The Chicago City Council Proceedings shows election returns dated July 10, 1835. Two Polish-looking names are on it, and both are hard to read. The first one only records the last name and looks like Snyseski.[190] Snyseski might be a poor spelling of Sadowski. Someone named Stawecke was also living in Chicago around this time. A letter for Takop Stawecke showed up at the post office on February 13, 1836.[191] Stawecke might have been one of the 234 Polish exiles from Trieste. Lerski's list of Polish exiles contains the similar-sounding name of Sawicki.[192] The other name is spelled Jacob Artenbuski.[193] There is a record of a similar-sounding name in 1846. Vital records from Chicago newspapers 1833-45 writes that the *Chicago Daily Journal* printed a list of officers and agents employed by the board of commissioners for the Illinois and Michigan Canal. J Froscoboski was employed as a "rodman" on the canal on October 8, 1845.[194] The *New World Dictionary* describes a *rodman* as a person who carries the leveling rod in surveying.

A few other people with Polish-looking names showed up in 1835. John Kulozjcky witnessed the marriage of John Latzky to Potily Morris on October 1, 1835.[195] A letter showed up at the post office for Mr. Michriski on May 20, 1835.[196] A Louis Malaskey signed a petition on August 29, 1845, protesting a new tax by the city.[197] It also looks like R. Michriski signed a petition on

188 General Directory of the City of Chicago 1844. P. 31.

189 1850 Federal Census of Jones County, Iowa: [National Archives Roll 185, p. 198]

190 Chicago City Council Proceedings 1833-1871, Roll 1, Document 164.

191 Chicago Genealogical Society, List of Letters Remaining in the Post Office Chicago and Vicinity January 1834-July 1836: [Chicago, Illinois 1970] P. 50.

192 Jerzy Jan Lerski, p. 177, No. 201.

193 Chicago City Council Proceedings 1833-1871, Roll 1, Document 164.

194 Vital Records From Chicago Newspapers 1833-1845: [Compiled by the Newspaper Research Committee, Chicago Genealogical Society, Chicago, Illinois 1976] p. 28.

195 Rev. Joseph J. Thompson, The First Chicago Church Records 1833-34: [Reprinted from the Illinois Historical Review and Catholic Directories, Baltimore, Maryland: Gateway Press] Index 1988 by Nancy C. Thornton] [Distributed by Heritage Enterprises, Lemont, Illinois] p. 28.

196 Chicago Genealogical Society, List of Letters Remaining in the Post Office, p. 17.

197 Chicago City Council Proceedings 1833-1871, Document 2429.

August 28, 1846, recommending that Mr. Joseph Smith be allowed to operate a ferry at Lake Street and the south branch of the Chicago River.[198] J. Morasky voted in the Eighth Ward during the Chicago General Elections on March 21, 1847.[199] Four more letters with Polish-looking names came in 1836. I already mentioned the letter to Takop Stawecke in the previous paragraph. A letter addressed to Pawlinski and Kurylowicz arrived on April 2, 1836.[200] Both these people were members of the 234 Polish exiles from Trieste and are numbers 83 and 147 in Lerski's book.[201] Aleksander Grobicki claims Franciszek Kurylowicz was from Lithuania and was a noncommissioned officer in the insurrection.[202] Stanislaw Pawlinski was a second lieutenant in the insurrection.[203]

The last name in letters at the post office is Alfredoni Zakaszewski, whose letter was at the post office on January 2, 1836.[204] His real name has to be Alexander Zakrzewski, and he would go on to make quit a name for himself in California. According to Haiman, Alexander was born in Sandomierz, Poland, on January 1, 1799. He was a military engineer in the Polish Congress Kingdom Army in 1825, holding the rank of second lieutenant. Alexander took part in the 1830 Polish insurrection and was promoted to captain during the war. Alexander went to France when the rebellion ended with many other ex-Polish soldiers.

Alexander lived in Paris for a time and then became somewhat of a drifter. He moved around to such far-off places as Tahiti, the Reunion Islands, and Madagascar. It looks like he was in Chicago as well since a letter was waiting there for him. Alexander ended up in San Francisco, California, by 1849, the same year that so many gold prospectors came to California. San Francisco City records for 1850 shows Alexander living on Clay Street and his occupation lithographer. You readers will have to read your dictionaries to figure out what exactly a lithographer does. It is difficult to explain, but a lithographer makes some type of prints or pictures. He was a mapmaker or (cartographer) as well and made a number of them in Warsaw, Poland, and Paris before he left Europe.[205]

198 Chicago City Council Proceedings 1833-1871, Roll 18, Document 3344.

199 Chicago City Council Proceedings 1833-1871, Document 3415.

200 Chicago Genealogical Society, List of Letters Remaining in the Post Office, p. 59.

201 Jerzy Jan Lerski, p. 174 & 176.

202 Aleksander Grobicki, Proba Biografii, Sodalis: [St. Mary's College Library, Orchard Lake, Michigan] Letter K. p. 20.

203 Aleksander Grobicki, Letter P. p. 20.

204 Chicago Genealogical Society, List of Letters Remaining in the Post Office, p. 47.

205 Miecislaus Haiman, Polish Pioneers of California: [Copyright, 1940, by the Archives and Museum of the Polish Roman Catholic Union, Chicago, Illinois] p. 49.

Polish Americans in California 1827-1977 adds more. Alexander created the official map of the city of San Francisco in 1849. He made other maps of San Francisco as well as various California towns and the California countryside. His maps helped the earlier Spanish and Mexican citizens of California prove ownership of their land grants to the American government. He was also one of the founders of the Polish Society of San Francisco in the 1860s.[206]

Ferdinand Krizoski is recorded in the Chicago Fourth Ward election returns for March 21, 1847.[207] Rev. Joseph J. Thompson recorded the baptism of Ferdinand Pogd on March 25, 1838. The parents were John Pogd and Catherine Molden. One of the sponsors was Ferdinand Sebisky.[208] Julian Hulanicki, one of the 234 Polish exiles from Trieste, settled in Chicago by 1839. You will find out more about him in my story about Julian Hulanicki. Vital records from Chicago newspapers 1833-45 records one Polish name. On May 7, 8, and 9, 1840, "Stephen Owaska, the Polander" was a juror in a murder trial.[209] John Stone was tried for the murder of Mrs. Lucretia Thompson. Andeas writes that Stone was convicted and hung on July 10.[210] Vital records from Chicago newspapers 1833-45 lists the marriage of Thomas Giawaski to Cecilia Shaw on May 12, 1841.[211] According to the First Church records of Chicago, Basil Ignatius Joursky was baptized on May 1, 1842. The Reverend Maurice De St. Palais performed the baptism.[212]

Besides Michael Sadowski, only one other Pole comes close as to number of mentions in Chicago City Council Proceedings Files. Thomas Jaworski was also one of the 234 Polish exiles from Trieste.[213] I wrote a story about him titled Thomas Jaworski but will tell you about some of his experiences in Chicago. He settled in Cook County a few miles north of the city in 1839.[214] Thomas moved to the north side of Chicago by at least 1846. He signed a petition on July 3, 1846, to grade Des Plaines Street in the Third Ward between First and

---

206 Polish American Historical Association, California Chapter, Loyola Marymount University Los Angeles, California [Polish Americans in California 1827-1977 and who's who 1978] p. 36.

207 Chicago City Council Proceedings 1833-1871, Document 3415.

208 Rev. Joseph J. Thompson, p. 9.

209 Vital Records From Chicago Newspapers 1833-1845, p. 5.

210 A. T. Andreas, p. 386.

211 Vital Records From Chicago Newspapers 1833-1845, p. 24.

212 Rev. Joseph J. Thompson, p. 43.

213 Jerzy Jan Lerski, p. 174, number 69.

214 Andreas, p. 471.

Second streets. The area was flooding badly, and it was hoped that the water could be drained along First Street into the Chicago River. Thomas was the first person to sign the petition.[215] Thomas was living in the Fifth Ward when he voted in the March 2, 1847, election.[216] He signed another petition on April 23, 1847. This time to build a sidewalk on Jefferson Street. He was the fifth person to sign the petition.[217] Thomas signed a petition to build a sidewalk on Canal Street on June 16, 1848.[218] A month later, he signed another petition to extend Jefferson Street from First to Second streets.[219] There is also an 1850 census for the Jaworski family, but I will leave it in my story about Thomas.

Charles Pznosovsky signed a petition on February 26, 1849. Chicago was in the midst of a cholera epidemic, and the petition urged the city newspapers to start printing an edition in the German language. The city had a large German population, and many could not read English. It was thought that the entire population of the city should have "full knowledge of everything."[220] The *Chicago Daily News Almanac and Year-Book for 1914* contains the name of William F. Blocki. He arrived in Chicago in 1850. William died on August 22, 1913.[221] According to Edmund L. Kowalczyk, Anthony Polenski settled in Chicago in 1850. He was a lieutenant of Hussars in the Hungarian revolt of 1848.[222]

The teachers' reports in the Chicago City Council Proceedings Files 1833-1871 contain some names that could be Polish. Keep in mind these records are hard to read. The February 27, 1841, teachers report for school District Number 4 records the name Michael Collinsk (Collinski?). He was a nineteen-year-old student.[223] District Number 4, School Number 9 recorded the name Barbara Levanbrske, six years old, on October 25, 1843.[224] District Number

---

215 Chicago City Council Proceedings 1833-1871, Document 3277.

216 Chicago City Council Proceedings 1833-1877, Document 3713.

217 Chicago City Council Proceedings 1833-1877, Document 6464.

218 Chicago City Council Proceedings 1833-1871, Document 4664.

219 Chicago City Council Proceedings 1833-1871, Document 6824.

220 Chicago City Council Proceedings 1833-1871, Roll 29, Document 5729.

221 The Chicago Daily News Almanac and Year-Book for 1944: [Compiled by James Langland, M. A.] [Copyright, 1913, by The Chicago Daily News Company] p. 640, died in 1913.

222 Edmund L. Kowalczyk, Polish American Studies, [The Polish American Historical Association of the Polish Institute of Arts and Sciences in America, St. Mary's College, Orchard Lake, Michigan Volume XL 1-2 January-June 1954] p. 38.

223 Chicago City Council Proceedings 1833-1871, Roll 6, Document 1094.

224 Chicago City Council Proceedings 1833-1871, Document 1800.

4 contains the name Leirski on February 24, 1844.[225] I cannot make out the first name. There was a Liepski living north of Chicago in Niles Township in 1847.[226] Nancy Annosky, six years old, is listed on the District Number 4 teachers report on January 29, 1848.[227] The District Number 3, School Number 2 teachers report for October 27, 1849, has the name Brazila E. Weiska, seven years old.[228]

Captain Bernard Stempoffski was probably the most well-known Pole in Chicago's Polish community in 1850. Haiman calls him "the most active person in the economic development of Poles in Chicago in the years 1846 to the Civil War, was a land agent, Captain Bernard Stempoffski, whose office was located at 73 W. Randolph Street."[229] According to Julie Joan Giertuga, Captain Stempoffski served in both the Polish and American armies. In America he participated in the Seminole War from 1835 to 1937 and spent eight months in Company F, Second United States Dragoons in the Mexican War of 1847-48. In the Mexican War, he took part in the battles of Palo Alto and Resaca de la Palma. When the Civil War started, Captain Stempoffski was ready to serve again. Bernard and two other men, Marland L. Perkins and Dwight S. Heald, recruited a company of men from Chicago and the surrounding area during the summer of 1861.

Stempoffski was made captain of the ninety-four-man company. On October 7, 1861, Stempoffski's company was assigned to Company F, Ninth Illinois Cavalry. Captain Stempoffski was supposed to have been a real stickler for drilling his troops, and Julie Joan Giertuga states, "He was a very strict disciplinarian . . . The command, 'Wollensack to the rear, column march' was often heard with more dread than pleasure by his Co. F."[230] Captain Stempoffski only served in Company F until May 29, 1862. The army discharged him before his company had seen any action. After his discharge, he went back to his land agent job in Chicago. I have not been able to find out why he was discharged, but maybe he was just too old. I also cannot find the date of his death. He was still alive when the City of Chicago took a special census in 1871.[231]

---

225 Chicago City Council Proceedings 1833-1871, Roll 12, Document 2298.

226 Jacob Kercher, Niles Center Pioneers in the 1800's.

227 Chicago City Council Proceedings 1833-1871, Roll 23, Document 4234

228 Chicago City Council Proceedings 1833-1871, Document 5410.

229 Miencislaus Haiman, Poles of Chicago 1837-1937, p. 12.

230 Julie Joan Giertuga, p. 46.

231 Maryellen Tobiasiewicz, Poles in Chicago Part 111: [Chicago, Illinois: Chicago Genealogist Magazine, Summer, 1983] [Publication of the Chicago Genealogical Society] p. 180.

The 1850 Federal Census of the City of Chicago is my last source of information for Poles in Chicago. As I mentioned earlier, most Poles on the 1850 census are probably Polish Jews. I tried to weed out the Polish Catholics from the Polish Jews, so I am only making an educated guess. After mentioning the probable Polish Catholics, I will also write about the first Polish neighborhood in Chicago.

Living in the First Ward, John Sieawske, twenty-nine years old, occupation shoemaker and born in Poland.[232]

Living in the Fourth Ward, M. Cattinsky, thirty years old and born in Poland. His wife is twenty years old and born in Poland.[233] This might be the Michael Collinski who was a nineteen-year-old student on the February 27, 1841, teachers report for School District Number 4.

Living in the Fourth Ward, Kukkosky, thirty-five years old and a laborer.[234]

Christina Cronkosky, no ward listed. Her occupation is cook, and it looks like she works on a ship. Christina is twenty-one years old and born in Germany.[235]

According to the Polish Genealogical Society, Antoni Scherman (Smagorzewski) is considered the founder of the Polish community in Chicago. He was born on May 24, 1818, in Wagrowiec, Duchy of Poznan. He brought his wife Frederica and three children with him from Poland and settled in Chicago on June 1, 1851. The children's names were Ludwika, Dorota, and Stanislaw. He was a carpenter, and his first job was building Pullman sleeping cars. Antoni built a house, store, and buffet on the northwest side of Chicago in 1867. His property was located at Noble and Bradley streets, near the future Milwaukee Avenue.[236] Maryellen Tobiasiewicz claims that Antoni owned a saloon and "appears in the records of the Cook County Recorder of Deeds as the owner of many parcels of land during this time period."[237] Parot claims that Antoni was living at the Noble and Bradley streets location during the Civil War.[238]

---

232 1850 Federal Census of Chicago, Illinois: [National Archives, Roll 102, p. 147]

233 1850 Federal Census of Chicago, Illinois: [National Archives, Roll 102, p. 251]

234 1850 Federal Census of Chicago, Illinois: [National Archives, Roll 102, p. 244]

235 1850 Federal Census of Chicago, Illinois: [National Archives, Roll 102, p. 455]

236 Rodziny, Polish Genealogical Society Newsletter: [Fall, 1986] p. 29.

237 Maryellen Tobiasiewicz, Poles in Chicago Part 11: [Chicago, Illinois: Chicago Genealogist, Spring 1983] p. 119.

238 Joseph John Parot, Polish Catholics in Chicago, 1850-1920: [DeKalb, Illinois: Northern Illinois University Press 1981] p. 20.

Twenty-four to thirty Polish families lived around him, and a large number of German emigrants were living in the vicinity. Antoni changed his name to Scherman from Smagorzewski at some point to attract more German customers. Antoni's land was on the edge of the city and Parot writes,

> Schermann's property and surrounding environment must have reminded him of many Polish farming communities. From the still undeveloped and sparsely settled prairie on the outskirts of ante-bellum Chicago, he could see nothing but grassland stretching westward to the horizon. East of his land stood a thickly wooded area guarding both banks of the nearby North Branch of the Chicago River which swung noose-like around Goose Island. The virgin land between Schermann's settlement and the river was populated at the time by chickens and cattle belonging to neighboring farms.[239]

Antoni was one of the founders of St. Stanislaw Kostka Church. Built in 1868, Antoni was appointed the first president of the church. Also in 1868, Antoni switched occupations and became a shipping agent. The position allowed Antoni either the time or the influence to assist Poles trying to immigrate to America. He is supposed to be responsible for helping over one hundred thousand people immigrate to America, most but not all Poles. Antoni died in 1900 and was eighty-two years old.[240]

Polish Jews

Even though Poland had not existed for over fifty years, the Polish Jews still listed Poland as their place of birth on the 1850 census. The Catholic Poles at the same time considered the Jews Polish but of the Jewish faith. The Society of Poles in America created by the Polish exiles from Trieste actively recruited Polish Jews. The *Societies Manifesto* wrote, "Every émigré Pole regardless of position and faith had the right to become a member of the association, its primary goal being mutual aid and brotherhood."[241] Henryk Sienkiewicz, the famous Polish writer, wrote an interesting observation in the 1870s about Polish Jews in America.

---

239 Joseph John Parot, p. 20.

240 Rodziny, Polish Genealogical Society Newsletter [Fall 1986] p.29

241 Stanislaw Osada, Historia Zwiaks Narodowego Polskiego I rozwoju ruchu narodwego pulsing w Ameryce Polnocnej. [Chicago: Polish National Alliance, 1905] p. 3 & 4.

> It was only here that I became convinced what an energetic and enterprising people they are . . . here where the population is extremely industrious . . . and the struggle for survival is conducted ruthlessly, and real commercial abilities of the Jews become fully evident. In trade and commerce the Polish Jews hold their own against Yankee competition, and if need be, could do so against the devil himself. They come here in most instances without a cent, without a knowledge of language or conditions, in other words with only their two hands and a good head on their shoulders . . . I do not know a single Jew who after a year's residence, is still in poverty . . . Each of them has money; each as the Americans say, "is making a living"; . . . Some of them manage to make millions.[242]

The first Jews came to Chicago in the late 1830s and early 1840s, most from Bavaria. Polish Jews started arriving in the late 1840s. The Jewish population of Chicago was less than one hundred in 1847. Chicago's population in 1847 was about seventeen thousand. Despite their small numbers, they owned a number of businesses on Lake Street. The first Jewish worship took place in 1845. The first Jewish cemetery was established in 1846 and was used often during the cholera epidemic of 1848-49. Many Jews were supposed to have died then. Those who made it through the epidemic lived in a constant state of anxiety that the sickness would come back. Jews continued to settle in Chicago despite the epidemic, and by 1850, the Jewish population was close to two hundred people.

The first Polish Jews immigrated to Chicago in the late 1840s. They were from Posen in German-occupied Poland and spoke German. The Bavarian Jews also spoke German but refused to have much to do with the Polish Jews. A different group of Jews from Russia, Lithuania, Romania, and Poland came to Chicago after the Polish Jews. This group spoke Yiddish as opposed to German. The Bavarian Jews were from cities in Bavaria and had a higher standard of living as compared to the latter group of Polish Jews who came from villages or small towns and had lived in poverty. As a result, the Bavarian Jews must have thought this last group of Polish Jews were all hicks and refused to have anything to do with them.

The Polish Jews established their own synagogue called Kehilath B'nai Shalom (Congregation of Men of Peace), in May 1852. H. L. Meites writes,

[242] Henryk Sienkiewicz, Portrait of America: Letters of Henryk Sienkiewicz, Edited and translated by Charles Morley, New York: [Columbia University Press, 1959] p. 219 & 220.

"The charter members were S. Harris, Casper Summerfield, Jacob Pieser, Jacob Frost and Jacob Auerbach."[243] The Polish synagogue was located on Clark Street, a couple of blocks from the Bavarian synagogue. They each used different prayer books. Over the years, Kehilath B'nar Shalom expanded its membership, and according to H. L. Meites, "At one time having the finest Jewish house of worship in Chicago."[244]

The first Polish Jews in Chicago were S. Marks and J. Marks who came in 1846 and whose names appear on the 1846 Chicago Directory.[245] On the 1850 Federal Census for the City of Chicago, James Marks is a Merchant and born in Poland. I cannot read his age. His wife is twenty-two years old.[246] The 1848 Chicago Directory contains the name David Witkowski.[247] David did well for himself and in 1858 "was the proud owner of four clothing stores at 97 and 102 Lake Street and at 33 North Clark and 311 South Clark Street, and lived at 111 Monroe Street, Conrad Witkowsky then being engaged as a clerk at 102 Lake Street."[248] The 1850 Federal Census of the City of Chicago has more people who are most likely Polish Jews. I translated their names to the best of my ability.

Conrad Wovlbiske, thirty-three years old, occupation tailor, and born in Germany. Conrad lived in the Second Ward.[249] This might be David Witkowski's brother.

Nithorowsky, twenty-nine years old, occupation tailor, and born in Germany. His wife Eutrine, twenty-five years old and born in Germany. They lived in the Third Ward.[250]

John Bauman, twenty-two years old, occupation barkeeper? Born in Poland and lives in the First Ward.[251]

Isaac Cohen, thirty-five years old, occupation grocer and born in Poland. Lives in the Second Ward.[252]

---

243 H. L. Meites, History of the Jews in Chicago: [Chicago, Illinois: Chicago Jewish Historical Society: Wellington Publishers 1990] p. 53.

244 H. L. Meites, p. 54.

245 H. L. Meites, p. 53.

246 1850 Federal Census of Chicago, Illinois: [Roll 102, p,216]

247 H. L. Meites, p. 53.

248 H. L. Meites, p. 67.

249 1850 Federal Census of Chicago, Illinois: [Roll 102, p. 196]

250 1850 Federal Census of Chicago, Illinois: [Roll 102, p. 205]

251 1850 Federal Census of Chicago, Illinois: [Roll 102, p. 164]

252 1850 Federal Census of Chicago, Illinois: [Roll 102, p. 164]

E. Long, thirty years old, occupation tailor and born in Poland. Lives in the Third Ward.[253]

N. Cohen, thirty-one years old and born in Poland. His wife M. is thirty-one years old born in Poland. Two daughters, a six-year-old and a nine-month-old. Both were born in Poland. They live in the Fourth Ward.[254]

M. Goodman, twenty-one years old, occupation merchant and born in Poland. Lives in the Fourth Ward.[255]

J. Kenny, thirty-six years old, occupation musician and born in Poland. Lives in the Fourth Ward.[256]

Some Polish Jews spent time in Quincy, Adams County, Illinois, before coming to Chicago.

Casper Summerfield: the 1850 Federal Census of Adams County, Illinois, lists Casper's age as twenty-one, occupation peddler and born in Poland. He was living with the Samuel Marks family in Quincy's South Ward.[257] I mentioned earlier that Casper was a charter member of Kehilath B'nai Sholom, which came into being in Chicago in May 1852.[258] He was elected president of Kehilath B'nai Sholom in 1857.[259]

The 1850 Federal Census of Adams County, Illinois, lists the name Samuel Marks. This could be the S. Marks listed on the 1846 Chicago Directory.[260] Samuel's age on the 1850 census is twenty-six, occupation peddler and born in Poland. His wife Sarah is twenty-eight years old and born in Poland. Daughter Eliza is seven years old, and son Ephram is three years old. Both of them were born in Poland.[261] If Ephraim is only three in 1850, this might not be the same S. Marks. It is possible the census taker recorded the Marks family for the 1850 census while Ephram was still three years old.

---

253 1850 Federal Census of Chicago, Illinois: [Roll 102, p. 212]

254 1850 Federal census of Chicago, Illinois: [Roll 102, p. 243]

255 1850 Federal Census of Chicago, Illinois: [Roll 102, p. 250]

256 1850 Federal Census of Chicago, Illinois: [Roll 102, p. 251]

257 Great River Genealogical Society, 1850 Federal Census of Adams Country, Illinois: [Volume 3, 1984] p. 106

258 H. L. Meites, p. 53.

259 H. L. Meites, p. 66.

260 H. L. Meites, p. 53.

261 Great River Genealogical Society, 1850 Federal Census of Adams County, Illinois: [Volume 3, 1984] p. 106.

Soloman Harris was living next door to Samuel Marks in Quincy. On the 1850 Federal Census of Adams County, Illinois, he is twenty-two years old, occupation peddler and born in Poland. His wife Hannah is eighteen years old and born in Poland.[262] Solomon was a charter member of Kehilath B'nai Sholom.[263] He was also the first president of Kehilath B'nai Sholom, and the new synagogue "met in rooms above the clothing store of Solomon Harris."[264]

Isaac Levy was another ex-Quincy resident. On the 1850 Federal Census of Adams County, Illinois, Isaac is forty years old, occupation merchant and born in Poland. His wife Henretta is thirty years old and born in Germany.[265] Isaac is recorded as one of the founders of Chevra Kaddisha Ubiklur Cholim, an organization conceived to help poorer Jews pay medical bills and burial costs.[266]

Poles have lived in Chicago almost from the beginning. I think there was probably more living in Chicago before 1850 than we will ever know because they left no records of themselves. Maybe they avoided the census or were just missed. This is all speculation. The two main settlements of Polish Jews in Illinois before 1850 were Chicago and Quincy in Adams County.

262 Great River Genealogical Society, 1850 Federal Census, p. 106.

263 H. L. Meites, p. 53.

264 H. L. Meites, p. 53.

265 Great River Genealogical Society, 1850 Federal Census, p. 90.

266 H. L. Meites, p. 87.

DeKalb County

DeKalb County had one Pole before 1850, Francis Easinski. I felt all along that he was one of the Polish exiles from Trieste but could not match his name to any names on the various lists of exiles. I am reasonably certain that Francis was one of the 234 Polish exiles from Trieste named Francizek Jan Jasinski.[267] The 1840 Winnebago County Census spells the Easinski name as Ysinscka. Whoever took the census down must have thought the name began with a "Y." The letter "J" is pronounced as "Y" in the Polish language. The 1850 and 1860 censuses spell his name as either Easinski or Edsinski. According to Aleksander Grobicki, Francis was a noncommissioned officer in the 1830 uprising.[268] Francis actually lived in Winnebago County first, which is located just a little northwest of DeKalb County. Francis might have settled in Winnebago County as early as 1836.[269] In 1846, Francis bought land on the prairie in Mayfield Township, DeKalb County.

DeKalb County was created from Kane County on March 4, 1837. Sycamore is the county seat. DeKalb County is located in northeastern Illinois, sixty miles west of Chicago. The settlement of this part of Illinois occurred much later than the rest of the state. According to Al Westerman, the area was Indian territory until the Treaty of Chicago, September 26, 1833. This treaty forced the Potawatomi, Ottawa, and Chippewa Indian tribes to cede their lands to the Federal government. The government paid them fourteen and one-half cents an acre. The land involved consisted of five million acres in northeastern and north-central Illinois and southeastern

267 Maria J. E. Copson-Niecko, Orthography and the Polish Emigrants from Triest 1834-1835: [Polish American Studies, Volume xxxi No. 2. Autumn 1974] p. 24.

268 Aleksander Grobicki, Proba Biografii, Sodalis: [St Mary's College, Orchard Lake, Michigan, letter "J"] p. 23.

269 Sycamore True Republican, August 26, 1903 P. 1 Col. 4. [Obituary located in the Obituary files of the Sycamore Public library, Sycamore, Illinois.]

and south central Wisconsin. In 1835, the tribes were resettled on land west of the Mississippi River.[270]

At the time of its settlement in 1835, most of DeKalb County was prairie. Boies wrote, "It is simply a plain parallelogram of rich rolling prairie, eighteen miles broad and thirty-six miles long, dotted with a few small groves and watered by a few small streams."[271] Otto John Tinzmann's book has a number of excerpts written about the prairie by early settlers.

> The prairies were often compared to the sea or ocean. The vastness and waving grass caused such comments as the following: The prairies strikingly resemble the solitary grandeur of the ocean. There is something, too, of a sternly striking character in the landscape of Illinois. The middle of these vast sweeping plains owing to their being destitute of trees, are indescribably silent and lonesome.[272]

Like the other prairie regions in Illinois, the first settlers to DeKalb County settled in groves and along the timbered areas of streams. No one thought prairie would ever be good for anything other than livestock pasture. The prairie was excellent pasture. The later settlers had to settle on the prairie, but this would prove to be a blessing in disguise. John Deere invented a new plow in 1837 that would turn the prairie into productive farmland. Prairie soil by the way is a more high-yielding soil as compared to a timber soil. Many of the settlers on the prairie had no stands of timber at all, and it became common to buy small plots of timber. Some of these woodlands were often ten to fifteen miles away. Easinske added a two-acre woodland to his holdings when he was able to buy one.

Living on the prairie was tough. The roads were bad. The only market for their farm produce was sixty miles away in Chicago. Prairie fires occurred every year. The roots of prairie grass were so thick that five yoke of oxen were needed to plow it. Many settlers often led a solitary existence. Sickness and disease were always prevalent. At different times cholera, erysipelas, scarlet fever, typhoid fever, and diphtheria passed through. Low, wet areas of the

---

270 Al Westerman, Public Domain Land Sales in Lake County, Illinois: [2006] p.8.

271 Henry L. Boies, History of DeKalb County, Illinois: [Chicago: O. P. Bassett 1868] [A Reproduction by Unigraphic, Inc. Evansville, Indiana: 1973] p. 5.

272 Otto John Tinzmann, Selected aspects of early social history of DeKalb County, Illinois: [Loyola University of Chicago, Illinois, Copyright by Otto John Tinzmann 1986] p. 106.

prairie were breeding grounds for malaria-carrying mosquitoes. This type of malaria was known as "ague" by the early pioneers. It rarely killed anyone but got the settlers very sick for a few days each year. Almost everyone had it.

Winter was an especially hard time on the prairie. Otto John Tinzmann's book includes a letter written by a Norwegian settler. "The country here is beautiful to look upon, but the long winter and the piercing cold such as I have never in my life experienced, together with the equally strong heat, cause me to advise that no person who has a good income in Norway to leave it."[273] A settler from neighboring Kane County wrote, "We have suffered this winter such intense cold in our log hut that I must raise every exertion to build a better house for my family and cattle . . . We lost a daughter this winter due to the cold."[274]

Helen Bingham's book has a letter from another Norwegian settler. It describes the hard life on the prairie but ends in a humorous way.

> "One feels the cold even more here than in Norway," wrote Johansen, "where there is no protection against the sharp, penetrating north wind," This wind drifted the heavy winter snows and packed them so hard, they would support almost any weight. One settler lived on the prairie in a sod house which was almost covered with snow. A man with a horse and sled drove over the corner one day and the owner stuck out his head and told him to stay off his house. The traveler replied that he would have to put up a sign.[275]

Though life on the prairie was tough; the settlers had plenty of good times too. Sleigh rides were popular in winter. There were church picnics, dances, singing clubs, and harvest balls. Debates were common. There were holidays to celebrate. Ira Douglas, Abigail Easinski's sister, also lived in Mayfield Township and hosted the annual agricultural picnic.[276] The prairie was full of wildlife, and the settlers made good use of them. The Easinskis lived in Mayfield Township, an area teeming with wild game. Deer, rattlesnakes, and coyotes were very common there. Helen Bingham wrote,

---

273 Otto John Tinzmann, p. 97.

274 Otto John Tinzmann, p. 98.

275 Helen Bingham, My Scrapbook of Collections and Recollections: [Copyright 1972 by Helen Bingham] p. 18.

276 Sycamore Tribune, August 25, 1903: [Book 1, page 125 of the Obituary books at the Sycamore Public library, Sycamore, Illinois.]

> During the first winter, my brother and I shot many prairie chickens and quail, just as many as we needed or could use. They were in such numbers that little skill was required in shooting them. Thus, we were supplied with fresh meat. Mother seldom used more than the breasts of the chickens, which she fried or broiled as steaks. Chickens would frequently light on the house, on the straw roof of the prairie stable and on the cow-yard fence. Quail did not venture so far out from the hazel brush which edged or bordered the timber.[277]

Before I start with Easinski, there is one more thing to mention. There was a serious crime problem in Dekalb County. Frontier regions are often lawless places, and the county was no exception. In the nearby counties of Lee, Winnebago, and Ogle, the situation was just as bad, if not worse. Crime was so bad in the area that Boies devoted a whole chapter on the subject called "The Banditti." According to Boies, the worst crimes occurred the first few years after the county opened up for settlement. Travelers and peddlers passing through the county were known to just vanish. Horse theft was endemic well into the 1850s. Counterfeiting and theft were also high on the list. There was even an incident of body snatching. Grave robbers dug up the bodies of the recently dead and sold them to a nearby medical college. Boies claims,

> A strong and well constructed net-work of organized crime at the time stretched over this whole section of country, and few were fortunate enough to preserve all their property from being swept up in its meshes. A good horse and his equipments was the most easily captured, and most readily concealed-consequently the most coveted and dangerous property in the country. No possessor of a fleet and famous horse dared leave him for a single night, unless secured in a strong, double-locked stable, guarded by faithful dogs, and oftentimes by the owner himself, who regularly slept in his stable.[278]

With very few or no lawmen around, the settlers did the only thing they could do to protect themselves; they turned to vigilantism. The Ogle County Lynching Club seems to have been the largest of such organization and had members in three different counties. The local population usually gave these

---

277 Helen Bingham, p. 28.

278 Henry L. Boies, p. 78 & 79.

clubs their backing. Lynching club members rode throughout the region watching for any suspicious activity and ordering those they considered bad characters or troublemakers out of the county. The suspected evildoer was given up to thirty days to leave or face lynching. A trial to prove your innocence was unheard-of, and if you could not sell your land in thirty days, too bad.

Now that you know a little about DeKalb County, I'll get back to Francis Easinski. Francis first lived in the city of Rockford in Winnebago County across the river from the Polish tract. He later moved to DeKalb County. Winnebago County is situated a little northwest of DeKalb County. I mentioned in the book foreword that the Polish tract was eighteen miles long, two miles wide, and located in three townships and on the west side of the Rock River.

Church claims, for years, the American settlers living on the Polish tract were not sure if they owned their land. The Polish tract was all located on the west side of the Rock River in Rockford, Owen, and Rockton townships. Those parts of Rockford and Rockton counties lying east of the Rock River were also kept off the market. The settlers living on the east side of the River all knew they owned their land but would need a new deed when the government put the east side up for sale. Daniel S. Haight platted the east side of Rockford in 1836 and sold the lots to settlers by quitclaim deed. Haight emigrated to Winnebago County in 1835 and was the first person to settle on the east side of the Rock River. When the Polish tract went on sale October 30, 1843,[279] the settlers on the east side were required to get new deeds. They sent Daniel S. Haight to bid on their lots on November 3, 1843. Haight successfully bid for their land and returned with their deeds on November 7, 1843.[280] Easinski paid Haight fifty dollars for his lot on the east side of the Rock River on November 17, 1843.[281]

The book *Early Days in Rockford* by John H. Thurston contains a lot of information about the early history of Rockford. Thurston came to Rockford in 1837 at the age of thirteen, so he would have lived in Rockford during the Polish tract dispute. You would think that the Polish tract would have been a major issue in Rockford at the time, but Thurston never writes anything about it. There is a hint that there were problems with land claims

---

279 Royal Brunson Way, The Rock River Valley: [Chicago: S. J. Clark Publishing Company, 1926] p. 480.

280 Charles A. Church, Past and Present of the City of Rockford and Winnebago County, Illinois: [Chicago: S. J. Clarke Publishing Co. 1905] [A reproduction by Unigraphic, Inc. Evansville, Indiana 1973] p. 50.

281 Winnebago Recorder of deeds, Rockford, Illinois: [Grantee Book 1, 1836-1849 Winnebago Country Book F. page 57.

in Rockford. According to Thurston, the year 1837 brought a lot more settlers to Winnebago County.

> At this time settlers began to come in very fast, and the few first settlers felt uneasy about their Claims, and some wanted to "unload," provided they could get their price, which was more than the Land would bring for years after. A great many claim-holders hung around "seeking whom they might Devour." If a wagon hove in sight, they would hold a council and decide what to do.[282]

Boies has an interesting comment about the Polish tract.

> The United States Government, in sympathy with the Poles who had just been overwhelmed in their contest for their independence by the power of Russia, had made a grant of a large tract of land on the banks of the Rock River to such of that nation as chose to settle on it. It was accordingly Surveyed some years earlier than most of this part of the State. Very few of that nation however, availed themselves of this privilege. Claims had been made on the same land by other and earlier settlers. These combined to drive away the new claimants. Numerous little stockade forts were built with loop holes for muskets, and a determination was expressed to drive the Polish emigrants out of the country, and they were entirely successful. They never occupied their grant.[283]

There must have been some hard feelings toward the Poles. Not knowing if you owned your land for eight years must have taken its toll. Nevertheless Francis chose to live in Rockford until 1846. The obituary of Francis's wife Abigail Douglas Easinski claims the Easinskis settled in Mayfield Township, Illinois, in 1836.[284] There is no mention of them ever living in Winnebago County, but Francis bought a lot there in 1843.[285] His son Alexander was born

---

282 John H. Thurston, Reminiscences, sporting and otherwise, of Early days in Rockford, Illinois: [Rockford, Illinois: Press of the Daily Republican 1819] Reprinted by The North Central Illinois Genealogical Society of Rockford, Illinois, [Dixon, Illinois: the Print shop] p. 24

283 Boies, p. 383-84

284 Sycamore True Republican, August 26, 1903.

285 De Kalb County Illinois Probate records, Sycamore, Illinois: [Francis Easinski file, Chattel property.]

in Illinois in 1839. The 1840 Federal Census for Winnebago County includes the Francis Easinski family. The census spells Francis's last name Ysinscka instead of Easinski. The census shows one boy between the ages of zero and five years old, two boys between the ages of five and ten years old, and one man between the ages of twenty and thirty years old. On the women side of the census, there is one girl between the age of five and ten years old and one woman between the ages of thirty and forty years old. Francis worked in manufacturing and trades in Rockford.[286]

Some parts of the 1840 and 1850 census records do not match up. The 1850 Federal Census shows that Francis age is fifty-five. His occupation is farmer and his place of birth is Poland. Wife Abigail is forty-six years of age and born in Vermont. On the 1840 census, Abigail is older than Francis. Son Alexander's age is eleven on the 1850 census, so it matches the 1840 census. One source I have claims Alexander was born in 1840.[287] The 1850 census shows son Francis Jr. is six years old and his sister Harriet eight years old. All were born in Illinois. Hannah Daniels is also living with the family in 1850. She is seventeen years old and born in New York.[288] The ages of the whole family in the 1860 census match the ages on the 1850 census.[289]

Francis could be the Pole mentioned in *Past and Present of Winnebago County*. This county history claims that one of the Polish exiles worked at the Rockford Hotel. It states, "Only one of those exiles ever subsequently appeared in Rockford or Winnebago County. He was employed for a time as a cook, in 1837, by Henry Thurston, the landlord of the old Rockford House.[290] Henry Thurston was the father of John H. Thurston whom I mentioned earlier. Francis is the only Pole listed in the 1840 Winnebago County census, so there is a good chance that he was the Pole working at the Rockford House.

The Rockford house was the first hotel in Rockford. It was built by Daniel S. Haight and Charles S. Oliver. I mentioned earlier that Francis bought his lot from Haight. At first, the hotel was a tavern. In 1837, two more stories were built. Staying on the third floor made for an interesting story.

---

286 Ernest Harding Jackson, The 1840 Federal census Winnebago County, Illinois: [Evansville, Indiana: Whipporwill Publications] p. 30.

287 De Kalb Country Cemeteries, Genoa Township: [Indexed by the Genealogical Society of De Kalb Country, Illinois Sycamore, Illinois.] p. 53

288 Mrs. Bernice C. Richard, 1850 Federal census of DeKalb County, Illinois: p12

289 Marilyn Robinson, DeKalb County, Illinois 1860 Census: 1981-1982 p. 64.

290 Charles A. Church, p. 50.

According to Church, "the third story, which was divided into two rooms, was reached by a ladder, which was made by slats nailed to two pieces of the studding, in the first story of the main building. The proprietor's son John was an important functionary. He made the beds and escorted the guests up the ladder when they retired."[291]

The Easinski family moved to DeKalb County in 1846. DeKalb County Probate Records show that on February 1, 1846, Francis bought twenty-eight acres on the prairie in Mayfield Township.[292] He added thirteen and one-half acres of prairie on November 11, 1848.[293] Francis bought two acres of timberland March 21, 1854.[294] On the 1860 Agriculture Census of DeKalb County, Francis claims to have fifty-seven tillable acres and three unimproved acres which is probably timberland. There are four horses, three milk cows, three calves, and three pigs. His farm produced 173 bushels of wheat, 100 bushels of corn, 100 bushels of oats, 10 bushels of potatoes, and 14 tons of hay. Also 400 pounds of butter.[295]

Mayfield Township encompassed twenty-two thousand acres. Five thousand of those acres were wooded, the rest prairie. Mayfield Township was first named Liberty Township. Eunice Nickerson, one of the first teachers of the township, proposed changing the name to Mayfield because of the abundance of wildflowers.[296] Besides New Englanders, many Pennsylvania Dutch settled in Mayfield Township. A number of Swedish and Norwegian emigrants came in the late 1850s.

Writing about the settlers, Otto John Tinzmann wrote that "most lived relatively good lives, starting with little but adding to their acres so that in old age they could start their children on farms or rent to others."[297] Francis died January 26, 1864.[298] Abigail died August 14, 1903, at the ripe old age of

291 Charles A. Church, p. 24.

292 DeKalb County Probate records, Sycamore, Illinois: [Francis Easinski file, Chattel Property]

293 DeKalb County Probate records, Sycamore, Illinois: [Francis Easinski file, Chattel Property]

294 DeKalb County Probate records, Sycamore, Illinois: [Francis Easinski file, Chattel Property]

295 1860 Agriculture Census of De Kalb County, Illinois: Illinois State Archives, Springfield, Illinois [Roll 31-6]

296 Sycamore True Republican Newspaper, May 12, 1937: [At DeKalb Country Genealogical Society, Sycamore, Illinois]

297 Otto John Tinzmann. P. 116.

298 De Kalb County Probate records, Sycamore, Illinois: [Francis Easinski file.]

ninety-nine. She was living with her daughter Mrs. Hattie Denny in Sugar Grove, Kane County, Illinois.[299] Francis and Abigail are buried in Pleasant Hill Cemetery in Mayfield Township.[300] After Francis's death, the Easinski family name was changed to Senska. This really threw off my research, and it took me quit a while to figure it out.

The 1870 census shows Abigail, Alexander, Francis Jr. and Harriett (Hatti) still living on the farm. Francis Jr. operated the farm while Alexander learned the brick mason trade.[301] Francis Jr. moved to Silver Creek Township in Sanborn County, South Dakota, in 1883. He died in 1894, and his obituary writes that he was one of the first settlers in the county and a farmer by profession. The "deceased was an upright, honorable man, and had the respect of all who knew him. He leaves a wife, two sons, and two daughters to mourn his death."[302] Alexander married Lucy Shutts sometime in the 1870s and moved to the village of Genoa, De Kalb County, by 1880.[303] Their marriage produced at least three children that I know of, two daughters and one son. Alexander was elected Genoa village trustee in the years 1882 and 1883.[304] Alexander's grandson Claude was born in Genoa in 1889[305] and served as a Genoa alderman for a time.[306] He was also one of the founding members of the Genoa Gun Club and elected the club's first secretary in 1910.[307] Claude lived in Genoa until his death on May 20, 1985.[308] I tried to contact his daughter Billie Lou Roland but was not successful.

---

299 Sycamore Tribune, August 25, 1903: [In the Obituary files at the Sycamore Public Library, Sycamore, Illinois]

300 Cemeteries of Mayfield Township, County of De Kalb, State of Illinois: [Published by the Genealogical Society of De Kalb County, Illinois, Sycamore, Illinois.] p. 2.

301 Florence Houghton Marshall, 1870 Census Mayfield Township De Kalb County, Illinois. P. 22.

302 Sycamore Public Library, [Obituary book # 22, p. 52]

303 Florence Houghton Marshall, 1880 Census Genoa Township De Kalb County, Illinois. [1985] p. 443.

304 Shiela Rae Lenihan Larson, [Genoa, Illinois A History of its Township 1836-1986] p. 20.

305 Index to Birth Record Book - 2 of De Kalb Country, Illinois: [Published by Genealogical society of De Kalb Country, Illinois Sycamore, Illinois]

306 Sheila Rae Lanihan Larson, p. 21.

307 Sheila Rae Lanihan Larson, p. 83.

308 De Kalb County Cemeteries Genoa Township, p. 62.

Effingham and Shelby Counties

I combined these two counties because the Poles in both counties lived in close proximity to each other. Three Poles settled in this area. Alexander Bielaski lived in Effingham County and George Suprunowski and Stefan Jankiewicz in Shelby County. George Suprunowski resided near the town of Holland, which was located in both counties. The boundary between the two counties ran right through the middle of town. The southern part of town was in Liberty Township, where Alexander Bielaski lived. Stefan Jankiewicz bought land in Shelby County from George Suprunowski.

History of Effingham County 1910 claims that Alexander Bielaski and George Suprunowski were "very early settlers" in the county.[309] History of Effingham County 1883 states that Alexander Bielaski and George Suprunowski settled in Effingham County in 1840.[310] In addition, Joseph A. Wytrwal and Julie Joan Giertuga have written extensively about Alexander Bielaski.

Effingham County became a county February 15, 1831, from parts of Fayette and Crawford counties. It is located in south central Illinois. St. Louis is about one hundred miles to the southwest. The state capitol of Springfield is eighty-nine miles to the northwest. The first settlers found a little over half the county wooded, the rest prairie. Two-thirds of the prairie had standing water on it for much of the year. This made Effingham County an unhealthy place to live. These wetlands were breeding grounds for insects and snakes, especially for malaria-carrying mosquitoes. The wetlands are all tiled and

309 Effingham County Biographical: [Chicago: Munsell Publishing Company 1910] [St. Clair Chapter DAR. Reproduction by Unigraphic, Inc. Evansville, Indiana 1972] p. 639.

310 History of Effingham County, Illinois: [Chicago: O.L. Baskin & Co., 1883] [Ann Crooker, St. Clair Chapter DAR. Reproduction by Unigraphic, Inc. Evansville, Indiana 1972] p.239

drained now and productive farmland. The terrain is mainly flat to rolling. The land in Liberty Township in the northwest part of the county is more hilly than the rest of the county. The Little Wabash River is the main river in the county. Wolf Creek is the chief river in Liberty Township.

The prairies came in all different sizes. Flowers of all colors grew everywhere. Gerhard identified 186 prairies in central Illinois. The grass growing on them were anywhere from "very short, and at other times, five to six feet high."[311] Others claimed that some prairie grass was "as high as a man's head on horseback."[312] Prairie fires were an annual occurrence.

The first pioneers to the county settled in or along the wooded areas. Their fields were small, and much of their diet consisted of wild game. *History of Effingham County 1910* wrote, "Wild game was plentiful, and the woodman's gun was an important adjunct to the housekeeping outfit, for by means of it the housewife could have her larder supplied with game."[313] *Effingham County, Illinois—Past and Present* contains an interview with Aunt Fanny Evans, an early settler to the county. She was born December 19, 1845, in Union County. Aunt Fanny gives some insight into life in Effingham County. They had all the wild food they needed, fish, foul, and in particular wild hogs. Her family always kept a fire in the fireplace to keep panthers from coming down the chimney. Aunt Fanny claimed, "Panthers were the most dreaded of wild beasts." She lived to be one hundred years old. Aunt Fanny was the mother of 10 children and had 150 grandchildren and great-grandchildren.[314]

In 1829, the federal government started building the Cumberland Road through Effingham County. This road opened up the county to settlement. It was first constructed by the Jefferson administration and was the first road built by the federal government. The Cumberland Road in Effingham County was finished in 1831.

Alexander Bielaski

According to Julie Joan Giertuga, Alexander was Polish nobility. His family belonged to the clan "Jastrzebiec." In Poland, clan was similar to coat of arms. Alexander was born August 1, 1811, near Minsk, which is located

311 Robert P. Howard, Illinois, A History of the Prairie State: [Grand Rapids, Michigan: William B. Eerdman's Publishing Company 1972] p. 3.

312 Robert P. Howard, p. 2.

313 Effingham County Biographical 1910, p. 620.

314 Effingham Regional Historical Society, Effingham County Illinois-Past and Present: [Effingham, Illinois] 1968. P.321-23.

in the present country of Belarus. Alexander was accepted to the military academy in St. Petersburg at a young age. His field of study was engineering topography. After graduating, he enlisted in the Russian Army. While surveying for the Russian government near Vilno, he was caught up in the revolutionary spirit of the Vilno University students. He accompanied the students to Warsaw and participated in the beginning of the revolution when Grand Duke Constantine had to escape from Warsaw.

Alexander enlisted in the Polish Army as a lieutenant under the command of General Dembinski. Dembinski was a cavalry general and had been sent to Lithuania to carry on the rebellion there. After an unsuccessful attack on Vilna, Dembinski was forced to fall back to Warsaw. While passing through the village of Owanta, the Russians caught up with the Poles. The only way to get into Owanta was by one wooden bridge. Bielaski was given command of three hundred men. Their mission was to stop the Russians long enough for the army to cross the bridge. After the army crossed, they were supposed to destroy the bridge.

Bielaski's forces gave the Polish Army enough time to cross the bridge, but only Alexander and twenty-nine of his men survived their mission. To evade the Russians, they traveled by night and slept in the woods by day. They soon ran out of food, so Bielaski was forced to leave the woods and look for food in a nearby village. Alexander did not realize until it was too late that a regiment of Russian infantry was also in town. The place was full of Russians, but Bielaski remained calm and spoke with them as he walked through town. Alexander fled town the first chance he got, jumped over a fence, and ran for his life. His men saw him sprinting in their direction and shouted to him what happened. "Oh, nothing," replied Bielaski. "Nothing but a regiment of Russian infantry close at my heels." Everyone ran for it, but the Russians managed to kill or capture more of his men. Only Alexander and one of his men made it back to General Dembinski's camp. Alexander was promoted to captain for protecting the army's retreat.

After rejoining the army, Alexander participated in the battle of Grochow and was shot in the mouth during the battle. The bullet passed through the back of his neck and knocked out all the teeth on one side of his face. Alexander fell down and soon the Russians were passing by. One Russian soldier noticed Alexander and stabbed him in the shoulder with his bayonet. Alexander pretended to be dead until the Russians were gone, then left when it was safe. He was dazed and parched with thirst. He found a stone bench to rest on and asked a nearby girl for some water. She must have misunderstood him for instead of water she brought Vodka. Thinking it was water, he drank it all down. I'll bet his face wound felt good after that. It did bring him to his senses long enough for him to get to a hospital.

Alexander recovered from his wound, but his face was scared for life. After the rebellion was over, he left Poland and walked to Paris, France. Alexander enlisted in the French Army but after a few months left for America with another Pole named Stefan Jankiewicz. They landed in Portland, Maine, sometime in 1832.

After arriving in America, Alexander found work as a railroad engineer. He was working as a surveyor in Florida three years later on the first railroad built in that state. Alexander moved to Illinois in 1837. He found employment as an engineer on the Illinois Central Railroad and at the State Highway Department. Alexander became a citizen in June 1841. He also got married in Springfield on July 17, 1842, to Ann Carey. Alexander and his new bride went to Mexico in November of 1842 to work on a railroad. The president of Mexico at the time was Santa Anna. This was the same Santa Anna of the Alamo fame. Santa Anna was so impressed with Alexander's work; he "offered Bielaski Mexican citizenship and a high rank in the Mexican Army."[315] Alexander chose to stay a citizen of the United States and, after working eighteen months in Mexico, came back to Illinois.

Alexander had another good reason to come back to the United States. He owned a considerable amount of land in Illinois. I have records of him owning land in three different counties. His first land purchase was on March 12, 1838, when he bought eighty acres in Shelby County.[316] Alexander bought land in Shelby County on two more occasions the same year.[317] On December 8, 1838, he bought eighty acres in Edger County.[318] Edger County is located on the Illinois-Indiana state line around seventy miles northeast of Effingham County. The first record of Alexander buying land in Effingham County is January 18, 1840.[319] Land records show him buying land regularly until he left the state. The last record I have shows him selling 320 acres in March 1847.[320] This would have been two years after he left the state.

In Illinois, Alexander switched occupations and became a farmer. While in Illinois, Alexander met Abraham Lincoln. They became better friends when they were both living in Washington, D.C., Julie Giertuga thinks

---

315 Julie Joan Giertuga, Polish contributions in Illinois during the War between the States: [Peoria, Illinois Bradley University thesis] 1948 p. 21.

316 General Index Grantee, Shelby County Book 1 1833-1859: p. 1 Volume 146.

317 General Index Grantee, Shelby County Book 1 1833-1859: p. 12

318 Shelby County Historical and Genealogical Society, Illinois Public Domain Sales, Shelby County: 1982 p. 34.

319 General Index Grantee, Effingham Book 1 June 1, 1833-November 6, 1866.

320 Shelby County Granter, Book A p. 171.

that they met in Springfield. Springfield is eighty-nine miles northwest of Effingham County. In horse and buggy days, it would make for a long journey. After farming for two years in Illinois, a General Shields talked Alexander into working for the General Land Office in Washington, D.C. He started work there September 1, 1845, and would go on to become the chief draftsman at the Bureau of Patents.

At the start of the Civil War, the Union army had a shortage of engineers. Alexander chose to join the army at the age of fifty. General McClernand wanted Alexander on his staff and wrote a letter to General Winfield Scott. Scott was commander of the Union forces at the time. He urged the general to speak to President Lincoln about assigning Alexander as his aide-de-camp. President Lincoln wrote back on August 10, 1861, designating Alexander aide-de-camp to General McClernand as well as giving Alexander the rank of captain.[321]

An article by Joseph A. Wytrwal has a different version about how Alexander came to join the Army.

> Lincoln walked from the White House to the residence which Alexander Bielaski then occupied . . . sat down in the living room and persuaded Bielaski that his past training in military matters and his experience in the wars, would make him a very valuable man in the Union Army, and asked him if he would accept a commission as Captain in the Regular Army.[322]

Alexander had a wife and seven children to support. It sounds like Alexander was not all that wild about joining the army either. In the end, the president talked him into enlisting. Alexander's grandson Frank Bielaski saw a letter President Lincoln wrote to Alexander that ended with "Go and fight for your adopted country."[323]

I only have census records of the Bielaski family for the year 1860. The family lived in the Seventh Ward of the District of Columbia. Alexander is forty-seven years old and born in Warsaw, Poland. All the other sources I have say that Alexander was born near Minsk. Wife Mary is thirty-five and born in New York. I cannot determine the age or place of birth of their daughter

---

321 Julie Joan Giertuga, p. 18-26.

322 Joseph A. Wytrwal, Polish American Studies: [Vol. xiv, no. 3-4 July-December] [The Polish American Historical Association of the Polish Institute of arts and sciences in America St. Mary's College, Orchard Lake, Michigan] 1957. P. 65-67.

323 Joseph A. Wytrwal, p. 66.

Rosetta. Daughter Jane is seventeen and born in Illinois. Son Victor is fifteen, born in Illinois. Sons Oscar, thirteen; Alexander, nine; and Eugene, five, were all born in Washington. Daughter Agnes is elven and born in Washington. Also living with the family is Margaret Holland. She is twenty-five years old, born in Ireland and occupation servant.[324]

Julie Giertuga states that Alexander went with General McClernand to join General Grant's army in Cairo, Illinois. Cairo is located at the very bottom of the state. Alexander was assigned to Company F, Thirtieth Illinois Infantry. From Cairo, Grant's army moved twenty miles south to Belmont, Missouri, where the Battle of Belmont was fought on November 7, 1861.[325] The battle was General Grant's first battle of the Civil War.

Lansden gives the following account of the Battle of Belmont. The main Confederate army was camped at Columbus, Kentucky. A smaller force of rebels was camped across the Mississippi River at Belmont, Missouri. Grant divided his army into three parts. One part went by boat to Belmont. Another part went by land from Bird's Point to Belmont while the third part went by land to Columbus.

The boat troops arrived much sooner than the land troops. The boat troops did not bother to wait for the land troops and hastily attacked the rebel camp. They easily captured the camp but found it deserted except for a three-month-old baby girl sleeping on the ground. The baby was taken away and later brought back to Cairo where Catholic Father Lambert raised her. The troops started to destroy and loot the camp and were soon spread out in all directions. This is what the rebels were waiting for. While the Union troops were destroying the camp, additional rebel troops had crossed over from Columbus. The Union forces had marched into a trap. The rebels opened fire from the woods. At the same moment, the Union land troops arrived and joined the battle. After a short but intense fight, the rebels left their positions in the woods and attacked. The Union troops broke rank and ran back to the boats. The Union troops made it back to the boats by nightfall with the rebels in hot pursuit. Most but not all Union troops made it on the boats. As they were sailing down the river, the rebels continued firing at them from the shore. Those Union troops who failed to reach the boats in time had to find their own way back. Those troops made it back to Bird's Point in a couple days.[326]

324 1860 Federal Census for Washington D. C. [At the National Archives, Box 653 Roll 104 p. 739 & 740.

325 Julie Joan Giertuga, p. 24.

326 John M. Lansden, A History of the City of Cairo Illinois: [Carbondale Illinois: Southern Illinois University Press 1910.] p. 63-65.

Julie Giertuga's dissertation includes a number of letters written by General McClernand, Colonel Napoleon B. Buford, and Colonel John A. Logan about what happened to Alexander. According to General McClernand, Alexander was advancing with the Twenty-seventh Infantry. Colonel Buford commanded the Twenty-seventh. They had left the main army and had made a difficult trip around a lake to be the first to attack the enemy. According to Colonel Buford,

> While forming under fire the gallant Captain Bielaski on his charger, was seen animating the men and assisting in forming the line. His heroic bearing was observed by us all. After having his horse shot under him he seized a flag, and advancing with shouts, he fell mortally wounded.[327]

Alexander was hit by a cannon ball and so badly wounded that it was almost impossible to identify him. In a letter to Mrs. Bielaski November 8, 1861, General McClernand stated that Alexander was shouting, "Follow me," when he was killed. General McClernard then wrote, "While I deeply sympathize with you in your irreparable bereavement, it is consolation to know he died a hero, covered with glory."[328]

Colonel John A. Logan wrote to General McClernand about Alexander on November 11, 1861. "A braver man never fell on a field of battle. Alexander Bielaski's ardent zeal in the course of his adopted country has won him the admiration of all succeeding ages."[329]

I have one more thing to say about the Battle of Belmont. After finishing research on the Sandusky family in Kentucky, I drove through western Kentucky to see what the country looked like. We stopped for the night at a campground at Columbus, Kentucky. To my surprise, there was a memorial to the Battle of Belmont there. I had no idea it was there. We got another surprise later that night.

We slept in a tent on a bluff overlooking the Mississippi River. In the middle of the night, a hellacious storm blew in. The thunder sounded like cannons, and there was a first-rate lightning show over the Mississippi River. You would have thought the Battle of Belmont was being fought again. The rain came down in buckets, and soon my tent and everything in it was soaked. We slept in the car the rest of the night.

---

327 Julie Joan Giertuga, p. 24-25.

328 Julie Joan Giertuga, p. 25.

329 Julie Joan Giertuga, p. 26.

Shelby County

Shelby County had two Poles living there by 1850, George Suprunowski and Stefan Jankiewicz. I mentioned earlier in the story that George Suprunowski was living in Shelby County by at least 1840. George is probably one of the Polish exiles from Trieste. He also lived on the American Bottoms in St. Clair County for a number of years. Stefan Jankiewicz bought land from George Suprunowski in 1842. I only have a small amount of information about Stefan.

Shelby County is in central Illinois and located north and west of Effingham County. It is situated a short distance south of the center of the state. This area was part of Fayette County until its creation January 23, 1827. In 1829, Macon County was created from Shelby County. Shelby County was divided again in 1843, this time to establish Moultrie County. The county seat of Shelby County is Shelbyville.

George Suprunowski and probably Stefan Jankiewicz lived in the far southern part of the county. The soil there was not as fertile as compared to the northern part of the county. The land in the north is also more level. When it was first settled, two-thirds of the county was prairie and the rest wooded. The area around Holland were Suprunowski lived was mainly wooded at the time it was first settled. The Kaskaskia is the most extensive river and runs through the middle of the county.

The town of Holland where George Suprunowski lived was located in both Shelby and Effingham counties. The county line ran through the middle of town. At one time Holland was a thriving, though small, town. At its largest, there were twelve families living there. The railroad stopped every week to pick up hay and livestock. There was a popular church there with about a hundred members. *Effingham County Past and Present* wrote that "Holland as a town is no more."[330]

We drove around looking for Holland to see if anything was left of it. I am glad to say it is still there, barely. On the Effingham side of town, I counted three houses and one trailer. The church is still there. The railroad tracks run north and south with Holland to the west of the tracks. The Shelby side of town has one house and the Holland Community Building which was established in 1946.

Mrs. Isaac Rawlings is the expert on Suprunowski. According to her, George was born in Poland in 1810. His family was nobility and George was a count. He attended the University in Warsaw in 1829. George joined the

[330] Effingham Regional Historical Society, p. 45.

Polish Army when the 1830 November uprising started. After the insurrection failed, the army George served in crossed into Austria where the Austrians arrested him and threw him in prison. For serving in the Polish Army, the Russians confiscated everything he owned. After a few months in prison, he was released on the condition that he leave the country. George went first to France and then to America, landing in New York on Easter Sunday, 1833, with forty or fifty other Poles. I disagree with this version of how Suprunowski arrived here. A *Polish Chapter in Jacksonian America* contains a number of lists of Polish exiles from Trieste. The name Jan Suprunowski is listed as a passenger on the ship *Adria.*[331] The *Adria* landed in New York in May 1835 and contained thirty-nine Polish exiles. The exiles from Trieste had been imprisoned in Austria where they were given the choice of going back to Russia or being exiled to America. For some reason some of the exiles from Trieste changed their first names but not their last names. I think George was one of them. Maria J. E. Copson-Niecko published a list of Polish exiles in Polish-American Studies called *Orthography and the Polish Emigrants from Trieste 1834-35.* On this list, Suprunowski's first name is written as either Jan or Grzegarz.[332] Rawlings wrote that George's middle name was Gregory.

After landing in New York, George learned the skill of hatter. At some point, he left New York and moved to New Orleans. After some time there, George moved to St. Louis and worked as a hatter for the French families in town. A hatter makes, sells, cleans, and repairs hats. There used to be an expression "Mad as a hatter." Hatters were exposed to high levels of mercury on the job. I am not saying George was mad, just that hatter was a hazardous job. From St. Louis, George moved across the Mississippi River to Cahokia. There he switched occupations and became a surveyor for the state of Illinois. The mathematics he learned at the university prepared him for this trade. George could speak five languages but had never done any hard physical work in Poland. Nobility never did this type of work. It was beneath them. The servants or serfs did it all.

After losing all his wealth in Poland, George had to start all over again as so many other emigrants have. He also found out what it was like to do hard work for a living. This is a familiar story to me. My relatives told me much the same thing. Our ancestor was Polish nobility who did not know

331 Jerzy Jan Lerski,A Polish Chapter in Jacksonian America: [Madison: The University of Wisconsin Press 1958] p. 180.

332 Maria J.E. Compson - Niecko, Orthography and the Polish Emigrants from Trieste 1834-35: [Polish American Studies Volume XXXI number 2 1974 Autumn, Polish American Historical Association] p. 28.

how to do anything when he came here either. Anything seems to mean he did not know any trade. He did seem to know something about agriculture. He moved to Illinois and took up farming at the age of fifty, while supporting a wife and four children.

George went to work surveying in Shelby County for the government. While surveying in Shelby County, George met his future wife. According to Illinois Marriages 1825-1850, he married Elizabeth Rogers there on March 15, 1842.[333] Her father was Robert L. Rogers, an ex-slave owner from Tennessee. His disillusionment with slavery caused him to get rid of his slaves and move to Illinois. The family settled in Holland Township, Shelby County.

Soon after getting married, George and his new wife moved to the American Bottoms in St. Clair County. Helen Cox Tregillis writes that the Suprunowskis lived in Cahokia in a "large two-story house." Their farm was close to the "Cahokia Common Fields," which ran along the banks of the Mississippi River. The commons was a large open area where the local people pastured their livestock and gathered firewood.[334] In 1850, George's farm contained thirty-seven acres of tillable land and seventy acres of unimproved land. He had two horses, three milk cows, four calves, and six pigs. The farm produced eight hundred bushels of corn, three hundred bushels of oats, and one hundred bushels of potatoes. In addition, George raised vegetables to sell in town.[335]

On the 1850 St. Clair County census, George is forty years old and his occupation is farmer. Elizabeth is twenty-nine years old and born in Tennessee. Daughters Catherine, eight, and Casimira, six years old. Sons Jacob, five, and James, three. All were born in Illinois. Also living with the family is Joseph Rogers. He is seventy-three years old and his occupation is farmer.[336]

By the 1860 St. Clair County census, the family has grown larger. There are two more sons, Joseph, ten, and George, six, and one more daughter, Minerva, age seven. Also living with the family is Joe Oginsky. Joe is thirty-eight years old and born in Poland and a farmhand on George's farm.[337]

---

333 Liahona Research, Illinois Mariages 1826 to 1850: [Bountiful, Utah: Heritage Quest 1999] p.801

334 Helen Cox Tregillis, The Shelby County Book Shelby County, Illinois: [Decorah, Iowa: the Anundsen publishing co. 1986] p. 15.

335 1850 Agriculture Census of St. Clair County: [Illinois State Archives, Springfield, Illinois T1133 Roll 5]

336 Robert Buecher, St. Clair County, Illinois 1850 Census Index Volume 1: [Thomson, Illinois: Heritage House] p. 82.

337 Kay F. Jetton, 1860 Census St. Clair County, Illinois Volume 1: [Decorah, Iowa: The Anundsen Publishing Company 1981] p. 123.

The Suprunowski family moved back to Shelby County sometime in the 1870s. They had lived in St. Clair County for around thirty years. I could have put them in the story about St. Clair County but decided on Shelby County because George and Elizabeth are both buried there. The mentions in the *Effingham County Histories* was another factor. George had extraordinarily bad timing to start farming on the American Bottoms. The Mississippi River flooded in 1844, 1849, 1858, and 1862. In an interview with Count John Sobiesky, George talked about living on the American Bottoms.

> I believe in destiny and although mine has been rough, I have had many good things along with the bitter of life. After I came to America earning a rich farm in the Mississippi bottom, near East St. Louis, twice my possessions were swept away by the floods, now I must die a poor man, but my wife is my greatest comfort and the best woman in the world. For fifty years she has been my constant and tender help-mate and has shared my joys and my sorrows.[338]

Mrs. Rawlings wrote that George was a "quiet and unobtrusive man."[339] He was well-known in both Shelby and Effingham counties. George was always interested in the current events of the day concerning America. He switched from the Democratic to the Republican Party because of the slavery issue. The Republicans were against slavery. George and Dr. Illinski from St. Clair County were friends going back to Poland. They were no doubt in prison together.

George was active into his eighties. He lived until the age of eighty-five and died in 1895 in Holland. His wife Elizabeth died one year later on May 24, 1896.[340] George and Elizabeth are both buried in Hubbartt Cemetery in Holland Township.[341]

---

338 Mrs. Isaac D. Rawlings, Polish Exiles in Illinois: [Transactions of the Illinois State Historical Society for the year 1927, number 34] [Danville, Illinois: Danville Printing Co. 1927] p. 96.

339 Mrs Isaac D. Rawlings, Polish Exiles in Illinois: [Transactions of the Illinois State Historical Society for the year 1927, number 34] [Danville, Illinois: Danville Printing Co. 1927] p. 96.

340 Edward Boedecker, Inscriptions of Shelby County, Illinois Cemeteries Volume viii: 1984 Reread by Barbara Thomas in 1997. P.1.

341 Edward Boedecker, p. 1.

Stefan Jankiewicz

I only have one record of Stefan in Illinois. He bought land in Shelby County from George Suprunowski on March 17, 1842.[342] Stefan came to America with Alexander Bielaski. Proba Biografi contains a small story about a Josef Jankiewicz. Josef was a noncommissioned officer in the 1830 insurrection. In 1834-35, he was working at a cloth manufacturing factory in Lowell, Massachusetts. The Polish Committee of Boston, Massachusetts, helped him out for a time after which he went to New York.[343] There is no way to tell if Stefan and Josef are the same person. I have found a few Polish exiles that changed their first names. George Suprunowski being one of them.

It looks like the Suprunowski children all moved back to Shelby County with their parents. Only three of the children were living when George died, Jacob, Joseph, and George.[344] There is a number of records of the Suprunowski family in Shelby County. At some point son George Gregory Suprunowski moved back to St. Clair County where he is listed as an alderman in the Second Ward of East St. Louis, Illinois, in 1911.[345] I only have one more thing to mention about Alexander Bielaski. Edward C. Rozanski wrote that Alexander's son Oscar was the "first Polish major league ballplayer."[346]

342 Shelby County, General Index Granter Book 1 1833-1859: p. 178.

343 Aleksander Grobicki, Proba Biografii, Sodalis: [The Polish American Historical Association of the Polish Institute of arts and sciences in America: St. Mary's College, Orchard Lake, Michigan] J. p. 22.

344 Mrs. Isaac D. Rawling, p. 96.

345 East St. Louis Journal, [March 19, 1911]

346 Edward C. Rozanski, The Civil War Centennial and Polish Americans: [Polish American Studies, Volume XX, number I January - June 1963. p. 41.

Fayette County

Fayette County had one Pole before 1850, Antoni Gajkowski. He lived near the town of Vandalia. In 1834, at least ten Polish exiles were supposed to have stopped in Vandalia.[347] Only Gajkowski left any record of himself there. I first saw his name in *Polish Exiles in Illinois* by Mrs. Isaac Rawlings. She mentioned his name and that he was a Polish exile.[348] Antoni was one of the 234 Polish exiles from Trieste[349] I have to tell the readers that there is a mystery to this story.

Fayette County was formed from parts of Bond, Crawford, and Clark counties on February 14, 1821. It is situated in the valley of the Kaskaskia River. The banks of the river are low and subject to flooding. When first settled, the greater part of the county was prairie. Some parts were heavily wooded. According to *History of Fayette County*,

> At one time the timber industry in the county was quite extensive, and many a man got a good start in life, cutting ties for sale to the Illinois Central Railroad. Men were brought to the county for the purpose of working at lumbering, who afterwards became permanent settlers, taking agricultural pursuits or other occupations.[350]

---

347 Florian Stasik, Polish Political Emigres in the United States of America, 1831-1864: [New York: Columbia University Press 2002] p. 67.

348 Mrs. Isaac Rawlings, Polish exiles in Illinois: [Transactions of the Illinois State Historical Society for the year 1927, # 34 Danville, Illinois: Illinois Printing Co. 1927] p. 95.

349 Mieczyslaw Haiman, Slady Polskie W Ameryce: [Chicago, Illinois: Printed Daily Union 1938] p. 120.

350 Historical Encyclopedia of Illinois and History of Fayette County, Vol. 1: [Chicago: Munsell Publishing Company 1910] [A Reproduction by Unigraphic, Inc. Evansville, Indiana 1972] p. 618.

Vandalia was the state capital for twenty years. The first state capital being at Kaskaskia in Randolph County in Southern Illinois. The state capital was moved from Kaskaskia to Vandalia because the central part of the state was being settled and Kaskaskia was considered too far south. Kaskaskia was located on the Mississippi River and had a bad flooding problem. On March 3, 1819, Congress granted the state of Illinois four different sections of land. The state was to decide which section it would build the new capital on. When the board of commissioners was out looking for a new location, they shot a deer on one of the sections. While eating the deer, the commissioners liked the surrounding countryside so much they decided to build the capital on the spot were the deer was killed.

Vandalia is located on the west side of the Kaskaskia River. The town is seventy miles east of St. Louis and ninety miles west of the Illinois-Indiana border. The present population is 5,338. In 1825, Loomis wrote that "the road for three miles east of town is impossible with a wagon and almost impossible on horseback."[351] While I was leaving Vandalia in the wet spring of 2002, I found the roads almost impassible myself. There was flooding as far as the eye could see and the water was up to the edges of each side of the road. It looked more like we were driving over a bridge. James Hall wrote in 1832 that

> it is surrounded by timber; on the north and west the prairies approach its boundaries, and in some places cross the town line; to the south is a extensive belt of timber, which skirts the river, and on the east, the forest widens, with slight intervals of prairie, to a distance of from eight to twelve miles. The surrounding country is good, but does not contain so continuous a body of fine land as is found in many other parts of the state.[352]

Vandalia was supposed to be the permanent site of the state capital. Within ten years, a movement started to place the capital farther north. Settlers had begun to move into the northern part of the state and now Vandalia was considered too far south. The Illinois legislature voted to move the capital to Springfield on February 28, 1837. Springfield became the capital in 1839.

---

351 Documentary History of Vandalia, Illinois: [The State Capital of Illinois from 1819 to 1839: October, 1954] p. 93.

352 Documentary History of Vandalia. Illinois: p. 43.

Antoni Gajkowski

According to Bielecki, before the 1830 November uprising, Antoni was a low-ranking engineer in the bridge department. He was a lieutenant in the insurrection and one of the 234 Polish exiles from Trieste.[353] Florian Stasik has written that in May 1834, Gajkowski settled in Philadelphia with twenty-five other Polish exiles. On June 30, 1834, the United States Congress granted land in either Michigan or Illinois to the 234 Polish exiles from Trieste. The Polish National Committee chose Barron Ludwik Chlopicki and Jan Prehal to select a site in Illinois. They arrived in Illinois in the fall of 1834 and picked out land on the Rock River in Winnebago County.

Soon after Congress granted them land, a group of about seventy Polish exiles set out for Illinois and the Polish land tract. Most were from New York and Philadelphia and had set out in small groups rather than one large one. Gajkowski must have been in one of these groups. Most went by steamship the first leg of the journey, then on foot. The farther they went, the worse the trip got. Most could not speak English, had little money, and were soon starving. Many also got sick from being exposed to the elements. Wojcieh Rostkowski, the oldest of the 234 exiles, committed suicide when he could not go on. The harshness of the trip finally became too much. Groups of exiles began settling in the cities along the way or went back. Small bands of exiles settled in Cincinnati, Louisville, Vandalia, and St. Louis. Ten exiles were supposed to have stopped in Vandalia;[354] Only Gajkowski left any evidence of himself there.

In May 1834, the citizens of Vandalia had sent a letter to the exiles inviting them to settle in Illinois. The letter contained such language as "Noble descendents of a brave nation come to us. Heroes of freedom come to us. We greet you with a brother like embrace. Come and share the abundant fruits of the land and of the freedom which your forefathers helped us acquire."[355] The citizens of Vandalia also formed a committee to assist the Poles. The committee appointed groups to solicit and receive donations of money, grain, livestock, and farm equipment. On December 6, 1834, Barron Chlopicki addressed the Vandalia Committee thanking them for their aid.[356]

---

353 Robert Bielecki, Slownik Biograficzny Oficerow Powstania Listopadowego E-K: [Warszawa: Naczekcja Archiwow Panstwowych 1996] p. 53.

354 Florian Stasik, p. 66-67.

355 Biblioteka Polskiej Akademii Nauk w Krakow, Ms 5500, 25-27; Kronika Emigracji Polskiej, 1835, 11, 191.

356 The Sangamo Journal Newspaper, January 10, 1835.

Unfortunately, the Vandalia Committee's sympathy and help for the Poles stopped when they found out about the plight of the American squatters living on the Polish land grant. Chlopicki had selected land with some American citizens living under squatter title.

This was the situation when Gajkowski was living in Vandalia. There could have been some hard feelings about the Polish land grant versus the Americans living there. It would take eight years before the situation was resolved. On May 12, 1838, the *Sangamo Journal* carried the following account of this incident in Vandalia.

> From the Vandalia Register horrid murder—On Saturday last, our town was the theatre of what was in all appearance the most cold blooded and deliberate murder we ever remember to have read in the annals of time. About three o'clock p.m. on Saturday, in the grocery of Mr. Brown, some dozen or more persons being present, A. Gajkowski and Nelson Riall were standing at the counter apparently drinking together in friendship. Suddenly the former drew a pistol, cocked it, and presenting it at Riall, shot him through the right breast, the ball passing downwards in the direction of the heart. The unfortunate man reeled round, placed his hand on the wound, fixed his glazed eyes on the murderer, fell, and instantly expired. Gajkowski was immediately arrested and committed to trial. He is a Polander by birth, and among those exiles to whom the liberality of our government was extended at the time they sought refuge among us from the power of Russia. He lived about a mile and a half from this place, on the Kaskaskia bluff. Mr. Riall was a highly respectable, worthy, and industrious citizen of our county. He was in the prime of life and has left a widow and four children to deplore his untimely fate. We forbear to comment upon this transaction pending the trial of the prisoner, which it is thought will take place at the special term of the court; the regular being nearly six month distant.[357]

This incident must have made the citizens of Vandalia real happy. Gajkowski's lucky they did not lynch (hang) him on the spot. The result of the trial is in the November 9, 1838, *Sangamo Journal*. Gajkowski was found guilty and sentenced to death. The execution to take place the fifth of next month.[358] Gajkowski's lawyer requested a supersedeas at the Illinois

---

[357] The Sangamo Journal Newspaper, May 12, 1838.

[358] The Sangamo Journal Newspaper, November 9, 1838.

Supreme Court. A supersedeas suspends an execution to appeal the case. What happened next? I cannot tell you because I have never been able to find out anything more about the case. This could be the end of the story, but maybe not.

I happened to buy a book called *Poles in the 19th Century Southwest* by Francis Casimir Kajencki. The book contains a story about a Polish exile named William Geck. Geck was born on June 4, 1818, in Warsaw, Kingdom of Poland. In the same book, Geck's granddaughter Lillian Weir Dukeminier claims that Geck's name was originally Gajkowski. According to Lillian, William Geck came to America as a stowaway in the 1830s. Speaking about the 234 Polish exiles from Trieste, Kajencki writes, "I believe that Geck, a sixteen-year-old lad, found himself among those exiles. As a minor and subject of the tsar, he was not listed on the passenger manifest."[359] Stasik's book contains a list of the 234 Polish exiles from Trieste. The name Antoni Gajkowski is on the list.[360] Mr. Kajencki and the Geck descendants all think that William Geck was Antoni Gajkowski's son.

According to Kajencki, William Geck was supposed to have been a servant to Robert E. Lee of Civil War fame. Lee was stationed in St. Louis during the years 1837-1840. Geck enlisted in the army for five years on January 12, 1841. His age was twenty-three. He was stationed at Fort Leavenworth, Kansas, in Company H, First United States Dragoons commanded by Captain Nathan Boone. Boone was the youngest son of frontiersman Daniel Boone.

Company H was sent to Fort Gibson in Indian territory, which is near the present city of Muskogee, Oklahoma. The fort was known as a great place to catch malaria. During the time Geck was stationed at the fort, Company H went on a sixty-nine-day reconnaissance mission. The expedition left on May 14, 1843, and traveled through Kansas to the Santa Fe Trail. There they turned southwest into Indian Territory. The expedition had little trouble with Indians, except for an incidence of stealing. The soldiers spent much of the time hunting buffalo for food and made it back to Fort Gibson on July 31.

Geck was discharged from the army on January 12, 1846. He did not stay out very long for he reenlisted in the army for five more years on February 16, 1846. Geck was assigned to his old unit, Company H. The Mexican War started in 1846. Company H was not sent to Mexico, but remained on the frontier. They were stationed first at Camp Dragoon, Arkansas, and then ordered back to Fort Gibson. Their mission was to protect the frontier from Indians.

---

359 Francis Casimir Kajencki, Poles in the 19th Century Southwest: [El Paso, Texas: Southwest Polonia Press 1990] p. 3.

360 Florian Stasik, p. 207.

Sometime before 1848, Geck married a German woman named Mamie. She accompanied him back to Fort Gibson. There a son was born to them whom they named Charles. A freak accident at the fort destroyed Geck's family when Mamie fell into a well and drowned. At the same time, the Mexican War had ended and Company H was transferred to New Mexico. Not being able to care for Charles himself, Geck left him with friends. After Geck's second enlistment was up, he came back to Fort Gibson to get Charles. His friends had left and he never saw Charles again.

New Mexico had been a part of Mexico before the war. Geck was among a group of twenty-five soldiers stationed at the village of Dona Ana. Geck must have liked his new assignment for he made it his permanent home. He was discharged from the army at Dona Ana on February 6, 1851. Mexican war veterans received a land bounty for their service, and Geck obtained his near Dona Ana. He went to work building a good-sized adobe house, which he also used as a trading post. His house became the most impressive house in Dona Ana. Geck became a very successful trader and eventually owned four stores. At the same time, he also increased his land holdings. Geck became a citizen on November 1, 1851.

Geck also found himself another wife. On April 24, 1851, he married Margarita Severiana de Jesus Barrio. Margarita was born on February 21, 1838, in Juarez, Mexico. She died two years later during childbirth. The baby girl survived. She was given the name of Jesusita. In 1854, Geck married Beatriz Aguirre. History repeated itself when Beatriz died in childbirth on July 11, 1856. The baby, a son, named William Cidrono Peter lived.

Geck's fourth and final marriage occurred on December 31, 1859. Maybe I should say he robbed the cradle on that date instead. He married Beatriz's first cousin Sarah Aguirre. She was not quite thirteen years old. It is not as bad as it looks. He treated her more like a daughter at first. In fact, he enrolled her in a Catholic school in Missouri along with his own daughter Jesusita. In 1863, Sarah left school and came back home to Dona Ana. A daughter was born to William and Sarah on April 9, 1864. They named her Beatriz, but she died nine days later. On April 25, 1866, son Samuel was born. In 1868, son Marion was born. He only lived to be sixteen months old. Four more daughters were born to the Gecks, Caroline in 1870, Wilhemina in 1872, Mary in 1874, and Sarah in 1879.

Geck was a justice of the peace for a short time during the Civil War. In 1861, the southern half of New Mexico was part of the Confederacy. The rebels appointed Geck justice of the peace for Dona Ana County. He also sold supplies to the rebels from his store. This arrangement did not last long. Before the year was over, Union troops took New Mexico back. Geck found himself in serious trouble. The United States charged him with treason. According to

Kajencki, "the Union army seized and confiscated much of Geck's property and goods in retaliation for his collaboration with the Confederates."[361] Geck's own house was used to house a company of Union soldiers. Geck did not need the house anyway. He had already been escorted to Fort Craig where the army gave him a new home in the Brig. In February 1863, the judicial district court took up Geck's case. He was acquitted of treason and all his property returned to him.

Geck died on June 9, 1890. Sarah died December 18, 1924. They are both buried in the Geck family cemetery. The cemetery was located about two hundred feet from the Geck house. The cemetery is on private property at the present time. Daughter Caroline lived in the Geck home until 1955. In the 1960s, the house was destroyed. Geck was into education in a big way and sent all his children to Catholic schools in Missouri. Geck is supposed to have a large number of descendants, mainly living in the southwest.

After researching this story, I do not think that Louis William Geck ever had a dull day in his life. I am not sure if I agree with the Geck family descendants or Mr. Krjencki about Gajkowski's origins. The exiles' descendants do not always have the story right. My theory is that Louis William Geck was Antoni Gajkowski. Geck would have been twelve years old at the time of the 1830 November uprising. Twelve is a young age to be a soldier, but not unheard-of in the Polish Army. At least two other Polish exiles from Trieste, Pavel Sobelewski and August A. Jakubowski, also served in the army at young ages. I think Gajkowski was acquitted of murder in a second trial. Maybe the murder was ruled an accident? He then moved to St. Louis and changed his name.

361 Francis Casimir Kajencki, p. 27.

Greene and Jersey Counties

I combined these two counties because two of our subjects lived in both counties. John Polaski and Francis Mulaski lived in both counties at one time or another. Michael Cohen lived in Greene County. One of the Sandusky families also lived in Greene County. There is also a special mention of the Wardynski family. There is no evidence that either John Polaski or Francis Mulaski was Polish, other than their names look like it.

Greene County became a county on January 20, 1821. Madison County is its parent county. The county is in the southwestern part of the state with the Illinois River its western boundary. Carrollton is the county seat. Most of the county was wooded when it was first settled, the prairies being very small. The land is rolling until you get to the western boundary where bluffs run along the Illinois River.

Jersey County was created March 26, 1839, from Greene County. It is the next county south of Greene County and lies at the junction of the Illinois and Mississippi rivers. The central and eastern part of the county is level or rolling prairie while the western boundary has wooded bluffs along the Mississippi River. Jerseyville is the county seat. Most of the early settlers came from New Jersey, which is where the name Jersey came from.

John Polaski

According to the Greene County Historical Society, John was born May 17, 1816, in Eisenach, Germany.[362] The first record I have of him is his marriage to Ruth Ann Sevene. They were married on January 12, 1842, in Greene County.[363] At various times, the Polaskis lived in Greene and Jersey

---

362 Green County Historical Society, Carrollton, Illinois: [The White Hall Register April 2, 1875] P. 4.

363 Illinois Marriages: 1825 through 1850: [Copyright 1998 by AGLL, Inc. Boundtiful, Utah] p. 652.

counties as well as St. Louis.[364] They settled in the town of White Hall, Greene County, for good in 1859.

David Barrow founded White Hall in 1832. White Hall grew fast and by 1840 had a population of three hundred. The town was known for its top-quality clay. History of Greene County 1879 wrote, "By far the most important business interest of White Hall is her manufacture of and trade in the drain tile, fire brick, sewer pipe, terra cotta ware and other forms of clay."[365] These fireclays were sold all over the country.

On the 1850 Jersey County Census, John is thirty-four years old and born in Saxony. His occupation is tailor. Ruth is forty-four years old and born in Ohio. She might have had two daughters from a previous marriage. In addition, Henrietta, eighteen, and Sarah, twelve, Levin were also living in the Polaski household. They were both born in Illinois. John and Ruth also have two sons on the census. William Alonzo, eight, and Nelson J., four, years old. Both were born in Illinois. Nelson was born in Jerseyville, Jersey County, in 1845.[366]

At some point after Nelson was born, the Polaskis moved to St. Louis. They did not stay long. By 1850, they were back in Jerseyville buying land.[367] They would have been back in Jersey County in time for one of my favorite stories about the county. The Hog War took place in 1853. There was a small corn crop that year and there was not enough feed for all the pigs in the county. A group of farmers got together and herded all their pigs to a government-owned woods located in a different part of the county. Originally, pigs in Illinois were fattened on mast, which is acorns, hickory nuts, beech nuts, etc. This alarmed the local farmers living near the woods who thought they were entitled to use the woods for their own pigs. *History of Jersey County* tells what happened next: the locals "promptly armed themselves to protect their rights, to the last extremity. The intruders also armed themselves to protect their property and their rights. Luckily, a suit for trespass was instituted before a justice of the peace, and a change of venue gave time for wiser counsel to prevail, and the intruders withdrew and took their hogs home, which

---

364 Jersey County Recorder of deeds, Jerseyville, Illinois: [Grantee Book G pages 606 & 607]

365 History of Greene County, Illinois: [Chicago: Donnelley, Gassette & Loyd 1879] [Reproduced under the sponsorship of The Greene County Historical Society of Illinois by Unigraphic, Inc. Evansville, Indiana 1974] p. 404.

366 Index to the 1850 census of Jersey County, Illinois: [Yakima, Washington: Yakima Valley Genealogical Society 1976] p. 3.

367 Jersey County Recorder of Deeds, [Grantee Book G pages 607 & 608]

ended, what, at the beginning, promised to result in much bloodshed."[368] It would have made for a much better story if they would have fought it out but you can't have everything.

In 1859, the Polaskis moved for the last time to White Hall in Greene County.[369] On the 1860 Green County Census, John is forty-four years old and a tailor. Ruth is fifty-four years old. Henrietta and Sarah are gone. Nelson is fifteen years old.[370] Son William is on a different census. He is a farm laborer living on the Griswald farm. The census writes his last name Perlaski instead of Polaski.[371]

Julie Joan Giertuga informs us that both of the Polaski sons served in the Civil War. William enlisted in the Sixty-first Infantry in White Hall on February 4, 1862. He was discharged from the army on February 7, 1865. Younger brother Nelson actually enlisted in the army first on January 3, 1862. He enlisted in the Sixty-first Infantry in White Hall at the age of sixteen. Nelson was the company drummer and was discharged from the army on September 8, 1865.[372]

John died March 27, 1875, in White Hall.[373] Frank Sobeck bought John's tailor shop on April 24, 1875.[374] William died December 28, 1881, in White Hall leaving a wife and several children.[375] Nelson died May 9, 1882, in White Hall. His wife died in 1880. He was survived by his mother and three children.[376]

---

368 History of Jersey County Illinois, edited by Oscar B. Hamilton: [Chicago: Munsell Publishing Company 1919] [Reprinted by Higginson Book Company Salem, Massachusetts] p. 493.

369 Greene County Historical Society, Carrollton, Illinois: [The White Hall Register April 2, 1875] p. 4.

370 1860 Federal census of Greene County, Illinois: [National Archives: Box 653 Roll 178 Page 724]

371 George B. King, 1860 Census of Greene County, Illinois: [Lee-Baker-Hodges House 1993] p. 49.

372 Julie Joan Giertuga, Polish contributions in Illinois during the War between the states: [Thesis, Bradley University: Peoria, Illinois 1948] p. 60.

373 Greene County Historical Society, Carrollton, Illinois: [The White Hall Register April 2, 1875] p. 4.

374 Greene County Historical Society, Carrollton, Illinois: [The White Hall Register April 2, 1875] p. 4.

375 Greene County Historical Society, Carrollton, Illinois: [The White Hall Register December 31, 1881] p. 3.

376 Greene County Historical Society, Carrollton, Illinois: [The White Hall Register May 13, 1882] p. 3.

Michael Cohen

Michael lived in Carrollton, the county seat for Greene County. The year 1821 saw a large influx of settlers to Carrollton. In 1832, thirty out of a population of three hundred died of cholera. Carrollton was a very thriving town when the Cohen's lived there. *History of Greene County* printed an article from the October 18, 1851, Carrollton Gazette describing the town.

> Carrollton has not over eight hundred inhabitants, and there are four churches, and besides these, there are five ministers living in the town, and men of no ordinary abilities. Each of these denominations has regular meetings every Sabbath. So much for the moral character of Carrollton. In regard to her literary character, we can boast of three excellent schools, all in successful operation, and a large academy now in progress of building, soon to be completed. We have also two printing offices, both doing a smashing business; also a telegraph office, doing a fine business. We have eight dry goods stores, two drug and fancy stores, one family grocery, one bakery, three taverns, and one private boarding house; one tin and stove store, three boot and shoe makers, six blacksmith and wagon shops, two gunsmiths, two jewelers, two house and sign painters, two saddle and harness makers, two lumber yards, and twelve carpenters; one hat store; two carding machines, one propelled by steam, with saw attached; one cooper shop, four tailor shops, and one clothing store; a large number of stone and brick masons, brick makers and plasterers, four lawyers and the district judge; two cabinet shops, eight doctors, one dentist [and a good one at that] ; a Masonic lodge building owned by the fraternity; a Sons of Temperance hall, a fine brick building, owned by the Order, and one hundred and fifty Sons of Temperance, and the Grand Scribe, a section of the Cadets of Temperance, numbering between forty and fifty, and no groggeries; a first class brass band, and a regular set of amateurs.[377]

With a last name of Cohen, I think it is safe to say that Michael is a Polish Jew. He married Matilda Canstant[378] in 1850.[379] On the 1850 Green

377 History of Green County, Illinois, p. 336.

378 Greene County Recorder of Deeds, Carrollton, Illinois: [Granter Book V page 215]

379 Mabel Tucker Sheffer, 1850 Greene County, Illinois census: [At the Greene County, Illinois Historical and Genealogical Society, Carrollton, Illinois] p. 26.

County Census, Michael is thirty-eight years old, occupation farmer and born in Poland. Matilda is thirty-eight years old and born in Kentucky. Also living with the Cohens' were Adeline, nineteen, and Norman, nine. They were both born in Illinois.[380] If this census is right, Michael is the only Polish Jewish farmer I have ever found living in Illinois. The Cohens sold their farm in 1850 for $160.[381] If this is all their farm was worth, it could not have been much of a farm. It looks like Michael or a relative stayed around Carrollton and vicinity for a time. There were some Cohen businessmen in Carrollton well into the 1900s. William Cohen's obituary is in the September 17, 1909, *White Hall Register Newspaper*.[382] Mike Cohen left White Hall in 1923 and married Lizzie Sanders in Ottawa, Illinois, in 1924.[383]

Francis Muliski

Greene County Marriage Index has a Polish-looking name before 1850. In 1836, Milniskie married Waldon.[384] The 1840 Jersey County Census contains the name Francis Muliski. He is between the ages of twenty and thirty. His wife's age is also between the ages of twenty and thirty. There is also a daughter under five years old.[385] There is no more information about him and I cannot prove that he was Polish.

Sandusky

A large Sandusky family lived in Green County at this time. On the 1850 Census, Jacob Sandusky is a forty-six-year old farmer, born in Kentucky. His wife Malinda is forty-four years old and born in Kentucky. Their sons are Wyley, twenty; Alexander, twelve; and James, eight. Daughters are Nancy, eighteen; Elizabeth, fifteen; Maltilda, ten; and another daughter, four years old. I cannot make out her name.[386] The Sanduskys lived in Morgan County before moving to Greene. Jacob had a good-sized farm. The 1850 Agriculture Census shows that Jacob had 110 improved acres and 170 unimproved acres. He owned eight horses, six milk cows, ten other cows, twenty-seven sheep,

380 Mabel Tucker Sheffer, p. 26.

381 Greene County Recorder of Deeds, Carrollton, Illinois: [Granter Book V p. 215.]

382 The White Hall Register Newspaper, White Hall, Illinois: [September 17, 1909]

383 The White Hall Register Newspaper, October 3, 1924.

384 Greene County Marriage Index: [May 6, 1821-January 1, 1840.] p. 7.

385 1840 Jersey County Census: [Box 704, Roll 61, Page 332]

386 1850 Federal Census of Greene County, Illinois: [National Archives, Box M432 Roll 108 Page 121]

and forty-five pigs. The farm produced 253 bushels of wheat, 3,000 bushels of corn, 45 pounds of wool, 8 bushels of potatoes, 60 pounds of butter, and 10 tons of hay.[387]

Wardynski

The Wardynskis were a little past the date of 1850, when this book is supposed to end. I included it anyways. *History of Greene and Jersey Counties* has a mention of the Wardynskis. According to *History of Greene and Jersey Counties*, "John B. Logan was married on February 5, 1867 to Frances Wardinski, a native of Polish Germany, born near Posen. Her father, John Wardinski, a Union sympathizer, was killed at Columbiana, this county, during the war, by bushwhackers."[388]

I also found two different stories about them at the Greene County Historical Society. Each story has a different date for when the Wardnskis first arrived in America. The first story was an obituary of Mrs. Mary Wardynski in the Wardinski file at the historical society. Mary died on December 21, 1906. She was the wife of John Wardynski. He being the one killed by bushwhackers. "She was born February 2, 1823, near Posen, Poland, a province of Prussia. She came to America in 1849 and settled in St. Louis for 12 years and then came to Columbiana. Her husband was killed by bushwhackers in 1862. She was the mother of six children—three boys and three girls."[389]

Ben Logan Jr., a descendant of the Wardynskis, wrote the second story. John Wardynski immigrated to America in 1853. In Poland, he had been a shoemaker, but in Columbiana had a general store. In 1854, his wife Mary left Poland for America. With her were her daughter Frances and two sons. John's brother Thomas and his family came with them. One of John's sons died during the trip and was "buried at sea."

After the two Wardynski families landed in New Orleans, they went to St. Louis. John's family went to Columbiana, Greene County, while brother Thomas and family stayed in St. Louis. Two more daughters were born to

---

387 1850 Agriculture Census of Green County, Illinois: [Roll No. 31-2]

388 History of Greene and Jersey Counties, Illinois: [Springfield, Illinois: Continental Historical Co. 1885] [The reproduction of this book has been made possible through the sponsorship of the Greene County Historical and Genealogical Society, Carrollton, Illinois by Unigraphic, Inc. Evansville, Indiana 1980] p. 876.

389 Greene County Historical Society, Carrollton, Illinois: Wardynski file [Patriot, December 21, 1906] p. 21.

Mary after arriving here, Florence and Mary. All three of the Wardynski girls attended Catholic school in St. Louis.[390]

I have no research linking John Polaski with Poland. Polaski looks like a Polish name to me. Maybe John had some German blood in him. Some Cohens were still living in Carrollton into the early nineteen hundreds. Hainsfurther and Cohen opened a new store there on April 6, 1867.[391] The obituary of William Cohen occurred in Carrollton on September 17, 1909.[392] There was also Cohens living in Jacksonville, Illinois, in the late 1800s.[393] The 1840 census does not contain much information about Francis Muliski. There is no 1850 census, so Francis must have left the state. I thought the Wardynskis should be mentioned because they managed to get themselves into the Greene and Jersey counties history books and because I like their story. Thanks to the Greene County Historical Society. They were very helpful researching this story.

---

390 Ben Logan Jr. The Wardynski Family: Greene County Historical Society, Carrollton, Illinois: p. 52.

391 Greene County Historical Society, Carrollton, Illinois: Cohen file [The Carrollton Gazette April 6, 1867] p. 7.

392 Greene County Historical Society, Carrollton, Illinois: Cohen file [The Carrollton Gazette April 6, 1867] p. 7.

393 Greene County Historical Society, Carrollton, Illinois: [Cohen file, The Carrollton Gazette November 7, 1902] p. 7.

Hancock County

Hancock County had one member of the well-known Zabriskie family. Lewis Curtis Zabriskie came to the county with the Mormon exodus in 1838-39. Hancock County was also home to three women with Polish-looking last names. I suspect they are sisters, but each one spells their last name different. I believe the correct spelling of their name is Avadawski. Avadawski might be an Americanized version of Ivanoffski. The 1850 Federal Census has the names Jean Powlowiez and Maxwell, first name unknown. Both state Poland as place of birth. In addition, there is a man named Matthieu Maximilian Potochi or Potocki? It looks more like Potocki to me on the census at the National Archives. Powlowiez and Potocki were both members of a communist group known as the "Icarians."

Hancock County was created from Pike County January 13, 1825. Carthage is the county seat. Hancock County is located in central Illinois in the western side of the state. The Mississippi River is its western boundary. Two-thirds of the county was one large prairie known as Hancock Prairie and situated in the center of the county. The wooded areas of Hancock County were in the southern and eastern parts of the county and on bluffs along the Mississippi River.

The big story of Hancock County has to be the Mormon settlement at Nauvoo. It is a long and complicated story, so I will only give a brief outline. The Mormons first came to Illinois in 1839-1840. They had to leave Missouri running for their lives and most of their possessions were left behind. The citizens of Illinois were sympathetic to their plight at first, but that would quickly change. After leaving Missouri, the Mormons did not intend to settle in Illinois permanently but planned to buy land in the half-breed tract located across the Mississippi River from Nauvoo in Lee County, Iowa. Problems with land titles ended this venture, and most Mormons remained in Hancock County. About one hundred families did settle in Lee County, Iowa, however, some of them Zabriskies. By 1840, the large Mormon emigration had caused the population of Hancock County to rise to almost ten thousand. Five years later the population was anywhere from fifteen to thirty thousand people and still growing. Most Mormons lived at or near Nauvoo, which is on the banks of the Mississippi River. For a time Nauvoo had double the population of Chicago.

Joseph Smith was the founder and prophet of the Mormon Church, which he started in Palmyra, New York. Before their arrival in Illinois, the church had spent short periods in Ohio and Missouri. Whenever the church settled, they managed to raise the ire of the local populace.

Most of the Mormons living in Nauvoo were described as industrious people. They built the town of Nauvoo and established a university there as well. Every Mormon volunteered to work one day in ten to build the temple. Some lived in other parts of the county and worked on the local farms. The church also sent missionaries to all parts of America and Europe.

There were some problems. *History of Hancock County* wrote, "The new citizens of Nauvoo were generally an orderly and well disposed people; but they had a few ruffians among them, who, by their violence and intemperate conduct made themselves generally obnoxious."[394] Most of these crimes against non-Mormons were supposed to be minor. What upset the locals more was the belief that Mormon leadership shielded these criminals from prosecution. The Mormon Church's undoing in Illinois was probably their involvement in state politics. They voted in a block for whomever Joseph Smith told them to. The large and fast growing population could sway elections. This was an increasing source of anxiety to the rest of the state. The state of Illinois allowed the Mormons to govern and police themselves which created a state within a state. The Mormons were also allowed their own militia which at full strength numbered six hundred men.

In 1844, a group of ex-Mormons formed a newspaper in the nearby town of Carthage called the *Expositor*. Some of these people had been higher-ups in the church. They began publishing anti-Mormon articles, which only helped to stir up the evermore fearful non-Mormons. This was too much for Joseph Smith. He, along with his brother Hyrum, led a mob to Carthage and destroyed the newspaper's presses. The local sheriff charged Joseph and Hyrum Smith and some members of their mob with rioting. On June 24, 1844, Smith and the others turned themselves in and were immediately locked up in the Carthage jail. On June 27, a mob stormed the jail and killed both Joseph and Hyrum Smith.

The Mormon Church was now leaderless but others stepped up. Brigham Young would rise to the top of the church leadership. The Mormons stayed in Nauvoo for the time being and continued to build their temple. The temple was finished May 28, 1845, and dedicated April 1846.

---

394 Thomas Gregg, History of Hancock County, Illinois: [Chicago: Chas. C. Chapman & Co. 1880] Reprinted by [The Anundsen Publishing Co. Decorah, Iowa 1984] p.347.

In 1845, the Illinois State legislature disbanded the charters. The charters allowed the church to govern themselves. The church soon realized that leaving the state was in their best interest and started to look for a new place to live. Tension between Mormons and locals continued to worsen. The period known as the "Mormon wars" started in the fall of 1845 when anti-Mormon mobs began setting fires to the houses of church members on the outskirts of Nauvoo. At least one hundred houses were burned down. The famous trek to Utah would soon begin, and by 1846, most Mormons had left Illinois.

Lewis Curtis Zabriskie

According to George Olin Zabriskie, Lewis was born in Hamilton County, Ohio, on September 17, 1817. He converted to the Mormon faith April 19, 1836. Lewis fled Missouri during the Mormon exodus of 1838-39. He settled in Adams County, Illinois, first but later moved to Hancock County. Lewis was not done moving yet, and at some point moved across the Mississippi River to Lee County, Iowa. Lewis's father, uncle, and brother were all living in Lee County at the time.

Lewis was married twice. His first marriage was to Mary Keziah Higbee on April 5, 1839. Mary was born in Clermont County, Ohio, September 5, 1821. The marriage produced six children. William, Isaac, Eleanor, Huldah, John, and Mary. Mary Higbee Zabriskie died March 2, 1847, in Council Bluffs, Iowa. Lewis's second marriage was to Sarah Ann Park. Their marriage took place in Council Bluffs, Iowa, on July 25, 1847. Nine children were born from this marriage. Hyrum, Joseph, Matilda, George, David, Louisa, Sara, Esther, and Charles.

Lewis and his family participated in the famous Mormon trek to Utah in 1846. The family took up residence in Provo, Utah, September 23, 1851. Lewis's father was also living in Provo. Lewis moved several times after arriving in Utah. In 1859, he moved to Salem, Utah County. In 1860, he moved to Fairview, Sanpate County, Utah. Lewis made his last move in 1862, his final destination Spring City, Utah. Lewis died in Spring City November 17, 1872.[395]

Awadawski

I first saw the names Awadawski and Aversky in *Pioneers of the Prairie* by Brunenn.

---

395 George Olin Zabriskie, The Zabriskie Family, [Copyright 1963 by George Olin Zabriskie] p. 348-349.

> McDonald, Alexander—born ca 1822 in Indiana, was married at Carthage, Illinois, in 1848 to Mary Jane Aversky, born ca 1825 in Indiana. A daughter, Laura was born 1849 in the township.
>
> Mr. McDonald was elected supervisor of St. Albans Township in 1850 and again in 1856. He was appointed Post Master of the St. Albans Post Office on December 5, 1856 and served until May 5, 1857.[396]

St. Albans Township is located in the center of Hancock County on its southern boundary. It does not look like there was a town in St. Albans Township until 1856. According to Thomas Gregg, Alexander Mc Donald was an early settler of St. Albans Township.[397] That is if this is the right Alexander McDonald. There were two Alexander McDonalds living almost next door to each other. Both of their wives were named Mary Jane, and each family has a Margaret living there.

On the 1850 Federal Census, Alexander is twenty-eight years old, farmer, born in Indiana. Mary Jane is nineteen years old and born in Indiana. Daughter Laura is two years old, born in Illinois. Also living with the family is Margaret Everdiska, sixteen years old. Her place of birth is not readable. I believe Margaret is Mary Janes's sister.[398] The other Alexander McDonald is sixty-one years old on the 1850 census. He was a farmer and born in New Jersey. Jane is fifty-nine years old and born in Kentucky. Margaret is twenty-four years old and born in Indiana.[399] These two McDonalds gave me fits. Our Alexander McDonald moved away in the 1850s but the older Alexander McDonald is still around in 1860.

Pioneers of the Prairie also lists the marriage of Abigail Awadawski to Samuel (Solomon) Davis. Solomon's marriage to Abigail was his second marriage.

> Mr. Davis married March 28, 1839 to Abigail Awadawski, b. in Ohio, she died August 1879. They were the parents of five children: 1—Abraham, b. January 23, 1840. 2—Yegellin M, b. June 6, 1841. 3—Sevana, b. October 29, 1842, died November

396 Wilma Brunenn, Pioneers of the Prairie, p. 587.

397 Thomas Gregg p. 548.

398 1850 Federal Census of Hancock County, Illinois: [At the National Archives, Roll 109, p. 348]

399 1850 Federal Census of Hancock County, Illinois: [At the National Archives, Roll 109, p. 348]

11, 1845. 4—Sinthia A, b. August 1, 1844. 5—Charles, b. January 30, 1851.

Mr. Davis was appointed Post Master of the St. Albans Post Office May 5, 1857, he served in That capacity one year. He was also a merchant in St. Albans Township, the business was in his home. Among his wares were "Cuba Sixes" cigars, "Long Green" and "Peachy Dew" tobacco.[400]

Solomon took over the St. Albans post office from Alexander McDonald May 5, 1857. On the 1850 census, Solomon's occupation is farmer. The McDonald and Davis farms were located very close to each other.

Both Mary Jane Aversky and Margaret Everdiska were born in Indiana. I checked early Indiana census records and found the name John Awnvdonski on the 1830 Federal Census. He was forty to fifty years old. A woman twenty to thirty years old was also living in the house.[401] Could John be a relative of the three women I just mentioned? I think so. The census takers at this time frequently misspelled names, and I think that the Awadawski spelling used by Abigail is probably the most accurate spelling.

Maxwell

I know next to nothing about Maxwell, not even his first name. The1850 Federal Census for Hancock County has the name Maxwell. His age is thirty-five and his occupation is grocer. Maxwell's place of birth is Poland. He was living in a hotel owned by Thomas G. Hill.[402] I have not found anything else about him and he probably left the county.

Powlowiez and Potocki

Both Powlowiez and Potocki were members of a socialist group called the "Icarians." The Icarians settled in Nauvoo in 1849. They had recently been cheated out of the title for lands in Texas. *The History of Adams County, Illinois* documented the Icarians landing in Quincy on their way to Nauvoo.

---

400 Wilma Brunenn, p. 320

401 1830 Federal census of Vermillion County, Indiana: [At the National Archives Roll 26, p. 211]

402 The 1850 Census of Illinois, Hancock County: [The Tri-City Genealogical Society, Locust Grove Press p. 74]

> Communists—The "American Eagle" landed at the Quincy wharf on Tuesday, April 13, 1849, 281 French Communists who were on their way to Nauvoo with a view of making a permanent location. They were composed mostly of merchants and farmers, having with them their Implements of husbandry and a variety of tools suited to their various trades.
>
> The steamboat officers reported them to be the most cleanly and industrious emigrants they ever met. The company was headed by Monsieur Cabet, who was many years a leader in the French House of Deputies, and was once banished from France by Louis Phillippe. They bought from the retiring Mormons some of their property, but did not make a great success of their settlement.[403]

Descendants of Icarians, Illinois office of tourism states that Etienne Cabet was the founder and leader of the Icarians. Cabet was born in Dijon, France, in 1788. His father was a barrel maker. Cabet studied medicine but changed over to law because of his interest in social causes. Cabet's support for the French middle class got him in hot water with King Louis Philippe. Cabet managed to aggravate King Louis so much that he was given the option of jail or exile to England. In England, he wrote the novel *Voyage to Icaria* in 1840. The book became very popular in France and most of Europe. His topic was about living the socialist life in a fantasyland.

Thousands of people urged Cabet to create an "Icarian" society in America. Cabet decided to give it a try and left France with a group of followers on February 3, 1848. The group was composed of people from six different European counties. Their first attempt to buy land in Texas failed. They found out about the now-vacated Nauvoo and bought a tract of land around the Mormon temple. Hundreds more Icarians settled in Nauvoo over the next five years. The Icarians were big on education, medical care, and music. They ate their meals together in a dining room that held four hundred people. During their leisure time, they read poetry, attended plays, or held discussions about Icarian philosophy. Their thirty-four-member orchestra performed concerts on Sundays and holidays.

Over time, a number of problems arouse which would fragment the settlement. Some disliked the Midwest winter and thought life at Nauvoo too harsh. Quite a few returned to France after King Louis Philippe was dethroned. The main reason for the Icarians' demise was disagreement over their constitution. A generation gap between young and old added to the

---

403 The History of Adams County, Illinois. [Chicago: Murray, Williamson & Phelps 1879] [A Reproduction by Unigraphic, Inc. Evansville, Indiana 1977] p. 425

problem. Cabet had enough of it all and left Nauvoo in 1856 with 180 of the older members. The group went to St. Louis where an untimely event occurred. Two days after arriving, Cabet died of apoplexy "stroke." The group stayed together eight more years then disbanded. Those who stayed in Nauvoo did not make it much longer and dissolved in 1860.

A faction of Icarians did survive a while longer. In 1853, a band of Icarians organized a settlement in Corning, Iowa. The group managed to carry on until 1878. They moved to a ranch in California in 1881 and disbanded in 1898. The Icarian venture lasted about fifty years.[404]

History of Hancock County, Illinois 1818-1868 has an interesting comment about the Icarians.

> On the heels of the departing Mormons came the Commune Icarie, a socialistic group from France, headed by an idealistic Etienne Cabet. They were thrifty and law abiding, but the beautiful ideal of every man working at the trade or profession that he loved best and each receiving according to his need, just didn't work out. There weren't enough who loved to chop wood and hoe corn to meet the basic needs of food and fuel.[405]

The only information I have about Powlowiez or Potocki is the 1850 Federal Census. They were both Icarians. Jean Powlowiez is listed as forty-four years of age. His occupation is typographer and he was born in Poland.[406] Matthieu Maximilian Potocki is thirty-nine years old and his occupation is gardener. Potocki lists France as place of birth.[407]

Lewis Curtis Zabriskie only lived in Hancock County a short but exciting time. The Avadawskis have a Polish-looking name. When they came to America is unknown. Maxwell is probably a Polish Jew. Who knows what became of Powlowiez and Potocki? Did they go west with the Icarians or drop out of the sect. According to the Illinois Department of Tourism, the Icarians' descendants meet once a year at Nauvoo State Park. The public is invited.[408]

---

404 Descendants of Icarians, [Nauvoo, Illinois] accession number 80013100: [Illinois Office of Tourism, The Icarian Community in Nauvoo: At the Lincoln Library, Springfield, Illinois] p.2-4

405 Board of Supervisors of Hancock County, Illinois, History of Hancock County, Illinois 1818-1968: [Carthage, Illinois: Journal 1968]

406 Tri-City Genealogical Society, 1850 Census of Hancock County p. 148.

407 1850 Federal Census of Hancock County, Illinois: [At the National Archives, Roll 109 p. 358.

408 Illinois Office of Tourism, p. 4.

Julian Hulanicki

Julian was living in Chicago by at least October 11, 1839. His oldest son Julian Jr. was born there on that date.[409] Julian was one of the 234 Polish exiles from Trieste. For some reason, the Hulanicki name is not mentioned on any of the lists of the 234 Polish exiles in either Lerski's or Stacik's books. Haiman does have a list of the 234 Polish exiles with the Hulanicki name on it.[410] According to Robert Bielecki, Julian was born in 1809 in Braranov, in the province of Galicia. His father's name was Leon. Julian went to school for a time in the town of Radom, then became a student at the University of Warsaw in 1829. There he majored in administration and law.

Julian was a lieutenant in the 1830 Polish uprising and a subordinate of General Paz in May 1831. In October 1831, Julian fled to Prussia with General Rybinski. At some point he left Prussia for Krakow, Poland, were the Austrians arrested him in 1833.[411] About four months after his arrest, he was deported to America with 233 Polish exiles. The group left Trieste, Italy, on two ships November 22, 1833, and arrived in America on March 28, 1834. Julian Jr. claimed his father's estate was confiscated by the Russians for his participation in the insurrection and he lost a "vast fortune."[412]

Julian was also a member of the small but influential left-wing Patriotic Society. A notation next to his name claims he was a passionate revolutionary.[413]

---

409 William M. Worth, Descendents of Julian Hulanicki: p. 1.

410 Mieczyalaw Haiman, Slady Polskie W Ameryce: [Chicago, Illinois: Drukiem Dziennika Zjednoczenia 1938] Number 139, p.122.

411 Robert Bielecki, Slownik Biograficzny Oficerow Powstania Listopadowego: Volume two, Number E-K [Warszawa: 1996] p. 166.

412 Rufus Blanchard, History of Du Page County, Illinois: [Chicago: O. L. Baskin & Co. 1882] [Reproduced by Duopage Process in the U. S. of America, Cleveland, Ohio] p. 99.

413 Wladyslaw Smolenski, Studja Historyczne Zaklady Drukarskie F. Wyszynskiego I S-Ki: [Warszawa, Warecka 15. 1925] Towarzystwo Patrjotyczne Podczas Powstania Listopadowego p. 245.

God's Playground wrote that the Patriotic Society scared the hell out of the conservatives. They were hawks for war with Russia and had ideas like freeing the serfs. Their motto was "For your freedom and ours."[414] The Patriotic Society also published a periodical called *New Poland. God's Playground* claims, "They frightened as many people as they converted."[415] Leslie adds more: the Patriotic Society created seven areas of operation to plan for war with Russia. Everyone took an oath to unite all of Poland and support the constitution, and then sent out to organize the resistance in the seven different zones.[416]

Julius Jr. claims that his father's first job in America was a civil engineer in New York. At some point he moved to Virginia where he became a professor of languages at the University of Richmond.[417] Julius married Marcia Tuttle on November 13, 1838, in Auburn, New York. Their marriage produced six children. Julian Jr., born in Chicago October 11, 1839. Charles, born in Chicago in 1841, but died young. Polonia, born around 1843. Thaddeus, born around 1846. Edmund, born June 19, 1848, in Dowagiac, Michigan. And Frederick, born January 30, 1860, in Sandusky, Iowa.[418]

History of Iroquois County, Illinois wrote that Julius resurveyed the Illinois-Indiana state line in Iroquois County in 1842.[419] Iroquois County is located in north-central Illinois on the east side of the state. The Hulanicki family was living in Dowagiac, Michigan, when their son Edmund was born in 1848. The Hulanickis moved at least once more, this time to Sandusky, Iowa. This would be the final move for Julius who died in Sandusky on November 30, 1859.[420] The 1860 Iowa Mortality Schedule lists "accidental drowning" as cause of death.[421] The *Gate City Daily* printed the Coroner's inquest, which mentioned that Julius "was a Polander by birth, a first rate Civil Engineer by profession, a man of fine natural feelings and superior acquirements."[422]

---

414 Norman Davies, God's Playground A History of Poland: Volume ii [New York: Columbia University Press 1982] p. 323.

415 Norman Davies, p. 323.

416 R. F. Leslie, Polish Politics and the Revolution of November 1830: [Westport, Connecticut: Greenwood Press Publishers 1969] [Reprinted by permission of The Athlone Press] p. 111.

417 Rufus Blanchard, p. 99.

418 William A. Worth, p. 1.

419 H. W. Beckwith, History of Iroquois County: [Chicago: H. H. Hill and Company 1880] [A Reproduction by Unigraphic, Inc. Evansville, Indiana 1972] p. 334.

420 William A. Worth, p. 1.

421 1860 Iowa Mortality Schedule.

422 The Gate City Daily Newspaper: [Keokuk, Iowa February 27, 1860]

Sandusky is five miles north of Keokuk, Iowa, and located on small bluffs overlooking the Mississippi River. Keokuk is in the far southeast corner of Iowa. The Burlington and Quincy Railroad runs through the village of Sandusky. Its first settler was a French trader named Lemoliese who established a trading post there in 1820. Sandusky has been a very small town for most of its history. It did have its moments. From 1870 to 1878, a large number of canal workers lived in Sandusky, possibly in the hundreds. This in turn brought new business to town. After the canal workers left, the village shrunk in size again. I drove through Sandusky a couple years ago and saw maybe ten to fifteen houses. No one knows how Sandusky got its name, possibly from Sandusky, Ohio, or Sandusky, Illinois.

There is quite a bit written about Julius's sons. Julian Jr. went to school in Keokuk where he studied business and literature. He also worked with his father on civil engineering jobs. Julian Jr. moved to Chicago in 1861 where he was employed at the post office for two years. He went to work for the Burlington and Quincy Railroad in 1863, holding the title of chief clerk of the general freight department for ten years. Julian Jr. worked at a variety of jobs for the railroad until June 1, 1882. On August 1 of the same year, Julian went into business himself in Hinsdale, Illinois. According to Blanchard,

> He is doing some building, as well as dealing in lime, cement, brick, lumber and real estate. In 1861, he married Miss Fannie Hugunin, by whom he has one child-Dora, who keeps house for him, her mother having died in 1871. In 1869, Mr. Hulanicki bought his present property and erected buildings at Hinsdale, where he is one of the Village Trustees. His daughter is a Congregationalist; he is a Unitarian, and a member of the Board of Village Trustees.[423]

Julian and Fannie also had a son Julian, born in Chicago on May 1, 1871. He only lived for three months, dying on August 3, 1871. Julian's second marriage was to Jennie Plummer of Wheaton, Illinois. They were married in Hinsdale on October 3, 1882. They had one son, Frank, born in 1883, but died the same year.[424] Hinsdale by Timothy H. Bakken has a small mention concerning Julian.

> As early as 1876 vagrants were reported to have raided the cellars of local farmers, stealing crocks of butter, salt pork, canned

423 Rufus Blanchard, p. 99.

424 William A. Worth, p. 1.

> fruit and whatever . . ." In November 1882 some were said to have carried off small quantities of goods from Julian Hulanicki's lumber yard in downtown Hinsdale, taking corn and potatoes for food and $15 worth of lumber, maybe to build a shelter of some sort. We need more policemen," was the village's reaction, but little was actually done.[425]

Hinsdale is very close to your author's home in Lisle, being about seven or eight miles to the east. The current population is about seventeen thousand. Hinsdale is a wealthy town and you need big bucks to live there.

Julian's son Thaddeus was an outstanding soldier in the Union army during the Civil War. Julie Joan Giertuga writes that Thaddeus enlisted in the Union army in Chicago on March 31, 1862. He started out as a private but by the time he left the army three years later held the rank of captain. Thaddeus served in Battery L of the Second Illinois Light Artillery until the end of the war. Captain William Bolton raised Battery L in Chicago in 1862.

On March 31, 1862, Battery L got orders to proceed to Benton Barracks in St. Louis, Missouri. On April 9, they moved to Pittsburg Landing. There they were assigned to the Fourth Division, Army of Tennessee under the command of Brigadier General S. A. Hurlbut. Battery L took part in the battle of Corinth in Mississippi on October 3-4, 1862. Some of my great-grandfather's brothers and cousins also participated in this battle. They were members of the Seventeenth Regiment of fighting Irish from Kenosha, Wisconsin. At Corinth, the Seventeenth was cited for heroism for driving the rebels off the battlefield with a bayonet charge.[426]

After Corinth, Battery L hooked up with General Sherman and advanced to Memphis, Tennessee. Battery L next fought at the battles of Newcome Creek and Hatchie. At Hatchie, they captured four cannons and a rebel flag. The rebel flag was later given to the city of Chicago. On November 26, Battery L was reassigned to the Third Division, under the command of Brigadier General John A. Logan. They went along with General Grant on all his battles in Mississippi including forty-seven days at the siege of Vicksburg.

According to Julie Joan Giertuga, "Hulanicki's fearlessness and gallantry on the field of battle were not overlooked. Promotions came in swift succession.

---

[425] Timothy H. Bakken, Hinsdale: [Published by J. Peter Teschner, Timothy H. Bakken, Kristi Cook and the Hinsdale Doings. 1976] p. 141.

[426] Frank L. Klement, Wisconsin in the Civil War: [Madison: The State Historical Society of Wisconsin 1877] p. 88.

From private he rose to Sergeant on April 18, 1864, and seventeen days later received his second lieutenant's bars."[427] Thaddeus was promoted to senior first lieutenant on March 13, 1865, also becoming the commander of Battery L. On June 12, 1865, he was promoted to captain at Vicksburg, Mississippi. At the end of the war, Battery L was discharged in Chicago on August 9, 1865. There were only 130 men left from the 450 men Battery L started out with in 1862.[428]

Thaddeus married Molly Finney in 1866. He died the same year leaving Molly a widow after less than a year of marriage. Thaddeus survived the Civil War, but civilian life must have been bad for his health. The Hulanicki family tree does not have the cause of his death.[429]

Julius's son Edmund was also in the Civil War, enlisting in the same outfit as his brother Thaddeus. Edmund participated in all the same battles up to the siege of Vicksburg, and then discharged because of disability on November 5, 1864. Edmund is supposed to have reenlisted in the Twelfth United States Heavy Artillery and like his brother promoted to captain. I cannot understand why the army would let him enlist again after they discharged him, but that is what it says.[430] Edward C. Rozanski claims the Twelfth Heavy Artillery was a Negro regiment.[431]

Edmund married Charlotte Felicia Lowthe in Chicago on June 10, 1866. Edmund and Charlotte had one son, Thaddeus Charles, born in 1870 but died the following year. Charlotte died in Ottumwa, Iowa, in 1873. Edmund married Rosabelle McGaw in Ogden, Utah, on February 28, 1877. Two daughters were born to their marriage. Adah, born in Utah in 1877, and Rosa, born in Utah on January 26, 1878. Adah died in 1878.[432]

Julius's youngest son Frederick was born January 30, 1860, two months after Julius died. He married Ruth Kerr in Cauker City, Kansas, on October 12, 1880. Four children were born from the marriage. Ofal Polonia, born August 1, 1881. Paul, born February 23, 1883, but died April 18 of the same

427 Julie Joan Giertuga, Polish Contributions in Illinois during the war between the states: [Peoria, Illinois: A Thesis submitted to the Department of History at Bradley University 1948] p. 37.

428 Julie Joan Giertuga, p. 36, 37 & 38.

429 William A. Worth, p. 2.

430 Julie Joan Giertuga, p. 15.

431 Edward C. Rozanski, Civil War Poles of Illinois: [Polish-American Studies Volume xxiii, No. 2 July-December, 1966: The Polish American Historical Association of the Polish institute of Arts and Sciences in America St. Mary's College, Orchard Lake, Michigan] p. 112.

432 William A. Worth, p. 2.

year. Ruth Mary, born October 2, 1885. Marcia, born March 12, 1893.[433] I also have Frederick's obituary from the February 23, 1928, *Keokuk Daily Gate City and Constitution-Democrat.*

Publisher who was born here died recently

> Frederick J. Hulaniski whose birthplace was Keokuk, died last week in California, and his funeral was held there last Friday. Death resulted an attack of influenza, Says the Martinez, California., Standard:
>
> Hulaniski was born at Keokuk, Iowa, and was 68 years old on January 30 last. Early in life he began his career as many of the old school of journalists did in the printing shop, and at 21 he was employed in Cawker City, Kansas, where he met Miss Ruth Kerr, daughter of Gordon and Flora Kerr. They were united in marriage in 1880.
>
> He founded the Western Empire at Alton, Kansas, and made it a wide reputation. It is still published at that place. He was the editor and publisher of the Plaindealer at Ouray, Colo. For 20 years and during that period was also engaged in mining enterprises in Colorado. His mining enterprises profited him greatly at one time and he had offices in New York.
>
> He moved to Richmond with his family fifteen years ago and took an active part in the development of Richmond and Contra Costa county and became known to every one by his writings and activities. He purchased the plant of a labor paper published at Point Richmond and started the Richmond Morning News and published it until a newspaper merger was effected.
>
> He published in book form and then as a monthly in San Francisco the "Thinkograph," Which was a fair companion to Elbert Hubbard's Phillistine.[434]

I managed to find a descendant of Julius Hulanicki and contacted him. William M. Worth, of Clarksville, Tennessee, was nice enough to send me the Hulanicki family tree. The family tree was a great help in writing this story, and we are all indebted to Mr. Worth.

433 William A. Worth, p. 2.

434 Keokuk Daily Gate City and Constitution-Democrat Newspaper: [Keokuk, Iowa, February 23, 1928]

Jackson County

Jackson County had one Pole by 1850 named Julius Bamberger. He was in Jackson County by at least 1844. Julius lived in the town of Murphysboro, which is also the county seat. I have only been able to find a small amount of information about him and a small amount is all you are going to get too. About the only source I have for him is the 1850 census, and the rest of the story is more like a history of Jackson County.

Jackson County was formed from parts of Randolph and Johnson counties January 10. 1816. The county is located deep in the southwestern part of the state with the Mississippi River its western boundary. The center of the county where Murphysboro is located is rolling hills and high ground. To the east and west, the countryside is mostly flat. In its undeveloped state most of the county was wooded with the exception of the northeastern portion of the county which was prairie. The Big Muddy is the most important river. The current population of Murphysboro is 13,295.

The first county seat in Jackson County was the town of Brownsville. Brownsville was not located in the center of the county, and many people wanted the county seat moved to a more central location. They got their chance when the courthouse in Brownsville burned down January 10, 1843. Moving a county seat takes state legislation. Those wanting a new county seat wasted no time and immediately petitioned the Illinois General Assembly. On February 24, 1843, the Illinois General Assembly signed legislation to move the county seat to the center of the county. Three county commissioners checked different sites in the center of the county and on August 17, 1843, chose a twenty-acre tract located four miles upstream of Brownsville on the Big Muddy River. Dr. John Logan, who happened to be one of those pushing for a new county seat, donated the parcel to build on. To figure out a name for the new town, the three commissioners' names were put in a hat and commissioner Murphy's name picked out.

In the middle of the tract, a square was designed with the center reserved for the courthouse. The first day that lots went on sale, thirty-four lots were sold for from ten to forty dollars apiece. The new courthouse was built by the fall of 1845. This time the courthouse was built out of brick. Most of the population of Brownsville moved to Murphysboro in 1843-44. Some brought their houses with them. By 1850 Murphysboro had a population of 150 while Brownsville was completely deserted. Newsome wrote some very interesting accounts of the early years of Murphysboro.

> Murphysboro was a very dull place usually when there was neither court nor election in progress. Circuit court was only held one week in the spring and one week in the fall, and elections were only once a year; but at these times the farmers from the whole county would crowd in, and the town would then be lively, yes! Very lively-for even at that time there were several "groceries" as they were then called; for they were not yet dignified by name of "saloons," but in them whisky was cheap and abundant; drunkenness and fighting were very common occurrences. It was often the case, that during the time that an earnest counselor was making his best effort before a jury, a fight would begin just outside of the courthouse, which soon became exciting and general; the crowd shouting, the audience in the courtroom rushing out, even the judge and jury peep out through the windows. For a time the counsel pleads in vain; no one hears him as long as the fight continues.[435]

Jackson County was a rural county and Murphysboro the only town in the county until 1850 when Dorchester was built. Dorchester was located just across the Big Muddy River from Murphysboro and was also know as Scottown. The Jackson County Coal Company built Dorchester. Most of the employees were Scotch or Welch emigrants, hence the name Scottown. After the coal mine opened, New England Yankees along with German, Irish and English emigrants, came on the scene. Before 1850, most of the inhabitants of Murphysboro and Jackson County were Southerners. They were mainly from the states of Kentucky, Tennessee, the Carolinas, and Virginia.[436] Julius might have been one of the first foreign-born persons in town.

Now that you know something about Murphysboro, I will write about the small amount of information I have about Julius Bamburger. Julius was

[435] Newsome, Historical Sketches of Jackson County, Illinois: 1894 [Reprinted by Jackson County Historical Society, Murphysboro, Illinois. 1987] p. 167 and 168.

[436] Woodson W. Fishback, A History of Murphysboro, Illinois 1843-1882. [Brandon, Mississippi: Quail Ridge Press, Inc. 1982] p.9.

living in Murphysboro by at least 1844 when he married Sara Ann Kunce on July 28, 1844.[437] It was the second marriage for Sara whose maiden name was Hiers.[438] The 1850 Federal Census of Jackson County shows that Julius is thirty-five, occupation tailor and born in Poland. At the time, he was the only tailor in town. His wife Sara Ann is twenty-five and born in Illinois. Sons William Morris is four and Julius nine months old. Both were born in Illinois. Daughter Elizabeth is three and born in Illinois.[439]

There are no other census records of the Bamburgers after 1850, but some of the Bamburgers were still around until 1900. The Jackson County Historical Society managed to find two records of the Bamburgers. On November 26, 1871, Nicholas Bamburger married Anna Vancil.[440] The other is the death of Albert Bamburger on January 26, 1900. Albert died of meningitis at fourteen days of age.[441]

With the last name of Bamburger, Julius must have been either a Polish Jew or a German from Poland. Julius and Sara were not married in a church but by a justice of the peace. I have some records of the Kunces and they are all members of various Proteatant faiths. I would like to thank Kenneth E. Cochran of the Jackson County Historical Society for his help with this story.

---

437 Liahona Research, Illinois Marriages: 1826-1850. [Bountiful, Utah: Heritage Quest, 1999] p. 36.

438 Kenneth E. Cochran, Jackson County Historical Society, Research Committee.

439 John W.D. Wright, Jackson County, Illinois, Residents in 1850 [Carbondale, Illinois: 1972] p. 5.

440 Kenneth E. Cochran, Research Committee.

441 Kenneth E. Cochran, Research Committee.

THOMAS JAWORSKI

Thomas settled at Dutchman's Point, now Skokie, in Cook County. The city of Chicago is also in Cook County and was located about eight or ten miles south of Dutchman's Point. Over the years, Chicago's boundary has moved farther north. Thomas was one of the 234 Polish exiles from Trieste and is number 69 on Lerski's list of Polish exiles.[442] According to Aleksander Grobicki, Thomas was either a soldier or a young noncommissioned officer in the 1830 uprising.[443] He is also listed as an early settler of Niles Township. Andreas writes, "Thomas Jawarski, a native of Poland settled on the southern half of Section 27 in 1839."[444] There might have been another Pole living in Niles Township before 1850. *Niles Center Pioneers in the 1800's* contains the name Liepski.[445] The teacher's report for Chicago district number 4 has a student with the similar-sounding name of Leirski.[446]

This area was under the control of the Potawatomi Indians until the Treaty of Chicago on September 26, 1833. They where allowed to stay until 1835, then moved west. Cook became a county on January 15, 1831; Putnam County is the parent county.. Cook was later divided into Mc Henry and Will counties in 1836 and Du Page County in 1839. Chicago is the county seat.

The first settler in Niles Township was an Englishman named Joseph Curtis, who settled in the spring of 1831. John Dewes, another Englishman, came in 1832-33. They only stayed a couple years, and then both went back to England. More well-known was John Ruland, who came to Niles Township

---

442 Jerzy Jan Lerski, A Polish Chapter in Jacksonian America: [Madison, Wisconsin: The University of Wisconsin Press 1958] p. 174.

443 Aleksander Grobicki, Proba Biografii, Sodalis: [St. Mary's College Library, Orchard Lake, Michigan] Number J, p. 23.

444 A. T. Andreas, [Chicago: A. T. Andreas Publisher 1884] [Reproduction by South Suburban Genealogical and Historical Society, South Holland, Illinois, Evansville, Indiana: Unigrafic, Inc. 1976] p. 471.

445 Jacob Kercher, Niles Center Pioneers in the 1800's:

446 Chicago City Council Proceedings Files 1833-1871: [Document 2298]

in 1834 and managed to get himself renamed "Wrong Way Ruland." Ruland had intended to settle in Chicago. Chicago was still a small town of about one thousand people in 1834.The captain of the ship Ruland was a passenger on sailed along the shore of Lake Michigan looking for Chicago but could not find it. Ruland decided to get off the ship anyways, probably thinking he would eventually find Chicago. Ruland did not know at the time but his location was north of Chicago. He headed west through the forest for about four miles and built himself "a sort of cave in a sand bank which he partially walled and roofed with sod and bark."[447] Ruland later went on to build a real house and lived in Niles Township the rest of his life, dying there August 24, 1880.

I mentioned in the beginning of the story that Thomas settled in Dutchman's Point. Dutchman's Point got its name from four German families who settled there on a wooded ridge in 1834. The ridge extended from the North Branch of the Chicago River and ended in a point in Niles Township where the four German families settled. The other settlers in the area mistakenly called the Germans "Dutchmen," which was a common occurrence in those days. Pennsylvania Dutch is another example. They were actually Germans. Dutchman's Point grew very slowly, and by 1850, the population was still so small that it was not considered a village. It was not until 1888 that there were enough people living there to incorporate into a village. At the same time, the name Dutchman's Point was dropped and the name changed to Niles Center. It would remain Niles Center until 1940, and then changed to Skokie. The settlers of Dutchman's Point-Niles Center were mainly of German descent until the 1940s when large numbers of Jewish people moved into town. Skokie still has a sizable Jewish community and its population is around sixty thousand.

The west side of Niles Township was heavily wooded, and over time much of it was cut down and sold as firewood in Chicago. The Skokie River ran through the north end of the township. The Skokie River Valley was located to the east of the timbered area and named "East Prairie." East Prairie had little timber and was a large swamp for much of the year. The word *Skokie* is supposed to be from the Algonquin Indian word *Wabskokie,*(wet prairie) or *Che-Wabskokie* (big wet prairie).[448] Big it was. It started from around Oakton Street in Skokie and extended north into Lake County. In 1908, Lake County drained most of the swamp.[449]

---

447 Skokie, Illinois History Government: [School District seventy-three and one-half, Skokie Historical Society, Skokie, Illinois] p. 1.

448 Skokie, Illinois History Government, p. 12.

449 Waukegan Daily Sun Newspaper [Waukegan, Illinois August 28, 1908] p.2.

Thomas Jaworski is recorded as being an early settler of East Prairie, coming there in 1840.[450] Andreas claims Thomas settled in the southern half of Section 27 in 1839.[451] The southern part of Section 27 would have been right at the southern end of the swamp. Niles Township was surveyed and its boundary lines established in 1838; however it did not go on sale by the government until 1841-42.[452] Thomas bought 160 acres from the government on February 17, 1841, at one dollar and twenty-five cents an acre.[453] The land was located on Lincoln Avenue, the main road to Chicago at the time. Thomas might have been a squatter. If he was already living on the same land he bought in 1841, he was definitely a squatter. The 234 Polish exiles from Trieste lost their land grant to squatters, but here a Pole was doing the same thing. Squatting on public land was very common in Illinois. Pease writes,

> Long before the country was put on sale by the federal land officers, squatters had established claims on the most desirable combinations of timber, prairie, springs, and healthful sites. Such claims the rough and ready custom of the frontier accepted as valid, and another settler coming on the land was forced by public opinion to recognize the claim by buying off the occupying clamant.[454]

The government also accepted squatter titles. History of the Niles Township area states, "The parties who had located themselves on lands by preemption made good their claim by purchasing it from the government if they had the necessary funds"[455] Thomas might have made an excellent choice to settle on. Might because I am not sure how often it was underwater. The soil from drained swampland is known as "muck" soil and is very fertile. Because of its close proximity to Chicago, Niles Township was an ideal location for

450 Jacob Kercher, Niles Center Pioneers 1800's

451 Andreas, p. 471.

452 History of the Niles Township Area 1881: [Niles Centre Maennerchor] [At the Skokie Historical Society, Skokie, Illinois] p. 2 & 3.

453 State of Illinois Archives Division Public Domain Sales Land Tract Record: [At the Skokie Historical Society, Skokie, Illinois] p. 4681.

454 Theodore Calvin Pease, The Frontier State: [Chicago: A. C. McClure & Co. 1922] p, 181.

455 History of the Niles Township Area 1881: [At the Skokie Historical Society, Skokie, Illinois] p. 3.

market farms "vegetable farms." Skokie, Illinois, by School District 73 and a half-wrote,

> This place had wide prairies where often you could see a whole mile. The sky was blue instead of smoky, birds sang all summer, you could hear the shrill cry of the kill-deer and the call of quail and prairie chickens in the grass. Squirrels frisked through the trees and rabbits scuttled through the grass. It was quite like the country, yet had the advantage of being less than an hour from the loop.[456]

It was not all roses. The roads were muddy much of the year. According to *A Chronological Index to Skokie History 1666-1976*, East Prairie "was essentially a marsh, so deep, that one John Schneider lost his horse in East Prairie and was nearly drowned himself."[457] Early Skokie claims, "In Spring when the swamp rose, one could row a boat to Evanston."[458] Bertha Rosche writes, "In years of extreme high water the lake sturgeon sometimes came up the Chicago River and the North Branch into the East Prairie swamp."[459] Wetlands can be unhealthy places to live in because of malaria, but none of the Skokie histories mention any problems with the disease.

The Jaworski family only lived in Niles Township for about seven years. The family was living in Chicago's Fifth Ward by 1846. An article in the *Chicago Genealogist* titled "Old Residents of Chicago Nov. 15, 1918" lists Thomas's son Stephen D. Jaworski as a resident of Chicago in 1849.[460] The 1850 Federal Census record of the Jaworski family is hard to read, but I will do my best to translate it. Thomas is sixty years old, occupation laborer and born in Poland. His wife Cecilia is forty years old, born in Scotland. A son, whom I cannot make out his name is nine years old and born in Illinois. Son J. Valentine and daughter Rosalie are twins, six years old and born in Illinois. Stephen D., two years old and born in Illinois. Deborah, thirteen

---

456 Skokie, Illinois History Government, p. 10.

457 A Chronological Index To Skokie History 1666-1976 [Skokie Public Library Skokie, Illinois] p. 2.

458 Roberta Kaye Sweetow, Early Skokie: [compiled by the League of Women Voters of Skokie-Lincolnwood and published by the Village of Skokie] p. 1.

459 Bertha Rosche, Before the White Men Came: [History of Skokie binder at the Skokie Historical Society, Skokie, Illinois] p. 1.

460 Chicago Genealogist, Spring 1983: [Abstracted by June B. Barekman and Bernice C. Richard Old Residents of Chicago November 15, 1918] p. 144.

years old and born in New York. Cecilia and Ferdinand, one-year-old twins born in Illinois.[461]

I could not find any other census records of the Jaworskis after 1850, but there is plenty of evidence of the Jaworskis living in Chicago before then. Thomas signed a petition in Chicago's Third Ward on July 3, 1846, requesting the city grade Des Plains St. between First and Second Street. The area had a bad flooding problem, and it was hoped that grading would enable all the water to drain down First Street into the Chicago River. Thomas was the first person to sign the petition.[462] Thomas was a resident of the Fifth Ward when he voted in the city elections on March 2, 1847.[463] He signed another petition on April 23, 1847, urging the city to build a sidewalk on Jefferson Street.[464] Thomas signed a petition to build another sidewalk on June 16, 1848. This time to build a sidewalk on Canal Street.[465] The last petition he signed on July 24, 1848, requested that Jefferson Street be extended from first to Second Street.[466] Thomas took an active interest in improving living conditions in Chicago. Maybe he moved to Chicago to get out of the Skokie marsh and did not want to live in mud anymore.

Thomas died sometime in the 1850s. His wife Cecilia is listed in *Deceased Estates in Cook County, 1871-1892.*[467] Son Stephen was living at 2743 Warren Avenue in Chicago in 1918.[468] It also looks like one of the Jaworskis either stayed or moved back to Niles Township. Five Jaworskis are buried in the St. Paul's Lutheran Cemetery in Skokie. The last burial took place on April 24, 1942.[469] Lee County in north-central Illinois had a Polish pioneer named Nickolas Jaworski living there before 1850. I have not been able to determine if he was related to Thomas. There is no more information about Liepski.

---

461 1850 Federal Census of the City of Chicago, 5th Ward: [At the National Archives, Roll 102 p. 284]

462 Chicago City Council Proceedings Files 1833-1871: [Northeastern Illinois University Irad, Chicago, Illinois, Document 3277]

463 Chicago City Council Proceedings Files 1833-1871, Document 3713.

464 Chicago City Council Proceedings Files 1833-1871, Document 6464.

465 Chicago City Council Proceedings Files 1833-1871, Document 4664.

466 Chicago City Council Proceedings Files 1833-1871, Document 6824.

467 Probate Division [p 5358, Docket 22, Page 90 Estate of Cecilia Jaworski] [On the 12th floor of the Daly building, Chicago, Illinois]

468 Chicago Genealogist, Spring 1983, p. 144.

469 Record of Tombstones, St. Paul's Lutheran Church, Skokie, Illinois: [At the Skokie Historical Society, Skokie, Illinois] p. 7.

Jo Daviess County

Jo Daviess County is located in the northwest corner of the state. Galena is the county seat and the most famous town in the area. Jo Daviess County was created from parts of Mercer, Henry, and Putnam counties on February 27, 1827. It was divided itself a number of times. Rock Island County was formed from Jo Daviess County in 1831. Ogle, Whiteside, and Winnebago counties were created from Joe Daviess County in 1836. Carroll and Stevenson counties were also a part of Joe Daviess County until they came into being in 1837.

This part of the state is known as the "Driftless Area" and is much different from the rest of northern and central Illinois. Southwest Wisconsin, northeast Iowa, and southeast Minnesota are also a part of the Driftless Area. Glaciers missed this area and left the region's hills and valleys intact. Galena and the rest of the Driftless Area were famous for its lead mines. This was the greatest lead mining region in the world during the 1840s. Lead was easy to mine there because it was close to the surface of the ground and it was of a high quality being 90 percent pure lead. Anyone with a diggers permit, pick, shovel, and bucket to haul it out of the ground could excavate it. Once mined and smelted, the lead was transported down the Fever River to the Mississippi River, a distance of four miles. The Mississippi River then moved it to markets around the world. Most of the exported lead ended up as bullets.

The French were the first Europeans to explore the area, coming in 1634. La Sueur saw the site of the future Galena in 1700 and wrote that the Indians were mining lead there. In 1721, the French brought in five hundred slaves from San Domingo and two hundred white miners to start a mining venture there. The undertaking was a failure, and the slaves were sent back to San Domingo after a short time. A few of the miners chose to stay.

In 1804, the United States government purchased the lands between the Illinois and Wisconsin rivers from the Sac and Fox Indians. The lead region came under direct control of the government in 1807. All mining claims were by lease only, with the government taking 10 percent of the profits. Large numbers of miners came in the 1820s, and the leases brought the government a nice profit. The government changed the policy in 1838 and allowed miners to purchase their claims.

The first Americans to immigrate to Jo Daviess County were mainly Southerners from Kentucky, Missouri, and Southern Illinois. They came by Keelboat up the Mississippi River each spring, mined until late fall, and then returned home before winter set in. Colonel James Johnson of Kentucky was one of the first people to acquire a lease. In 1822, he transported 150 slaves and 20 white miners from the south to work his claim. Colonel Johnson failed to make a go of it using slave labor and sent most of his slaves south. Other southerners did use slaves in the mines until slavery was finally outlawed in 1845. Slavery was supposed to be illegal in 1787, but Illinois managed to find a loophole in the law by claiming the slaves were "indentured servants."

Galena became the most influential city for a one-hundred-mile radius. Only 100 people lived in the Galena area in July 1825, but the number rose to 151 by December. This increase came after the miners had gone back south. The population was 200 by the spring of 1826, and 550 by the fall. Stagecoach service to and from Chicago began in 1829. By 1830, Galena's permanent population stood at 900 with an additional 1,600 people working in the mines. Some miners lived in Galena while other miners chose to live near their claims in hillside caves.

During this time, no one was sure if Galena was in Illinois or Wisconsin (Wisconsin was a part of Michigan territory then). At first, mail was addressed to the "Fever River Settlement" rather than Galena. The name of Galena came into use after 1827. The Illinois-Wisconsin border was still under dispute when Wisconsin became a state in 1848. Many people in Galena felt they had more in common with the lead mines in Wisconsin than the prairies of Illinois. An attempt was made to secede from Illinois in the 1840s, but Congress put an end to it.

Galena was a boomtown well into the early 1830s, and a typical frontier town. People from all over the country and Europe came to make their fortunes there. *History of Jo Daviess County* claims, "Every language was spoken, every costume worn."[470] In the early days of settlement, a great many miners were Southerners, Irish, or French. Women and families were scarce. Soon Cornish, English, Canadians, Welch, and Swiss came on the scene. The Cornish had been lead miners in Cornwall. Northerners came in large numbers in the 1840s. They stayed away from the mining camps and became the town's businessmen and farmers.

---

470 The History of Joe Daviess County Illinois: [Chicago: H. F. Kett and Co. 1878] [Reproduction by Unigraphic, Inc. Evansville, Indiana 1973] p. 828.

The docks along Galena's riverfront brought in a great variety of characters. The workers were mainly free blacks, Irish, and Welch. The Welch were famous for their novel approach at conflict resolution. Each person stood next to a pile of stones and engaged in the "stone duel." The duelists threw stones at each other until someone was either "unconscious or dead."[471] The riverboat crews tended to be "shanty Irish" who had a reputation for getting drunk for any occasion. Everyone on the dock probably got drunk for any occasion. Philip Williams writes,

> Liquor flowed freely along the waterfront, and in the "lighthouses" [saloons] the miners and river men found their relaxation. They were particularly fond of cock fights and wolf fights which were generally held in the back rooms of these saloons with bets running high. The amazing thing about the rough life of the riverfront was that even the hardest characters had a definite "law of honor". Debts, gambling and otherwise, were practically always paid. Merchants of Galena rarely bothered to lock the doors of their stores, because burglary was so infrequent.[472]

The steamboats in those days were particularly dangerous places to work in. Each wheel needed its own boiler and the boilers were notorious for blowing up. Thirty blew up on the upper Mississippi River between the 1830s and 1840s. The ship captains used any means necessary to keep their mainly Irish crews in line. Captain Billy Wilson knew how to run his ship. He used a large paddle made out of a barrel stave to keep order. The paddle contained a number of holes and each hole left a blood blister on the backside of any crew member unfortunate enough to rile Captain Billy. The captain always carried a pistol as well but never had to use it, preferring his paddle instead. I have worked in a number of jobs over the years and would have delighted in seeing some of my lazier coworkers treated in this manner.

Galena could not keep its prominent position. Lead mining production increased every year until 1845, and then started falling. A number of factors contributed to the lower amounts of lead. Planning for a Galena to Chicago railroad started in 1845, but did not reach the area until 1855. Then the Illinois Central Railroad decided to change course and bypassed Galena for Dubuque, Iowa, leaving Galena without a railroad. After years of mining, the shallow lead deposits were all mined out and new shafts had to be sunk much deeper. Lead

---

471 Philip Williams, Galena, Illinois A Footnote to History: [1941] p. 19

472 Philip Williams, p. 19.

deposits found in other parts of the world sent the price of lead lower. Many of the miners left in 1849 when gold was discovered in California. Others went to work in Minnesota iron mines or the silver mines in the Black Hills of South Dakota. In addition, erosion from mining Galena's hills started to fill up the Fever River. Today the river is only one-fifth its original width.

Galena held on and remained an important city. Farmers became more numerous and their produce became a major source of income. Galena's population actually increased to fourteen thousand by 1858. It was always a major center for trade with the towns on the Mississippi River, especially those to the north. Galena was the central point for the shipping of agriculture products farther north or south on the Mississippi River. A number of warehouses also operated out of Galena.

Galena's second wind only lasted a short time. River transportation could not compete with the railroad. Philip Williams wrote,

> But since 1857 and 1858 business has gradually declined. The opening of railroads from Chicago to Prairie du Chien and La Cross [Wisconsin] has diverted trade and travel from our city; the wholesale grocery and dry goods establishments which lined our levee and Main Street have disappeared and the large steamboat interest, which was concentrated in our city and gave animation to business, has almost ceased to exist."[473]

The Civil War added to Galena's problems when the Mississippi River was blockaded at New Orleans. Galena's fortunes continued to decline, and by 1865, the city had very little importance at all. Its population decreased as well and stood at three thousand when Philip Williams wrote his book in 1941. The population is currently about four thousand.

Jo Daviess County had a number of Poles settling there over the years, but none stayed for very long. James Reed (Rydnowski) is the first person of Polish descent to make an appearance in the county. The *History of Sangamon County* claims James came to Galena in 1820.[474] Applications for digger's permits contain the name James F. Reed requesting a permit to mine for lead in July 1827.[475] James stayed until 1831, and then moved to Springfield,

---

[473] Philip Williams, p. 26.

[474] History of Sangamon County, Illinois: [Chicago: Inter-state Publishing Company, 1881] p. 853.

[475] Robert Hansen & Alfred Mueller, Smith Paper, apply for diggers permit 1977: [at the Galena Public Library] p. 30.

Illinois. James would go on to be a participant in one of the most infamous incidents in American history, but you have to read my story about Sangamon County to find out what happened.

Vincent Dziewanowski arrived in Galena in November 1835. He was one of the 234 Polish exiles from Trieste. Vincent left a detailed story of himself titled "A Polish Pioneer's Story." My cousin Joe gets the credit for finding this story, which has inspired me so much. "A Polish Pioneer's Story" was one of the first stories I read about the Polish exiles from Trieste and got me thinking that there must be more of these stories out there. I had read *A Polish Chapter in Jacksonian America*, by Lerski, but had never seen anything like "A Polish Pioneer's Story." I am only going to write a small amount of Vincent's story because he only spent a short time in Galena. He lived most of his life in Wisconsin, so his story must be written about in my book about Wisconsin Poles, if I ever have the time to write it, that is.

Vincent was born April 5, 1804, in Podolia, Russian Poland. His family was nobility and owned an estate containing five hundred serfs. Vincent was exiled to America for participating in the 1830 Polish insurrection. He arrived in New York with 233 other Polish exiles on March 28, 1834. Being nobility, he was not used to doing any type of manual labor. Serfs did all that type of work in Poland. He quickly learned that life would be much more different here and took any job he could find. He soon learned the English language. Vincent worked at various jobs in the states of New York and New Jersey for about a year, and then resolved to go west. He did not have much money, so he decided to walk, working along the way. In western Pennsylvania Vincent befriended a peddler who offered him a job as his assistant. They traveled around the countryside selling household goods to farmers' wives, and Vincent managed to save some money. Vincent still longed to go west and came up with a plan. With the help of his employer, Vincent went into the peddler business himself and worked his way out to Galena, stopping at farms along the way.

After arriving in Galena, Vincent sold his business and took a job as a lead smelter for the William S. Hamilton Company. He put all his effort into his new occupation and quickly mastered the trade. By spring, he had learned enough to take on his own customers and soon had all the work he could handle. During Vincent's first winter in Galena, he heard stories about the beautiful country of southwest Wisconsin. Southwest Wisconsin was also a lead mining region. Vincent got his chance to see the area for himself when the William S. Hamilton Company built a new plant in Muscoda, Wisconsin, in November 1836. Muscoda is located along the southern bank of the Wisconsin River.

Vincent left Galena for good and moved to Muscoda where he worked for the William S. Hamilton Company until 1839. He also found some unclaimed land in Iowa County, which he purchased from the government in September 1838. On February 7, 1843, Vincent married Mary Jane McKown. They started a family and became a very well-known family in the area. Vincent became an expert dairy farmer and operated the farm until his death on February 22, 1883. Mary died May 15, 1890.

Extracts from the Galena and Northwest gazettes contains one Polish name and one other name that might be Polish. Letters at the Galena Post Office on October 1, 1838, lists the name Alex Vandebesky.[476] There is no way to know if he was a Pole, and the first part of the name almost looks like a Dutch name. The other name is definitely Polish. Letters at the Galena Post Office for July 3, 1841, contains the name Stainiat Birbauski.[477] This is really Stanislaus Bielowski, who married Mary Ann Mariah James in Winnebago County on August 23, 1841.[478] What little I know about Stanislaus is in my story about Winnebago County.

Joseph Krokowski either passed through or spent some time in Galena. He applied for a license there to marry Mary Moore on May 13, 1841.[479] The Krokowskis lived most of their lives in Fairfield Township, Jones County, Iowa. Joe's nephew Michael Sadowski was one of the 234 Polish exiles from Trieste and lived in Fairfield Township as well.[480] Joe might have been the oldest Pole to enlist in the Civil War. He joined the army when he was sixty-one years old.[481]

The last Pole to leave any record of himself in Joe Daviess County is Rudolf Soloski. Rudolf is listed on the 1850 Federal Census of Joe Daviess County. He was thirty-three years old, occupation farm laborer at the Francis

---

476 Wisconsin State Historical Society, Extracts from the Northwest Gazette and Galena Advertiser 1834-1845: [Madison, Wisconsin: microfilm collection]

477 Wisconsin State Historical Society, Extracts from the Galena & Northwest Gazette and Galena Advertiser 1834-1845] p. 7.

478 Liahona Research, Illinois Marriages 1826-1850: [Bountiful, Utah: Heritage Quest 1999] p. 63.

479 Joe Daviess County Marriages, Marriage Applications 1828-1849: part 3,[at the Galena Public Library] p. 1.

480 Aleksander Grobicki, Proba Biografii, Sodalis: The Polish American Historical Association of the Polish institute of Arts and sciences in America St. Mary's College, Orchard Lake, Michigan [letter S] p. 26.

481 Joseph A. Wytrwal, Poles in American History and Tradition: [Detroit: Endurance Press 1969] p. 188.

Longgates farm and born in Poland. Francis had a good-size farm. He had four other people besides Rudolph working for him.[482] Other Poles worked in the lead mining regions of Iowa and Wisconsin, but they belong in books about those states instead of in an Illinois history. Thousands of miners came and left Galena during its lead mining years, and I would not be surprised if other Poles worked there at some point but left no records of it.

Galena is a popular tourist destination for people from the Chicago area. It still looks like it did in the 1800s and has a number of antique shops. The current population is four thousand, and its high school football team has won three state championships since 1997. Galena was also the home of Ulysses S. Grant before the Civil War. Grant was appointed commander in chief of the Union army during the Civil War. He later became the president of the United States. Grant's home is still there and a well-known tourist attraction. Galena also produced eight other generals during the Civil War.[483] I'd like to thank Steve Repp, of Galena, for his help with this story.

482 1850 Federal Census of Joe Daviess County, Illinois: [National Archives, Box 432 Roll 111, Page 236]

483 Philip Williams, p. 24.

Lake County

Now we come to the county that your author was born and raised in. Lake County had a number of Poles before 1850, including my ancestor Franciszek. The first Polish settlers to the county were Hanson and Robert Minskey who were of Polish descent. Their father was a Polish exile. Six Polish exiles settled in Lake County. Five were members of the 234 exiles from Trieste while the sixth came over from Trieste on a different ship. Stanislaus Lisiecki and Stefan Gasiorowski settled in Waukegan. Alexander Bilinski lived in Waukegan and Diamond Lake. Theodor Dombski settled in Hainesville. My ancestor, Franciszek Wlodecki, settled in Warren Township. Basil Jaroshinski settled in Newport, "the present town of Wadsworth." Basil was not one of the 234 exiles but came over on a different ship in July 1834. In addition, Thaddeus Pienkowski, another one of the 234 Polish exiles from Trieste, was living north of the other exiles on the Wisconsin side of the Illinois-Wisconsin state line.

Lake County was originally a part of Cook County. Mc Henry County was created from Cook on January 16, 1836, and Lake County was created from Mc Henry County on March 1, 1839. Lake County is located in the far northeastern corner of Illinois. Its northern border is the Wisconsin state line and its eastern border Lake Michigan. The county got its name because fifty lakes are located there, all west of the Des Plaines River. The Des Plaines River is six miles west of Lake Michigan and is the main river in the county flowing in a north-south direction through the entire length of the county. The north branch of the Chicago River begins in Lake County and a small part of the Fox River flows through the western edge of the county. The topography is level to rolling and the soil black. When first settled, hardwood forest covered all the area east of the Des Plaines River. The land west of the Des Plaines River was about one-half prairie and one-half wooded, the prairie being interspersed with large groves of trees. The northwestern part of the county had much wetland.

This part of Illinois was Indian Territory until the Treaty of Chicago on September 26, 1833. The land involved encompassed five million acres in northeast and north-central Illinois and southeast and south central

Wisconsin. The Pottawatomie, Chippewa, and Ottawa Indian tribes lived in this region and were paid fourteen and one-half cents an acre for their land. The government moved these tribes to land west of the Mississippi River when President Andrew Jackson signed the treaty on February 23, 1835.[484] The Pottawatomie Indian tribe inhabited Lake County.

Lake County was a favorite Indian hunting ground. The Indians managed it by setting yearly fires on the prairies and wooded areas. The first white pioneers could drive their wagons through the forests without being caught in undergrowth. The rivers and lakes abounded with fish and waterfowl. The following story from the October 25, 1868, *Waukegan Gazette* shows what a week of hunting was like for hunters in Lake County. The blue boat club spent a week hunting and fishing on Grass Lake. The "club numbers fifteen members and owns ten boats. Going rather early, the club met with rather indifferent success, killing only about two-hundred fifty ducks. In fishing, luck was good. About two hundred pounds of pickerel and bass were taken."[485] The Nippersink club did much better the next week, killing 329 ducks during the week of October 31, 1868.[486] The Nippersink club outdid itself two years later when they killed 450 ducks during the week of October 22, 1870.[487]

The largest game, bear and elk, were all hunted out within the first couple years of settlement.[488] Mountain lions were occasionally seen. The last record of a mountain lion killed in the county is February 12, 1898.[489] Lynxes and bobcats lived in the most remote parts of the county well into the early 1900s. Whitetail deer roamed throughout the county in abundance. Clarke Coarser, an early settler of Benton Township, claimed, "Deer were running so thickly that you couldn't walk twenty rods without running into one." "And prairie wolves, why they were running so wild that the country was over-run by them."[490] The county had two kinds of wolves, grey or timber and prairie or "coyotes." All would prove to be a nuisance to the county's farmers well into the early 1900s. A number of large wolf hunts took place

484 Al Westerman, Public Domain Land Sales in Lake County, Illinois: [Copyright 2006, by Al Westerman, Zion, Illinois] p. 8 & 9.

485 The Waukegan Gazette Newspaper, [Waukegan, Illinois] [Blue Boat Club] October 25, 1868.

486 The Waukegan Gazette, [Nippersink Club] October 31, 1868.

487 The Waukegan Gazette, October 22, 1870.

488 The Waukegan Daily Sun, [Waukegan, Illinois] [The Oldest Surviving Settler of Lake County.] September 15, 1905.

489 The Waukegan Gazette, [A Desperate Fight With a Panther.] February 12, 1898.

490 The Waukegan Daily Sun, [Only man who defies Zion's law.] January 4, 1906.

in the 1870s, all unsuccessful. Individual hunters killed most of the wolves. Do not feel too sorry for the wolves. The farmers of Somers, Wisconsin, lost about three hundred sheep to wolves during the summer and fall of 1872.[491] The December 20, 1909, *Waukegan Daily Sun* contains a very enlightening story about wolves in Indiana.

> Simon Helms, farmer, near Elkinsville, fourteen miles south of here, battled for almost an hour with a pack of wolves, which killed several sheep, raided a chicken coop and drove Helms family into the house after they had been severely injured by the enraged animals, which were finally driven off.
>
> Last winter a pack of wolves gave the southern part of the county a great deal of trouble. It became necessary for farmers to accompany their children to and from school.[492]

The Indians were required to move west when President Andrew Jackson signed the Treaty of Chicago on February 23, 1835. A few trappers and settlers were already living in Lake County by this time. The first settler was Captain Daniel Wright, who came out by himself on horseback from Ohio in May 1834. He built himself a log cabin on the west bank of the Des Plains River in Vernon Township and sent for his family. They arrived in late summer. The trip west was bad for their health and most were sick. His youngest son died on September 7, and three days later, his wife died. Captain Wright was supposed to have been on good terms with the Indians whose village was two miles away. He had a strange sense of humor though. Once for a joke he traded the Indians a barrel of rancid pork for fish and wild game. He claimed he would not feed it to his own family but figured the Indians would eat it. He was right and they apparently liked it too.

By August 1836, settlers had already built one hundred cabins throughout the county. They were all officially squatters. Much of Illinois was settled by squatters, however. Surveying began in Lake County in September 1837 and completed August 1840. The squatters were unsure of ownership until the land office put the county lands up for sale from September 10, 1840, to June 14, 1842.[493] One of these squatters was twenty-six-year-old Hanson Minskey, who arrived to the county June 20, 1835.[494]

---

[491] The Waukegan Gazette, [Wolves] January 25, 1873.

[492] The Waukegan Daily Sun, [Wolves and Farmer Fight] December 20, 1909.

[493] Al Westerman, p. 11.

[494] Al Westerman, [Personal Collection, Hanson Minskey] [Zion, Illinois]

Hanson Minskey

Hanson was one of the first settlers in Benton Township.[495] Benton Township is located in the far northeast corner of the county. Being a squatter, Hanson joined the claims commission in 1836 to defend his claim. Land claims in Benton Township did not go on sale until June 14, 1842. By November 1842, Hanson had bought 180 acres of mostly wooded land from the General Land Office. Hanson's brother Robert soon joined him in Benton Township and was here by 1837.[496] Their father Samuel was a "Polish refugee."[497] It looks like their last name was originally Dominski. The 1860 Federal Census for Lake County lists Robert's last name as Dominski.[498]

Benton Township was covered by woods. There were no lakes, except for the shores of Lake Michigan. The northwest corner of the Township did contain north prairie, a very fertile prairie with a radius of eight miles. Elijah Haines claimed north prairie was the finest prairie in the county. Hanson and Robert both lived in the forested area near the shores of Lake Michigan. For years, the township contained only one very small village named Benton. Steven L. Ragno wrote that in 1850, "The town of Benton is a district of the county not very prolific in historical events. It is strictly a rural town. It has no village in it, nor collection of houses that could be called such; nor has it a store, tavern, grocery, or public building of any kind within its limits save its churches and schools."[499] Elijah Haines called the town of Benton "the Garden of the county."[500] Most of the settlers in the township were from the northern states.

---

495 Hon. Charles A. Partridge. Historical Encyclopedia of Illinois and History of Lake County: [Chicago: Munsell Publishing Company 1902] p. 628. [Reproduction by Unigraphic, Inc. 1975]

496 Al Westerman, [Personal Collection, Robert Minskey]

497 John J. Halsey, A History of Lake County, Illinois: [Chicago: Harmegnies & Howell Copyright 1912, by Roy S. Bates] p. 820. [Reprinted by Higginson Book Company, Salem, Massachusetts]

498 Lake County Genealogical Society, 1860 Federal Census of Lake County, Illinois: [Mundelein, Illinois: Copy Systems 1984] p. 7.

499 Stephen L. Ragno, The Village of Winthop Harbor and Environs: [Part Two Early History 1835-1900] p. 61

500 Elijah M. Haines, Historical and Statistical Sketches, of Lake County, State of Illinois: [Waukegan, Illinois: E. G. Howe, 1952] p. 77.

Hanson was born on October 28, 1809, in Baltimore, Maryland. I already mentioned that Hanson's father Samuel was a Polish refugee. His mother's maiden name was Ann Merriken. They were the parents of four sons, Hanson, John, Samuel, and Robert and one daughter Harriet "Hattie."[501] Hanson was in the U.S. Navy before coming to Lake County. Evidently, someone back east convinced him to settle in the soon-to-be-opened-for-settlement northern Illinois.[502] Maybe Hanson realized that he could claim a farm on virgin land and sail on Lake Michigan as well. New settlers would create demand for products and he would haul them on the lake. Hanson's census records usually list his occupation as farmer, ship captain, or farmer/ship captain. On March 23, 1838, Hanson married Charlotte E. Porter. Charlotte had immigrated to Lake County with her parents on March 1, 1836. Their marriage produced six children, Annette, Jeremiah, Harriet, Samuel, Charlotte, and Nellie.[503]

Hanson was captain of the ship *James Mc Kay*. Built in Waukegan, the ship was named after one of the leading citizens of Waukegan and Lake County. Mc Kay was also part owner of the ship. Hanson hauled mainly lumber from Milwaukee to Waukegan. He also made runs to Chicago and even Buffalo, New York, to haul back provisions for the settlers. Buffalo, New York, ended up being the end of the line for the *James Mc Kay*. The ship was in Buffalo's harbor when another ship crashed into it. The *James Mc Kay* sunk to the bottom of the sea[504] after only a few years of service. Hanson went into business for himself in 1870. He bought a ship named the *Gazelle* in Manitowac, Wisconsin, and stuck to hauling lumber from Wisconsin to Waukegan. The *Gazelle* "carried one-hundred thousand feet of lumber" at a time.[505]

The *Waukegan Daily Gazette* recorded a number of Hanson's exploits over the years. The April 25, 1874, *Gazette* wrote that one of the captain's sailors fell overboard during a snowstorm near Two Rivers, Michigan. The storm prevented the ship from turning around and, in spite of throwing everything they could find to him, lost sight of the sailor in the falling snow. They never saw him again.[506] Another drowning almost took place two years later. Hanson let the young son of Martin Abbott go on a voyage to Michigan. Told to sleep

---

501 Al Westerman, [Personal Collection, Hanson Minskey]

502 Stephen L. Ragno, The Village of Winthop Harbor and Environs: [Part Two Early History 1835-1900] [p. 51]

503 Al Westerman, [Personal Collection, Hanson Minskey]

504 Ho. Charles A. Partridge, p. 641.

505 The Waukegan Gazette, May 28, 1870.

506 The Waukegan Gazette, April 25, 1874.

below deck, the boy did not listen and chose to sleep on deck with the crew. While asleep, the boy fell overboard. Luckily, the crew heard his screams and managed to save him. I'll bet he slept below deck after that.[507] In the spring of 1874, the *Gazelle* made four voyages to Muskegon, Michigan, and back to Waukegan in twelve days.[508] On June 20, 1874, Captain Minskey hurt his shoulder so bad he had to put F. M. Porter in charge.[509] On October 3, 1874, a bad storm blew in while the *Gazelle* was unloading a cargo of lumber in Waukegan. The captain had to scuttle the ship. Scuttling is opening the hatchways on a ship's deck or hulls and sinking the ship on purpose to prevent it from blowing to shore and getting stuck or damaged.[510] The mishap cost him four hundred dollars. Captain Minskey must have been relieved when the year 1874 ended. The weather was bad all summer and the cost of hauling cargo meager. He secured his ship on the Chicago River around December 1 and called it quits for the year. It also looks like Hanson was in the process of turning the *Gazelle* over to his son Jeremiah in 1874. I found a mention of Captain Judd Minskey tying up the *Gazelle* and going home for the winter in the December 5, 1874, *Waukegan Gazette*.[511]

Captain Minskey's bad luck carried over into 1875. The May 1, 1875, *Waukegan Gazette* notes that Captain Minskey left on his first voyage of the year knowing his family was in good health. His young son Johnny died while he was gone. Hanson only learned of his son's death after docking in Chicago on the return trip.[512] On October 2, 1875, the *Waukegan Gazette* reported that the *Gazelle* "was wrecked on the beach in front of this city during the terrible gale of three weeks ago." Hanson dismantled all the masts and rigging from the *Gazelle* to use on a new ship,[513] the *Eclipse*. The *Eclipse* was a much larger ship and could carry sixty more tons of cargo than the *Gazelle*. The *Waukegan Gazette* recorded that the *Eclipse*'s first voyage to Waukegan's harbor occurred on October 23, 1875.[514] Hanson retired in 1878. He sold most of his farm and moved to Waukegan where he lived for the next two years. Al Westerman claims that Captain Minskey defaulted on the rest of his farmland in 1879. The captain moved to Wharton County, Texas, in

507 The Waukegan Gezette, [Narrow Escape] June 30, 1876.

508 The Waukegan Gazette, May 30, 1874.

509 The Waukegan Gazette, June 20, 1874.

510 The Waukegan Gazette, October 3, 1874.

511 The Waukegan Gazette, December 5, 1874.

512 The Waukegan Gazette, May 1, 1875.

513 The Waukegan Gazette, October 2, 1875.

514 The Waukegan Gazette, October 23, 1875.

1880. He left his family behind in Waukegan until he could get established in Texas.[515] According to the *Waukegan Gazette*, "The Captain was an honest, industrious man. For many years he sailed upon the lakes, and he was always so conscientious that he never allowed his vessel to be loaded or unloaded on the Sabbath and rarely sailed upon that day. Leaving the lakes he attempted farming but was not successful here, and, going South where land is cheap to make a new start, he survived but a few months."[516]

Captain Minskey's life had a tragic ending. He had sent for his family in the spring of 1881. His sons stayed in Lake County, however. By the fall of the same year, both he and his wife were sick. Hanson's wife Charlotte soon died of paralysis of the brain on September 19. The distraught Hanson died two days later. Adding to the grief, Hanson's sister Hattie died two days later on September 23. The trip to Texas was too much for Hattie and she had been sick ever since. Three of the Minskeys dead in one week.[517]

Both Hanson's sons became ship's captains. I mentioned earlier that it looked like Hanson was preparing Jeremiah to become the captain of the *Gazelle*. The January 8, 1881, *Waukegan Gazette* claims that right after Jeremiah recovered from a bout of diphtheria, he pulled his arm out of joint at the shoulder while getting off the train.[518] The year 1881 was not Jeremiah's best year. According to the August 13, 1881, *Gazette*, "Capt. J. P. Minsky, of this city, is again fairly convalescent after a long and serious illness from typhoid fever. The Captain has had his full share of sickness during the last year, and we trust that his recovery at this time may be full and complete."[519] Jeremiah had a couple bad months in 1882. In April, his ship was stuck in ten inches of ice at the port of Garden Bay.[520] In May, he caught his foot in a coil of rope on the ship's deck. The rope yanked Jeremiah high in the air before he fell off and suffered three broken ribs, a dislocated shoulder, and some bad bruises. It did not stop Jeremiah from working, and he went out on the next voyage even though "badly crippled."[521] Jeremiah was captain of the ship *Barbarian* in 1885 when the ship was caught in a bad storm at sea. Luckily, he managed to sail into the port at Northport, Michigan, and wait out the storm. Jeremiah had not seen his family in three months and, after

---

515 Al Westerman, [Personal Collection, Hanson Minskey]

516 The Waukegan Gazette, [Death of the Minski Family] October 15, 1881.

517 The Waukegan Gazette, [Death of the Minski Family] October 15, 1881.

518 The Waukegan Gazette, January 8, 1881.

519 The Waukegan Gazette, August 13, 1881.

520 The Waukegan Gazette, April 29, 1882.

521 The Waukegan Gazette, May 6, 1882.

the storm was over, went home as soon as possible.[522] In 1898, Jeremiah was captain of one of the largest cargo ships owned by the Gilcrist Company.[523] The last mention of Jeremiah in 1908 wrote, "The Captain of the Steamer City of Genoa having been summoned home because of the death of a child, the owners of the boat telegraphed Captain Minskey of Waukegan to take charge of the steamer and he is in command back to Buffalo. He is one of the oldest lake captains and one of the most capable."[524]

Hanson's son Samuel has fewer mentions in the *Gazette*, but what I have found about him is usually major news. Samuel was Jeremiah's younger brother and there was a twelve-year difference in their ages. His first mention in the *Gazette* was in 1881 when he spent a month in the hospital in Chicago because of fever.[525] The whole Samuel Minskey family almost went down with the ship in 1902.

> Monday Willard Wilder received a three-line note from his brother-in-law Samuel Minskey, to the effect that while his boat lies in the bottom of the Gulf of Mexico, the captain and his wife and son are safe. The letter contained no details further than to state that all persons on the boat were saved by a "heir's breadth" and that the boat and all of its contents went down. Capt. Sam Minskey and family are well known in Waukegan where they have resided for many years. Mrs. Minskey and son had joined the Captain but a few days before the accident in which they nearly lost their lives.[526]

Sam was in another bad accident at the Western Coal and Dock Company in 1910. A *Gazette* article titled, "Saved Eyes from Steam" tells the story.

Explosion at Western Coal and Dock Company a Serious one.

> The condition of Captain Samuel N. Minskey is reported as better today. He suffered greatly from the severe burns on his face and hands yesterday but is more comfortable today. He was burned

[522] The Waukegan Gazette, December 12, 1885.
[523] The Waukegan Daily Sun, April 2, 1898.
[524] The Waukegan Daily Sun, August 18, 1908.
[525] The Waukegan Gazette, [Personalities] September 3, 1881.
[526] The Waukegan Daily Sun, December 26, 1902.

by escaping steam when a valve blew out on Dock No. 2 at the Western Coal and Dock Company's plant early Saturday morning. He was the engineer at the plant and had repeatedly spoken about the danger from the valve which exploded, it is claimed. The valve had been patched up several times.

The force of the explosion was so great that the windows in the boiler-room were blown out. Captain Minskey, who is a well known lake captain, was knocked down and saved himself by crawling on his hands and knees to a place of safety. He saved his eyes by closing them at the start when the steam burst forth. The burns have proved to be much more serious than at first thought and it is believed that he will be confined to his bed at the hospital for three of four weeks. His face is swollen so badly that he can scarcely see.[527]

Robert Minskey

There is not a whole lot of information about Robert. I owe Al Westerman for most of what little I know about Robert. He was the younger brother of Hanson and born in 1812 in Baltimore, Maryland. Robert was in Lake County by 1837 and seems to be either buying or selling land until he left the county in 1877. He married Sarah Anderson on April 29, 1846.[528] Their marriage produced two children, George, born around 1847, and daughter Amorett, born around 1858. The census records always list Robert's occupation as farmer. His son George was a sailor; maybe he worked for his uncle Hanson.[529] Robert and Sarah sold their farm on March 21, 1877, and moved to Chicago. Sarah died in Chicago on August 15, 1888, and Robert died soon after on September 9, 1888.[530] George also became a ship's captain, but I have found only one mention of him in the *Gazette*. George also lived in Waukegan.[531] The Minskeys were a very well-known and influential family in Lake County for about one hundred years.

---

527 The Waukegan Daily Sun, [Saved Eyes from Steam] January 17, 1910.

528 Al Westerman, [Personal Collection, Robert Minskey]

529 Lake County Genealogical Society, 1870 Federal Census of the Town of Benton: [Mundelein, Illinois: Copy Systems 1985] p. 2.

530 Al Westerman, [Personal Collection, Robert Minskey]

531 The Waukegan News Sun, [Waukegan, Illinois] July 16, 1920.

Stanislaus Lisiecki

The earliest record I have of Stanislaus is the 1840 Federal Census of Lake County. I believe Stanislaus was there at least two years sooner and will explain my case later. He settled near the small village of Little Fort, now named Waukegan. Stanislaus is probably one of the 234 Polish exiles from Trieste. His name is not on any of the passenger lists of the 234 Polish exiles from Trieste, but he claimed to be one. The numbers 207 and 208 in Lerski's list of Polish exiles are blank, so it is possible his name was not recorded.[532] Stanislaus signed his name on a letter sent by six Polish exiles to the General Land Office on December 22, 1836, and claims to be one of the 234 Polish exiles from Trieste. Two of the other signers also settled in Lake County, Theodor Domski and Alexander Bilinski. Maria J. E. Copson-Niecko published their letter to the General Land Office.

> We the Undersigned Polish Exiles, having come to America on two Austrian Frigates under Admiral Bandiera, and landed at New York City on the 30th day of March 1834; Having been informed, that, the Hon the Congress of the United States, by an act passed on the 30th day of June 1834, did grant unto us certain lands in the state of Illinois, to be possessed by us on certain conditions. But in consequence of the said land being unmeasured, and of our impoverished [sic] circumstances at the time of the passage of said Act, we were unable to possess said land or to furnish ourselves with the necessary implements and utensils required in Agriculture, and therefore could not occupy the lands, so kindly proterred to us by Congress, and were under the necessity of enlisting in the service of the United States, in a Company of Ordnance at Watervliet Arsenal, for the period of three years—The term of our enlistments has now nearly expired, and having carefully saved our earnings for services rendered to the United States, feel in a measure prepared to furnish Ourselves with implements to possess the aforesaid land-And therefore most respectfully solicit information, whether the Aforesaid Act is such as to allow us the said lands; . . .[533]

---

532 Jerzy Jan Lerski, A Polish Chapter in Jacksonian America: [Madison: The University of Wisconsin Press 1958] p. 177.

533 N.A., RG, Bureau of Land Management, Special Acts, Box 38, Polish Exiles. J. Worth to Commissioner of the General Land Office, Watervliet Arsenal,

Stanislaus enlisted in the U.S. Army on January 9, 1835, nine months after he arrived in America. He was thirty-one years old and signed up for three years. His enlistment papers name Sochaizew, Poland, as place of birth. Stanislaus claimed to be a carpenter in Poland.[534] He had blue eyes, light hair, and was 5'8" tall. Stanislaus spent most of his time in the army in Ordnance at Watervliet Arsenal. Watervliet is located near Troy, New York.[535] Ordnance stores and handles weapons and ammunition. In 1837, Stanislaus was temporarily assigned to Ordnance at Gareys Ferry in Florida during the Seminole War. The army discharged Stanislaus on January 9, 1838.[536]

The first record of Stanislaus in the county is the 1840 Federal Census of Lake County, Illinois. Stanislaus is the head of household. His age is from thirty to forty years old and his occupation is trades. Wife Maria is from thirty to forty years old. There is one son under five years old.[537]

On the 1850 census, Stanislaus is a forty-six-year-old carpenter, born in Poland. His wife Maria is forty-one years old and born in New York. Son Philip is eleven years old and born in Illinois. Also living with the family was Margaret Bradbury, an eighteen-year-old woman born in New York, and Stefan Gasiorowski, a sixty-two-year-old farmer born in Poland. Stefan was one of the 234 Polish exiles. I have a little more information about Stefan and will write more about him later. It looks like Margaret Bradbury's three brothers and two sisters were living next door in Sophia Rochead's home.[538] Philip's age means that the Lisieckis were here before 1840. I believe Stanislaus came to Lake County with Teodor Dombski, although I cannot prove it. Teodor Dombski was also stationed in Ordnance at Watervliet. He immigrated to Lake County in July 1838.[539]

December 23, 1836. [In The Poles in America from the 1830's to 1870's by Maria J. E. Copson-Niecko: [Also in Poles in America Bicentenial Essays: by Frank Mocha, Stevens Point, Wisconsin 1978] p. 181

534 National Archives, M233, Roll 19, Volume 40, p. 113.

535 National Archives, [M233, Roll 19, Page 113]

536 Maria J. E. Copson-Niecko, The Poles in America from the 1830's to 1870's: [In Poles in America Bicentenial Essays by Frank Mocha, Stevens Point, Wisconsin 1978] p. 279.

537 1840 Federal Census of Lake County, Illinois: [National Archives, Box 704, Roll 62, Page 95]

538 D. F. Thompson, 1850 Federal Census of Lake County, Illinois: [1976] p. 245.

539 Reflections of Hainesville Past and Present: [Published by the Village of Hainesville, Bi-centennial Commission 1976] p. LXX.

According to Al Westerman, Stanislaus bought eighty wooded acres in Little Fort (now Waukegan) from the General Land Office on October 19, 1841. He bought eighty more wooded acres on June 14, 1842. On May 27, 1846, Stanislaus sold eighty acres to his neighbor Sophia Rochead. Margaret Bradbury's brothers and sisters were living with Sophia on the 1850 census.[540]

Little Fort got its name from a small French fort and trading post located on the bluffs overlooking Lake Michigan. There is disagreement over when the fort was built. Once source claims 1695, while another states 1721-1725. It was deserted long before the first pioneers came in 1835, the only remains being a rotting wood foundation. The town of Little Fort was built on the bluffs overlooking Lake Michigan. The bluffs are from 45' to 62' high and located about a mile from Lake Michigan. The area between the bluffs and Lake Michigan is called the flats. Little Fort was heavily wooded and contained many ravines. The ravines all needed bridges, which cost Little Fort a bundle over the years. Waukegan's favorite son is the late comedian Jack Benny whose real name was Benny Kubelsky.

Before the arrival of the first settlers, at least four white trappers lived in Little Fort. The date of their arrival is a mystery but folklore says 1833. The first settlers to the region knew them. One of the trappers known as English John seems to have been a real character. Thomas Jenkins was a boy when his parents settled in Little Fort in 1835. He and his friends used to visit English John, and Thomas claimed that English John used to live in a hole he had dug out of the side of a bluff. His choice of food was on par with his choice of lodging. With all the wild game available, English John preferred to eat snake meat, the snake's heart in particular.

Thomas Jenkins father opened the first store in Little Fort in 1835. Only four or five families were living there at the time. The associate editor of the *Waukegan Gazette* claimed that when he first came to Little Fort in 1837, there were only three cabins. Possibly a net loss in population but he also wrote that most people lived in tents on the shore of Lake Michigan and engaged in fishing. Waukegan has always had the best fishing in Lake Michigan. Little Fort became the county seat on April 5, 1841. The population had grown to fifty people by then. Little Fort really started its growth in 1844 when D. O. Dickinson built the first pier. By the end of 1844, 151 ships had docked in the Little Fort Harbor bringing almost 1 million feet of lumber and 250 tons of miscellaneous merchandise. The same ships left Little Fort with 66,000 bushels of wheat, 200 bushels of oats, 200 pounds of furs, 8,000 pounds of

---

540 Al Westerman, [Personal Collection, Stanislaus Lisiecki]

hides and 15 barrels of pork. Hundreds of wagons hauling wheat, etc., were soon making the trip to Waukegan every fall.

By 1845, the population had grown to 450, and 62 buildings were built. A year later, there were 180 houses in town and the population stood at 759. Little Fort continued growing steadily, and its present population is 87,901. Now it's known by the name of Waukegan, however, having changed the town's name on March 31, 1849.

The following event would have occurred at the time Stanislaus lived in Little Fort. The winter of 1842 was a particularly bad one. It was intensely cold and deep snow covered the ground for almost five months. The farmers all ran out of hay and large numbers of their livestock died. At the same time, a man named Miller appeared in Little Fort claiming to be a prophet and predicting that the world would end in March 1843. An egg with the words "Time ends in 1843" written on it was found at Chauncey King's farm. The whole town was in an uproar, so the residents called for a meeting. One settler realized the whole thing was a fraud and wrote "Repent and Be Baptized" on a different egg. Everyone calmed down and Little Fort went back to normal.

Maria Lisiecki died of liver disease January 2, 1860.[541] Stanislaus died three years later in Minnesota.[542] Why he was in Minnesota is a mystery but I have another one of my theories. His son Philip inherited the farm but sold it two years later and moved to Menominee, Michigan. Maybe Waukegan had become too big for the Lisieckis and they longed for the wilderness. Minnesota would not have had a very large population in 1863 and Menominee is located in the Upper Peninsula of Michigan where the winters are long and the snow deep. The October 25, 1885, *Waukegan Gazette* mentioned that Philip Lisiecki and his two sons stopped in Waukegan and were thinking of moving back.[543] Philip's son Will got married in Waukegan on February 20, 1886.[544]

Stefan Gasiorowski

I have only been able to find out a small amount of information about Stefan. He was a lieutenant in the Polish Army in the 1830 uprising and was

[541] Lake County Genealogical Society, 1860 Census and Mortality Schedule of Lake County, Illinois: [Mundelein, Illinois: Copy Systems 1984] p. 213.

[542] Al Westerman, [Personal Collection, Stanislaus Lisiecki]

[543] The Waukegan Gazette, October 25, 1885.

[544] The Waukegan Gazette, [Married] February 20, 1886.

one of the 234 Polish exiles from Trieste.[545] Stefan enlisted in the U.S. Army for three years on June 30, 1834, only three months after his arrival to New York. His enlistment papers show his age is thirty-four and he was a farmer in Poland. He was a private of artillery in the U.S. Army and discharged at Fort Harlee, Florida, on June 30, 1837.[546]

Stefan showed up in Waukegan sometime in the 1840s and went to work on Stanislaus Lisiecki's farm. Stefan claimed to be sixty-two years old on the 1850 Federal Census for Lake County.[547] He claimed to be thirty-four years old sixteen years earlier on his enlistment papers. I think the census is wrong because it looks like Stefan reenlisted in the army sometime in the 1850s. He was a private at Fort Simpson when he either died or deserted on June 21, 1857.[548] It is hard to make out what happened to him.

If Stefan's age actually was sixty-two in 1850, he would have been one of the oldest Polish exiles from Trieste. My ancestor Franciszek was also one of the older exiles being fifty-six years old in 1850. On Haiman's list of Polish exiles, their names are right next to each other.[549] Franciszek and Stefan might well have known each other good since people usually hang out with other people of similar age.

Theodore Dombski

Theodore was a second lieutenant in the 1830 Polish uprising and might have been a member of the same army as my ancestor Franciszek.[550] Theodore was born around 1804 near the city of Zytomierz, in the province of Kiev.[551] On the map, Zytomierz seems to be around seventy to eighty miles straight west of the present city of Kiev. Two different groups rebelled in Kiev province, and I am not sure which one Theodore belonged in. The first group was a small band of 130 men under the command of K. Rozycki. They fought their way west through Russian lines and united with the Polish Army commanded by General Dwernicki. Count Henry Krasinski wrote, "Charles Rozycki, a military officer inhabiting the Ukraine, succeeded in forming and organizing a regiment

545 Mieczyslaw Haiman, Slady Polskie W Ameryce: [Chicago, Illinois: Druiem Dziennika Zjednoczenia 1938] p. 123.

546 National Archives, M233, Roll 19, Volume 40, p. 76.

547 D. F. Thompson, 1850 Federal Census of Lake County, Illinois: p. 245.

548 National Archives, [Box 233, Roll 19, Page 76]

549 Mieczyslaw Haiman, p. 123.

550 Mieczyslaw Haiman, p. 120.

551 National Archives, M233, Roll 19, Volume 40, p.56.

of light cavalry, armed in the Cossack fashion, and with such wild enthusiasm did he inspire his followers, that when he was surrounded by the Russian Army on every side, he overthrew everything that opposed him, gained every battle that he fought, and after incredible difficulties and twenty-five days' march, joined the Polish Army at Zamosc."[552] Dwernicki's army fought the Russians at the battle of Boromel on April 18, 1831. The battle so weakened the Polish Army that they had to withdraw west, the Russians in pursuit. Dwernicki's army crossed the Austrian border on April 27, 1831. The Austrians forced the Poles to lay down their arms and arrested Dwernicki. They let the rest of his army leave Austria, and most went back to the Polish Congress Kingdom.[553]

The other group of soldiers from Kiev province was members of General Benedykt Kolyszko's army. My ancestor was also in Kolyszko's army. This army was composed of two thousand men from the provinces of Kiev and lower Podolia. The men from Kiev united with the soldiers from lower Podolia on May 13, 1831, at the small town of Krasnosiolka. The next day the Poles set out for Byelaya Tserkov. On the way there, they were attacked by a Russian Army near the town of Dashov. Despite poor organization and green troops, the Poles should have won the battle but managed to snatch defeat from victory. After Dashov, most of the army dissolved except for about four or five hundred men. This group headed west and fought three more battles in nine days before crossing the Austrian border on May 23 to avoid a large Russian Army.[554] The Austrians imprisoned most of the officers and let the enlisted men "not officers" go. The highest-ranking officers either escaped or were sent to the city of Lviv. The lower-ranking officers were imprisoned in a castle at Chortkow, Ukraine.[555]

Theodore arrived in New York on March 28, 1834, one of the 234 Polish exiles from Trieste. Six weeks later, on May 12, Theodor enlisted in the U.S. Army for three years. He was twenty-six years old and assigned to Ordnance at the Watervliet Arsenal in Troy, New York.[556] Ordnance is military weapons.

552 Henry Krasinski, The Poles in the Seventeenth Century: [London: T.C. Newly 1843]

553 R. F. Leslie, Polish Politics and the Revolution of November 1830: [Westport, Connecticut: Greenwood Press, Publishers 1969] [Reprinted by permission of the Athlone Press] p. 199.

554 R. F. Leslie, p. 201 & 202

555 Jozef Bialynia Cholodecki, General Kolyazko and his subordinates in the area of Galicia: [Lwow: Printed by Polonia 1912] [At the Library of the Jagiellonian University in Krakow] p. 1.

556 National Archives, M233, Roll 19, Volume 40, p. 56.

Theodor's enlistment papers show that he was 5' 6" tall, light brown hair, and blue eyes. The army discharged him when his three-year enlistment was up on May 12, 1837.[557]

Theodore moved west to Lake County, Illinois, in July 1838, settling in Avon Township.[558] I mentioned earlier that I think he came out here with Stanislaus Lisiecki. He was thirty-two years old and accompanied by his eighteen-year-old Irish-born wife Sarah.[559] Their marriage produced five children. Amelia, born in 1840. Henry, born in January 23, 1842. Ann, born in 1843. Theodora, born in 1848. And Emma, born in March 9, 1851.[560] They also adopted a daughter, Mary Ann, born in 1838. Theodore was a farmer in Illinois. He bought 160 acres of land on July 2, 1841, and added 80 more acres on June 10, 1842.[561] The present Illinois Route 120 runs next to the site of the old Dombski farm. The farm was sold long ago and most of what's left is now housing subdivisions.[562] It looks like Theodore was a good farmer. He had a small mention in the April 28, 1922, *County Gentleman* magazine. "In 1847 a Pole by the name of Domski invented a crooked handle cradle from which the grain would slip off easily without the aid of the operator."[563] Theodor's farm was always ahead of the other Lake Country Polish exiles' farms. He owned five horses in 1850 when all the others just owned oxen.[564] All of Theodor's land was improved (tillable) by 1860.[565]

Theodore settled in the north-central part of Lake County in the small village of Hainesville, ten miles west of Lake Michigan. For most of its existence, the village was very small, but the population has grown a lot recently and its present population is 2129. Hainesville was the first village incorporated in Lake County in the years 1846-1847. It was named after the Honerable Elijah Haines, who settled on the future site of Hainesville

557 National Archives, [Box 233, Roll 19, Page 56]

558 Reflections of Hainesville Past and Present: [Published by the village of Hainesville, Bi-centennial Commission 1976] p. LXX.

559 D. F. Thompson, 1850 Federal Census of Lake County, Illinois p. 336.

560 Charlotte K. Renehan, Absent but ever Present: p. 68.

561 Charlotte K. Renehan, p. 68.

562 Charlotte K. Renehan, p. 68.

563 S. F. Vose, In the course of a Lifetime: [printed in the County Gentleman on April 28, 1922, located at the Warren Township Historical Society]

564 1850 Agriculture Census of Lake County, Illinois: [Illinois State Archives, Roll No. 31-2]

565 1860 Agriculture Census of Lake County, Illinois: [Illinois State Archives, T1133]

with his stepfather and mother in May 1836. Elijah's stepfather soon died, and Elijah became the man of the family. He ran the farm during the day and self-educated himself at night. Elijah became schoolmaster of Little Fort School the winter of 1841-1842. He was soon the county school commissioner as well as justice of the peace. Elijah also taught himself surveying and platted the village of Hainesville in 1846 as well as other parts of Lake County. He also established two newspapers, the *Patriot*, a weekly paper, and the *Legal Adviser*, a legal newspaper. Elijah wrote three books, *The American Indian*, *The Red Man*, and *Historical and Statistical Sketchs of Lake County*. The county histories refer to him as the "Honorable Elijah Haines" because of his great service to Lake County. Elijah died April 25, 1889. Theodor would definitely have known him.

After its incorporation, Hainesville became the chief town in the central part of the county. The plank road from Waukegan to Mc Henry County ran right through Hainesville. Construction of the plank road began in Waukegan in 1848 and made it out to Hainesville by 1850. It is now Illinois Route 120. The road had three tollgates, one in Hainesville. Theodor's name is on a list of Hainesville landowners who donated land for the roads' right of way.[566] The plank road brought in commerce, and soon Hainesville had a blacksmith shop, post office, two hotels, and various other enterprises. Unfortunately, Hainesville's prosperity did not last long. In 1886, the Wisconsin Central Railroad bypassed Hainesville for nearby Grayslake. Hainesville diminished in importance and soon became a very small village, which is how I remember it.

An unfortunate and rare for the times, event occurred to the Dombski family on June 25, 1864. Theodor and Sarah divorced.[567] The 1865 state census shows that they were living next door to each other, the children all living with Sarah.[568] On the 1880 Federal census, Theodore, his son Henry, and Sarah all lived next door to each other.[569] Theodore died October 18, 1884, and Sarah died on May 31, 1891. They are both buried in the Grayslake Cemetery.[570] I found a small article written by Marion Parker, one of Teodore's descendants at the Grayslake Historical Society. She claims Theodore was

566 Ruth Drummomd Mogg, Glimpses of the old Grayslake Area: [1976] p. 47.

567 The Waukegan Gazette, June 25, 1864.

568 Lake County Genealogical Society, 1865 Illinois State Census, [Mundelein, Illinois: Copy Systems 1989] p. 39.

569 Lake County Genealogical Society,1880 Federal Census of Lake County, Illinois: [Mundelein, Illinois: Copy Systems 1987] Avon Township: p. 48.

570 Charlotte K. Renehan, p. 68.

nobility and I have to agree with her. The officers in the Polish Army were always nobility.[571] I also found his name in a book called *Les confiscations des Polonais Sovs le Regne de Empereur Nicholas Ier L. Lubliner.* Theodor's name is mentioned in the section about the province of Kiev. The book contains an "alphabetical chart by name of Poles whose possessions and properties were confiscated but are not included in the official public documents either by the number of serfs or by sums of money."[572] The Theodor Dombski estate was valued at twelve serfs. A serf in Russia was valued at 175 silver rubles, so Theodor's estate was valued at 2,100 silver rubles.[573] Our estate in Podolia was valued at seven serfs.

The Dombskis adopted their oldest daughter Mary Ann. Her obituary on May 11, 1918, wrote her name as Mary A. Barton Dombski and claims she was the only daughter of John and Sarah Barton. She married a Civil War veteran from Vermont named Fayett Thompson on November 28, 1867. Thompson was one of the first dentists in Little Fort. Fayett Thompson died in 1899. Mary Ann ran her own millinery and dressmaking shop in Waukegan for twenty-five years, and the *Waukegan News Sun* called her "one of the business pioneers of this city."[574] A millinery makes women's hats. She belonged to the Congregational Church of Waukegan and was a charter member of the Order of the Eastern Star and the Rebekah Lodge. Mary Ann was one of the founders of the Rebekah Lodge, donating all the money needed to start up the lodge.[575] The June 4, 1918, *Waukegan News Sun* called Mary Ann "an eccentric old lady, although approaching her final end denied herself the necessities of life because she didn't want to spend the money."[576] The *News Sun* also claimed, "Because of her eccentricities and general peculiarities and penury was 'hard to get along with.'"[577] She did have a good friend from the Rebekah Lodge named Jenny Polmateer, who looked after her for most of the winter of 1918 until her death on May 11. Mary

571 A visit with Marion Parker, Belvidere Road, Grayslake: [At the Grayslake Historical Society, Grayslake, Illinois] p. 5.

572 Les Confications des biens des Polonais Sovs le Regne de L' Empereur Nickolas Ier L, Lubliner [Brussels-Leipzig 1861] p. 35.

573 R.F. Leslie, p. 267.

574 The Waukegan Daily Sun, [Mary A. Thompson Obituary] May 11, 1918.

575 The Waukegan Daily Sun, [Mary A. Thompson Obituary] May 11, 1918.

576 The Waukegan Daily Sun, [Solicitude for sick woman is rewarded by gift] June 4, 1918.

577 The Waukegan Daily Sun, [Solicitude for sick woman is rewarded by gift] June 4, 1918.

Ann was so grateful for Jenny's help that she willed her a two-flat building on Utica Street worth a considerable amount of money. Mary Ann willed her brother Henry the lion's share of her estate but the *News Sun* mentioned that "this is the first time in some years in Waukegan where an outsider has received such a big bequest from a Waukegan resident."[578]

Amelia Dombski married Frank Root on August 29, 1859.[579] She had a number of tragic events in her life. Her son Willie died when he was only twenty-six days old on September 10, 1863. Another son, Frank Jr., died on February 22, 1878. He was seventeen years old. A daughter Annie only lived fourteen years, dying August 25, 1878.[580] Her husband Frank was an engineer for the Pittsburg and Fort Wayne Railroad. On August 20, 1864, he was uncoupling train cars and managed to get his foot caught in the frog of a track. The train's cars ran over Frank and killed him.[581] They had only been married five years. It looks like one daughter named Sarah, born in 1864, did survive. She was living at Grandma Dombski's house in 1870.[582] Amelia Dombski Root died on June 13, 1891.[583]

Annie Dombski was a well-known and admired schoolteacher. She married W. N. Smith, of Clinton, Iowa, in 1880. Teaching turned out to be bad for her health, and she switched occupations and became a milliner. On September 26, 1882, she gave birth to stillborn twins. She died two days later on September 28. They buried Annie and her twins in the same coffin.[584] Annie's sister Theodora (Dora) Dombski died of consumption (tuberculosis) on February 18, 1867. She was nineteen years old.[585] Emma, the youngest daughter, never married. She was a noted milliner in Lake County. I have seen her advertisements in the old Waukegan newspapers a number of times. She died July 15, 1919, in Grayslake.[586]

Theodore's son Henry had an interesting life. Henry was a farmer all his life and a patriot like his father, super patriot would be a better description.

---

578 The Waukegan Daily Sun, [Solicitude for sick woman is rewarded by gift] June 4, 1918.

579 Charlotte K. Renehan, p. 57.

580 Charlotte K. Renehan, p. 57.

581 The Waukegan Gazette, [Died] August 20, 1864.

582 Charlotte K. Renehan, p. 57.

583 Charlotte K. Renehan, p. 57.

584 The Waukegan Gazette, [Obituary] October 7, 1882.

585 The Waukegan Gazette, [Died] March 2, 1867.

586 The Waukegan Daily Sun, [Find woman dead on floor of home] July 15, 1919.

According to *History of Lake County, Illinois*, "Mr. Henry Domski enlisted in Company B, Ninety-Sixth Illinois volunteer infantry on the 26th of July, 1862. He had never missed a day's service to the end of the war."[587] Henry held the rank of private, and his only injury in the war was a minor wound to the right cheek at Lookout Mountain. History of the Ninety-sixth Regiment wrote that "was with the Regimental pioneers from March, 1864, until the close of the war, but was always at the front. Had a remarkable career, in that he was never disabled or sick to the extent that unfitted him for active duty."[588] Henry was understandably proud of his service in the war. His tombstone has 96th Illinois Infantry Com. B carved on it. Henry was a charter member of the Grand Army of the Republic post in Waukegan and held a number of offices there over the years. He was also involved with the Rising Sun Lodge in Grayslake.[589]

Henry was good at an old Polish specialty, breeding horses. Writing about the 1878 Lake County Fair, the *Waukegan Gazette* noted that "a pair of spotted colts, one of them the property of Henry Dombski and the other belonging to Mr. Huson attracted considerable attention. They were the get of Slasser's Arabian stallion and were good colts. An offer of $75 apiece was made for them on the ground by Chicago parties."[590] My great-grandfather Frank also entered horses in the fair during the 1870s, winning first and second places with his teams. The *Waukegan Gazette* also mentioned that Henry was involved in an incident that occurred at the 1877 Lake County fair. Two men attacked a Lake County Marshal named Ballard on the fair racetrack in front of the judges' stand. One of the men was supposed to be hitting the marshal with a hammer but some people alleged the two used only their fists. Henry jumped in and disarmed the man with the hammer. Henry seems like a real take-charge guy to me. Marshal Ballard's face was cut up pretty badly during the fight. Nowadays, attacking a policeman would result in a lengthy prison stay, but apparently not then. One offender was escorted off the fair grounds while the other was told not to cause any more trouble.[591]

Henry married Ella Cable on September 22, 1870. They were the parents of two daughters, Bernice and Jennie. Ella only lived to the age of thirty-eight, dying on March 7, 1889.[592] Bernice married Clarence Doolittle on December

---

587 Hon. Charles Partridge, p. 736.

588 History of the Ninety-Sixth Regiment: [Chicago: Edited by Charles A. Partridge 1887] p. 721.

589 Hon. Charles Partridge, p. 736.

590 The Waukegan Gazette, [County Fair Notes] September 21,1878.

591 The Waukegan Gazette, [Lake County Fair] September 15, 1877.

592 Charlotte K. Renehan, p. 49.

21, 1904.[593] Henry was always highly involved at the post of the Grand Army of the Republic in Waukegan. The *Waukegan Daily Sun* mentions Henry's trips to the post a number of times over the years and refers to him as "a leading citizen of Avon Township."[594] In 1907, the village of Grayslake considered offering Henry the job of police commissioner.[595] Henry would have been sixty-six years old in 1907 so was a little past his prime.

Henry was also involved in one of early Grayslake's most sensational trials and one of my favorites. First, I have to explain the events leading up to the trial. In 1898, Henry volunteered to help put up a flagpole in Grayslake. Henry picked up the 60' long flagpole with his team of horses and brought it back to Grayslake. He also hauled all the gravel needed to put the pole in place.[596] The *Waukegan Daily Sun* wrote about an incident that occurred while raising the flag in Grayslake in 1901.

> "A telephone wire was strung across the village flag-pole in such a manner that the flag struck it in waving to and fro. Old veterans protested and one of the most vociferous was Dombski. He asserted the flag would be ultimately torn to shreds. He was consequently arrested on a charge of disorderly conduct, the passage in law being the one in which arrest is possible on account of use of profane language."[597]

Henry lost his temper and swore in public. A trial was necessary. His trial got underway at 7:00 a.m. on Monday, the village of Grayslake being the prosecutors. Hundreds of people from the county showed up. The jury announced a verdict of not guilty at 2:00 a.m. the next morning. The *Daily Sun* wrote, "Old soldiers and Old glory win out. The real people pay the costs and ain't kicking."[598] The Village of Grayslake had to pay $15.00 for the cost of the trial. Little did Henry know that the very flagpole he put up three years earlier would cause him so much trouble. How a trial for swearing in public could last eighteen hours is a complete mystery to me, but that is what it says.

Henry ran into some problems in his old age. The September 4, 1914, *Waukegan Daily Sun* reported that Henry was hit by a car going

593 The Waukegan Daily Sun, [Grayslake Locals] December 30, 1904.

594 The Waukegan Daily Sun, [Personal Mention] April 23, 1898.

595 The Waukegan Daily Sun, [Fitch will run for mayor of Grayslake] February 1, 1907.

596 The Waukegan Daily Sun, May 6, 1898.

597 The Waukegan Daily Sun, [All Night] July 30, 1901.

598 The Waukegan Daily Sun, [All Night] July 30, 1901.

thirty-five to forty miles an hour. He was standing on a street corner near the Congregational Church in Grayslake when Frank Eddy of Waukegan plowed into him. Henry was seventy-four years old at the time and knocked unconscious. The September 4, 1914, Waukegan *News Sun* claims Eddy and two other cars were racing through Grayslake. Witnesses said Eddy's car tried to pass the other cars at the corner by cutting across the curb and hit Henry who was standing there.[599] Eddy disputed the story in the September 5, 1914, *News Sun*. He claimed the other two cars were racing and ran him off the road. Eddy visited Henry the next day and Henry cleared him of all blame for the accident. Henry claimed that he looked away when someone called his name and walked in front of Eddy's car. Eddy also said his car had almost stopped when the accident occurred. Luckily, Henry ended up with only bruises and no broken bones.[600]

Henry died March 16, 1919.[601] The *Waukegan Daily Sun* writes that the year before, Henry was visiting his sick sister in Waukegan. He left her house at 5:00 p.m. and walked downtown to eat. On the way, a boy on a bike ran into Henry, knocking him to the ground and breaking his hip. The sidewalks were icy and it was probably an accident.[602] The boy on the bike "made off as fast as he could.[603] "Two sailors came to Henry's aid."[604] Henry never recovered from the accident and died a year later.[605]

Alexander Bilinski

Alexander was one of the 234 Polish exiles from Trieste. He is classified as a Comune in the 1830 uprising on Haiman's list of Polish exiles.[606] The Polish exiles' names are all written in Italian on Haiman's list. The crew of

599 The Waukegan Daily Sun, [Aged man living at Grayslake hit by Waukegan auto] September 4, 1914.

600 The Waukegan Daily Sun, [Eddy makes explanation about his auto accident] September 5, 1914.

601 Charlotte K. Renehan, p. 49.

602 The Waukegan Daily Sun, [Boy on a bike crashed into aged man; hip broken?] February 25, 1918.

603 The Waukegan Daily Sun, February 25, 1918.

604 The Waukegan Daily Sun, [Boy on a bike crashed into aged man; hip broken?] February 25, 1918.

605 The Waukegan Daily Sun, [Brother of Mrs. Mary Thomson died on Sunday] March 17, 1919.

606 Mieczyslaw Haiman, p. 124.

the two ships used to transport the exiles to America were all Italians, and they recorded all the names of their passengers in Italian. If my translation from Italian to English is right, Alexander was a private in the army. The Italians might have gotten Alexander's rank wrong because he was nobility and nobility were usually officers. The Wlodeckis (my family) and the Bilinskis might go back a long way. I personally know some of Alexander's descendants. In Podolia, we lived relatively close to the Bilinskis. In Illinois, the Bilinskis lived in Diamond Lake while we lived in Gurnee, probably eight or nine miles apart. Herbarz Polski records the Bilinski name as belonging to the Clan SAS.[607] Clan in Poland is similar to coat of arms in Western Europe. We were also members of SAS.[608] There is no telling how close we ever were because we had lost all contact with each other for probably a hundred years. Despite living so close, neither family knew anything about each other until I made contact.

Alexander was born January 1, 1812, near Balta,[609] the province of Podolia. Balta was a major market for wheat and was a part of Turkey until 1791. The region was under Russia rule since the second partition of Poland in 1793. Under Polish rule, this area was known as Lower Podolia or Bratslav. It is located in the present country of Ukraine in the southwestern part of the country. Alexander joined the rebellion when he was twenty years old.[610] He was almost certainly in the army from Lower Podolia led by General Benedykt Kolyszko. We were in the same army. I mentioned what happened to General Kolyszko's army in my story about Theodor Dombski and our family's story, so I will not go into it again. The Austrians imprisoned Alexander for two years at the termination of the rebellion.[611] He was moved to Trieste with the rest of the Polish prisoners and then sent to America on November 22, 1833.

The Bilinskis claim Alexander was nobility. The book Les *Confiscations des biens des Polonais Sovs le Regne de L' Empereur Nicholas Ier L. Lubliner La Pologne* records the names of four Bilinskis who participated in the 1830 rebellion. I mentioned earlier that Theodor Dombski's name was also in this book. The book contains an "alphabetical chart by name of Poles whose possessions and properties were confiscated but are not included in the Official Public Documents either by the number of serfs or by sums

607 Kaspra Niesieckiego S. J. Herbarz Polski: [Volume 8, W Lipsku, Nakladem I Drukiem Breitkopfa I Hertela 1841] p. 284.

608 Lodesky Family signet ring.

609 Al Westerman, [Personal Collection, Alexander Bilinski]

610 Carlson Family History Manuscript: [Libertyville, Illinois]

611 Carlson Family History Manuscript:

of money."[612] The four Bilinskis, their names written in French, are Jean, Alexandre, Leon, and Nicolas. The whole book is written in French. Each one's estate is valued at seven male serfs. One male serf is worth 175 silver rubles in Russia, so they were each worth 1,225 silver rubles. The number 7 must be an estimate since every name in section B has a seven after it, including my family.[613] Those mentioned in *Les Confiscations* are all nobility. A very few serfs owned land in Poland, but the vast majority of land was owned by a few very wealthy nobles, the Catholic Church, or the king.

Alexander's name also appears on a notice that we found in the Krakow, Poland, Archives. The notice was a supplement to the publication of "Liquidation of Podolie" published in the *Gazette of Saint Petersburg, and Moscow* on December 26, 1852. The *Courier of Lithuania* published the list on November 21, 1852, and the *Gazette of Varsovie* (Warsaw) on December 16, 1852. List number 2 contains the names "of those persons whose estates are possible for sequestration and confiscation but have not been discovered."[614] Alexander and Jean Bilinski are both on this notice, as is my family's last name. General Kolyszko's name is also on the notice. I think they all covered their backsides before the war began so the Russians would not know what they owned. It looks like the Russians eventually found our land.

The Bilinski family manuscript contains a story as told by Alexander. The Austrians asked him when he was a prisoner which country he preferred to go to, Russia or America. One of the Austrian guards told him that America was a land of black people. The first person Alexander saw when they arrived to the port of New York was a black man working on the dock. He ran back to his fellow passengers and said, "It is true, the people here are black. After embarking though, he did not see any blacks."[615]

After landing in New York with the other exiles on March 28, 1834, he was supposed to have gone to New Orleans.[616] If he did, he did not stay long. His descendants never knew anything about it either. Alexander enlisted

612 Les Confiscations des biens des Polonais Sovs le Regne de L' Empererеur Nicholas Ier L. Lubliner: [Brussels-Leipzig] p.44.

613 Les Confiscations, p. 44.

614 Supplement a l' Annonce de la Commission de Liquidation de Podolie, publice dans les Gazettes de St. Petersbourg et de Moscow du 26 December, dans le Courier de Lithuanie du 21 November et dans la Gazette de Varsovie du 16 December 1852: List 2: [At the Krakow Historical Archives, Krakow, Poland]

615 Carlson Family History Manuscript:

616 Aleksander Grobicki, Proba Biografii, Sodalis: [St. Mary's College Library, Orchard Lake, Michigan] Number B, p. 26.

in the U.S. Army for three years at Watervliet Arsenal in Troy, New York, on November 7, 1834. His enlistment papers state that he is twenty-two years old, his occupation soldier and born in Balta, Poland.[617] He had blue eyes, brown hair, and was 5'8" tall. If he were twenty-two years old when he enlisted in the U.S. Army, then he would have been eighteen years old during the Polish rebellion.

Alexander married Jane Lundy in 1835, the first of his three marriages. The marriage produced five children. Julia, born April 2, 1836. She is thought to have died the same year. William, born March 1, 1837. Henry, born March 20, 1839. Henrietta, born February 20, 1843. And Ferdinand, born May 31, 1844.[618]

Alexander enlisted in the army for three more years on October 1, 1837. He was twenty-five years old. His occupation was a carpenter/carriage maker, and he was assigned to Ordnance at Watervliet Arsenal. Theodor Dombski and Stanislaus Lisiecki were also in Ordnance at Watervliet. The army discharged Alexander from Watervliet Armory on October 1, 1840, after six years in the army.[619] Right after getting discharged, Alexander left for Illinois. Records show Alexander settled there in 1840.[620] The Bilinskis came west via the Erie Canal, then on the Great Lakes by steamboat to Chicago. They planned to settle in Chicago but, after seeing the mud of early Chicago, decided to look elsewhere. Dombski and Lisiecki were already living forty miles north of Chicago, so it would have been logical for Alexander to head north. He was supposed to have settled in the small village of Machanics Grove and constructed one of the first stores/taverns there.[621]

The first record of the Bilinskis in Lake County is when Alexander bought eighty acres in Little Fort (Waukegan) from the General Land Office June 1, 1842. The whole tract was wooded and located near Stanislaus Lisiecki's farm. Six weeks later on July 13, he sold the north forty acres to Silas Stevens. The Bilinskis lived on the south forty until February 21, 1850, then sold their farm to Ira Porter and moved into town. Alexander worked as a joiner in Little Fort.[622] The Bilinskis originally thought that Alexander's first wife Jane Lundy Bilinski died in 1845. After they cleaned her headstone, they found out she died on November 16, 1899. It appears that Alexander

617 National Archives, M233, Roll 20, Volume 41, p. 27.

618 Carlson Family History Manuscript:

619 National Archives, M233, Roll 19, Volume 40, p. 28.

620 Carlson Family History Manuscript

621 Carlson Family History Manuscript:

622 Al Westerman, [Personal Collection, Alexander Bilinski]

and Jane were divorced in 1845, a rare occurrence in those days.[623] The 1850 census shows that all the children born to Jane and Alexander lived with Alexander.

Alexander married Hester Ann Guyles on March 7, 1848. Hester was seventeen years old while Alexander was thirty-six years old. She was born in Pennsylvania and had come west with her parents to settle in Little Fort. Two more children were born from this marriage, Julia Ann, born March 1, 1849, and Charles A., born February 16, 1852.[624] The Bilinskis lived in Waukegan for two years. They sold their house on December 3, 1851, and moved to Diamond Lake near the small village of Mechanics Grove in Fremont Township. Alexander bought forty acres on the north side of Diamond Lake for $500.00 from Enos Covalt.[625]

Mechanics Grove (now Mundelein) is located in Fremont Township and is in the center of Lake County. Lake Michigan is about ten miles to the east. Diamond Lake is a little south of Mundelein. Originally the eastern part of Fremont Township was prairie, the western part wooded. Emigrants from England were the first settlers in Mechanics Grove. They came here because there was a depression in England and were tired of oppressive taxes. Most were all skilled tradesmen but became farmers in America. In the old days, the name for tradesmen was mechanic, hence the name Mechanics Grove. Diamond Lakes present population is 1,500. Mundelein's present population is 17,053. Both towns probably have larger populations by now.

Alexander went to California to mine gold in 1852. Hester stayed with her brother John Guyles in Waukegan while Alexander was gone. John was a sheriff in Waukegan, and the Bilinski family lived in an apartment above the jail. Charles A. Bilinski was born above the jail. Alexander's route to California took him through Salt Lake City, Utah, where he had dinner with Brigham Young. Alexander only stayed in California a short while because of health problems.[626] He did earn enough money mining gold to expand his farm in Diamond Lake to 155 acres.[627] Misfortune befell Alexander shortly after his return to Lake County. Hester Ann died in 1854, leaving him with the two young children, Julie Ann, six, and Charles, two, as well as the four children from his first marriage.[628] Henrietta would have been eleven years old

[623] Carlson Family History Manuscript:

[624] Carlson Family History Manuscript:

[625] Al Westerman, [Personal Collection, Alexander Bilinski]

[626] Carlson Family History Manuscript:

[627] Al Westerman, [Personal Collection, Alexander Bilinski]

[628] Carlson Family History Manuscript:

at the time, but I'll bet she had to grow up fast and take care of her younger brothers and sister.

Alexander Married Clarissa (Clara) Cary February 4, 1857. Clara was born May 22, 1824, in Belcher, Washington County, New York.[629] They were supposed to have been married in Troy, Rensselaer County, New York. Two children were born to this marriage, Jennie, born May 28, 1858, and Anna, born December 25, 1859 (Christmas day). Clara outlived Alexander in this marriage.[630]

I thought the Bilinskis would be Catholics, but there is no record of them ever going to any Catholic church in Lake County. Instead, Alexander was a charter member of the Diamond Lake Free Church. The church cost $969 to build in 1858-59, with Alexander donating money for its construction. He gave a very generous contribution to the church in 1882. The Bilinskis are mentioned a number of times in the church's records.[631]

Alexander was in a serious train accident in January 1881. An earlier train accident in Chicago had delayed the train to Libertyville by almost three hours. The next train, the express, was due to leave at the usual time of 9:00 p.m., but the Libertyville train was leaving then. The conductors of both trains met and decided that the express train would leave eighteen minutes after the Libertyville train. The first train stopped at one of its normal stops at the Oak Glen station. Alexander was due to get off there and his son Charles was waiting for him. The conductor thought there was enough time before the other train arrived and never sent a brakeman to the back with a lamp. It was also a foggy night. According to the *Waukegan Gazette*, "the express train came thundering along at full speed, crashing into the standing train with such force as to push it about 30 rods, the locomotive tearing its way half through the single passenger car."[632] Thirty rods is 170 yards or 510 feet. One person was killed and others hurt. Alexander sustained a bruised shoulder and was badly shaken up. He was sixty-nine years old at the time. Charles was standing on the rear platform waiting for his father and had to jump for his life when the trains hit.[633] Alexander put his farm up for sale six months later. The *Gazette* reported that he had not "fully recovered from the shock of his railroad accident."[634] He must have kept his land on the shore of Diamond Lake, however.

629 Al Westerman, [Personal Collection, Alexander Bilinski]

630 Carlson Family History Manuscript:

631 Memories of Mundelein 1909-1984: [Mundelein Community Days Committee] p.5.

632 The Waukegan Gazette, [Railroad Accident] January 22, 1881.

633 The Waukegan Gazette, [Railroad Accident] January 22, 1881.

634 The Waukegan Gazette, [Diamond Lake] June 4, 1881.

Alexander lived to the age of seventy-four, dying August 13, 1886. Clara lived to the ripe old age of ninety-four, dying on September 15, 1918. Both are buried at the Diamond Lake Cemetery.[635] I have been to the cemetery with Mrs. Yngve Carlson, one of Alexander's descendants. Alexander's gravestone reads, "Exiled to this country in 1833 for participating in the Polish uprising."

A month after Alexander's death there was more bad news. Alexander's house burned down. None of the Bilinskis lived in the house at the time but were renting it to the Buchanan brothers' farm whose foreman lived there.[636] No one was hurt, but the Bilinskis found out a week later that the insurance had expired when Alexander died.[637]

Two of Alexander's sons served in the Civil War. Henry enlisted in the Union army on August 19, 1861. He was a private in Company F, Thirty-seventh Illinois Infantry until he was discharged because of wounds. I have not been able to find the date of his discharge.[638] Charles enlisted in Company F, Twelfth Illinois Cavalry on October 27, 1863. Charles was not quite twelve years old when he enlisted.[639] I had to read this twice but it is correct. After three years of service, Charles was discharged on May 29, 1866, a fourteen-year-old army veteran![640] After the war, Charles went back to work on his father's farm.[641]

The *Waukegan Gazette* newspaper frequently mentions Charles. He continued to work on his father's forty-seven-acre farm on Diamond Lake and was in total control of the farm by the late 1870s. Charles and a partner named Wenban operated a dry goods store in Diamond Lake.[642] They had to pick up their stock in Chicago, which was a one-day drive each way. The *Waukegan Gazette* wrote in 1877, "Wenban and Bilinski are having a good run of custom. They are obliging gentlemen, and honorable dealers."[643] One of their customers wrote a glowing account of the store in the *Gazette* in 1879. "It is those who

---

635 Carlson Family History Manuscript:

636 The Waukegan Gazette, September 11, 1886.

637 The Waukegan Gazette, September 25, 1886.

638 John J. Halsey, p. 444.

639 Lake County Discovery Museum Library, Waconda, Illinois: Card catalog of Civil War Enlistees in Illinois Regiments A-O] Charles Bilinski:

640 Julie Joan Giertuga, Polish Contributions in Illinois during the war between the states: [Peoria, Illinois: A thesis submitted to the Department of History in the Graduate Division of Bradley University in candidacy for the degree of Master of Arts 1948] p. 49.

641 Carlson Family History Manuscript:

642 The Past and Present of Lake County 1877: p. 448.

643 The Waukegan Gazette, [Diamond Lake] June 16, 1877.

know and appreciate a good thing at home, who knows when a tradesman is looking out for the interest of his patrons, who take pains to inform themselves of prices and quality of goods, and who patronize hard-working, pains-taking, careful and honest merchants."[644] According to the customer, the store was known for its choice butter. Charles paid the surrounding farmers above-average prices for their butter, even higher than Chicago prices.[645]

Charles married Ida Darby sometime in the late 1870s. They were the parents of Alberta, born in 1879. Maurine, born September 3, 1881. Emmett, born February 20, 1885. Esther, born July 8, 1886. Justin born January 11, 1888. Ida, born September 26, 1893. One child Gladys died in infancy in 1899.[646] Ida had a scare in 1900 when she came down with a bad case of typhoid fever.[647] I think Mrs. Carlson said she was a descendant of Emmett.

Charles's store must have done a good business for he built a new 24' × 50' two-story building in 1880. It was larger than the old building and about a half-mile north of the old store on the east shore of Diamond Lake.[648] It looks like the east shore was sparsely populated when Charles built his store there. The *Gazette* mentioned that when the store was complete, "a new village will be inaugurated."[649] Charles was appointed postmaster of Diamond Lake on February 4, 1879.[650] He also developed a resort (Bilinski's Grove) on the east shore and continued to operate the farm for some time as well. The *Gazette* wrote in 1899, "C. A. Bilinski is doing a rushing business with his cabbage crop."[651] In 1882, Charles somehow found time to run the dining hall at the Lake County Fair.[652] The 1901 *Waukegan Daily Sun* wrote,

Where to Eat

> C. A. Bilinski, who will run the dinning hall at the fair, next week desires us to state he will have accomodation for all who come. He is making extensive preparations to feed the crowds and

644 The Waukegan Gazette, [Trade at Home] July 26, 1879.

645 The Waukegan Gazette, [Trade at Home] July 26, 1879.

646 Carlson Family History Manuscript:

647 The Lake County Independent, [Diamond Lake] [Libertyville, Illinois] May 4, 1900.

648 The Waukegan Gazette, [Diamond Lake] May 8, 1880.

649 The Waukegan Gazette, [Diamond Lake] May 8, 1880.

650 John J. Halsey, p. 591.

651 The Lake County Independent, [Diamond lake] December 15, 1899.

652 The Waukegan Gazette, [Little Locals] October 14, 1882.

> promises to furnish good meals at prices no one can find fault with.
> get your meals on the grounds, you can't do better.[653]

The newspapers note many events occurring at Bilinski Grove throughout the years. There were dances every Saturday night in July and August. The Waukegan foresters had their dances there. I found mentions of harvest dances, picnics, school picnics, bands, Fourth of July celebrations, Sunday school conventions, and the reunion of the Grand Army of the Republic. Charles built a hotel by at least 1896.[654] The hotel included a bar and restaurant. He was also the manager of the Knickerbocker Ice Company in 1899.[655] The Bilinskis built a new house in 1899 as well as a new bathhouse at the resort.[656] Charles might have gone into the ice business himself. He built an addition to his own icehouse in 1905[657] and by 1906 had twelve men cutting ice for him on Diamond Lake.[658] Ida died in 1910 and Charles died in 1934.[659]

Alexander's daughter Henrietta married John A. Singer, of New York City, on May 18, 1866. The marriage took place at Diamond Lake on Alexander's property.[660] John Singer's father, Isaac, invented the Singer sewing machine.[661] Sometime after they were married, Singer bought 170 acres of land on the east shore of Diamond Lake. He built three houses and two large barns on the property. The Singers' residence was one of the largest and most modern houses in the county. They converted one of the houses into a large hotel.[662] Henrietta died at thirty-three years of age on August 29, 1876. There is no mention of any children.[663] Henrietta's half-sister Jenny married John Singer on May 28, 1877. She was nineteen years old.[664] In 1880, John put the estate up for sale at half the value of the property and moved back east.[665] Known as

---

653 The Lake County Independent, [Where to eat] August 30. 1901.
654 The Waukegan Daily Sun, [Diamond lake] August 14, 1896.
655 The Waukegan Daily Sun, [Diamond Lake] March 10, 1899.
656 The Waukegan Daily Sun, [Diamond Lake] March 3, 1899.
657 The Lake County Independent, [Diamond Lake] January 13, 1905.
658 The Lake County Independent, [Diamond Lake] February 9, 1906.
659 The Carlson Family History Manuscript:
660 The Waukegan Gazette, [Married] June 9, 1866.
661 The Carlson Family History Manuscript:
662 The Waukegan Gazette, [A Delightful Suburban Home for sale] June 12, 1880.
663 The Waukegan Gazette, [Died] September 2, 1876.
664 The Carlson Family History Manuscript:
665 The Waukegan Gazette, [A Delightful Suburban Home for sale] June 12, 1880.

the Singer house ever since, the house was destroyed by fire in 1901. There was no insurance on it either.[666]

Alexander's youngest daughter Anna was a well-known poet in the county. The book *Poems by Residents of Lake County, Illinois* by Robert Darrow contains four of her poems.[667] The 1910 *Waukegan News Sun* wrote a small article about Anna. "She early manifested the possession of the gift of poetry and for several years she was a prolific writer of verse, her productions being welcomed generally by the press."[668] The same article included her poem "The Plaint of the Frogs." Anna was living in Chicago at the time.[669]

I have to mention one more thing about the Bilinski family. When I first started my research, I assumed that we (my family) were the only Polish exiles to settle in the county. After discovering the others and their stories, I learned that the Bilinskis lived near us in Podolia. I found out something else as well. About twenty years earlier, I had worked in a small factory in Northbrook, Illinois, called Pace. Also working at the factory was a guy named Sam Carlson from Libertyville, Illinois, whom I got to know pretty well. Years later while researching the Alexander Bilinski story, I noticed that one of his descendants was Mary Ellen Carlson, of Libertyville, Illinois. This really got me thinking, so I found the Carlson's phone number and called. Sam answered, which confirmed to me that I had unwittingly worked with one of Alexander's descendants. I visited the Carlsons soon after. Sam and I swapped stories about Pace, and Mrs. Carlson gave me a copy of the *Bilinski Family History*. I would like to thank the Carlsons and Al Westerman for their help with this story.

Basil Jaroshinski

Basil was born in Lithuania, Poland, in 1810.[670] He participated in the 1830 Polish uprising and was one of the Polish exiles from Trieste. Basil did not come over with the 234 Polish exiles but came to New York on the ship *Lipsia* in July 1834.[671] He was living in New York City's Ninth Ward in

666 The Waukegan Daily Sun, [Singer House burns down] April 26, 1901.

667 Robert Darrow, Poems by Residents of Lake County, Illinois: [Waukegan, Illinois: Register Print Co. 1896] Index

668 The Waukegan News Sun, [Gems of Verse from Lake County Poets] April 30, 1910.

669 The Waukegan News Sun, [Gems of Verse from Lake County Poets] April 30, 1910.

670 Ancestral File 4. 19. [Copyright 1987 by Intellectual Reserve, Inc.]

671 Jerzy Jan Lerski, p. 178.

1840[672] and working as a "hatter."[673] Basil was highly involved in New York's Polish organizations. In 1840, he was a member of "Unification of Polish Emigration."[674] Basil was elected an officer in the "Association of Poles in America" in March 1842.[675]

Basil married Catherine Morgan in 1839. Catherine was born in 1819 in Belfast, Ireland. They were the parents of seven children. Joseph Boleslaw, born in New York in 1840. Mary T., born in 1842 in New York. Basil Jr., born in 1844 in New York. Adeline, born in 1847 in Illinois. Elizebeth, born 1849 in Illinois. Jacob, born in 1851 in Illinois. And John, born 1857 in Illinois. The Jaroshinskis had their share of sad events. John Jaroshinski died April 14, 1860. He was only three years old. Mary T. died at twenty-three years of age on September 8, 1865, in Emmetsburg, Maryland. Adeline married Ignatius Mitschler on October 24, 1869. She died in April 1877 at thirty years of age.[676]

The first record of Basil in Illinois is when he bought two parcels of wooded land in Newport Township, Lake County, on August 23, 1845. Each parcel was forty acres in size.[677] The land was located about one mile west of the present town of Wadsworth and another mile north of the small village of Mill Creek. Both Wadsworth and Mill Creek are forty-five miles northwest of Chicago. The populations of Wadsworth or Mill Creek are not in my atlas; maybe I need a new atlas. I do not ever remember Wadsworth having more then five hundred people living there when I was a kid, but Wadsworth's population has grown in recent years. I am not sure if Mill Creek is even considered a village anymore. There cannot be more than a few houses there. Temple Steel bought up almost every house and farm in Mill Creek after World War II and destroyed most of them. Now most of Mill Creek is just open farmland.

Newport Township is located in the far northern part of Lake County and close to its center. Its northern boundary is the Wisconsin Stateline. The Des Plaines River runs through the middle of Newport Township. The

672 Maria J. E. Copson-Niecko, p. 84.

673 Aleksander Grobicki, p. [J 23]

674 Florian Stasik, Polish Political Emigres in the United States of America, 1831-1864. [Polish American Historical Association 2002] [Distributed by Columbia University Press, New York] p. 90.

675 Jerzy Jan Lerski, p. 156.

676 Family Group Record, Ancestral File [T M - ver 4.19. [Copyright 1987, June 1998 by Intellectual Reserve, Inc.]

677 Al Westerman, [Personal Collection, Basil Jaroshinski]

Des Plaines River is the main river in Lake County running north to south through the whole county. Most of Newport Township was wooded in its original state. The first settlers to Lake County came up the valley of the Des Plaines River in 1835. Being the furthest north in the county, Newport Township was one of the last ones settled. The first settlers were mainly New England Yankees, but soon a large number of Irish settled around the town of Newport "Wadsworth" and Mill Creek. Quite a few Germans came as well. A small log cabin served as the Catholic church in Mill Creek in 1849. It was named after an early Mill Creek settler named Andrew Tougher, who had donated land for the church. In turn, the church was given the name of "St. Andrew Mission." The church had no priest at first, but the pastor of the Immaculate Conception Catholic Church in Waukegan would make trips there.[678]

Basil lived a mile west of the small town of Newport. Newport is on the east side of the Des Plaines River, and there was no bridge over the river when Basil first settled there. A bridge was built over the river in 1850.[679] Most of the records I have found about Basil show him doing all his business in the town of Millburn, about two miles west of Mill Creek. Millburn was a Scotch settlement. Some of my ancestors on my mother's side were from Millburn. My great-great-grandfather James Bater and Basil Jaroshinski are both on the same list of credit customers at Robert Strang's store in Millburn.[680]

The 1850 census of Lake County, Illinois, records Basil's occupation as a "farmer."[681] By at least the late 1860s, and possibly in 1859, Basil was a grade school teacher. The Lake County Teachers Association elected him secretary in 1866. The same article writes that Basil, his daughter Elizabeth, and son Joseph were all teachers in Newport Township.[682] The April 13, 1867, *Waukegan Gazette* records Basil and his daughter Elizabeth as being teachers in Millburn. Son Joseph is a teacher in Newport, possibly the village of Newport.[683] An article in the March 6, 1869, *Gazette* might have confused

---

678 Bridge to the Past, Wadsworth, Illinois Bicentennial Book. [At the Lake County, Illinois Discovery Museum and Library, Wauconda, Illinois] P. 20.

679 Bridge to the Past, p. 1.

680 The Story of a Landmark: [published in commemoration of the 100th anniversary of the founding, in 1856, of the Millburn Corner Store] p. 4.

681 D. F. Thompson, The 1850 Census of Lake, County, Illinois: [Evanston, Illinois: November, 1976] p. 64.

682 The Waukegan Gazette, [Lake County Teachers' Association] April 14, 1866.

683 The Waukegan Gazette, April 13, 1867.

Basil with his son Joseph. It mentions Joseph as a teacher in Newport District Number 7. The district's western boundary was the Des Plains River, which would include the village of Newport. Basil was a teacher in Millburn two years earlier. District Number 7 had thirty-five students, and the inside and outside of the school building was supposed to be "far from inviting."[684] The article goes on to say,

> The physical features of the county in the immediate neighborhood of the school house are not so pleasant to the eye as are some sections of the county, being broken and woody, with some quite extensive sloughs. Still there are some very good farms in the district, and sufficient wealth to afford better school accommodations than they have. Mr. Jaroshinski is an old man, having taught some ten years, I think, and if he would make teaching his business, would be one of the best. His school is orderly, and as well conducted as one can be with the accommodations at his command."[685]

Basil was fifty-nine years old in 1869, while Joe was twenty-nine. Unless twenty-nine was old in 1869, at least part of the article was about Basil. It looks like either Basil or Joseph was teaching in a dump. The same article lists Joseph as a director of School District Number 5.[686] Catherine Morgan Jaroshinski died October 1, 1868. Basil died in Libertyville, Illinois, on November 28, 1869. Both are buried in the Old St. Patrick's Cemetery in Wadsworth.[687]

I have a little information about Basil's offspring. Joseph was a private in the Seventeenth Illinois Cavalry Company F in the Civil War. Nathaniel Vose organized the Seventeenth Illinois Cavalry, and it was mainly composed of men from Warren Township.[688] After the war, he was a member of the Waukegan post of Grand Army of the Republic. Henry Dombski was also a member there.[689]

---

684 The Waukegan Gazette, [Our County Schools] March 6, 1869.

685 The Waukegan Gazette, [Our County Schools] March 6, 1869.

686 The Waukegan Gazette, [Our County Schools] March 6, 1869.

687 Al Westerman, [Personal Collection, Basil Jaroshinski]

688 The Waukegan Gazette, [Members of Company F. 17th, Illinois Cavalry] February 13, 1864.

689 The Waukegan Daily News, [Members of Waukegan Post, G. A. R.] March 31, 1899.

Joe lived with the Jaroshinski family on the 1860 census of Newport Township.[690] On the 1870 census, it looks like Joe lived in two different places at the same time. The 1870 City of Waukegan Census shows Joe and his younger brother Jacob living at their sister Mrs. Adeline Mitchler's house. Her husband, Ignatius, is thirty-three years old, born in France, and occupation fishing. Adeline keeps house. Joe is a thirty-year-old teacher. Jacob is eighteen years old and occupation fishing.[691] The 1870 Newport Township Census has Joe living in the town of Newport (Wadsworth). He is thirty years old and occupation farmer. His wife Lucia is thirty years old, born in New York, and keeps house. They have a seven-year-old daughter named Viola and a three-year-old son named Ira.[692] Sometime in the 1860s, Joe changed his name to Suminski. In the 1870 Waukegan census, his name is still Jaroshinski, while the 1870 Newport census gives the name Suminski.

It looks like Joe was also a stagecoach driver. The census never reports it, but the *Waukegan Gazette* has a few mentions. The *Gazette* wrote on October 26, 1872, that "Sumerski, the Antioch stage driver, says that since the October elections, even the wild geese as they fly over are crying out Grant! Grant!! Grant!!!"[693] Joe was talking about General and President Grant. The February 1, 1873, *Gazette* claims that A. T. Cribb of Antioch just sold his horse and a lot to "J. H. Sumerski, the stage-driver."[694] Joe's middle name was Boleslaw, but I have seen an H. used for a middle initial on other sources. The same article writes that the train between Kenosha and Rockford could not run for four days because of the deep snow. The only people to get mail were what Joe's stagecoach brought them.[695]

Joe might have been running a small boarding house in 1880. In the 1880 Newport Township Census, Joe is thirty-nine years old and occupation farmer. Wife Lucy keeps house. Viola is seventeen years old and Ira is thirteen. There is a new member of the family, Benjamin, three years old. Samantha Hoskins, sixty-three years old and born in New York, was also living in the Jaroshinski household. George Hall, a thirty-three-year-old shoemaker from New York, lived there along with his wife Jennie. She was twenty-three years old, born in

690 Lake County Genealogical Society, The 1860 Census and Mortality Schedule of Lake County, Illinois: [Mundelein, Illinois: Copy Systems 1984] p. 18.

691 Lake County Genealogical Society, The 1870 Census of Lake County, Illinois: [Mundelein, Illinois: Copy Systems 1985] p. 68.

692 Lake County Genealogical Society, The 1870 Census of Lake County, Illinois, p. 87.

693 The Waukegan Gazette, October 26, 1872.

694 The Waukegan Gazette, [Antioch] February 1, 1873.

695 The Waukegan gazette, [Antioch] February 1, 1873.

Illinois and a housekeeper. The Halls might have been relatives. Paul Carney was also living with the Jaroshinskis. He was seventy years old, a retired farmer and born in Ireland.[696] The January 1, 1881, *Gazette* notes that Joe was living in the small village of Hickory on the Newport-Antioch Township border close to the state line. Once Joe was trying to get his dog to go home when his team of horses spooked. The team almost ran to Waukegan. This is a distance of probably seven miles as the crow flies. Near Waukegan, one horse fell on "the frozen ground so hard as to lame it considerably and almost make it blind."[697] The *Gazette* also reported in 1881 that even though the roads were bad, the Suminskis hosted a large Christmas party on December 31, which was attended by friends and relatives.[698]

The year 1885 was a good year for the Suminskis. Their daughter Viola got married on May 28 to E. Eddy.[699] A history of Russell, Illinois, a nearby town, has an interesting account of how Viola met Eddy.

> Joseph Sumeriski was a stage driver. His daughter, Viola often rode with him. A change of horses was made at Eddy where a post office was located. The post office at Eddy was named Newport. It was located just west of the Northwestern Freight line. This is now route 173. It was on the south side of the road. E. W. Eddy was the postmaster there until the Russell P. O. was established.
>
> Remember Eddy met Viola Sumeriski there and fell in love with her. They married and their son, Everett Eddy, of Waukegan, Ill. Gave us this information. Remember Eddy was the son of E. F. W. Eddy.[700]

The Suminskis might have moved to the small village of Rosecrans, located about three to four miles straight east of Hickory on Route 173 in 1886.[701] The *Gazette* printed a story from Gages Lake in 1898. "Mr. and Mrs. Suminski when returning from the reunion last Thursday met with a severe accident. The horse became frightened and ran away tipping the buggy and

696 Lake County Genealogical Society, The 1880 Census of Lake County, Illinois: Volume 1 [Mundelein, Illinois: Copy Systems 1987] p. 53.

697 The Waukegan Gazette, [Hickory] January 1, 1881.

698 The Waukegan Gazette, [West Newport] December 31, 1881.

699 The Waukegan Gazette, [Millburn] May 30, 1885.

700 Russell, Illinois 100 years of Memories 1873-1973: [At Warren Township Historical Society, Gurnee, Illinois] p. 9.

701 The Waukegan Gazette, [Rosecrans] September 25, 1886.

throwing them out. Mrs. Suminski had her arm broken and was otherwise injured, while Mr. Suminski escaped injury."[702] Gages Lake is a probably five or six miles southwest of Rosecrans and located in Warren Township. There is no census for 1890, and I have not found much about the Suminskis in the 1890s. By 1900, they were living in Libertyville, Illinois, a few more miles southeast of Gages Lake. It looks like Lucy died sometime in the 1880s. Joe has a new wife named Emma on the 1900 Federal Census of Libertyville, Illinois. She is thirty-nine years old, while Joe is a fifty-nine-year-old farmer. There is also another son, one-year-old Dewey. None of Joe's other children were living with him at the time.[703] Emma must have been Joe's wife hurt in the accident in Gages Lake. Joe's occupation on the 1900 census is farmer, but it looks like he was starting his own picnic grove. The August 30, 1905, *Daily Sun* mentioned that "the Women's Relief Corps held their annual picnic at Shamerski's Grove in Libertyville." The Shamerski place is a beautiful one and the ladies enjoyed themselves much.[704]

Joe's story ends in a surprising manner. According to the May 4, 1906, *Waukegan Daily Sun*, "Because the rheumatism made life unbearable to him, this noon Joseph Suminski, residing about two and a half miles north of Libertyville, committeed suicide by hanging himself in a hay chute in the barn back of his residence.

"The suicide is all the more remarkable as Suminski is over seventy years old and was krown the width and breadth of the county as one of its cheeriest men. He was a musician in the Civil war and an old veteran."[705]

I have a little information about Basil's son Jacob. I mentioned earlier that in 1870, Jacob was an eighteen-year-old fisherman living in Waukegan at his sister's house.[706] He changed his last name at some point and went by the name of "Shinski." He married Mary Oswald in Waukegan on October 13, 1874.[707] The July 5, 1873, *Waukegan Gazette* wrote, "Another Fish Story—Lake Michigan yielded up a good share of its contents to Messrs. Shinski, Arno & Co. on Tuesday last. Those gentlemen had not taken in their net for two days and were somewhat surprised to find, on Tuesday morning,

702 The Waukegan Daily Sun, [Gages Lake] September 9, 1898.

703 Lake County Genealogical Society, 1900 Federal Population Census, Lake County, Illinois: [Mundelein, Illinois: Copy Systems 1995] p. 45.

704 The Waukegan Daily Sun, [Relief Corps Picnic] August 30, 1905.

705 The Waukegan Daily Sun, [Aged man of seventy suicides by hanging self in the hay chute in the barn] May 4, 1906.

706 Lake County Genealogical Society, The 1870 Census of Lake County, Illinois, p. 68

707 00262 I. G. I. Fiche Illinois F. H. L.: p. 17,047.

that they had captured about three and one half tons of fish in one net. Those Evanston fisermen that made the big haul a few days since are respectfully requested to take in their colors, surrender the belt and try again."[708] A list of Lake County taxpayers and voters records Jacobs's occupation as "farmer" in 1877.[709] The June 29, 1878, *Waukegan Gazette* wrote an informative article about the Waukegan fishing industry.

> The fishing interest of Waukegan is by no means a small one. There are no less than six firms at this place engaged in fishing, and at times doing a lucrative business. Quite an amount of food for man is annually taken from our beautiful lake, furnishing employment to a large number of hands. Occasionally our fishermen suffer from a storm that the landsman thinks little of. Such was the case on Thursday night and Friday of last week, when the waves ran with such force as to damage their nets greatly, and in some instances almost entirely destroy them, taking the piles from their moorings and so breaking up things that a week or ten days will be required to place their nets back into position. The damage to the different firms amounts in the aggregate to over a thousand dollars. They are taking advantage of the fine days to stick their piles, mend their nets and prepare fore the future as though no strange thing had happened.[710]

Jacob might have had enough of fishing and got into a different line of work. The 1879 *Waukegan Gazette* claims that Kranz and Shinski shut down their meat market because there was too much competition.[711] The 1880 Waukegan census lists Jacob's occupation as fisherman. His wife Mary is twenty-three years old and keeps house. They have two daughters, Anna four, and Mary, three years old.[712] Jacob and family must have moved to California right after the 1880 census. Their son Jacob was born there in 1880. Other children born in California were Florence, Frank, George, and Henry.[713]

---

708 The Waukegan Gazette, [Another Fish Story] July 5, 1873.

709 Past and Present of Lake County 1877, p. 336.

710 The Waukegan Gazette, June 29, 1878.

711 The Waukegan Gazette, September 13, 1879.

712 Lake County Genealogical Society, 1880 Census of Lake County, Illinois: [Mundelein, Illinois: Copy Systems 1987] p. 88.

713 Jaroshinski Ancestral File 4. 19. [Copyright 1987, June 1998 by Intellectual Reserve, Inc. [Family History Library]

Thaddeus Pienkowski

Thaddeus actually lived in Wisconsin. My book is about Polish settlers in Illinois but I will have to make an exception this time. The Pienkowski family lived in Kenosha County, Wisconsin, on the Illinois-Wisconsin state line. Kenosha County is located directly north of Lake County, Illinois. All Thaddeus had to do was walk across the street and he would be in Illinois. He was also one of the 234 Polish exiles from Trieste as were all the Polish exiles in Lake County. Thaddeus lived about four miles as the crow flies from Basil Jaroshinski in Newport Township. I also have another reason to write about Thaddeus. I contacted his descendants and they gave me a copy of their family history titled *A Brief Sketch of the Life History of our Father and Mother.* Thaddeus's adopted daughter Sara and his daughter Minnie were the authors. The ladies did a great job. The manuscript is seventeen pages long and covers Thaddeus's life in Poland as well as in America. The Pienkowski family knows more about their family history than any of the descendants of Polish exiles I have researched to date.

The Pienkowski family was Catholic and a nobility in Poland. Thaddeus was born November 28, 1802, in Szarvgood, Poland. His mother died when he was an infant, and his father died when he was seven years old. Thaddeus's father gave his son some great advice right before he died. "My son promise your Father that you will be a good boy; that you will be truthful and honest; that you will say your prayers; that you will not drink liquor or go in bad company, or do anything which you know to be wrong; and that you will obey your brother when your Father is gone. You will have a hard time, but be true to your God and to your country."[714]

Thaddeus went to live with his oldest brother and his wife. The couple was childless and they treated him like their own son. There he received a good education and went on to study at the University in Krakow, Poland. Thaddeus and two of his brothers joined the Polish Army during the 1830 uprising. He held the rank of noncommissioned officer in the army.[715] In one of the battles, the same cannon ball killed his brother and Thaddeus's horse. Thaddeus himself was knocked senseless and blinded in the right eye. He was carried off the battlefield, his right eye blinded for the rest of his life. His senses came back to him fast and he rejoined the battle. A cannon ball

[714] Mrs. Sarah Norton Lockhart Young and Mrs. Minnie Eliza Pienkowski Buckley, A Brief Sketch of the life history of our Father and Mother. P. 1.

[715] Aleksander Grobicki, [letter P] p. 21.

killed his second horse as well, so he found a riderless horse wondering around the battlefield and used it. Thaddeus's other brother is thought to have been killed in the battle too. Thaddeus never saw him again.

The army Thaddeus belonged to crossed into Austria at the end of the war. The Austrians arrested many of them, Thaddeus being one of those arrested. He spent one year in jail waiting to find out what the Austrians would do with them. Thaddeus claimed the Austrians treated them humanly while they were in jail. He made the most of his time in jail by designing a beaded bag made out of velvet. "He put a white eagle on the top, the emblem of Poland, a weeping willow tree, indicative of the downfall of his county, an oak tree loaded with acorns, typical of a great strength which would not bend; a butterfly, implying that prayers would ascend; a monogram composed of four letters, and other emblems of his own country."[716] One of the jailers had watched Thaddeus make the bag the whole time and told him either give me the bag or put a Russian crown on the white eagle. The crown signified the Russian domination of Poland. Thaddeus did not want to lose the bag so had to comply, planning to take the crown off when he got out of prison. It never was taken off. His wife liked it the way it was and asked him to leave it that way. The Pienkowskis still have the bag and sent me pictures of it. It is beautiful workmanship.

Thaddeus found a job in a paper mill/factory soon after arriving to America. He did not know the English language yet, but his university education helped him and he was quickly promoted to the foreman of his department. Thaddeus managed to save up some money and get himself established. He also went looking for a wife. Thaddeus met Emily Ellen Norton and they were married on July 14, 1834, at Christ's Episcopal Church in New York City. They were introduced to each other by Emily's half sister Eliza, who was married to a Pole named Komorninski. Emily was born June 10, 1818, in New York City. She had a good education and was already interested in Polish history before she met Thaddeus. Emily's ancestors immigrated to America from England in 1635, and her grandfather was a captain in the Revolutionary War.

A son, Thaddeus Edward, was born to the new family on September 8, 1835. Another son, Thomas Joseph, was born October 1, 1837. Emily's mother Elizabeth also moved in. She was a widow and Emily was her favorite daughter. Elizabeth also brought her adopted daughter, Sarah. Both Sarah's parents had died from tuberculosis, leaving their three daughters orphans. The Pienkowski family was starting to feel comfortable when a friend of the family came to visit. He ran a dairy farm on the western side of the state in Onondaga County,

716 Mrs. Sarah Norton Lockhart Young and Mrs. Minnie Eliza Pienkowski Buckley, p. 4.

New York. This friend talked Thaddeus and Emily into moving on the farm and becoming partners. Neither Thaddeus nor Emily knew anything about dairy farming but decided to give it a try and moved in the spring. The first two years on the farm went very good. The crops were good and Thaddeus developed an interest in raising livestock. Emily became an expert in making butter and cooking. A daughter, Ellen Catherine, was born to the Pienkowskis on Christmas day 1839. A couple weeks after Ellen was born, Emily came down with rheumatoid arthritis and was sick all winter.

The Pienkowskis had a real bad spring. Thaddeus had trusted his partner with the farm's finances. His partner never really paid Thaddeus any money during the last two years. Thaddeus asked him a number of times but the partner always had some excuse and assured him there would soon be money. Thaddeus later found out that his partner had lost some money in a business deal with another friend. One day a neighbor came over and told Emily she heard that a sheriff auction would sell the Pienkowski farm tomorrow (a foreclosure). The sheriff showed up the next day. The so-called partner had already sold the farmland but everything else was slotted for auction. Thaddeus's partner had also taken some of the livestock away before the auction and sold them, pocketing all the money. He told Thaddeus not to worry about the auction, that it was a normal thing in this country. After selling all the farm implements, livestock, grain, etc., the sale moved inside the house. The Pienkowskis' personal possessions were next. The Pienkowskis now knew what was really going on and that the partner had lied to them about everything. The Pienkowskis tell what happened next:

> Then God spoke through an old Quaker gentleman. First he demanded attention. When It was quiet he said, "Mr. Sheriff, this business stops right here. Any one who dares to disturb a thing in this house does it at his peril. This is the most shameful disgraceful piece of work that ever happened in this county. Not satisfied by robbing this family because my friend does not understand the tricks of this country, you enter the home and have not the decency to respect the suffering wife and helpless little children. I have seen more than I can stand today, and if one article is touched in this house by you men, I will prosecute you if it takes all I have. "Then repeating the words over and over "leave this house immediately" he ordered them out.[717]

[717] Mrs. Sarah Norton Lockhart Young and Mrs. Minnie Eliza Pienkowski Buckley, p. 7.

Thank God for the Quakers. The Pienkowskis barely knew him but he saved all their possessions. The same Quaker urged Thaddeus to buy his own farm. Thaddeus went back to New York to withdraw what money he still had in a bank there. The paper factory offered him his job back, but Thaddeus decided to go back into farming and bought a farm in Onondaga County. The first year on the farm produced a good crop and the year was very successful. The fall of the second year brought tragedy to the family. The Pienkowskis were using a thrashing machine to thrash their grain in the barn, the first time they had ever used one. The two boys, Eddy, now six years old, and Thomas, four, years old, were of course very curious to see such a machine. The boys were told to stay out of the barn while the machine was running. The men shut the machine down for a moment to switch over to a different grain. Thinking the thrashing done, Eddy ran into the barn just as a hired man threw a pitchfork full of straw out the barn door. He ran right into the pitchfork, getting stabbed in the temple. They sent for a doctor, but after seeing the wound, he said there was nothing he could do. Eddy died the next morning. Thaddeus would not go into the barn for weeks. Another son was born to the Pienkowskis that fall, Victor Alexander, born November 14, 1841.

The Pienkowskis farmed for another year, then sold the farm and moved to the city of Syracuse. There Thaddeus bought a cargo barge and hauled mainly salt to Buffalo, New York. He stayed at the freight business for a little over a year when Emily got sick. She was not expected to live but managed to pull out of it anyways. Next, their young son Victor caught a bad virus that crippled his leg. No doctors could cure him, and the Pienkowskis took a chance and hired an old Indian woman to try it. She lived with the family for three months and completely healed Victor. On January 9, 1843, Emily also gave birth to another son, Willis, who died the next day. Besides all this, someone burglarized the Pienkowskis' house. Emily wanted a change, so it was decided to go west in the spring.

The Pienkowskis headed for Wisconsin in the spring of 1843 via the Erie Canal and by schooner on the great lakes. The trip took three weeks. Bad weather prevented landing in South Port (Kenosha), so the schooner headed to the port of Racine, about ten miles north. After landing, they were contacted by friends from Salem, Wisconsin, who invited them to stay in their house. Thaddeus found some land to rent near Salem within a few days of their arrival. Salem is close to the Illinois state line and about fifteen miles from Lake Michigan. The Pienkowski family stayed with their friends for the time being. The next year Thaddeus found a different farm to rent some distance from Salem. This one had a small house on it. They had a prosperous year but decided to move to a farm closer to a school and church.

The farm's owner wanted them to stay and offered to give them the farm if they would look after him. He was old and did not want to leave the farm to his only relative. Years later, Thaddeus and Emily declared that moving from this farm was one of their worst blunders.

In November 1844, one of the Polish exiles from Trieste paid Thaddeus a visit. The exile had recently purchased a large farm about eight miles east of Salem near Bristol, Wisconsin.[718] The manuscript does not record who it was, but it must have been Pavel Sobolewski. The 1850 Federal Census for Kenosha County, Wisconsin, shows Pavel living near Bristol, Wisconsin.[719] Pavel was one of the 234 Polish exiles from Trieste and would become one of the most famous exiles. You can read more about him in my story about Boone County. Pavel had made a lot of money in the east and had bought himself a large farm and wanted to go into partnership with Thaddeus. Thaddeus and Emily still had bad memories from their last partnership and declined Pavel's offer. They did agree to run the farm on shares. Shares means that Thaddeus operates the farm while Pavel supplies the land, fertilizer, seed, etc. They split the profits. The Pienkowskis moved into a large log cabin located on Pavel's land and went to work. Much of the farm had not been cultivated yet and the soil was very fertile. Another son, George Anthony, was born in the cabin on December 11, 1844. They moved to a newly built one-and-a-half-story frame house in the spring and would live there for the next four years. Another son, Robert Samual, was born there on November 30, 1846.

The Pienkowskis lived on the prairie in Wisconsin and encountered the same problems as Illinois pioneers did. The occasional Prairie fire, bad roads, cold winters, sickness, and the like. In addition, the prairie was overrun with deer, rattlesnakes, coyotes, and wolves, plus the usual birds and small game. Thaddeus always said the nightly howling of the grey wolf reminded him of an incident in Poland. When Thaddeus was a young boy, he went to town with one of his brother's peasants. It was winter and they were carrying some beef to sell in town. According to Thaddeus, "While driving along, all at once the shrill cry of a wolf was heard immediately behind us. Although we went at full speed, we were soon overtaken. The wolf jumped into the sleigh and fortunately went to work on the meat instead of us. We of course had no weapons, it being against the law to carry any, and we dared not move to show any signs of life, not even to look behind us. Finally the wolf managed

---

718 Mrs. Sarah Norton Lockhart Young and Mrs. Minnie Eliza Pienkowski Buckley, p. 10.

719 1850 Federal Census of Kenosha County, Wisconsin: [National Archives, Box 432 Roll 1000, Page 210]

to get a quarter of beef out of the sleigh onto the ground." The wolf's howling attracted more wolves, and soon other wolf packs came on the scene. It was full speed ahead for Thaddeus and the peasant. They made it to town safely and from then on Thaddeus was terrified of wolves. He later claimed that fighting on the battlefield was nothing as compared to the thought of being eaten by wolves.[720]

Thaddeus bought his own farm in 1848. This was the farm on the Illinois-Wisconsin state line. It was 120 acres in size but had no house. The owner of the farm next door invited them to move into his cabin until they could build their own house. While living in the cabin, a new son, Edward Thaddeus, was born to them on February 25, 1849. The Pienkowskis could not get along with the farmer's hired man and moved to the new house before it was finished. There were still no doors or windows in the new house, but they hung up blankets and carpets. None of the land on this farm had ever been cultivated, and fourteen-year-old Thomas had to use five yoke of oxen to plow it all up. They moved in November 1850 and were all glad to be out of the cabin and into their own house. Grandma Elizabeth Norton lived two more years after moving into the new house, dying September 27, 1852.[721]

The schoolhouse was two miles away. During bad weather, however, Thaddeus would have to take all his and the neighbor's children to school by wagon. Thaddeus was also the commissioner of roads and a school director. Five more daughters were born in the new house, Elizabeth Theresa, born February 3, 1851; Adeline Emilia, born December 27, 1853; and Minnie, born April 25, 1856. The last two, Leah Rosetta, born April 6, 1858, and Edith Evelyn, born February 3, 1859, each died before they were a year old. A bad epidemic of bloody dysentery broke out in the area in the fall of 1857. Almost every family lost someone to the sickness, and eight of the Pienkowski children came down with it. Sixteen-year-old Victor died on October 21, 1857. A doctor actually declared Minnie dead, but she surprised everyone and survived. In addition, the crops were also bad. During this time, Thaddeus and Emily converted to the Baptist faith. Their new preacher had to chop a hole in the ice of the Des Plaines River in order to baptize them. I hope they didn't have to stand in the river to get baptized. I think I'd wait until summer myself. The church was supposed to be in Illinois. Your author grew up a block away from the Des Plains River.

---

720 Mrs. Sarah Norton Lockhart Young and Mrs. Minnie Eliza Pienkowski Buckley, p. 2 & 3.

721 South Bristol Cemetery in Bristol Township Kenosha County Wisconsin: [Records kept by Samuel Kempf, Kenosha, Wisconsin. P. 7.

The next year was not much better. The crops failed again. No money came in but plenty went out to pay bills. Thaddeus had to borrow money to keep afloat. Instead of borrowing from a bank, Thaddeus went to a lawyer in Kenosha whom he must have thought was a friend. Loan shark would be a better description. The loan was due in the fall. Thaddeus intended to pay the loan off from the sale of his grain crop but could not harvest the crop because of wet weather. Thaddeus was not worried though. The lawyer had told him when he got the loan that he could pay it back when he had the money. Thaddeus and a friend hauled a newly thrashed load of wheat to Kenosha and sold it. Afterwards he went straight to the lawyer's office and paid off the loan. After taking Thaddeus's money, the lawyer told him the loan was past due. Thaddeus thought he was joking until the police came and took his team of horses and wagon. Thaddeus was devastated. His friend managed to find a ride to Bristol but had to practically pick up Thaddeus and throw him into the wagon. Thaddeus was so upset he was still standing in the same spot where the police had taken his team. The next day was even worse. The police came out to the farm and took all the livestock. Thaddeus's neighbors came to his aid the following day and helped thrash the remaining wheat crop. Thaddeus was able to buy another team and wagon with the profits from the wheat.

The problems did not end there; they were also behind on the farm mortgage payment. A man named Mason held the mortgage on the farm. Thaddeus went to see him and thought he had worked out a deal to pay only the mortgage interest for the time being. Thaddeus later found out that someone from Kenosha was trying to persuade Mason to sell him the farm. Thaddeus went back to Mason to find out just what was going on. Mason had changed his mind and told him that if the mortgage was not paid on time, he would sell the farm. Mason then chewed out Thaddeus for being crazy enough to send his kids off to school in the city. Then Mason went on, "I can't read or write my own name and my youngsters can't either but we have made lots of money. This education is all nonsense."[722] The neighbors soon found out and offered to help raise the needed money. Emily also suggested they ask a friend named Delos Larabee for help. Delos secured enough money to pay off Mason and Thaddeus was back in business. Delos was soon paid back everything, interest included. That was the last time they ever owed money to anyone.

[722] Mrs. Sarah Norton Lockhart Young and Mrs. Minnie Eliza Pien Kowski Buckley, p. 15

Thaddeus died December 14, 1868. Emily rented the farm out and moved to Kenosha so Adeline and Minnie could go to high school. All the boys were already gone and working in town. Apparently, none wanted to farm. Son Robert was an aspiring businessman in Princeton, Illinois, where he died on February 11, 1875. Emily eventually sold the farm. Part of the payment for the farm included a brick house at Grand Avenue and Ash Street in Waukegan. My great-grandmother lived a couple blocks away from there. Emily died on November 10, 1884. She was survived by Thomas, George, Edward, Sarah, Ellen, Elizabeth, Adeline, and Minnie. The *Daughters of the American Revolution Lineage Book* contains the names of Ellen, Elizabeth, Adeline, and Minnie.[723] The 1943 *Who's Who in Polish America* lists Arthur Thaddeus Pienkowski. He was a physicist and in education: Arthur earned a PhD from the University of Chicago in 1898 and was a high school teacher in Illinois and Indiana during the years 1898-1903. He was also a physicist at the U.S. Bureau of Standards in 1906.[724] I have to thank Mrs. Mary Ann Cole, of Kenosha, Wisconsin, for all her help with this story. Two of Thaddeus's descendants were also most helpful. Robert Pienkowski, of Blacksburg, Virginia, sent me the *Life Sketch of the Pienkowski Family*. His brother Steven, of St. Charles, Illinois, invited me to his home to discuss the Pienkowski family history. Al Westerman was particularly helpful for sending me his stories about the first Polish landowners in Lake County.

723 Daughters of the American Revolution Lineage Book: [Volumes V11, C, XXX11, XC1X and LXV]

724 The Rev. Francis Bolek, Who's who in Polish America: [New York: Harbinger House 1943] p. 346.

LaSalle County

LaSalle County had three Poles and possibly two others before 1850. John Morris, Aaron Neustadt. and a Mr. Oppenheim all list Poland as place of birth. They were all most likely Polish Jews. There might have been two Russians living there too. My book concerns Poles, not Russians, but finding any Russians in Illinois before 1850 is rare.

LaSalle became a county on January 15, 1831, from parts of Vermillion and Putnam counties. Ottawa is the county seat. LaSalle County is located in northern Illinois in the center of the state. The Illinois River flows through the middle of the county. Two large rivers, the Fox and the Vermillion, flow into the Illinois River there. The banks along the Illinois River have sandstone bluffs up to 140 feet high, making this part of the river very scenic. Starved Rock state park is also located there. I will write more about Starved Rock later.

The French were the first white men in LaSalle County. Father Jacques Marquette and Louis Joliet landed at the "Grand Kaskaskia Indian Village" near the present town of Utica in 1673. The village contained seventy-four lodges and a population of twelve hundred. The Indians were members of the twelve-tribe Illinois Confederacy. The Confederacy controlled most of Illinois and parts of Iowa, Missouri, and Arkansas. Marquette and Joliet did not stay permanently, but told the Indians they would be back to start a trading post. They came back in 1675 and built a mission and trading post. Between Marquette and Joliet's first and second trip, eleven of the twelve Confederacy tribes had moved to Grand Kaskaskia Village in anticipation of the trading post. By 1680, the village contained 460 lodges.

In September 1680, an Iroquois war party showed up at the Grand Kaskaskia Village. Most of the Illinois warriors were gone at the time. The village's inhabitants fled west to the Mississippi River. The Iroquois razed the village, and then came in pursuit. Three Illinois tribes were caught at the junction of the Illinois and Mississippi rivers. Many were killed or captured. One of the tribes, the Espeminkia, was never heard of again.

In 1682, the French built Fort Saint Lewis on top of a high bluff now known as Starved Rock. The site of the now destroyed Grand Kaskaskia Village was nearby. The Illinois tribes soon regrouped across the Illinois River from the fort and built a new village. Other bands of non-Illinois Confederacy tribes fleeing the Iroquois also joined them. The new village could boast four thousand warriors. Unfortunately, the tribes could not get along with each other. By 1689, all the non-Illinois Confederacy tribes had left. The whole village was vacated in 1691 and rebuilt farther down the river. The French fort and trading post moved with them and set up close by. Now friction started to develop between the Confederacy tribes. The tribes who had converted to Christianity could not get along with those tribes who had not.

In 1700, the Christian tribes moved to Southern Illinois. The Peoria and Moingwena tribes stayed behind. The Moingwena soon merged with the Peoria. The Peoria managed to hold on until 1769. That year, an assassin from the Kaskaskia Tribe in Southern Illinois murdered Pontiac, a popular chief of the Ottawa Tribe. The Ottawa were not members of the Illinois Confederacy. To avenge Pontiac, the Pottowatomi, Ottawa, Chippewa, Fox, Winnebago, and other tribes attacked the Peoria. According to the *Handbook of North American Indians*, "a war of extermination was begun which, in a few years, reduced them to a mere handful, who took refuge with the French settlers at Kaskaskia while the Sauk, Foxes, Kickapoo and Potawatomi took possession of their country."[725] The siege at Starved Rock occurred at this time. The Peoria lost a battle to the northern alliance and retreated to the top of a large rock on the banks of the Illinois River. The rock is 125 feet tall and the top about an acre in size. The summit can only be reached after a very strenuous climb up one side. The northern alliance decided to starve the Peoria out and stopped all food and water from reaching them. Before long, the Peoria were starving. Many died but one group tried to escape, and according to Baldwin, on "a dark and stormy night, left their fastness, and encountered the foe; but being few in number and in a weakened condition, they were no match for their well fed, and numerous enemies, and were soon dispatched; but it is said that in the darkness and confusion, a few individuals escaped."[726]

Those who escaped made their way to the Mississippi River and crossed to the other side. There is some dispute as to whether the events I just described ever happened. The Indians living here when the first white settlers arrived in the county completely believed it. The earliest white settlers claimed Starved Rock was littered with bones.

The remaining Peoria settled with the Confederacy tribes living near the town of Kaskaskia in Southern Illinois. French missionaries and settlers were

725 Handbook of American Indians north of Mexico: [part 1, Edited by Frederick Webb Hodge] [New York: Pageant Books, Inc. 1959] p. 598

726 Elmer Baldwin, History of La Salle County, Illinois: [Chicago: Rand, McNally & Co. 1877] p. 71.

also living in the area, mainly at Kaskaskia and a few other settlements along the Mississippi River. The French and Kaskaskia tribe had good relations. They frequently intermarried and were allies. Enemy tribes to the north and south of the Illinois continued the attacks. In 1714, sickness killed one-quarter of the Illinois. Alcoholism also became a problem. In 1832, the Illinois left the state and moved west. By 1850, all that was left of the once-powerful twelve-tribe Illinois Confederacy was eighty-four people.[727]

In 1762, the treaty of Fountain Bleau ceded everything east of the Mississippi River to Great Britain. After the French left, there were no white settlers in the county until 1823. Dr. Davidson came in the summer of that year and settled in south Ottawa. During this period, LaSalle County was a part of Peoria County. Large-scale emigration to the future LaSalle County did not begin until the end of the Winnebago Indian War of 1827. Most of the first settlers were from Southern Illinois or the south. New Englanders came next, but LaSalle County would end up with settlers from almost every state. Large numbers of Irish, Norwegians, and Germans followed next.

Some Russians were also supposed to be early settlers. This is unusual to see any Russians in the state at this time. I tried to find out who they were. According to Baldwin, John and Henry Sherman emigrated from Russia to LaSalle County in 1835.[728] *Biographical and Genealogical Record of LaSalle County* claims Henry and a Joseph Sherman were from Germany, not Russia.[729] There is a name on the 1840 LaSalle County Census that looks like a Russian name, Ivan Oskevith (Oskevich?). The 1840 census does not contain much more than head of household. He was between the ages of thirty and forty. His wife is also between the ages of thirty and forty. There are three sons and two daughters.[730] Enough of the sidetracking, this book is about Poles.

John Morris

John lived in the town of Peru. Peru was known as Salisbury when John first came to town and is located where the Illinois and Michigan Canal

727 History of St. Clair County, Illinois: [Philadelphia: Brink, McDonough & Co. 1881] p. 44.

728 Elmer Baldwin, History of LaSalle County Illinois: [Chicago: Rand, McNally & Co. 1877] p.428.

729 Biographical and Genealogical Record of LaSalle County Illinois: Volume 1, [Chicago: The Lewis Publishing Company 1900] p. 587 & 755.

730 1840 Federal Census of LaSalle County: [At the National Archives, Box 704 Roll 63 p. 137]

meets the Illinois River. It was platted in 1834 but did not become a city until 1851. By 1838, the population was 426, with most people working on the canal. Peru went through some tough times because of a national financial crisis starting in 1840. Many people in town lost their jobs and moved away. The town's population fell to two hundred. The good times came back when the financial crisis ended, and by 1844-45, Peru was almost a boomtown. The Illinois and Michigan Canal was finished in 1848 but was supposed to have helped the town of LaSalle more than Peru. LaSalle is located a very short distance east of Peru. They call both towns the "Twin Cities." The year 1849 brought some problems. In January, rain came down in torrents and the Illinois River overflowed its banks. Then frigid weather set in and the river froze. Heavy rains and warm temperatures in spring caused the ice to break up into large chunks. The swift current brought the chunks of ice crashing into buildings and knocked down everything in its path. Also in 1849, Peru had a bad episode with cholera which killed one-sixth of the population. Cholera left as fast as it came, and the population increased to about 3,000 in 1850. Peru's present population is 10,886.

John came to Peru by at least 1845 and possibly sooner. His occupation was a merchant. He married Esther Hobart McQuigg Slack in 1845-46. Esther was born in Spencer, Tioga County, New York, on August 8, 1814. It was her second marriage. Her first marriage was to Artemus Slack, who was killed in a railroad accident in 1843. Esther inherited some land Artemus owned in Peru and decided to move to Illinois with her son Archie.[731] The 1850 LaSalle County Census shows John's age as thirty-three, his occupation merchant, and born in Poland. His wife Esther is thirty-two and born in New York. Their son John is one year old and born in Illinois. Archibald Slack is seven years old. It also looks like John was running a boarding house. Living at the Morris home were

> Catherine Matroin, 22 years old, born in Germany.
> Emily Curtis, 23, born in New York.
> Charles Vose, 17 years old. His occupation is clerk and he was born in New York.
> Charles Hewlet, 17 years old, and born in New York.[732]

731 Morris file: [La Salle County Genealogy Guild, Ottawa, Illinois] [Letter from Karen S. Dickenson to Jenan Jobst]

732 The 1850 Federal Census of LaSalle County, Illinois: [Yakima, Washington: Yakima Valley Genealogical Society] p. 219.

I have found a few records of John H. Morris buying land in LaSalle County starting December 18, 1839.[733] John would have been only twenty-two years old in 1839. If this is the same John Morris, he might be the first Polish Jew to settle in Illinois. There are two entries of John Morris buying land in Peru in 1850.[734] *The Past and Present of La Salle County, Illinois* shows a John Morris elected councilman of the Second Ward in 1851.[735] John and Esther had three children, all boys. The oldest boy John died young. The other two boys, Robert and Edward, were twins. John and his stepson Archibald went to mine for gold in Wyoming in 1868. They sent for the family the next year.[736]

Neustadt

The Neustadts became a very well-known family in the town of La Salle and the surrounding area for years. La Salle is also located where the Illinois and Michigan Canal meets the Illinois River. The first white settler was Simon Crozier, who lived and traded with the Indians. Samuel Lapsley was next, settling in 1830. Some of the first settlers were killed off by Indians during the Black Hawk War in 1832. About one hundred pioneers came during the winter months of 1837-38. La Salle's population was about two hundred by the fall of 1838, but many of them died when some type of fever came through. Despite everything, the town was platted in 1837 and lots sold in 1838. Pooley has an interesting comment about La Salle. "Its two-hundred inhabitants were, according to accounts, of none too good a class." One traveler says that upon inquiry at one or two of the stores he "ascertained that there were Christians in the place."[737] Many of the canal workers lived in La Salle, and the town continued to grow. The 1840 financial crisis hurt La Salle hard, but the town came on strong at the end of the crisis. The local grain trade chose to ship their crop from La Salle rather than Peru. Two different railroads were constructed through La Salle in 1853-54. The canal and railroads soon made La Salle the transportation hub of the region. Industry gravitated to La Salle not only because of the great transportation opportunities but also

---

733 LaSalle County Recorder of Deeds, Ottawa, Illinois: [Book 4, p.93]

734 LaSalle County Recorder of Deeds, Book 20, p. 511 &512.

735 The Past and Present of LaSalle County, Illinois: [Chicago: H. F. Kett & Co., 1877] p. 309.

736 Morris file: [La Salle County Genealogy Guild, Ottawa, Illinois]

737 William V. Pooley, The Settlement of Illinois from 1830 to 1850: [Madison, Wisconsin: May, 1908] [Ann Arbor, Michigan: University Microfilms 1968] p. 103.

to take advantage of the large coal fields situated nearby. La Salle's current population is 10, 347.

Aaron Neustadt is first mentioned on the 1850 census. He is thirty-six years old and his occupation is merchant. Aaron was born in Poland and was living at a hotel owned by John H. McFarren. Another resident of the hotel has the name Oppenheim. He is a merchant and lists Germany as place of birth.[738] He might have been born in Poland because the 1850 census for the town of Ottawa lists three Oppenheims, no first names. All are clerks and born in Poland.[739]

The big story about the Neustadts is not Aaron but rather Robert M. Neustadt, a pioneer businessman of La Salle. The 1850 census is the only information I have about Aaron, but the Neustadt file at the La Salle County Genealogical Society is full of information about Robert. I am not sure what the relationship was between Aaron and Robert. Aaron was much older and might have been Robert's uncle.

Robert was born April 6, 1854, in Koobytan, Kries Krotoschin, Posen Province, Germany. Posen is in Poland. Robert came to America when he was fourteen years old with his mother; his father was already dead. They went to Chicago first, but soon moved to Galva, Illinois, where Robert found employment in a clothing store. I have been to Galva, and it is a small town located right in the middle of farm country. Robert worked there a few years, then went back to Chicago. He did not stay in Chicago long and moved to the city of La Salle in 1874 and worked at his uncle's clothing store. His uncle was a partner in the Bergheim & Lachmann Clothing Store. His uncle was Bergheim. Robert bought out his uncle the next year and went into a partnership with Lachmann that lasted until 1889. After Lachmann left, Robert named his store the Golden Eagle. He was now in total control of the store and implemented all of his own concepts, with a heavy emphasis on all forms of advertising. Before long, everyone within forty miles knew about the store. The Golden Eagle grew so fast that Robert had to build a new building within two years and an even bigger store in 1893. This last store was state-of-the-art for its day. It was a magnificent, massive two-story building which employed sixteen people. Robert also built himself a fine house on the same block as the store. The *La Salle Tribune* wrote in 1911, "The Golden Eagle has always been noted for its square dealing, and this has been a great factor in its growth and prosperity."[740]

---

738 The 1850 Federal Census of LaSalle County, p. 61.

739 The 1850 Federal Census of LaSalle County, p. 218.

740 The La Salle Tribune Newspaper, [Twentieth Anniversary Edition July, 1911]

Robert married Rosa Auerbach in 1879. They had four children together. David, born in1880. Bertold, born 1881. George, born in 1886. And Jean, born in 1890.[741] His sons continued to work in the clothing business. Robert died on December 22, 1941.[742] Rosa died February 19, 1946.[743] According to Robert's obituary in the *Daily Post-Tribune Newspaper*,

> Mr. Neustadt was of a friendly nature and numbered hundred's from all sections of the Illinois Valley among his acquaintances. He has been assisted in the management of the local store by his son, Bert R. Neustadt. For more than 65 years a member of the La Salle lodge of Odd Fellows. Mr. Neustadt was presented with a 65-year jewel by members of the lodge at a meeting last week. Mr. Nuestadt of course was unable to be present at the ceremonies because of his illness.
>
> He was for 60 years a member of DeSoto lodge, Knights of Pythisa, and had been quite active in the program of that organization. Mr. Neustadt was a stockholder and at the time of his death, president of the La Salle Inn company, owners of the Hotel Kaskaskia building. He was a member of the Illinois Valley manufacturers club, Illinois Chapter, B'nai Brith, and Temple B'nai Moshe, La Salle.[744]

It is not possible to know if Oskevith was a Russian. John Morris seems to be an enterprising person. He worked as a merchant and conducted a boarding house. Robert Neustadt had to have been the most widely known Polish Jew in the county. I have not found any other information about the Oppenheims.

741 Letter from Stephen F. Wheeler to Jean Jobst of the La Salle County Genealogy Guild: [In the Neustadt file at the La Salle County Genealogy Guild, Ottawa, Illinois]

742 The Daily Post-Tribune Newspaper, La Salle, Illinois: December 22, 1941.

743 The Daily Post Tribune Newspaper: February 19, 1946.

744 The Daily Post-Tribune Newspaper, La Salle, Illinois: December 22, 1941.

Lee County

Lee County had one Polish settler before 1850, Mikolay Jaworski. Mikolay was born in Warsaw on May 30, 1803.[745] He changed his name to Nicholas in America, so I will refer to him as Nicholas from now on. Nicholas was a soldier in the 1830 Polish insurrection. He was one of the 234 Polish exiles from Triest, which landed in New York City March 28, 1834.[746] Nicholas was also a veteran of the United States Army and the Mexican War. Nicholas settled in Wyoming Township, Lee County, by at least August 1848.[747]

Lee County was created from Ogle County February 27, 1839. It is sixty-two miles west of Chicago. According to Al Westerman, Lee County was Indian Territory until the Treaty of Chicago September 26, 1833.The treaty forced the Potawatomi, Ottawa, and Chippewa Indian tribes to cede their land to the federal government. The land was located in the present states of Illinois and Wisconsin. It consisted of five million acres in northeastern and north-central Illinois and southeastern and south central Wisconsin. The tribes were paid fourteen and one-half cents an acre and resettled on land west of the Mississippi River.[748]

Most of Lee County was prairie. The wooded tracts were alongside rivers or in groves scattered throughout the prairie. The two main rivers are the Rock and Green. The Green River originates in Lee County while the Rock River enters from the north. The Polish land grant was located farther north along the Rock River in Winnebago County. To find out more about the Polish land grant, you will have to read my story about Winnebago County.

---

745 Lee County Genealogical Society: Dixon, Illinois [Cemetery Records 1997] p. 435.

746 Mieczyslaw Haiman, Slady Polskie W Ameryce: [Chicago, Illinois: Drukiem Dziennika Zjednoczenia, 1938] p. 124.

747 National Archives and Records Administration, 700 Pennsylvania Ave. Washington D. C. [Nicholas Jaworski file] [F368311, 000125]

748 Al Westerman, Public Domain Land Sales in Lake County, Illinois, [Al Westerman 2006] p. 8.

Nicholas lived in Wyoming Township, which is located in the eastern section of Lee County. Wyoming Township was known for Paw Paw Grove, a two-thousand-acre forest in the middle of the prairie. Paw Paw Grove was named after the pawpaw tree. This tree needs a lot of sunlight and usually grows on the edge of the forest, and its fruit was known as the poor man's banana.[749] After a trip on the prairie, Paw Paw Grove was a welcome sight. It must have stood out like an oasis. The grove was full of the most valuable types of trees and a spring with exceptional water was located on the east side of the grove. Bardwell has a small comment about Paw Paw Grove.

> In 1840, Paw Paw Grove was the focus of the largest settlement in the county—Dixon and, possibly Sugar Grove, in Palmyra, excepted. This is accounted for by two facts: that it was on the stage road from Chicago to Galena, and also was one of the largest, most beautiful and attractive pieces of timber in all the county. All the early settlers sought the shelter and other advantages of groves, and were slow to reach out for the now valuable prairie lands.[750]

The first white settlers to arrive at Paw Paw Grove were Levi Kelsey and Joel Griggs. They came during the winter of 1833-34. After building a cabin, they abruptly left because they thought the cabin was on an Indian reservation. The first permanent settler was David A. Town. He came in the fall of 1834 with his wife and four children. They settled on the east side of the grove.

Three different villages sprang up around Paw Paw Grove. On the west side of the grove was the village of West Paw Paw. West Paw Paw was platted August 1, 1871, and renamed Paw Paw Grove. South of the grove was the village of South Paw Paw. It was located in DeKalb County on the boundary line of Lee and DeKalb counties. To the east of the grove was the village of East Paw Paw. Our story about Nicholas Jaworski takes place in this area. East Paw Paw was located in both Lee and DeKalb counties. In 1840, thirteen families lived in the Lee side and five on the DeKalb side. Stevens wrote, "So late as the spring of 1847, the place contained but half a dozen families and its business interests all were comprised in the smithy and a shingle mill. But

---

749 Roger B. Yepsen, Jr., Trees for the Yard, Orchard, and Woodlot: [Emmaus, Pennsylvania: Rodale Press, Inc. 1976] p. 124-125.

750 1904 History of Lee County Illinois: [Edited by A. C. Bardwell] [Chicago: Munsell Publishing Company, 1904] p. 700.

beginning with this year the settlers came in rapidly and the place showed rapid improvement."[751] East Paw Paw's name was changed to Wyoming in 1850.The township was also renamed Wyoming on May 14, 1851.

Paw Paw Grove was an attractive place for everyone. The Indians loved it. Wyoming Township contained more Indians than any other part of Lee County when the first whites arrived. The Indian burial ground was located in the southeastern section of Paw Paw Grove. Shabona and Waubansie, two of the most famous chiefs in northern Illinois, lived there as well. Bardwell claims,

> In 1834 a thousand Indians were encamped for a week at the Big Spring, at the northwest corner of the grove. They were being moved from Indiana west, and the Government made them a payment here. The local Indians had already been sent to their western reservation the same year, but the old chief Shabbona, who is held in grateful memory for the protection he afforded the settlement in the days of the Black Hawk Wăr, afterwards returned to the scenes of his early life and died on the Illinois River July 17, 1859, aged eighty-four.[752]

Outlaws liked Paw Paw Grove too. After northern Illinois was open to settlement, four of the newly created counties had a large amount of criminal activity. Lee, Ogle, Winnebago, and DeKalb counties were dangerous places in the 1830s and 1840s. Ogle County, which is north of Lee County, was supposed to be the worst. Paw Paw Grove was a favorite destination for horse thieves. Bardwell wrote, "As a settler of 1837 put it: Paw Paw was a strange place then. It seemed to me that every other man I met was hunting a horse thief, and you couldn't tell which was the thief-generally it was both."[753]

The settlers reacted to crime by forming vigilante bands like the "Ogle County Lynching Club" and the Regulators. These groups combed the area looking for bandits. Anyone suspected of criminal activity was given the option of leaving the county in thirty days or be hanged. Stevens writes, "David A Town was the terror to horse thieves and the Banditti, and for that more than any other reason, early Paw Paw was not much disturbed."[754]

751 Frank E. Stevens, History of Lee County Illinois, Volume 1: [Chicago: S. J. Clarke Publishing Company, 1914] p. 505.

752 1904 History of Lee County, Illinois, p. 700.

753 1904 History of Lee County, Illinois, p. 700.

754 Frank E. Stevens, p. 500.

David A. Town as I wrote earlier was the first permanent settler in Paw Paw Grove. Crime had largely been cleaned up by the time Nicholas came on the scene in 1848.

In Lee County records, Nicholas's last name is spelled Jawoski, Jawaski, or Jewaska. It was not until I sent away for Nicholas's military records that I found out the right spelling. Nicholas must have liked military life since he enlisted three different times in the United States Army. According to Maria J. R. Copson-Niecko, Nicholas enlisted in the army six weeks after arriving in New York and joined the Second New York Infantry on May 12, 1834. He enlisted for a term of three years. His enlistment papers give his age as twenty-four and born in Warsaw. His occupation is soldier. He was discharged three years later on May 12, 1837. Nicholas spent the next two years in civilian life but enlisted in the army again on March 27, 1839. He joined in Dearbornville, Michigan, this time and signed up for a five-year term. Nicholas spent his second enlistment in an artillery unit and was discharged at Fort Columbus, New York, on March 26, 1844. His five-year enlistment completed. A little over a year of civilian life must have been too much for Nicholas and he enlisted in the army for a third time in Buffalo, New York, on May 5, 1845. Nicholas signed up for five more years. He was forty-two years old and ordered back to the Second New York Infantry, the same unit he first served in. Nicholas remained in the Second New York until his discharge February 23, 1848, at the rank of corporal. All together Nicholas served about eleven years in the United States Army.[755]

Nicholas was discharged in Mexico City during the Mexican War. His military career ended when he sustained a wound on August 20, 1847, at the battle of Churousco. It is hard to read the medical description of his injury, but it appears to have been an eye injury. Nicholas was awarded a disability pension of four dollars a month. A full disability pension was eight dollars a month at the time.

After his discharge, Nicholas lived in New York a short time before going to Lee County, Illinois. On August 12, 1848, Justice of the Peace Isaac Harding wrote a letter to the Department of the Interior asking them to send Nicholas's military pension to Illinois. On the same letter is the name of John Edwards. John declared, "He is personally acquainted with Nicholas Jaworski and knows him to be the same person described in the above affidavit."[756]

---

755 Maria J. E. Copson-Niecko, The Poles in America from the 1830's to 1870's: [Frank Mocha, Poles in America Bicentennial Essays: Stevens Point, Wisconsin: Worzalla Publishing Company 1978] p. 184 & 286.

756 National Archives and Records Administration, [Nicholas Jaworski file]

This will not be the last time we see John Edwards's name. In a letter to the Department of the Interior on May 24, 1849, Nicholas wrote that he "located my bounty land in the state of Illinois."[757]

It looks like Nicholas might have been married when he first came out to Lee County, or was married soon after arriving. The only records I have to prove it are Lee County Cemetery records. The records show three Jaworskis buried in Wyoming Township, Nicholas, Laura, and Martha. There is not much to write about Laura or Martha. There is no date of birth for either of them. The date of Laura's death is June 19, 1850. The cemetery records also write that Martha "could not read." Because Martha could not read, she must be Nicholas's wife. Neither one's tombstone is readable. Laura's tombstone is larger than Martha's. My theory is that the recently married Martha died in childbirth or shortly thereafter. For some reason, Nicholas is not buried with his family. He was buried in Hasting's Cemetery[758] while Laura and Martha were buried in Wyoming Cemetery.[759]

Nicholas was living with the John Edwards family on the 1850 Federal Census of Lee County.[760] I cannot determine if Nicholas continued living at the Edwards home or returned to his farm. Nicholas's farm was next door to John Edwards's farm.[761] According to Lee County Probate Records, Nicholas lived at least the last sixty-two weeks of his life at the Edwards house and was paying the Edwardses for room and board. From March 7, 1854, to May 29, 1855, the Edwardses nursed Nicholas who was sick and dying. During the last four months of his life, he paid an extra twenty-five cents a night for "attending on him during his sickness." Nicholas also paid Mrs. Edwards seventy-five cents a week for "washing and mending" his clothes.

Nicholas hired Daniel Harris to work his farm for him while he was sick. Harris did not get paid until after Nicholas died. The money came from Nicholas's estate. Harris earned twenty-two cents for one day of planting corn. He spent ten days harvesting corn and was paid one dollar a day. Six days of work husking corn amounted to four dollars and fifty cents.[762] The 1850 Agriculture Census of Lee County shows that Nicholas had fifty-two

---

757 National Archives and Records Administration, [Nicholas Jaworski file]

758 Lee County Genealogical Society, Cemetery Records p. 435.

759 Lee County Genealogical Society, Wyoming Cemetery Records p. 5.

760 Marjorie Smith, Lee County, Illinois 1850 Census: [Thomson, Illinois: Heritage House 1972] p. 51.

761 1850 Illinois Agricultural Census: [T1133, No. 2]

762 Lee County Clerk, Probate Records: [Lee County Courthouse, Dixon, Illinois [Nicholas Jaworski file]

tillable acres and twenty-eight unimproved acres. Unimproved acres are usually pasture or hayfields. He had four oxen but no horses. Oxen were used to plow virgin prairie because they are much stronger. His farm produced 235 bushels of wheat, 70 bushels of corn, and 8 tons of hay. The farm was valued at $450.[763] James Woodbridge bought Nicholas's farm for $950 five years later. Nicholas never left a will, and John Edwards was appointed executor of the estate.

Nicholas died May 29, 1855. For eight weeks starting May 3, 1860, the *Amboy Times* ran a notice about Nicholas's estate. The notice stated that the estate of Nicholas Jawaski has a balance of $724.29. Anyone with any claims to the estate has six months to show proof. After six months, the balance of the estate will be paid to the Lee County Treasury. By November 28, 1860, no claims had been made on Nicholas's estate, and John Edwards turned the money over to the Lee County Treasurer.[764]

Before I end, let me write a little about John Edwards. *History of Lee County 1881* wrote,

> John Edwards resides at East Paw Paw. For six terms he was elected supervisor of Wyoming, and has served nineteen years as commissioner of highways here. He was born in the parish of Locherly, county of Hampshire, England, November 21, 1821. His parents names were William and Phebe. They were poor, and labored upon a farm. His school privileges were quite limited. In 1837 he sailed for the Island of Barbadoes, in the West Indies, where he was two years in the service of the British government, in the navy yard, and taking care of navel stores. Thence he went to Canada, where he was still employed by the government, at Montreal and Quebec. A year and a half later he came to Syracuse, New York, worked in the county, and in the spring of 1846 enlisted in the United States Army, 5th Inf. His regiment joined Gen. Worth's division, under Gen. Scott, at Vera Cruz, in the Mexican war, and was in all the engagements that followed to the capture of the city of Mexico. A ball from a sharpshooter took off his forefinger here. Each man wounded in entering the capital was presented by Gen. Scott with $10 from his own purse. Mr. Edwards received his discharge February 22, 1848, with a pension certificate

[763] 1850 Illinois Agricultural Census: [T1133, No. 2]

[764] Lee County Clerk, Probate Records: [Lee County Courthouse, Dixon, Illinois [Nicholas Jaworski file]

> for $96 a year, and a land warrant. The latter he soon after located in Wyoming, on Sec. 6. In September, 1848, he married Eliza Ann, daughter of Henry Merwine, of East Paw Paw. They have three children. Mr. Edwards is a member of the Methodist Episcopal church, and a worker in the Sunday school.[765]

History of Lee County 1881 also went on the say that during the Civil War, John drilled the Union League. The Union League was organized in 1862 and consisted of about seventy of the local citizens. Its mission was to protect the area in case of an attack by the Confederacy.[766] John died in July 1890. He was seventy years old and living in Paw Paw at the time. His obituary from the Dixon Telegraph writes that, John "was much respected throughout the County."[767]

I have not been able to find the cause of death for any of the Jaworskis. It seems civilian life never agreed with Nicholas. His time spent in Illinois did not work out either. John Edwards played a big role in Nicholas's life in Illinois from beginning to end. Both were wounded in action. Both had disability pensions. John Edwards was discharged from the army February 22, 1848, and Nicholas Jaworski on February 23, 1848. They could have known each other in Mexico City. Did they come out to Illinois together to claim their land warrant too? Did each one marry a local girl? Now I am really speculating. The appraiser's bill for the estate of Nicholas Jaworski lists a Polish Bible. Its value was appraised at one dollar and fifty cents.[768] Perhaps that Bible will turn up in someone's attic someday.

765 History of Lee County: [Chicago: H. H. Hill and Company, 1881] p. 699-700.

766 History of Lee County, 1881 p. 775.

767 Dixon Telegraph, July 23, 1890 p. 1. Column 2.

768 Lee County Probate file, [Nicholas Jaworski file] Dixon, Illinois

Logan County

Logan County had two Polish/German families, the Wodetzkis/Wodeskis and the Seicks. Both families were related. It appears that the Wodetzkis and Seicks were a Polish-German combination. The Seicks were first on the scene, settling in 1840. The Wodetzkis came in 1847. I was completely surprised to find the Wodeski name in the 1850 census. My family's last name has undergone many changes in spelling since we have been here. Wodeski was probably the most common, until Lodesky became the permanent spelling. In Poland, the Wodeskis wrote their name as Wodetzki. Our last name is impossible to spell or pronounce correctly in English, and I would need a Polish typewriter to spell it right. The name Wodetzki is the closest pronunciation of my family name from Polish to English. Our last name probably should have been spelled this way too.

I immediately thought the Wodeskis could be relatives. You might be wondering why I would be so surprised to find someone with a last name this similar to ours. At the present time, a little over fifty people out of forty million Poles use our last name. The Wodetzkis came to Illinois in the 1840s as we did, and they were Polish nobility. The similarity ends there, however. After researching them, it is doubtful we are related. The Wodetzkis were from Gdansk (Danzig). Most of the Wodetzkis living in Poland at the present time live in the northwest part of Poland not far from Gdansk. We lived in Southeastern Poland, in the region known as Podolia. This area is located in the present Ukraine. We were members of the Clan SAS, which is native to Eastern Poland (Ukraine). Clan insignia is similar to a coat of arms. If it turned out that the Wodetzkis in Logan County used SAS, I wound consider them relatives. In Poland, our families would have lived hundreds of miles from each other.

Logan County was created from parts of Sangamon and Tazewell counties on February 15, 1839, and is located in the center of the state. Mt. Pulaski is the county seat. About one-fifth of the area was wooded when first settled, the rest prairie. The wooded areas were along streams or in groves. Since most of the county was prairie, most everything written about it in the county histories concerns the prairie. According to Samuel Hoblit, "no one who had not seen it could imagine the beauty of the primeval landscape, the undulating wave of prairie grass with light and shadow on its surface; the brilliance of every variety of wild flowers, in great masses, giving the effect of a glorified patch work quilt over the land."[769]

To the early settlers, the prairie was the most beautiful place in the world. Part of their diet consisted of wild game. Deer, wildcats, foxes, badgers, and prairie wolves were numerous. Prairie wolves were supposed to be particularly fond of melon patches. Who would have guessed that? The pioneers did not have to cut down trees or remove stumps. John Deere invented a new plow to turn prairie sod in 1837, making it much easier to turn the prairie sod. Deere's plow was not mass-produced until the 1840s, however. Draining low, swampy areas produced the most fertile soil anywhere. Soil from areas that were formally swampland is known as a muck soil.

The prairie could also be a dangerous place. It was easy to get lost traveling through the prairie on a foggy night or in snowfall. Once lost, you could roam around the prairie in circles for days. Just like in the desert, mirages are seen on prairies too. Every year brought prairie fires. A prairie fire occurring miles away was supposed to be able to light up the night sky bright enough to read a book. Prairie fires became less frequent as more land was taken out of prairie and turned into cropland. The work was endless. The pioneers had to build cabins, barns, fences, and roads, as well as dig wells. There were no bridges, so fording a river risked drowning. There was also sickness to contend with. Bouts of fever and ague occurred annually. Ague was a form of malaria. It usually did not kill you, but would get you real sick every year. According to *History of Logan County*, the settlers "thought that drinking liquor would keep the ague off, so everyone attended to that."[770]

Logan County had two very large landowners, John D. Gillett and William Scully. Gillett's daughter was married to Governor Oglesby. Gillett owned thousands of acres of land in the southern part of the county. William Scully was an absentee landlord who lived in London, England. He was supposed to have owned forty-five thousand acres of land in the county. At first, he rented his land to Irish emigrants. Gillett had some bad experiences with the Irish and wrote that he "has had so much trouble with the Irish that he does not encourage their applications."[771] He rented to mostly German

---

769 The Namesake Town, A Centennial History of Lincoln, Illinois: Published by Centennial Booklet Committee, [Lincoln, Illinois: Feldman Print Shop 1953] p.5&6.

770 History of Logan County, Illinois: [Chicago: Inter-state Publishing Co. 1886] p. 237.

771 History of Logan County, Illinois 1886 p. 367.

emigrants after that. Logan County was still lightly populated when the Seicks and Wodetzkis arrived. I do not have any doubts about that. Two people owned most of it. The county's population had its biggest increase after the railroad came in 1853-54.

Edward L. Wodeski

Edward L. and his son Edward E. Wodeski are both mentioned in *History of Logan County, Illinois*. Edward L. was born in Poland on May 30, 1819. His father's name was Johann Gottlieb Wodeski. Ed's mother was a Syke (Seick). Johann Gottlieb owned a farm in Poland. The family left Poland for America when Ed was eighteen years old and settled in Baltimore, Maryland. Ed worked at a number of jobs in America before settling on the trade of wagon maker. He married Ms. I. V. Davis on October 12, 1847. She was the daughter of Major Samuel Davis, a veteran of the Revolutionary War.

It goes on to say that the Wodeskis had nine children. Seven were still living as of 1886 and their names are all listed. Ed was a Lutheran while his wife a Presbyterian. Politically, Ed was a Democrat. Ed must have enjoyed being a pioneer. He bought and sold four different farms in the county from the time he came here, until he retired. They were all undeveloped prairie farms when Ed purchased them. He brought them all into cultivation, constructed buildings, and made other improvements, etc. After eight or nine years, he would sell the farm, and buy another piece of undeveloped land to bring into cultivation.[772]

The best source of information about the Wodetzkis is found in a book written by Cecil Calvert Pryor. He researched and wrote a genealogy of the Smith-Clark and Wodetzki-Seick-Davis families. Pryor's wife was a Wodetzki, and Pryor wanted his wife and children to know their family history. According to Cecil, the Wodetzkis and Seicks lived near Danzig (Gdansk). This area was a part of Prussia during this time. Both families consider themselves Polish but spoke German to each other. The Seicks pronounced their name "Sik." Edward Sr. preferred to spell his last name Wodeski, while his family favored the Wodetzki spelling.

Edwards's mother was Julia Anna Seick. Her father's name is thought to be John. Julia's marriage to Johann Gottlieb Wodeski was her second marriage. According to the Church of the Latter-Day Saints family search, Ed's father, Johann Gottlieb, was born in Germany in 1793. Johann Gottlieb's father was Martin Gabriel, born in Germany in 1757. If this is correct, the Wodetzkis

---

772 History of Logan County, Illinois 1886 p. 673&674.

were living in Germany before the partitions.[773] Pryor goes on to write the Wodetzkis were nobility and could use "Von" in front of their name. Johann Gottlieb's occupation was miller. Two children were born to Johann and Julia, Gottlieb Emanuel, on April 6, 1816, and Edward Ludovic on May 30, 1819. In America, Ed used Lewis for his middle name. Johann died when his mill caught on fire and burned down.

Julia Anna was married for a third time to J. T. Schmidt. Five more children were born from the marriage. As Gottlieb and Edward got older, Julia Anna worried her sons would be drafted into the Prussian Army. She decided the best thing to do was to go to America. Julia Anna, J. T. Schmidt, and the Wodetski/Schmidt children all immigrated to America in 1832. Their ship left from Danzig and, after six weeks at sea, arrived in Baltimore. The family lived in or near Baltimore.

When Edward first met his future wife, Josephine Davis, she was engaged to a major in the U.S. Army. She was seventeen years old. Josephine broke up with him and married Ed instead on October 12, 1847. Edward and his bride left for Logan County, Illinois, two weeks after getting married. Ed's uncle John Seick was already living in Logan County at the time. The trip to Illinois was their honeymoon. Ed told Josephine that if she did not like Illinois, they would go back to Maryland. She must have liked Illinois for it would be twenty years before she came back to Maryland.

The Wodetzkis took the train from Baltimore to Cumberland, Maryland. They went by stagecoach from Cumberland to Brownville, Pennsylvania, and by steamboat from Brownville to Pittsburgh. They spent two weeks in Pittsburgh waiting for their furniture, etc., to catch up with them. Their furniture had to be hauled over the mountains and took longer to get to Pittsburgh. They left Pittsburgh by steamboat and sailed to St. Louis, Missouri. After reaching St. Louis, they boarded another ship headed for Pekin, Illinois.

While in Pekin, Ed was offered a job as a wagon maker. It paid six dollars a week, but he turned it down. The Wodetzkis were soon riding on the prairie in a wagon heading for Uncle John Seick's home in Postville. Between Pekin and Postville, only the town of Delavan had any kind of settlement at all. The distance between Pekin and Postville (Lincoln) seems to be about forty-five to fifty miles. The whole journey was through undisturbed prairie. When the Wodetzkis finally arrived in Postville, they found a courthouse surrounded by about twelve houses. The courthouse was the center of the community, and all the villages' weddings, funerals, religious services, and parties took place there.

[773] WWW FamilySearch.ORG [Family History Library]

Postville had its start in 1835. A settler from Baltimore, Russell Post, liked the countryside there and decided to build a town on the site. The town also took its name from him. According to Pease, "In 1839 a Catholic colony was projected at Postville in Logan County."[774] By 1839, Postville had a population of one hundred. It became the first county seat for Logan County. The stagecoach also ran through town on the Chicago to St. Louis road. Unfortunately, the citizens of Logan County voted to move the county seat to the town of Mount Pulaski in 1848. After the county seat moved, the value of land and homes decreased, and Postville was never the same. In 1865, Postville was incorporated into the new town of Lincoln. Its population was about two hundred at the time.

Ed resumed his wagon maker trade in Postville. He also became partners with a man named Zaddock Munday. They spent the next year building wagons, and then both changed occupations. Instead of building wagons, they built farms. They remained partners and spent many years together developing farms out of the wilderness. Ed and Zaddock would go on to develop five different farms out of the prairie.

The Wodetzkis had nine children. Edward Emanuel was the oldest. He was born July 20, 1848, and died August 20, 1930. Next is Mary Eugenia, born September 26, 1850, and died February 14, 1942. Juliana Constantia was born September 5, 1853, and died January 1, 1929. Number 4 is John Samuel, born May 5, 1857, and died September 17, 1883. William only lived three and a half years. He was born April 19, 1858, and died October 24, 1861. Catherine Anne, born January 25, 1861, and died August 28, 1947. Thomas Jefferson, born on July 25, 1865, and died August 9, 1937. Lucian Lewis, born May 10, 1867, and died March 21, 1938. Charles Chesterfield was the baby of the family. He was born July 8, 1869, and died March 9, 1947.

Josephine was comparably well educated for the time as compared to the neighbor women living around her. Josephine would teach them social skills such as sewing, dancing, etc. She was a southern sympathizer during the Civil War. Her father owned a few slaves and she always claimed that "in her state the colored people were well cared for."[775] Josephine did not care what the local Union supporters thought about her views during the Civil War.

Future President Abraham Lincoln spent quite a bit of time around Postville. He worked as an attorney at the courthouse and used to stay

[774] Theodore Calvin Pease, The Frontier State 1818-1848: [Urbana and Chicago: University of Illinois Press 1918] p. 179.

[775] Cecil Calvert Pryor, The Smith-Clark and Seick-Wodetzki-Davis Families: [At the Kewanee Public Library 1979] p. 153.

at a travelers' tavern in town. Josephine's brother-in-law Hugo Johnson and Abraham Lincoln were both attorneys and knew each other well. One time, while she was walking with Hugo, they ran into Abe. Hugo introduced Josephine to Mr. Lincoln. According to Josephine, "Mister Lincoln had great fun commenting upon what a beautiful girl she was to be with Johnson."[776]

The Wodetzkis recorded another story about Abraham Lincoln. One spring day, while court was out to lunch, they watched him play marbles with a group of boys. Someone hollered to Mr. Lincoln that court was back in session. "I don't care, said Lincoln, I'm not going to quit until I have finished this game,"[777] After the game, Abe went back into the courthouse "with his knuckles covered with mud from the wet ground."[778] He was defending a doctor accused of murder but got the doctor acquitted.

Some of Edwards's relatives also settled in Logan County. His brother Gottlieb Emanuel settled in the county sometime between 1857 and 1859. Gottlieb had been living in Baltimore until this time. He and his wife Sarah were the parents of ten children. In addition, Julia Anna and the Schmidts left Baltimore and moved to Logan County. The date for their coming to the county is unknown.

Edward died September 5, 1911. He had lived in Logan County sixty-four years. His obituary claims that he "was probably the oldest living person in the county at the time of his death."[779] Josephine died December 21, 1923, and was about ninety-three years old. She was a charter member of Daughters of the American Revolution. Josephine was supposed to have been the last person in the state whose father served in George Washington's army. A Chicago newspaper interviewed her two years before her death. According to the newspaper, Josephine is "the only known person now living in Illinois whose father served under Gen. George Washington in the Revolutionary War." It was published in 1922 in the Polish-American newsletter.[780] In the article, she told stories about her life and her father's life. There were seven Wodetzki children still living when Josephine died. She had twenty grandchildren and ten great-grandchildren.

---

776 Cecil Calvert Pryor, p. 154.

777 Cecil Calvert Pryor, p. 154.

778 Cecil Calvert Pryor, p. 154.

779 Old Union Cemetery records, [by the Logan County Genealogical & Historical Society Volume 5] p. 310.

780 Cecil Calvert Pryor, p. 152

Edward Emanuel Wodetzki

Edward Jr. is also mentioned in *History of Logan County*. He was born in Logan County on July 20. 1848. Ed left home in 1870. He was twenty-two years old and went to work in Lincoln for his cousin George Seick. The same year, he married Susan Anderson in August. Susan, however, died in April 1871. Edward became partners with George and John Seick in 1871. He sold his share of the business in 1876 and went into business for himself in 1877. His business sold paint and wallpaper. Edward got married again July 12, 1883, to Annie Simpson. The second marriage produced one son, Clifford.[781]

John Seick

Edward's uncle, John Seick, was an early settler of Postville. He bought land there on December 22, 1840.[782] The 1850 Logan County Census lists John's age as thirty-nine. His occupation was carpenter, and he was born in Danzig (Gdansk) in Prussia. His wife Margaret is thirty-two years old and born in Kentucky. They have three children, all boys. Ferdinand L, nine; John J. D., six; and George M., three. They were all born in Illinois.[783] Cecil Pryor recorded different facts as compared to the 1850 census. He claims that there were four children. The second one born was Theodore. All four were born from John's first wife Margaret. She died December 4, 1852. John's second wife was known to the Wodetzkis as "Auntie" Kerschnitski. There were two children from this marriage, Lewis and Mary.[784]

The Seicks and Wodetzkis were well-known around Lincoln for years. I checked the phone directory for the state of Illinois and found a number of people using the Seick and Wodetzki names. Thirty-two people use the last name of Wodetzki in Illinois. Ninety-three people used the last name of Seick. There is still a Wodetzki living in Lincoln. Most of the Wodetzkis now live around the Danville area. Some Wodetzkis moved to Nebraska. I think it is a good bet that all the Wodetzkis in Illinois are descendants of Edward and Gottlieb Emanuel. I have no idea how many people using the Seick last name are descendants of John Seick.

---

781 History of Logan County, Illinois 1886 p. 526&527.

782 Logan County Recorder of Deeds, [Logan General Index Grantee Book number 1 p. 186.]

783 United States Census 1850 Logan County, Illinois: Decatur Genealogical Society, Decatur, Illinois 1986 p. 50.

784 Cecil Calvert Pryor, p. 94.

Madison County

There are records of three Poles living in Madison County before 1850. None lived in the county any great length of time. Their names were Alexander A. Niewiardowski, Stefan A. Wyszomerski, and Maximilian Pendzinski. These last two only left a small amount of information about themselves.

Before I begin with their stories, let's take a look at Madison County. Madison County was formed from St. Clair County in 1812. It is located in southwestern Illinois directly across the Mississippi River from the north side of St. Louis, Missouri. The banks of the Mississippi River in Madison County are known as the American Bottoms. The American Bottoms was a one-hundred-mile-long body of alluvial soil that stretched from Alton to Chester and was from four to fifteen miles wide. Alluvial soil is soil deposited by moving water. The northern part of the county along the Mississippi River contains bluffs from 80 to 150 feet high. East of the bluffs were large prairies, the wooded areas mainly along the streams. The soil is black and was originally from one to six feet deep.

A number of different ethic groups settled in Madison County. The first settlers were mainly from the south along with a handful of Yankees from the northeast. Soon Pennsylvania Dutch and Irish arrived. In 1831, a large number of Swiss emigrated to the county. The Germans came in 1833. Starting in the early 1850s, a substantial group of Czechs settled there.

Alexander A. Niewiardowski

Alexander A. Niewiardowski was born in 1800[785] in Kolmei, Lithuania, Poland[786] Alexander was an army chaplain in the 1830 November uprising. He was living in Philadelphia, Pennsylvania, by 1835. Alexander was supposed

785 Joyce Meyer, Cemeteries and Tombstone Inscriptions of Madison County, Illinois Volume 3: [Madison County Genealogical Society 1986] p. 60.

786 Aleksander Grobicki, Proba Biografii, Sodalis: [St. Mary's College Library, Orchard Lake, Michigan] letter N, p. 26.

to have been a well-known figure around the "St. Jana Evangelical Church in Philadelphia.[787] The earliest record of Alexander living in Madison County is June 11, 1839, when he bought eighty acres from Curtiss Blakeman Jr.[788] This tract was located in the newly established town of Marine, located twenty-three miles northeast of St. Louis.

The town of Marine had an unusual beginning. J. Alonzo Matthews writes that in 1817, four ex-sea captains came by wagon train from Fairfield County, Connecticut, to Madison County. Their names were Captain Curtiss Blakeman, Captain George C. Allen, Captain James Breath, and Captain David Mead. They desired to become farmers and raise families.[789] Of these four, Captain Blakeman and his son Curtiss Jr. are the persons we are most concerned about in our story about Niewiardowski.

Matthews wrote, "Captain Blakeman, was a man of sound judgment on all questions of general interest; a man of great energy, commanding the respect of all who knew him."[790] Matthews goes on to say Captain Blakeman was born and educated in England. During his days as a ship captain, he crossed the equator forty-four times and made eleven trips to China. The citizens of Madison County elected him to the state legislature in 1822. Blakeman was also president of the Madison County Association to oppose slavery in Illinois. In 1816, he bought 1,120 acres of land in Madison County. Captain Blakeman, Captain George C. Allen, and others also established a town in the county named Madison. On November 18, 1820, they advertised the sale of one hundred lots. The venture never took off and the town was soon incorporated into Marine.[791] *History of Madison County, Illinois* writes that all the sea captains lived in the Marine settlement.[792] Captain Blakeman also donated two acres of land for the site of a school and church in 1820. Blakeman declared that the building was "open and free to all denominations of worshipping Christians that worship God agreeable to his written word as

---

787 Aleksander Grobicki, p. 26.

788 Madison County Grantee Index 1812-1873 [letters N, O, P, &Q] at the Madison County Courthouse, Edwardsville, Illinois: p. 65.

789 J. Alonzo Matthews, History of the Blakeman family Capt. Curtis Blakeman, Pioneer builder: [The collection of the Madison County Historical Society] p. 1 & 2.

790 J. Alonzo Matthews, p. 6.

791 J. Alonzo Matthews, p1-6.

792 History of Madison County, Illinois: [Edwardsville, Illinois: W. R. Brink & Company, 1882] [A Reproduction by Unigrafhic, Inc. Evansville, Indiana 1973 p.493.

contained in the Old and New Testaments as well as for the use of a school, as a majority of the subscribers and their proper assigns forever."[793] Known as "Union Church," it was the first school and church in Marine. It also might be of some interest to our story. A cholera epidemic came through Madison County in 1833 and hit the Blakeman family particularly hard. Captain Blakeman and one of his daughters died on May 20, 1833. His wife died the next day.

On June 11, 1839, Alexander bought eighty acres of land from Captain Blakeman's son Curtiss Jr. The land was in two separate parcels, one in section 32 and one on section 36. Alexander paid fifteen hundred dollars for his land.[794] Fifteen hundred dollars was a considerable amount of money for eighty acres in 1839. The grantee index for Madison County refers to land or lots. Maybe Alexander was speculating that Marine would grow in time and the value of his lots would be higher in the future. Located on Alexander's property was a schoolhouse. The schoolhouse and surrounding land was not part of the transaction. It was deeded by Philip Gatch to the county commissioner of Madison County.[795] According to Madison County land records, Captain Blakeman's son-in-law John L. Furguson deeded a tract of land to Philip Gatch October 4, 1834.[796] Alexander's farm might have had Union Church and school located on it, though he would not have owned it. In the late 1830s, the school at Union Church moved to a new brick one-room schoolhouse. Alexander would have bought his farm right after Union Church stopped being used as a school. *History of Madison County, Illinois* describes the Union Church as "a substantial frame building, with clapboard siding and split shingle roof, was the first erected. It was built in 1821, on section thirty-three, and was in constant use until a new Union church was built in the village of Marine."[797] Later on, John L. Furguson bought the building and turned it into a barn. Furguson was Captain Blakeman's son-in-law as well as the son of the first settler in Marine Township, Isaac H. Furguson.

History of Madison County, Illinois makes the matter confusing by stating that there was also an "empty cabin which stood between the houses of

---

793 Ronald W. Loos, A walk through Marine, from the past to the present 1813-1988: [1988] p. 16.

794 Madison County Grantee Index 1812-1873, p. 65.

795 Madison County Grantee Index 1812-1873, p. 66.

796 Madison County Granter Index1812-1873, letters L. M. N. & O. At the Madison County Courthouse, Edwardsville, Illinois: [November 3, 1857] p.636-642.

797 History of Madison County, Illinois 1882: p. 495 & 496.

Captain Blakeman and Rowland P. Allen, and for many years thereafter, the youth of the settlement were taught in an old cabin and the Union church."[798] One of these two buildings was on Alexander's property. Madison County land records show that Alexander's land was in two separate parcels, one tract in section 36 and the other tract in section 32. *History of Madison County, Illinois* states that Union Church was in section 33.[799] The land records are difficult to read. I would have been better off hiring a lawyer to figure it all out but did not want to spend the money. It turns out that an error was made when Alexander first bought the tract of land on section 32. He was supposed to have been given the northwest quarter of section 32 but ended up with the northeast quarter of 32 instead. The mistake was not corrected until October 27, 1857. Alexander's widow Martha was at the proceedings and was given different tracts of land in both sections 32 and 36.[800] Union Church might have been on Alexander's property by mistake. Having a church on his property would have been right up Alexander's alley.

The 1840 Federal Census lists four people living in the Niewiadowski household. There is one boy between the ages of ten and twenty years old and one man between thirty and forty years old. One woman between twenty and thirty years old and one woman between thirty and forty years old. Two people are employed in agriculture.[801]

The 1845 state census lists four people still living at the Niewiadowski residence. Two men between thirty and forty years of age. One woman between the age of thirty and forty and one woman between the age of forty and fifty. The census also lists two men in the militia.[802]

Alexander died in 1846. Martha is the head of household on the 1850 Federal Census. Her age is fifty-two and she was born in Pennsylvania. Martha's fifty-seven-year-old sister Anne Engles was also living there. She was also born in Pennsylvania. A farmhand named Charles Priegnitz lived there as well. He is thirty-two years old and born in Prussia.[803] Martha claims to have eighty improved acres and forty unimproved acres on the

---

798 History of Madison County, Illinois 1882: p. 495.

799 History of Madison County, Illinois 1882: p. 495.

800 Madison County Granter Index 1821-1873, p. 636-642.

801 1840 Federal Census of Madison County, Illinois: [Box 704 Roll 64 page 83] at the National Archives.

802 Elsie M. Wasser, 1845 census of Madison County, Illinois: [At the Madison County Historical Society, copyright by Elsie M. Wasser 1985] p. 20.

803 Maxine E. Wormer, Madison County, Illinois 1850 census: [Thomson, Illinois: Heritage House 1976] p. 29.

1850 Agriculture Census for Madison County, Illinois. She had five horses and four milk cows. The farm produced 90 bushels of wheat, 250 bushels of corn, 390 bushels of oats, and 36 pounds of butter.[804]

The Niewiadowskis never had any children. Alexander died December 2, 1846. Martha died April 11, 1863. Alexander and Martha are buried in the old section of the Marine City Cemetery.[805]

Stefan A. Wyszomirski

Stefan was born in Uacgrawice, Poland, August 2, 1811.[806] He was one of the Polish exiles from Trieste but was not in the group of 234 Polish exiles. Stefan was one of eleven Polish exiles on board the ship "Cherokee"[807] which landed in Boston, Massachusetts, on about September 27, 1834.[808] Stefan was in Illinois by 1838. He declared his intention to become a citizen January 26, 1839, in Alton, Madison County, Illinois, and became a citizen there on October 7, 1841. Stefan claimed he resided in Illinois for four years before becoming a citizen.[809] I have two conflicting circuit court records for Stefan. The Madison County Genealogical Societies newsletter, the *Stalker*, is the source of the first document. In the *Stalker*, Stefan claims to be from Prussia.[810] The other record is from the Archives of Southern Illinois University at Edwardsville, Illinois. On this document, Stefan swears his allegiance to the United States. He also absolutely and entirely renounces and abjures all allegiance and fidelity to every foreign prince, potentate, state, or sovereignty, whatever, and more particularly the allegiance and fidelity I in any way owe to "the emperor of Russia in Europe" whereof I was heretofore a citizen or subject.[811] This is all the information I have about Stefan and do not know what happened to him after he became a citizen.

---

804 1850 Agriculture Census of Madison County, Illinois: [Illinois State Archives, Roll No. 31-2]

805 Joyce Meyer: p. 60.

806 Madison County stalker: [Madison County Genealogical Society Quarterly, Madison County, Illinois Volume 8, Number 1, 1988] p14.

807 Jerzy Jan Lerski, A Polish Chapter in Jacksonian America: [Madison: The University of Wisconsin Press 1958] p.179.

808 Madison County stalker: p.14.

809 Madison County stalker: p.14.

810 Madison County stalker: p.14.

811 Southern Illinois University at Edwardsville Archives: [Naturalization and Intentions, Madison County B, 1 of 4 1837-1855]

Maximilion Pendzinski

The only record of Maximilion in Madison County is his marriage to Nanette Staffelbach on January 28, 1841.[812] He was a lieutenant or noncommissioned officer in the 1830 Polish uprising and one of the 234 Polish exiles from Trieste.[813] Max bought land a number of times in Salem, Marion County, Illinois, starting by at least November 19, 1839.[814] He sold it all by 1844[815] and moved to St. Louis, Missouri.[816] I write more about Maximilion in my story about Marion County.

Alexander Niewiadowski was a very religious man. In the rebellion, he was an army chaplain. In America, he hung around St. Jana's church in Philadelphia. In Illinois, he might have bought land with, guess what, a church on it. Stefan Wyszomerski lived in Illinois for at least four years. Maximilian Pendzinski lived in Illinois for five years then moved to St. Louis. I do not know what happened to either of them but hope to find out more about them in the future.

---

812 Liahona Research, Illinois Marriages: 1826 to 1850 [Bountiful, Utah: Heritage Quest 1999] p. 637.

813 Hejnal, Polish American Cultural Society of St. Louis: [Summer, 1964] p. 11.

814 Marion County Recorder of Deeds at the Marian County Courthouse, Salem, Illinois: [General Index Number 1 Grantee 1823-1857]

815 Marion County Recorder of Deeds, [General Index Number 1 Grantee 1823-1857]

816 Hajnal: p. 11.

Marion County

Marion County had three Poles living in the town of Salem before 1850, Felix Boczkiewiez, Joseph Wnorowski, and Maximilian Pendzinski. All three were members of the 234 Polish exiles from Triest that landed in New York March 28, 1834.[817] All three are mentioned in *History of Marion and Clinton Counties, Illinois.*

> The first foreigners that came to the county arrived in 1838. They were subjects of the Emperor of Russia, probably exiled Poles. Only three of them became naturalized citizens, Maximiliam Pendzinski, S. Joseph Wnorowski, and Felix Boczkiewicz-August term 1843. Boczkiewicz had landed in New York in 1833; he was a political refugee, and a man of polish and education.[818]

Marion County was created January 24, 1833, from parts of Fayette and Jefferson counties. The county is located in Southern Illinois in the central part of the state. Salem is the county seat and is located about sixty miles east of St. Louis, Missouri. Brinkerhoff claims that in its primitive state, two-thirds of the county was wooded and one-third prairie.[819] The *Gazetteer* by Beck claims two-thirds of the county was prairie and one-third wooded.[820] So I

---

817 Jerzy Jan Lerski, A Polish Chapter in Jacksonian America: [Madison: The University of Wisconsin 1958] p. 172,176, & 178.

818 History of Marion and Clinton Counties, Illinois: [Philadelphia: Brink, McDonough & Co. 1881] [Reproduction by Unigraphic, Inc.: Evansville, Indiana 1974] p. 31.

819 J.H.G. Brinkerhoff, Brinkerhoff's History of Marion County, Illinois: [Indianapolis, Indiana B.F. Bowen & Company 1909] [Republished by Marion County Genealogical and Historical Society: McDowell Publications, Hartford, Kentucky 1979] p. 114.

820 J. M. Peck, A. M., A Gazetteer of Illinois, in Three Parts: [Philadelphia: Grigg & Elliot 1837] [Facsimile Reprint, Heritage Books Inc. Bowie, Maryland 1993] p. 118.

am not sure what the county looked like, but I am sure that the countryside is level to rolling. The hilly areas are near the streams. Marion County has no major rivers. It does have a large number of small streams.

Southern Illinois is known as "Egypt." The name came from an event in the early years of the state's existence. In the 1820s, central Illinois had a poor corn crop while the southern part of the state had a large corn crop. The settlers from central Illinois had to make the journey south in wagon trains to buy their feed corn. The trip south reminded them of the biblical story of Joseph's brothers going to Egypt to buy corn. "Going down into Egypt" became a common term.[821]

All three of the exiles lived in Salem. Salem came into existence when Rufus Ricker and Mark Tulley donated the site for Salem on June 6, 1826. Tulley's house became a stop for the Vincennes stagecoach line. The stagecoach ran from Vincennes, Indiana, to St. Louis, Missouri, during the years 1820 to 1854. A number of the stagecoach drivers called Salem their home. During these years, Salem's growth was slow. Three or four years after its founding, only six families were living there. About ten houses had been built by 1838. Salem's population took off in 1854 when the railroad came through. By 1900 it had a population of 3,000. The current population of Salem is 7,909. Salem's favorite son is William Jennings Bryan. He was born there March 19, 1860, and gained nationwide fame as "the Great Commoner."[822]

Felix Boczkiewiez

In the 1830 uprising, Felix held the rank of lieutenant.[823] According to the *St. Louis Hejnal*, Felix was born in Kalisz, Poland. He enlisted in the United States Army January 1, 1835, at the St. Louis Arsenal. On his enlistment papers, Felix gave his age as twenty-two. Under occupation, he wrote student. Felix enlisted for three years but was discharged after nine months. During his time in the army, he served in ordnance, which is military weapons. Felix was married in Salem November 4, 1838, to Martha A. Ray. The marriage produced two children, Juliette and Alexander.[824] Felix's occupation was a

821 J.H.G. Brinkerhoff, p. 115-116.

822 History of Salem, Illinois and surrounding Territory: [by the Continental Historical Bureau of Mount Vernon, Illinois] p. B-4.

823 Mieczyslaw Haiman, Slady Polskie W Ameryce: [Chicago, Illinois: Drukiem Dziennika Zjednoczenia 1938] p. 123.

824 Hejnal, Polish American Cultural Society of St. Louis: [Winter 1986] p. 7.

saddler.[825] The first record of him buying land in Salem is November 19, 1839, when Felix and Maximilian Pendzinski bought some land together as partners.[826] Felix died in March 1850 while on a business trip. He is supposed to be buried in either St. Clair or Fayette counties, but no one knows which county or cemetery.[827] Felix died of consumption[828] which now goes by the name of tuberculosis.

The 1840 census does not provide much information about the Boczkiewicz family. Felix is not listed on the 1850 census. Martha is listed as head of household on the 1850 census. She is twenty-six years old, born in Kentucky. Daughter Juliette is eleven, born in Illinois. Son Alexander is nine and born in Illinois. Also living with the family is Thomas Ray, fourteen years old and born in Illinois. Thomas could have been Martha's brother. David Fisher is living with the family too. He is twenty-two years old, a farmer and born in Kentucky.[829] The Boczkiewiczs also farmed. In 1850, they had 40 tillable acres and 120 unimproved acres. They owned six horses, seven cows, a team of oxen, twenty-five other cattle, twenty sheep, and fifty pigs. The farm produced six hundred bushels of corn and three hundred pounds of butter.[830]

The Boczkiewicz family is mentioned in two different Marion County histories. *History of Richland, Clay and Marion Counties* and *Brinkerhoff's History of Marion County*. *History of Richland, Clay and Marion Counties* writes that Martha Boczkiewicz married William G. Williams March 15, 1852. It was the second marriage for both of them. Five children were born from this marriage. The new family was now living near the small town of Kinmundy, about twelve miles northeast of Salem. Its current population is 892. Daughter Juliette is also mentioned. She married T. W. Williams March 27, 1859. He was the son of the same William G. Williams, who married her mother. T. W. Williams was a successful farmer who in 1885 became postmaster in Kinmundy. Williams was the deputy circuit court for Marion

---

825 Ronald Vern Jackson, Illinois 1850 Mortality Schedule: [Bountiful, Utah: Accelerated Indexing Systems 1981] p. 66.

826 Marion County Recorder of Deeds, Salem, Illinois: [General Index Number 1 Grantee 1823-1857] p.2.

827 Hejnal, [Winter] p. 7.

828 Ronald Vern Jackson, p. 66.

829 Maxine E. Wormer, Marion County, Illinois 1850 census: [Thomson, Illinois: Heritage House 1972] p. 92.

830 1850 Agriculture Census of Marion County, Illinois: [Illinois State Archives, Springfield, Illinois Roll No. 31-2]

County in 1893. By 1900, he was a deputy sheriff in Salem. The account about Juliette's family goes on to say,

> She was a representative of a highly respected and well-known family of this county. By this union the following interesting children have been born; Henrietta, the wife of George M. Hargrove, of Fayette county, Illinois; Annetta, deceased; Alfe, the wife of W. W. Newis, of Salem; W. W. of Centralia, this state; Walter, of Ashland, Cass County, Illinois; T. S. of Salem. These children have received good educations and careful home training which is clearly reflected in their lives.[831]

Longin Joseph Wnorowski

Joe is the most written about of the three Polish exiles. In fact, I hardly had to do any work investigating the Wnorowski family. George Ross already had about everything covered in his story printed in the June 5, 1991, *Salem Times Commoner*. The story was also printed in "Vol. XVI, No 4 Footsteps in Marion County, Illinois." Mr. Ross wrote a great story.

Salem's Polish Carpenter

> Through its formative years, Salem had no better known nor valued citizen than Longin Joseph Wnorowski, a Polish carpenter, who specialized in constructing wagons, Carriages, and Cabinets. As he grew older, he became a source of information on Salem's early years, which he enjoyed sharing.
>
> Wnorowski was born March 19, 1804, at Dubnor, in Poland. At the age of twelve years, he commenced studying for the priesthood at Zubacesiner and continued the study until the death of his Mother when he was eighteen years old. He then returned to his home at Dubnor where he remained until he was twenty-one years old. In 1825, he became a Mason and, in the same year, enlisted in the Russian Army and served until the Polish Rebellion against their conquerors. During one of the battles, he saved the life of his commanding officer by knocking off the hammer of the enemy's gun with his saber as he was in the act of firing at close quarters.

831 History of Richland, Clay and Marion Counties, Illinois: [Indianapolis, Indiana: B. F. Bowen & Company 1909] [A Reproduction by The Richland County Genealogical and Historical Society 1987] p. 55-56.

After he left the Russian Army to fight for his own country in 1831, he was taken prisoner while carrying dispatches [but not before he had hidden the papers in a stump] and carried off to the bastile at Kazouri but escaped through the assistance of a Russian officer. The mother of Wnorowski had once found this officer upon a battle field seriously wounded, took care of and nursed him back to health, and recognizing the prisoner, determined to repay the kindness of the mother and told the prisoner to secrete a small paddle on his person and have his fellow prisoners do the same. He then showed them where to work, and, in time, they completed a tunnel to the base of a cliff on the Dnieper River, which was covered with a thin sheet of ice. They pushed boldly in but only a part of them reached the opposite shore. After arriving in Austria, they were informed by the authorities that they must go back or to some other country. Mr. Wnorowski was determined to come to the United States, and, in 1833, he landed in New York, moved on to Philadelphia, then worked his way to St. Louis. Here he enlisted in the U. S. Army and was stationed at a fort in the Iowa Territory. In the spring of 1834, he was sent to Florida where he took part in the Seminole War. Returning to St. Louis in 1835, he took up carpentry and became a master craftsman.

He had learned from stage coach drivers on the St. Louis to Vincennes Trail that a person with his skills was needed at Salem, and in 1839, he made the move and established his shop. The following year, he courted and won the hand of Miss Martha Jackson. When the hostilities with Mexico erupted in 1847, he immediately enlisted with the U. S. forces and did valiant service which required a march from Alton, Illinois to Santa Fe, New Mexico. It is related of him that while engaged in this long trek, he was the owner of a mule which was much given to "bucking," and in consequence thereof, he could not ride the animal. Wnorowski, however, could not be induced to part with him and showed his well known tenacity of purpose by leading him through all the weary stages of march. He returned home in the latter part of 1848 after his discharge. He resumed his wagon and cabinet making trade which he followed up until his death on January 27, 1891. It was said that he was never sick after the age of sixteen until his final brief illness.[832]

[832] George Ross, Footprints in Marion County [Volume xvi Number 4] p. 46-47. [Printed with the permission of the Morning Sentinel Newspaper, Centralia, Illinois]

I did manage to find a little about the Wnorowski family. According to the 1850, 1870, and 1880 Federal census of Marion County, Joe and Martha were the parents of four daughters and two sons. On the 1850 census, Daughter Lucy is seven years old. Elizabeth is six, Sophia five and Cecelia one.[833] The two sons were born much later than the girls. The 1870 census shows that son Frederick was born in 1866. Joe would have been sixty-two years old and Martha thirty-eight years old.[834] According to the 1880 census, son Frank was born about 1877 when Joe was seventy-two years old and Martha fifty-three. This seems almost too much to believe, but the census records list each one as son. I have to congratulate Joe and Martha for this great achievement. Joe also surpasses Charles Szirkowski, of Randolph County, who became a father at seventy-one.[835] The 1880 census also shows that Joe is still working as a carpenter. In addition, Albert Jackson, Joe's stepson is living in the Wnorowski home. Albert was born in Kentucky around 1850 and was only eight months old on the 1850 census.[836] He was still living with the family on the 1880 census and his occupation is carpenter.

Three different Marion County histories mention the Wnorowskis. *Brinkerhoff's History of Marion County, Illinois, History Richland, Clay and Marion Counties*, and *History of Marion and Clinton Counties*. Brinkerhoff's history mentions Joe's daughter Sophia. "Born and reared in Salem where she received a common school education and developed many praiseworthy characteristics." Sophia was the mother of six children. *Brinkerhoff's* goes on to say, "These children all received a good common schooling and were reared in a home of the most wholesome atmosphere, consequently they have developed characters of a very commendable type." Sophia's son, O. A. James, also has a small mention. "O. A. James, the popular and efficient cashier of the Salem state Bank." It also claims that his "grandfather on his mother's side was born in Russia and received his education in the city of Moscow."[837]

Joe died January 27, 1891. Martha died July 22, 1902. Joe and Martha are both buried in East Lawn Cemetery.[838] I have to return to George Ross to finish this story.

---

833 Maxine E. Wormer, 1850 census p. 135.

834 Maxine E. Wormer, Marion County, Illinois 1870 census: [Published by Marion County Genealogical & Historical Society, Salem, Illinois 1983] p. 95.

835 Maxine E. Wormer, Marion County, Illinois 1880 Census Part 1: [Salem, Illinois: Published by Marion County Genealogical & Historical Society 1985] p.14.

836 Maxine E. Wormer, 1850 census p. 135.

837 J.H.G. Brinkerhoff, p. 261.

838 Marion County Illinois Cemetery Inscriptions with Genealogical Notes Book # 5: [At the Marion County Genealogical & Historical Society, Salem, Illinois] p. 94.

The following notes appeared in the account of his death printed in the Salem Herald-Advocate. "The deceased was one of the oldest Masons in the country and was a member 66 years. He was the Tyler, a position he had held more than forty years and was buried by the members of Marion Lodge No. 130. A good man has gone to his reward.

"Uncle Joe, as he was called by everyone, lived in Salem more than fifty years and was known to all of the old settlers and many of the new. He was for many years coroner of the county . . . . He was of a remarkably pleasant disposition, always seeming to be happy and jovial . . . . His was a long and checkered life. Exposed as he was to the dangers of four wars on two continents, he passed through them with but two wounds, neither serious. He was also exposed to cholera while in Turkey when entire villages were depopulated by the scourge, yet he escaped."[839]

Maximilian Pendzinski

In the 1830 Polish uprising, Max was a lieutenant or noncommissioned officer.[840] He married Nanette Staffelbach on January 28, 1841, in Madison County, Illinois.[841] Max only lived in Salem a short time. He did make a number of land purchases during his time in Salem. I mentioned earlier in the story about Felix Boczkiewicz that Max and Felix bought land together on November 19, 1839. Max regularly bought land after that. He made two purchases in 1841 and two in 1842.[842] Max bought out Felix on one of the 1842 acquisitions. Max sold all his land in Salem on March 18, 1845.[843] He and Nanette had already moved to St. Louis, Missouri, in 1844.The *St. Louis Hejnal* states that by 1844, Max's name is in the St. Louis Directory. His occupation was a trunk manufacturer and he won first prize in 1848 at the Mechanics Institute in St. Louis.[844]

---

839 George Ross, p. 46-47.

840 Hejnal, Summer, 1964: p. 11.

841 Liahona Research, Illinois Marriages: 1826 to 1850 [Bountiful, Utah: Heritage Quest 1999] p. 637.

842 Marion County Recorder of Deeds, [General Index Number 1 Grantee 1823-1857]

843 Marion County Recorder of Deeds, [General Index Number 1 Granter 1824-1857]

844 Hejnal, Summer, 1964: p. 11.

Only Joe Wnorowski has any descendants left in Marion County. Unfortunately, I neglected to write down their last names, but none uses the last name of Wnorowski. I found the name E. Boczkiewicz in the 1891 Fayette County Landowners Index, but nothing more.[845] His occupation is farmer and stock raiser. Max left the state in 1844 and moved to St. Louis. I have not done any research in Missouri yet, but hope to someday. I would like to thank Harold Boyles of Salem for his help and the *Centralia Morning Sentinel* newspaper.

845 Mrs. Grace Middlesworth, Patron List-Landowners, Fayette County, Illinois Plat Book 1891: [Printed by the Decatur Genealogical Society 1981] p. 4.

Monroe County

I was not sure if I even needed to write about Monroe County. There were only two people living in the county that had Polish-looking names. There is no way to prove that either one was Polish. Most of the research I have is about Charles W. Kalowsky. The other person was August Duda. There is only one record of him.

Monroe County was created in 1816 from parts of Randolph and St. Clair counties. It lies in southwestern Illinois, and its western boundary is the Mississippi River. Waterloo is the county seat. Monroe County is located only a short distance southeast of St. Louis. The Kalowsky family lived in the town of Columbia, which is fourteen miles from St. Louis.

The western part of Monroe County along the Mississippi River is in the American Bottoms. The American Bottoms is a one-hundred-mile long body of alluvial soil that stretched from Alton to Chester. It was from four to fifteen miles wide. Alluvial soil is soil deposited by moving water. The American Bottoms was composed of forest, swamps, and prairies. It was full of malaria-carrying mosquitoes and frequently flooded, but the soil is very fertile. Bluffs rise above the Mississippi River. Originally most of Monroe County was wooded. The eastern portion of the county had a few small prairies.

The first white settlers were French. The first American settlers were from the southern states of Virginia, Maryland, North Carolina, and Kentucky. Many of the settlers from Virginia and Maryland were from wealthy families. They bought up most of the available land and created large farms hundreds of acres in size. The big story about emigration to Monroe County were the German settlers.

From 1835 to 1840, large numbers of Germans immigrated to Monroe County. Most of them sailed to New Orleans and from there came by boat to St. Louis. Some of them made their way across the Mississippi River to Monroe County. At first, there was some friction between the Germans and the earlier settlers. There were some bloody encounters but over time, both sides took on some of the customs of each other's culture. Laborers were needed to work on the large farms, and Germans filled the role. The first settlers to Monroe County owned most of the land but had little money.

The landowners solved the problem by paying their new German workers in land instead of money. The result was that over time the Germans owned most of the land in the county. So many Germans would immigrate to Monroe County that eventually the population became about three-quarters German.

Charles W. Kalowsky

Charles was born in Prussia around 1786.[846] The Kalowsky family immigrated to St. Clair County first. Charles bought sixty-two acres of land there on July 25, 1838. He purchased this tract from George Miller for $625.[847] The Kalowskys are in the 1840 census. Six people were living in the house. One male between the ages of ten and fifteen. One male between twenty and thirty years old and one male between the ages of fifty and sixty. On the female side, there is one female between the age of five and ten years old. One female twenty to thirty years old and one female between thirty and forty years old.[848] Looking at the 1860 census, I can only identify four of them. Charles and his wife Elizabeth, their son Charles and daughter Augusta.[849] There is no 1850 census for the Kalowskys. Charles Kalowsky Jr. wrote that his place of birth was Sasonia, Germany.[850]

Charles bought 113 acres in Monroe County on November 12, 1849.[851] This tract was near the town of Columbia. Columbia is located on a plateau five hundred feet above sea level. This location on the plateau protected it from the Mississippi's frequent flooding. Its present population is 4,269. Charles had eighteen tillable acres and eighty-two unimproved acres in 1850.

---

846 The Genealogy Society of Southern Illinois, Saga of Southern Illinois: [Volume 2, Number 4 October-December, 1975] p. 9-10.

847 St. Clair County Recorder of Deeds, Belleville, Illinois: [General Index Book Deeds 1790-1908: Book J-L Roll 6]

848 Robert Buecher, St. Clair County, Illinois 1840 census: [Thomson, Illinois: Heritage House] p.3.

849 Ruth Weilbacher Stewart,1860 Monroe County Illinois Federal Census: [Published by Genealogy Society of Southern Illinois] [Utica, Kentucky: Mc Dowell Publications 1998] p. 142.

850 Janet Flynn, The 1870 Monroe County, Illinois Census: [At the Morrison Talbott Library, Waterloo, Illinois 2002] p.404.

851 Monroe County Recorder of Deeds, Waterloo, Illinois: [General Index Book #1 May 1816-May 1858]

No livestock is listed on his farm at this time. He did grow eight hundred bushels of corn.[852]

Charles's wife Elizabeth had the German maiden name of Freitag.[853] Columbia had a Catholic church, but the Kalowskys were members of St. Paul's Evangelical Church. The German language was spoken at St. Paul's services.[854] Most of the Kalowskys are buried in St. Paul's Cemetery[855] Charles died in December 1859. He was seventy-three years old and his occupation is farmer.[856] Elizabeth died July 6, 1892.[857]

August Duda

There is only one record of August Duda in Monroe County. On July 18, 1850, he married Mrs. Luisa Cook.[858] I cannot determine if August is Polish or not, so we can only guess.

Charles Kalowsky still has descendants living in Monroe County. One of them, Vernon O. Ritter, of Columbia, sent me a copy of the family tree. While driving through Columbia, I saw a Kalowsky avenue and a Kalowsky subdivision. The Kalowsky name sure looks Polish to me, but all my research says they're Germans.

---

852 1850 Agriculture Census of Monroe County, Illinois: [Illinois State Archives, Springfield, Illinois, Roll No. 31-3]

853 Vernon O. Ritter, Kalowsky family tree: Columbia, Illinois

854 History of St. Paul's Evangelical Church of Waterloo, Illinois: [1931] [At the Morrison Talbott Library, Waterloo, Illinois]

855 The Columbia Area Historical Society: [Evangelical St. Paul Cemetery, Columbia, Illinois] Waterloo Public Library. Letter K.

856 The Genealogy Society of Southern Illinois, Saga of Southern Illinois: [Volume 2, Number 4 October-December 1975] p. 9-10.

857 The Columbia Area Historical Society, Letter K.

858 Roberta Sparwasser Hotz, Monroe County, Illinois Marriage Records 1816-1877: [Thomson, Illinois Heritage House 1976] p. 36.

Morgan County

Morgan County had three Poles before 1850, Napoleon Koscialowski, Edward Mlodzianowski, and Andrew Johnson. Napoleon Koscialowski and Edward Mlodzianowski were in the group of 234 Polish exiles from Trieste.[859] In addition, some members of the well-known Zabriskie family also lived in the county. The Zabriskies are one of the oldest Polish families in America, settling in New Jersey in 1662.[860]

Morgan County was a part of Sangamon County until it was created on January 31, 1823. The county is in central Illinois in the western part of the state. The Illinois River runs along the western boundary of Morgan County. Jacksonville is the county seat. The town was named after General Andrew Jackson, the same Andrew Jackson who would later become president of the United States. Originally, half of the county was wooded, the rest being prairie. The soil is dark and fertile.

Both Napoleon and Edward spent some time in Jacksonville, so we will take a brief look at the town. On January 16, 1825, the Illinois state legislature chose three commissioners to find a site in Morgan County for the seat of justice. They were to find a location in the center of the county. A beautiful site was picked on forty acres of land donated by Thomas Arnett and Isaac Dial. By 1830, Jacksonville's population was 446. A cholera epidemic in 1833 and a financial crisis in 1837 slowed the growth of the town for a while. By 1840 the population was 1,900. The current population is 20,284.

Almost twenty years after the founding of Jacksonville, the inhabitants represented almost every state of the Union. European-born settlers were mainly from the British Isles and Germany. New Englanders from Connecticut and Massachusetts made up the largest group of Yankees. The Southerners were mainly from Virginia and North Carolina via Kentucky

---

859 Jerzy Jan Lerski, A Polish Chapter in Jacksonian America: [Madison: The University of Wisconsin Press, 1958] p. 174&175.

860 George Olin Zabriskie, The Zabriskie Family [copyright 1963 by George Olin Zabriskie] p.11.

and Tennessee. If you did not know, Yankees and Southerners were usually at odds with each other wherever they met in Illinois. This was before the Civil War. *History of Randolph, Monroe and Perry Counties* wrote, "The Southerners regarded the Yankees as a skinning, tricky, penurious race of peddlers, filling the country with tinware, brass clocks, and wooden nutmegs. The Northerner thought of the Southerner as a lean, lank, lazy creature, burrowing in a hut, and rioting in whisky, dirt and ignorance."[861] Pease claims that despite everything written about northerners and southerners, there is not much evidence of confrontation between the two groups.[862]

Napoleon Koscialowski

Of the three Poles who settled in Morgan County, Napoleon is the most written about. The majority of information about Napoleon in this story comes from Francis Casimir Kajencki. Mr. Kajencki wrote an extensive story about Napoleon in his book *Poles in the 19th Century Southwest.*

Napoleon was born in Warsaw, Poland, on May 16, 1812. He was Polish nobility. Napoleon took part in the 1830 Polish uprising. His rank is unknown, but being nobility, he was most likely an officer. After the end of the rebellion, Napoleon fled to Austria. There he was arrested, jailed, and deported to America. Napoleon was one of the 234 Polish exiles from Trieste, who landed in New York March 28, 1834.

Soon after his arrival to America, Napoleon went to Albany, New York, to look for work with a group of twenty-five Polish exiles. Incidentally, my ancestor was also in this group. In Albany, Napoleon found a job as an artist but only worked at this job a short while. He then switched occupations, becoming a teacher at the Northampton Female Seminary in Massachusetts. Napoleon was living in Jacksonville, Illinois, by 1839. He went to Illinois hoping to claim his share of the Polish land grant.

Napoleon married Mary Ann D. Chenoworth in Morgan County on November 12, 1839.[863] He switched occupations in Illinois, this time becoming a farmer. The 1841 Morgan County, Illinois, tax list shows Napoleon had a partner named Tolfrey. They were both responsible for paying the taxes on

861 Combined History of Randolph, Monroe and Perry Counties, Illinois: [Philadelphia: J.L. McDonough & Co. 1883] p. 34.

862 Theodore Calvin Pease, The Frontier State: [Chicago: A.C. McClure & Co. 1922] p. 7.

863 Liahona Research, Illinois Marriages: 1826-1850: [Bountiful, Utah: Heritage Quest, 1999] p. 467.

140 acres of land worth ten dollars an acre.[864] Unfortunately, Napoleon's career in farming ended too soon, like the farming career of the author of this book. On February 1, 1842, Napoleon petitioned for bankruptcy.[865] The year 1842 had to be one of the worst years in Napoleon's life. His best friend, Edward Mlodzianowski, also died that year. The next year was not any better when his one-year-old daughter Clara Polonia died.

After his daughter died, Napoleon and his family packed it up and moved to St. Louis. Another daughter was born to the Koscialowskis in St. Louis on July 13, 1844. They named her Sophia Carah. A son Paul Casimir had been born while they were living in Illinois, and Napoleon now had a family of four to support. In St. Louis, Napoleon started a surveying and engineering business. Once again, he took on a partner, H. W. Leffingwell.

The Mexican War broke out in 1846, and President Polk asked for volunteers on July 16, 1846. Napoleon answered the call and joined the Third Missouri Regiment. He was conferred the rank of captain of a 130-man company named "the Kosciuszko Guards." On September 1, 1846, the Third Regiment went by ship from St. Louis to Fort Leavenworth, Kansas. They never left Fort Leavenworth because the War Department decided to dissolve the Third Regiment by the end of September. Dismissing the Third Regiment was very unpopular among the soldiers as well as the citizens of Missouri.

President Polk was calling for volunteers again in 1847 and asked Missouri Governor Edwards for assistance. A new battalion of men was needed to defend the Santa Fe Trail from the Indians. The Santa Fe Trail was the route that army supply wagons took to reach the southwest territories. The United States had recently acquired the area from Mexico.

Napoleon volunteered again. In fact, he even recruited his own company, which consisted of eighty-six men. Napoleon was captain of Company E, which was also known as Captain Koscialowski's Company. Company E was an infantry outfit. At the same time, four other companies were formed, two more infantry and two cavalry. The combined strength of the five companies was now five hundred men. On September 4, 1847, all five companies left St. Louis by ship headed for Fort Leavenworth. Their commanding officer was Lieutenant Colonel William Gilpin.

Gilpin did not waste any time after arriving in Fort Leavenworth. All five companies were on the Santa Fe Trail by October 6, 1847. In western

---

864 Wanda Warkins Allers and Eileen Lynch Gochanour, 1841 Morgan County, Illinois tax list: [August 1986] p. 17.

865 Illinois State Genealogical Society, Springfield, Illinois [Volume xxi, No.1 spring 1989] p. 15.

Kansas, Gilpin decided to winter his three infantry companies at Fort Mann. He left Captain William Pelzer in command there and took his two cavalry companies to Fort Bent in Colorado. The Cheyenne and Arapahoe Indians lived near Fort Bent, and Pelzer wanted to show them his forces.

Fort Mann must have been a real hole. According to Lieutenant Henry L. Routt, "Fort Mann is certainly the most desolate and uninteresting place upon the face of the earth."[866] Captain Pelzer was always drunk and troop morale was bad. In addition, the troops started fighting amongst themselves. Companies A, B, and E were made up of native-born Americans while Companies C and D were German emigrants. Hardly any could speak English. It got so bad that Thomas L. Karnes wrote, "A hostile nativism immediately developed in the other three companies, and the immigrants concluded that the 'Americans' would as soon attack them as they would the Indians."[867] They were even shooting at each other during hunting excursions.

A different kind of incident occurred in Company D. A private named Bill Newcome turned out to be a woman. Her real name was Caroline Newcome. This might not have been a secret to some of the troopers of Company D. She was the mistress of First Lieutenant Amandus Schnabel. Schnabel knocked up Caroline, so she had to desert.

Napoleon managed to get himself in hot water with Captain Pelzer. Pelzer had tricked some Pawnee Indians into entering the fort with the intension of capturing them. The Indians realized what was happening and tried to escape. Pelzer gave an order to shoot. Four Indians were killed and two captured. The rest escaped. Napoleon refused to order his company to shoot during the incident.

All this was too much for Napoleon. He sent a letter of resignation to the adjutant general. The adjutant general discharged Napoleon, but the discharge arrived too late. Gilpin had already ordered Company E to leave Fort Mann and go to Font Bent. Even though Napoleon had sent in his letter of resignation, he left with Company E anyways. At Fort Bent, the three companies set out for New Mexico on mules. Their total strength was three hundred men. Gilpin aimed to attack the Apache and Comanche Indian tribes and drive them away from the Santa Fe Trail. Both tribes found out

---

866 Francis Casimir Kajencki, Poles in the 19th Century Southwest: [El Paso, Texas: Southwest Polonia Press 1990] p. 208.

867 Leo E. Oliva, Soldiers on the Santa Fe Trail: [Norman: University of Oklahoma Press, 1967] p. 80. The Weekly Tribune [Liberty, Missouri], December 31, 1847; Karnes, William Gilpin, p. 192 and Gilpin to Jones, August 1, 1848. In Poles in the 19th Century Southwest by Francis Casimir Kajencki, p. 208.

that the troops were on the way and ran off. As the tribes were leaving, they set fire to hundreds of miles of the surrounding countryside. Gilpin returned to Fort Mann believing the Indian threat over.

Upon his arrival at Fort Mann, Napoleon decided to stay in the army. He would need help to be reinstated. H. W. Leffingwell, Napoleon's partner in the surveying and engineering company, came to his aid. Leffingwell convinced John M. Krum, mayor of St. Louis, Brigadier General William Milburn, and U.S. District Attorney Thomas T. Gantt to write a letter to the secretary of war. They managed to keep Napoleon on until July 1, 1848. Company E itself was discharged on September 30, 1848.

After his discharge, Napoleon and his family moved back to Jacksonville, Illinois, where he became an architect. Napoleon worked on such projects as the Illinois institution for the blind and the state capital in Springfield. By this time, his family had grown larger. There were two sons, Casimir and Edward, and three daughters, Sophia, Mary, and Pricilla. Unfortunately, Napoleon had wife problems. After the job in Springfield was over, Napoleon abandoned his family and moved back east. According to Francis Kajencki, "he did not even wait for his final pay. His Son Paul Casimir collected the money due his father."[868]

Napoleon ended up in New York where he enlisted in the marines on December 22, 1853. He spent five years in the marines until his discharge on May 5, 1858. After leaving the marines, Napoleon moved on to Washington, D.C. He was forty-seven years old and in poor health. Napoleon died on May 30, 1859.

Edward Mlodzianowski

Edward was one of the 234 Polish exiles from Trieste. He was also the good friend of Napoleon Koscialowski. According to Aleksander Grobicki, Edward was a lieutenant in the 1830 uprising. He was also Polish nobility.[869] During his time in Morgan County, Edward worked for the Northern Cross Railroad. *History of Morgan County* mentions Edward twice. Page 312 states that "the profile of the work was drawn by a Pole named Edward Malowginowskie, a noble by birth who had left Poland on account of some of the rebellions or persecutions there. He was a man of fine attainments

---

868 Francis Casimir Kajencki, p. 215.

869 Aleksander Grobicki, Proba Biografii: [The Polish American Historical Association of the Polish Institute of the arts and sciences in America, St. Mary's College, Orchard Lake, Michigan] M. p. 25.

and high character,"[870] On page 313, he is mentioned as a member of the corps of engineers."[871]

Congress granted land to the 234 exiles from Trieste on June 30, 1834. The land was to be chosen in either Illinois or Michigan. The Polish Committee sent out delegations to both states. Three delegates were dispatched to Michigan, Edward Mlodzianowski, Jan Rychlicki, and Michael Gorski. Their expedition had bad luck from beginning to end. Jan Rychlicki wrote a letter on September 9, 1834, to Napoleon Felix Zaba complaining about the trip. They took the train from Albany, New York, to the Erie Canal. The canal was supposed to take them to Buffalo, New York. About halfway through the trip to Buffalo, the canal was shut down for repairs. They had to make their way to Buffalo as best they could and spent most of their money doing so.

While in Buffalo, they stopped to see Niagara Falls. The weather was beautiful on the way to the falls, but halfway there it turned ugly. Rain came down in buckets. The three decided to go on anyways since they did not have the time or money to go back on another day. They walked through pouring rain but managed to see only half of the falls. On the way back, the rain stopped and the sun came out again. Rychlicki wrote, "You have to be a Pole to have such luck! We had it, and it still remains our constant companion."[872]

The letter continues; they finally made it to Detroit but were completely broke. Rychlicki assessed the situation in Michigan but did not think it would be a suitable location for a Polish colony. The best land there was already taken. They were also advised that Illinois would be a better location to put their plan into effect. Rychlicki had a few comments to add about the trip to Detroit. "There are swindlers and sharps all along the way; they strip you of your funds in an unheard of manner." He also wrote that they would probably leave Detroit but did not know where they would end up.[873]

Rychlicki would turn up in St. Louis. Edward moved to Jacksonville, Illinois, and found employment at the Northern Cross Railroad. It was the

[870] History of Morgan County, Illinois: 1878 [Chicago: Donnelley, Loyd & Co. 1878] [Reproduction by Unigraphic, Inc. Evansville, Indiana 1975] p. 312.

[871] History of Morgan County, Illinois: 1878 [Chicago: Donnelley, Loyd & Co. 1878] [Reproduction by Unigraphic, Inc. Evansville, Indiana 1975] p. 312.

[872] Adolph Pazik, A Polish American Letter: [Polish American Studies, Volume iii No. 3-4 July-December 1946] [The Polish American Historical Commission of the Polish Institute of arts and sciences in America St. Mary's College, Orchard Lake Michigan] p. 108-109.

[873] Adolph Pazik, p.109.

first railroad built in Illinois, and built with state money. The railroad was chartered February 5, 1835. The actual work did not start until May 9, 1838. It ran from Merodosia to the state capital of Springfield. The construction of the railroad was a very important event, and the groundbreaking was held in Merodosia in August 1837. Important men from all over the state attended. Area citizens and railroad workers showed up. There were speeches, and the oldest man in town dug up the first shovelful of dirt.

Grading started that winter. The *Jacksonville Journal Courier* states, "The first profile was that made by a Pole refugee, Edward Malowginowski."[874] Construction of the first track began May 9, 1838. The workers were paid nineteen dollars a month and eight jiggers of whisky a day. The first few miles of track ran straight through the prairie until it came to the Lazenby cabin. Mrs. Lazenby was known as a feisty woman.

Virginia Chamberlain writes, James Harkness, a contractor for the railroad, met with Mrs. Lazenby and explained that the railroad was supposed to go through her cabin. She told him, "Mister, if you think you're going to run your railroad thru my parlor, you're crazy."[875] Harkness told her the route was already drawn and that we did not know your house was in the way. "Well, you know it now," snapped Mrs. Lazenby, "and you can draw your line somewhere else."[876] In the end, Harkness gave in. Mrs. Lazenby would not be the last one to change the direction of the railroad. Whoever had the influence used it to change the course of the railroad to suit his or her needs. Instead of a straight run, the track winded through the countryside like a snake.

During his meeting with Mrs. Lazenby, Harkness had suggested to her that he had an idea she might want to consider. He made some eggnog for her and asked her if she would like to make some extra money selling the beverage to the railroad workers. Mrs. Lazenby recognized an opportunity when she saw one and agreed to the idea. The eggnog became so popular that the railroad workers started telling everyone they worked for the "eggnog railroad."

Sue Wilson wrote about another incident that occurred after the railroad was built. Sue was the great-great-granddaughter of Mrs. Lazenby. Sue claimed that once the Lazenbys' bull walked on the train tracks and refused to leave. The engineer stopped the train. After hollering and throwing sticks, the bull still refused to leave. The engineer got back into the engine

---

874 Journal Courier, Jacksonville, Illinois [November 28, 1976.

875 Virginia Chamberlain, Morgan Counties first Railroad: [Jacksonville Public Library Special Collections Room] [Railroad file] Jacksonville, Illinois: p. 4.

876 Virginia Chamberlain, p. 4.

and started to drive it forward. The bull was not going anywhere, and the two met on the tracks to decide the matter. With predictable results, the bull was knocked off the tracks and down the bank. It stayed away from the tracks after that.

Mrs. Lazenby decided to get even. The tracks on the return trip were upgrade. She put homemade soft soap on the tracks. On the way back, the train ran until it hit the soaped tracks. Its wheels just spun around, and the train was unable to go any farther. According to Sue, "this pleased Grandmother Lazenby to think she had gotten even with the engineer."[877]

Despite the politics, work on the railroad went fast. By November 8, 1838, eight miles of track had been completed. The first engine was shipped by sea, but disappeared on the way. The second engine was known as the "Rogers." It was sent in pieces from New Jersey and put together on the tracks at Naples, Illinois. Top speed was fifteen miles an hour. Twelve miles of track was completed by the spring of 1839. The railroad was finished January 1, 1840. It ran for twenty-four miles from Morgan City to Jacksonville.

After the first eight miles of track was completed, the railroad conducted its first trip. The passengers were local dignitaries, railroad workers, and contractors. Alcohol was flowing freely. The passengers "insisted the engineer should take something in honor of the auspicious occasion."[878] We now call this expression "twisted my arm." The engineer got so bent out of shape that "he had to be carried to a hotel to recover."[879]

The train riders were often used to help keep the train running. They were expected to draw water for the engine at stops and stack the firewood used for fuel. The train would stop at any point along the line to drop off or pick up riders or cargo. Freight for pickup was left alongside the tracks at the most convenient place. Accidents were a regular occurrence. Spikes in the railroad ties sometimes came out, causing what was known as "snake heads." The rail ends would then coil up and puncture the bottoms of the cars. Local farmers also found out that track rails made good sled runners and rails would mysteriously disappear. In 1839, a Galena newspaper wrote about train safety. "All persons, and ladies especially, should be careful to avoid stepping from the railroad cars when they are in motion."[880] Sounds like good advice to me.

---

877 Sue Wilson, The Wabash Railroad: [Jacksonville Public Library Special Collections Room] [Railroad File] Jacksonville, Illinois:

878 Virginia Chamberlain, p. 7.

879 Virginia Chamberlain, p. 7.

880 Virginia Chamberlain, p. 16.

By 1845, the railroad was in such bad condition it was almost useless. The engine derailed between New Berlin and Springfield. They could not get it back on track, so it sat rusting on the prairie for the next year and a half. They had to use mules to pull the cars for a time.

Mlodzianowski declared his intention to become a citizen on October 22, 1838.[881] He filed papers again on November 6, 1840.[882] Unfortunately, Edward did not live long enough to become a citizen. Mrs. Isaac Rawlings wrote an account of Edwards's death from the October 28, 1842, *Sangamo Journal.*

> In Jacksonville on Saturday the 8th, occurred the death of Lieutenant Edward Mlodzianowski, aged 30 years, a native of Poland. He was born a noble in Russian Poland and was just concluding his collegiate education at Wilno when the late revolution in Poland broke out. He left Wilno immediately and with much difficulty succeeded in reaching Warsaw where he entered the military service of his country. He was engaged in various battles of the brilliant and melancholy struggle and bore on his body till death the honorable memorials of his intrepidity and patriotism. By the fortune of war he was driven into Austrian Poland, from thence he reached Trieste and from thence United States.
>
> The manner of his death was painful. His first attack of sickness was by a slight eruption on his face on Wednesday. On Saturday the inflammation extended to his brain. A stupor accompanied with a partial paralysis had supervened and consciousness was gone. At 8 P.M. he expired. During that last melancholy day, he gave no signs of consciousness except when his brother in exile, Napoleon Koscialowski, who was constantly at his side, addressed him in his native tongue in tones of earnestness and affection. Then it seemed as though the memories of other years were stirred and for a moment he seemed to make a vain and painful effort to arouse himself. With many a bitter thought we laid him in his last resting place, thoughts not only of his personal worth and the loss our society had sustained in his decease, but on his

---

881 Jacksonville Area Genealogical & Historical Society, Jacksonville, Illinois: [Naturalization Records]

882 Jacksonville Area Genealogical & Historical Society, [Naturalization Records]

> and his nation's wrongs, wrongs that had bowed his country in the dust, and covered his own years with a cloud and sent him forth a wanderer amid the earth, to be buried by strangers in a strange land. Our tears fell not simply from the remembrance of his many personal virtues; we loved him for his sacrifices in the sacred cause of human liberty. Such is the vigilance of the Russian police, that the subject of this notice had never heard a word from his family since he was driven into exile.[883]

Andrew Johnson

I only have a very small amount of information about Andrew. The 1850 Morgan County Census lists Andrew's age as twenty-three. He was born in Poland and his occupation was a laborer. Andrew was working at the Samuel Lewis's family farm. Samuel was twenty-nine years old and born in Pennsylvania. His wife Louisa is twenty-seven years old and born in Kentucky. They have a five-year-old son, William, and a one-year-old son, James.[884] There are no more records of Andrew until the 1878 Morgan County Directory. On the directory, Andrew is a farmhand living in section 12.[885]

Zabriskie

Morgan County had some members of the Zabriskie family. Jacob Zabriskie was first on the scene and is recorded on the 1840 census.[886] His older brother Dr. Christian B. Zabriskie, along with his family, showed up in 1840.[887] This branch of the Zabriskies living in Morgan County were descendants of Jan, the second son of Albrecht Zabriskie. Another branch of the Zabriskie family also lived in Hancock County during the same period.

History of the Zabriskie family knows very little about Jacob. He was born April 11, 1817. Jacob was most likely born in Hackensack, New Jersey. He

---

883 Sangamo Journal, October 28, 1842

884 Margaret Sager Hohimer, Eileen Lynch Gochanour, Wanda Warkins Allers, Morgan County, Illinois 1850 Census: [Privately printed by Margaret Sager Hohimer, Eileen Lynch Gochanour and Wanda Warkins Allers, 1983] p. 72.

885 History of Morgan County, Illinois: 1878. P. 690.

886 Jacksonville Area Genealogical Society, 1830-1840 U.S. Census Morgan County, Illinois: Jacksonville, Illinois 1840 Census p. 440.

887 George Olin Zabriskie, p. 128.

had a twin brother named Albert. Jacob is mentioned in many Illinois County histories. These county histories contain a section called "History of Illinois." Jacob was a captain in the U.S. Army in the Mexican War. He was killed in the Battle of Buena Vista on February 23, 1847.[888] The Battle of Buena Vista is mentioned in the county histories as "the saddest, and, for Illinois, the most mournful event" of the battle-worn day.[889] The *History of Illinois* goes on to write, "Hardin, McKee, Clay, Willis, Zabriskie, Houghton-but why go on. It would be a sad task indeed to name over all who fell during this twenty minutes slaughter."[890]

Colonel John J. Hardin was the commander of the First Illinois Infantry. He was a well-known and distinguished man in Illinois. Colonel Hardin was born in Kentucky in 1810 and came to Jacksonville in 1830. He was chosen state attorney for Morgan County in 1832. Hardin was a veteran of the Black War in 1832-33. He was also picked by Governor Ford to command the state militia in the Mormon War of 1845-47. Hardin was one of the founders of the school for the deaf and dumb which was established in Jacksonville in 1839. He was a member of the Illinois House General Assembly in the years 1836, 1838, and 1840. Hardin was also the district representative to Congress in 1843. He was one of the first men to volunteer for the Mexican War and was appointed commander of the First Illinois Infantry. His death was a great loss to the state. The funerals of Elias Zabriskie and Colonel Hardin must have been held at the same time. Louis Scott Gard claims that "the funeral of these two men was the largest attended in Jacksonville up to that time."[891]

Jacob was elected first lieutenant in Company D, First Illinois Infantry at the beginning of the Mexican War. J. S. Roberts was captain and recruited the company. Roberts had to resign his commission because of a diseased limb. Jacob was promoted to captain and took over command of Company D.[892]

The Battle of Buena Vista started out looking good for the Americans. After fighting all day, the Mexican Army looked beaten. Santa Anna sent an

---

888 History of Fulton County, Illinois; [History of Illinois] [Peoria: Chas. C. Chapman & Co. 1879] p. 124.

889 History of Fulton County, Illinois, p. 120.

890 History of Fulton County, Illinois, p. 124.

891 Louis Scott Gard, Centennial History of Jacksonville 1825-1925: [Manuscript No. 8] p. 39 Bertha Mason, The Mexican War: Jacksonville Public Library p. 9, 34-37.

892 Charles M. Eames, Historic Morgan and Classic Jacksonville: [Jacksonville, Illinois, printed at the Daily Journal Steamjob Printers Office, 1885 p. 118

officer with a white flag over to the U.S. side. The American army ordered a cease-fire. American General Wool was sent out to talk with Santa Anna, but the Mexican artillery refused to stop firing and General Wool had to turn back. During the cease-fire, Santa Anna used the time to reorganize his army.

When the battle commenced, the right side of the Mexican Army retreated. Facing the Mexican right were the troops from Illinois and Kentucky. The Illinois and Kentucky troops had been itching to charge the enemy all day, and it now looked like the right time. Colonel Hardin was given the OK and the charge was on. The Americans charged and ran right into a trap. Mexican reserves were hiding in nearby ravines and had the Americans surrounded on three sides. A retreat was ordered, and the Americans ran into a ravine to escape. Colonel Harding was too tired to keep up and was killed by a Mexican lancer. I read somewhere that Captain Zabriskie was killed while standing right next to Colonel Hardin but neglected to write down the name of the book. The American troops in the ravine were ordered to fall to the ground so the artillery could open fire on the Mexican lancers. The battle went on until night fall. The next day, to the surprise of the Americans, the Mexican Army was gone.

Dr. Christian Zabriskie

The *Zabriskie Family History* writes that the doctor was born June 21, 1801, in Hackensack, New Jersey. He married Josephine Morrison on October 30, 1823, in New York City. The marriage produced four children, but two died young. The remaining children were son Elias and daughter Juliette. The family moved to Jacksonville, Illinois, in 1840. Both Dr. Christian and his son Elias joined the army when the Mexican War started. Christian was an assistant surgeon in the First Regiment of Illinois Infantry while Elias was a second lieutenant in the First and Fourth regiments of Illinois Infantry.[893]

The *History of Trinity Church, Jacksonville, Illinois* states, "Dr. C. B. Zabriskie & family removed to New York 1848."[894] They did not stay long for the *Zabriskie Family History* claims Dr. Christian and Elias were living in San Francisco by July 4, 1849. Wife Josephine and daughter Juliette, however, remained in Bergen County, New Jersey. Josephine died January 18, 1864. She is buried in Hackensack, New Jersey. Dr. Christian was living in Sacramento, California, in 1850. There are no more records of him until

893 George Olin Zabriskie, p. 288 & 128.

894 Jacksonville Genealogical & Historical Society Journal, [XI #4 December 1983] [The History of Trinity Church, Jacksonville, Illinois] p. 4.

he died. His date of death is in dispute. He died on either November 21, 1886, or June 1887.[895]

Elias and his father split up while in California. Elias reenlisted in the army and was an officer in the Indian wars and the Civil War. He married Justine Jackson on December 17, 1863. One son, Christian, was born October 16, 1864, at Fort Bridger, Wyoming. Elias was discharged from the army after the Civil War. He left the army with the rank of major and resided in Salt Lake City until 1870. Elias then moved to Carson City, Nevada, where he died on June 10, 1894.[896] Elias converted to the Mormon faith at some point. Virgil D. White claims that Elias was a member of "Hunter's Company Mormon Volunteer's."[897]

I have to comment on Napoleon Koscialowski's son Edward. He could have had one of the most difficult Polish names to pronounce in American history. With the exception of someone born in Poland, no American would stand a chance pronouncing his name. His full name is Edward Mlodzianowski Koscialowski. My relatively easy Polish last name has been butchered many times over the years, especially in the army. Edward might have gone through life never having anyone pronounce his name right.

Sandusky

The Jacob Sandusky family lived in Morgan County for a time. On the 1840 Federal Census of Morgan County, Illinois, Jacob is between the ages of thirty and forty. His wife is between the ages of twenty and thirty. There is one son under five and one son between five and ten. One girl is under five and two between five and ten.[898] The Sanduskys moved to Greene County by at least 1850.

Edward Mlodzianowski made quite an impression during his short time in America. The *Sangamo Journal* published an impressive obituary about him. *History of Morgan County* mentioned him in pretty much glowing terms too. Andrew Johnson must have changed his last name. The Zabriskies were of course Polish descent. Dr. Christian had the same amount of Polish blood as the author, one-sixteenth. The Zabriskies who lived in Morgan County were the descendants of Jan Zabriskie, the second son of Albrecht Zabriskie.

---

895 George Olin Zabriskie, p. 128.

896 George Olin Zabriskie, p. 288-289.

897 Virgil D. White, Index to Mexican War Pension Files: [Waynesboro, Tennessee: The National Publishing Company 1989] p. 596.

898 1840 Federal Census of Morgan County, Illinois: [National Archives, Box 704, Roll 66, page 450]

Montgomery County

Montgomery County had one Pole living there by 1850, John J. Lehmanowski. The earliest record I have of him shows that he immigrated to America in 1830. Lehmanowski was living in the town of Hillsboro, Illinois, in 1846.

Montgomery County is in the southwestern part of the state. On February 12, 1821, the county was established from parts of Bond and Madison counties. It has many hills and highlands, and in its original state was about one-half timber, one-half prairie. The main river is Shoal Creek. After Montgomery became a county, a site was needed for the county seat, and after much dispute, the area where Hillsboro is situated on was chosen. The terrain was full of craters and hilly but had a fine spring. Newton Coffey, one of the county commissioners who also helped chose the site of Hillsboro, contributed twenty acres to build the town on.

Hillsboro became the hub of business activity in the county. By 1834, the population was 250. Abraham Lincoln occasionally came through town on one of the two main roads, the Vandalia to Springfield road. Hillsboro is located about forty-five miles northeast of St. Louis, Missouri. Its current population is 4,359. I found the town to be very scenic.[899]

According to Lerski, Lehmanowski was a veteran of the Kosciuszko rebellion in Poland and the Nepoleonic wars. The highest rank he attained was colonel.[900] Wytrwal writes that Lehmanowski was a Polish Jew who converted to the Lutheran faith, becoming a minister.[901] Maria J. E. Copson-Niecko's book *The Poles in America from the 1830's to the 1870's* contains a letter written by Duff Green, editor of the *Washington United Telegraph Extra*, to

899 Workers of the Writers Program, Hillsboro Guide: [The Montgomery News, 1940.] p.12, 13, 15, 17, & 83.

900 Jerzy Jan Lerski, A Polish Chapter in Jacksonian America: [Madison: The University of Wisconsin Press, 1958] p. 23 &192.

901 Joseph A Wytrwal, Poles in American History and Tradition: [Detroit: Endurance Press, 1969] P. 131.

Martin Van Buren in 1830. Green was trying to help Lehmanowski get a permanent job.

> Late an officer in the French army, and the superior and friend of Young Layfayette. Condemned to be shot at the same time [December 7, 1815] and by the same tribunal, with the unfortunate [Marshal of France], Michael Ney, he more fortunate, fled to this Country to encounter new difficulties, and to make new sacrifices—The bounty of Layfayette gave him a farm in Pennsylvania which he generously sold to redeem a young brother from Turkish bondage, and he now seeks some employment however humble as the means of support for his family.[902]

It does not look like Duff was of much help. Lehmanowski was still a temporary worker two years later when he wrote the following letter to the secretary of state on January 25, 1832. He was working at the census bureau at the time but needed a more stable job.

> You had the kindness to recommend me to the Post Master General, but there is no vacancy in his Department at present. I am a Pole by birth, lost all my property at conquest of Poland by the Russians & am exiled from my native land. I am not mistaken in the belief that you entertain feelings of kindness towards the unfortunate Poles & will, if it is in your power, favor me with employment. By so doing you will lay me under an eternal obligation.[903]

Lehmanowski didn't get a job there either, but a turn of events brought him a different opportunity. In the early 1830s, large numbers of emigrants from Germany and France began settling in the Washington, D.C., area. No justice of the peace in town could understand either language, so it was obvious that someone who could speak both languages should be added to the

[902] N. A., RG 59, M639, Roll 14, frames 0108-0109 [D. Green to M. Van Buren, Washington, Feb. 23, 1830]. In The Poles in America from the 1830's to the 1870's by Maria J. E. Copson-Niecko: [Frank Mocha, Poles in America Bicentennial Essays, Stevens Point, Wisconsin: Worzalla Publishing Company, 1978] p. 118-119.

[903] N. A. RG 639, Roll 14, frames 0113-0114 [Lewis Lehmanowski to Edward Livingston, Washington, Jan. 25, 1832] Maria J. E. Copson-Niecko, p. 246.

staff. Lehmanowski was finally in the right place at the right time. He could speak both languages, a fact already known by some of the local businessmen in town. On August 28, 1833, one hundred of the citizens of Washington, D.C., recommended to President Andrew Jackson that Lehmanowski be hired as a justice of the peace. Three days later on August 31, Lehmanowski was appointed justice of the peace by President Jackson.[904] After only three years in this country, Lehmanowski had been recommended by one hundred citizens of the city to the president of the United States. Most were businessmen. How many emigrants to this country have something like that happen to them. Either he was an extremely sociable guy or there were other factors at work. A speech he gave in 1831 is a more likely reason why he was so well-known around town. Lerski adds more to the story.

The *Washington Globe* newspaper was very sympathetic to the 1830 uprising in Poland and sponsored a number of meetings to elicit aid for Poland. One meeting was convened "for the purpose of adopting measures for the relief of the brave but suffering Poles."[905] The meeting took place at the Washington, D.C., City Hall October 26, 1831. According to Haiman, "the Polish speaker, old Colonel Lehmanowski, when appealing for assistance for the country of his origin, pointed to his ten-year-old son and said that, should the United States ever be in danger, they would both give the last drop of their blood for the defense of American liberty."[906]

Lehmanowski only stayed in Washington, D.C., a few more years, moving west by at least 1837. Joseph A. Wytrwal's book contains a number of excerpts from Lehmanowski's autobiography. Lehmanowski's first love must have been education, for in 1837 he established elementary schools for German emigrant children in New Orleans, Louisiana, and Cincinnati, Ohio. Lehmanowski also started an academy in Corydon, Indiana, and wrote about his experiences in his autobiography.

> Just now I shall say a few words about my efforts for the causes of Education and Philanthropy. One of the greatest needs of the people of that Western region was for educational institutions, and especially for such in which a future ministry could be trained. I realized this fact to the extent of giving of my own means the money for the building of a brick academy, twenty-four by fifty

[904] Maria J. E. Copson-Niecko, p 246.

[905] Jerzy Jan Lerski, p. 23.

[906] Mieczyslaw Haiman, Polacy Wsrod Pionierow Ameryki: [Chicago, Illinois: Drukiem Dziennika Zjednoczenia 1930] p. 200.

> feet in size, at Corydon, Ind. And employing a qualified man as principal.[907]

This would not be the first time that Lehmanowski would have to spend his own money. I will have more about that later. After leaving Corydon,

> In 1839 he and George Yeager were appointed as a committee of two to draw up a constitution for the proposed seminary of the Evangelical Synod of the West. The following year Lehmanowski was reelected to serve as treasurer for the collections gathered for the seminary. In 1841 he was listed as appointed to a committee of five to locate a theological seminary of the West, and to report at the next meeting. He was also made agent of the Board of Trustees for the seminary.[908]

The earliest record of Lehmanowski in Illinois is 1846. He would have been traveling through the state before this date, looking for a site for the new seminary. The town of Hillsboro was probably selected because a school building had already been built there for Hillsboro Academy. Hillsboro Academy was first opened in 1837. Its founders built a two-story white building modeled after the Parthenon in Athens, Greece. The academy building is gone now, but the public library was built to resemble it. Hillsboro Academy was transferred to the Lutherans October 19, 1846. Lehmanowski took part in the proceedings and is listed as president. Hillsboro Academy was interdenominational and coeducational, and the Lutherans continued to run it that way. It was the first Lutheran college in Illinois and was named the Literary and Theological Institute of the Lutheran Church of the Far West. The college didn't stay in Hillsboro long, moving to Springfield, Illinois, in 1852.[909]

The Lutheran college at Hillsboro would prove to be a challenge to Lehmanowski's pocketbook as well as his purpose. Lehmanowski's autobiography offers some insight into the problems he had to deal with.

---

907 Fr. Ladislas J. Siekaniec OFM, The Polish Contribution to Early American Education: 1608-1865, [unpublished Ph. D. dissertation, Western Reserve University, 1962]. p. 46. [In Poles in History and Tradition, by Joseph A. Wytrwal, p. 132.

908 Fr. Ladislas J. Siekaniec, p. 47. [Joseph A. Wytrwal, p. 131]

909 Hillsboro Public Library, History of the City of Hillsboro: p. 41, 43, & 45.

> I also attempted the establishment of a college at Hillsboro, Ill., acted for some time as its Financial Agent, and out of my own means purchased a respectable library for it. However, this effort was a failure, as my means were limited, and I was practically the only one who took a living interest in the prospective college. There were some to whom the cause was presented whose means greatly exceeded mine, and others who out of love for their church should have labored early and late for the founding of the college. The reason these people did nothing at all, even when urged to help, I can find only in the ignorant and selfish prejudice of the one class against a liberal education and in the indifference and jealousy of the others.[910]

Our Constitution newspaper from Champaign County, Illinois, printed Lehmanowski's obituary on January 30, 1858. "Died: Col. Lehmanowski, the illustrious Pole who served under Napoleon, near Hamburg, Clark Co. Indiana, aged 88 years, a few days ago. Buried with Masonic honors."[911]

Lehmanowski came to Illinois in 1846. It's beyond dispute that he was a dedicated and generous man. The college that Lehmanowski helped found in Hillsboro didn't stay in Springfield long. The college moved to Carthage and was known as Carthage College.[912]

---

910 Fr. Ladislas J. Siekaniec, p. 131. [Joseph A. Wytrwal, p. 131]

911 Champaign Country Illinois Genealogical Society, Quarterly # 7-8, June-March 1985-87: p. 58

912 Workers of the Writers Program, Hillsboro Guide, [The Montgomery News, 1940] p. 54.

Randolph County

Randolph County had four Polish settlers before 1850. Joseph Baranowski was living in the town of Kaskaskia by 1836. Joe might also be one of the exiles from Triest. Otto Kaminski lived in the towns of Prairie Du Rocher, Kaskaskia, and Chester. The 1850 Federal Census is the first record of Otto in the county. Charles Szirkowski was in Illinois by 1837. He would live most of the time on a farm near the town of Chester. The fourth Pole is William Hall. The 1850 Federal Census lists William as a resident of Randolph County. He lived on a farm between Kaskaskia and Prairie Du Rocher.

Randolph County was established October 5, 1795. This was twenty-three years before Illinois became a state. Originally Randolph was a part of St. Clair County. The county is located in Southern Illinois with most of its western boundary the Mississippi River. The eastern and northern sections of the county were mostly flat prairies as opposed to the southern and western part that was tree-covered highlands. The Kaskaskia is the main river. Two-thirds of Randolph County's terrain alongside the Mississippi River was known as the "American Bottoms." The American Bottoms was the name given to the one-hundred-mile-long body of alluvial soil that stretched from Alton to Chester along the Mississippi River. Alluvial soil is soil deposited by moving water. In Randolph County, the American Bottoms was twenty miles long and from four to fifteen miles wide. It is very fertile soil but flooded frequently.

This part of Illinois has a rich history. The French were the first European settlers in Illinois. French missionaries and traders left their settlements along the St. Lawrence River in Canada and appeared in Illinois by 1673. They were very active along the Illinois and Mississippi rivers, establishing colonies along both rivers. The French settled in Randolph County at Kaskaskia in 1703 and at Prairie Du Rocher in 1722.[913] These French settlers have had a good deal of information written about them. *Illinois, a History of the Prairie*

[913] Mark Wyman. Immigration History and Ethnicity in Illinois: A Guide, [Springfield, Illinois 1990] From the Illinois State Historical Society] p. 2.

State by Robert P. Howard contains an excerpt written by Dr. John Francis Snyder about the early French pioneers. The doctor was a great-grandson of one of these French settlers.

> The native French on the American Bottom were, with few exceptions, non-progressive, indolent and generally illiterate, giving little thought to the problems of life beyond the gratification of present wants and comfort, trusting the future to Providence and the priest-the priests especially, who were their amanuensis, business adviser, and spiritual guide. They had no incentive to avarice, no inclination to depravity, nor ambition for wealth or distinction. Personal ease and festive amusement were apparently the chief objects of their existence. They were merry, friendly and hospitable, and while the broadest freedom of speech and action was tolerated in social intercourse, they were sober, honest, and virtuous .... They assimilated readily with inferior races, adopting unhesitatingly inferior methods, but their simple habits, manners and customs were little affected or improved by contact with people of advanced culture.[914]

Natalia Marse Belting adds more.

> Heavy drinking and gambling were common here, as in all pioneer communities, but on the whole the people were law abiding and the record of their courts does not reveal an excessive amount of crime. Disputes between them were readily submitted to the judge for settlement. The people in general were lighthearted and gay. Their carefree life shocked the self-righteous puritans who later came from the American colonies. Young and old, rich and poor danced on Sunday after mass. They played cards incessantly, and not always for money. They played billiards at all hours, and loved to gossip over a pipe and a mug both in their homes and in taverns. They celebrated every conceivable occasion with religious rituals and pagan ceremonies. They called upon the church to consecrate the newly built house, the plowed field and the harvested grain.

---

[914] John Francis Snyder, Adam W. Snyder and his Period in Illinois History 1817-1842. [Virginia: 1906] p. 24. In Illinois A History of the Prairie State by Robert P. Howard: [Grand Rapids, Michigan: William B. Eerdmans Publishing Company, 1972] p. 41-42.

> Twenty-seven holy days they celebrated with respite from labor, dressing in their best clothing and feasting.[915]

The French at Kaskaskia were also living side by side with the Kaskaskia Indian tribe. The Kaskaskia Indians originally lived along the Illinois River near Utica but moved south to get away from the Iroquois Indians. Father Marest, a French Jesuit missionary, came with them. They settled between the Kaskaskia and Mississippi rivers. This would be the future site of the town of Kaskaskia.[916]

Britain gained control of Illinois in 1765 and also control of the east bank of the Mississippi River. Most of the wealthy French families moved across the river at this time. By 1800, there were still five hundred French living in Kaskaskia and two hundred in Prairie Du Rocher. Shortly after 1800, American settlers mainly from southern states started coming to Kaskaskia via the Ohio River. By 1810-20, the population of Kaskaskia was over seven thousand and the destination of most emigrants. European-born settlers chiefly from Ireland also came in at this time. In 1809, Kaskaskia became the seat of justice for the Illinois Territory. A signpost at Kaskaskia State Park has a great introduction to the town of Kaskaskia.

> The historic village was once a thriving frontier community. Founded in 1703, before St. Louis or Chicago, this center of religion, trade, and government attracted settlers from all over the world. Known as "the Mother of a Thousand Cities" and the "Paris of the West," Kaskaskia is considered by many to be where the west began.[917]

Kaskaskia's time as seat of government for Illinois lasted only ten years, from 1809 to 1819. Pioneers were settling in Central Illinois and Kaskaskia was too far south. The city was however the county seat for Randolph County until June 7, 1847. In 1844, Kaskaskia experienced a devastating flood. It became clear that the county seat would have to move to a safer location. In 1847, the residents of Randolph County voted to move the county seat to Chester, where it still located. The flood of 1844 was the beginning of the end

---

915 Natalia Marse Belting, Kaskaskia Under the French Regime: [Urbana, 1948] p.68. In The History of Kaskaskia, Illinois 1809-1820 by Russell Fleet Combs: [Saint Louis, Missouri: Dissertation, June 1950] p 8-9.

916 Russell Fleet Combs, [St. Louis, Missouri: Dissertation, June 1950] p.10.

917 Kaskaskia State Park, Randolph County, Illinois.

for Kaskaskia. According to the *Combined History of Randolph, Monroe and Perry counties, Illinois*, the river was seven feet above normal. Everyone had to leave their homes and seek higher ground. A large number of houses washed away, and many people left town for good.[918] Randolph County, Illinois, *Bicentennial* wrote that the nuns from the sisters of the Visitation convent and school fled to the home of Col. Pierre Menard. Then the *Bicentennial* writes, "The Sisters, wishing to retrieve sacred articles, as well as personal items, sought the assistance of the riverboat, Indiana. During the attempt to return the Sisters, the riverboat ran into the school knocking a huge hole in the side. The Sisters left their ruined Academy for good and made a new home in St. Louis, Missouri."[919]

More floods came in 1851 and 1857. The flood of 1851 was not as bad as the flood of 1844, but it still managed to destroy all the crops in the surrounding area. The flood of 1857 destroyed the crops and part of the town. By this time most of the buildings in town were either destroyed or in deteriorating condition. The population had fallen to 350 by 1880. In 1881 the land located between the Mississippi and Kaskaskia rivers washed away, placing the town on an island.[920] I will turn to Kaskaskia State Park again. "The flood of 1881 did not instantly destroy the town, but little by little the Mississippi's swift current swept it away. Kaskaskia now lies at the bottom of the Mississippi."[921]

Joseph Baranowski

Joe could have been one of the Polish exiles from Triest. Lerski's book contains a "list of the Polish exiles who came from Triest to New York on the corvette Adria in May, 1835."[922] The name Jozef Baranowski is the second name recorded on that list. Joe probably is the same person, but his census records raise a question. He never states that he was born in Poland or Russia but either Germany or Prussia. The 1830 uprising took place in the Russian-occupied part of Poland, but some Poles from Poznan in Prussia did fight in the uprising. Maybe Joe was one of them.

---

918 Combined History of Randolph, Monroe and Perry Counties, Illinois: [Philadelphia: J. L. McDonough & Co. 1883] p. 119.

919 Randolph County Genealogical Society, Bicentennial 1795-1995: [Paducah, Kentucky: Turner Publishing Company 1995] p. 11.

920 Randolph County Genealogical Society, Bicentennial: p. 71.

921 Kaskaskia State Park:

922 Jerzy Jan Lerski, A Polish Chapter in Jacksonian America: [Madison, Wisconsin: The University of Wisconsin Press, 1958] p. 179.

The first record of Joe living in Kaskaskia is on October 12, 1836, when he bought a lot for twenty-five dollars.[923] Fourteen days later on October 26, 1836, Joe bought another lot for ninety dollars.[924] Kaskaskia probably seemed like a great place to buy land at the time. Who would know that one day the whole town would be underwater. Joe applied to become naturalized on April 29, 1841, and became a citizen April 29, 1843.[925] The census records always show Joe's occupation as a cabinetmaker. A cabinetmaker makes fine furniture and other woodwork. Montague's 1859 Directory of Randolph County records Joe's occupation as farmer.[926] In 1860, Joe owned a small farm of eight acres with a value of $160. He owned one horse, three milk cows, one team of oxen, and four pigs. The farm produced 320 bushels of corn, 10 bushels of potatoes, and 100 pounds of butter.[927] He was also a trustee of the Commons. The Commons was nine thousand acres of land located between the Kaskaskia and Mississippi rivers. All the people of Kaskaskia had equal access to the Commons for firewood and pasture for their livestock. The French created the Commons, and the American settlers continued the custom. In 1854, an act of legislature authorized the citizens of Kaskaskia to elect five trustees to manage the commons. Joe was one of the first five trustees elected. These first trustees leased most of the Commons and used the fees collected to support the local church and schools.[928]

Joe was born September 15, 1800, in Prussia. His wife Christina was also born in Prussia on April 24, 1802.[929] The Baranowskis were members of "the Church of the Immaculate Conception of the Blessed Virgin" Catholic Church. All four of their children were born in Illinois and baptized at Immaculate Conception of the Blessed Virgin. Daughter Marie Therese was born March 4, 1837. Son Joseph Jr. was born May 5, 1839. Joseph Jr. would

923 Randolph County Recorder, Book P, 1834-1837. p.374.

924 Randolph County Recorder, Book P, 1834-1837. p. 375.

925 Randolph County Clerk, Joseph Baranowski probate file. [Chester, Illinois]

926 E. J. Montague, A Directory, Business Mirror, and Historical Sketches of Randolph County 1859: [Alton, Illinois: Courier Steam Book and Job Printing House, 1859] [A Reproduction by Unigraphic, Inc. Evansville, Indiana 1974] p. 119.

927 1860 Agriculture Census of Randolph County, Illinois: [Illinois State Archives, Roll 31-10]

928 Combined History of Randolph, Monroe and Perry Counties, Illinois, p. 308.

929 Randolph County 1800-1850 information binder, [At the Randolph County Genealogical Society, Chester, Illinois] Cemetery Records: p. 219.

grow up to own a foundry and machine shop in Chester.[930] Daughter Marie Cornelia was born June 27, 1842. None of the census records has ever recorded her name, so she must have died at an early age. The youngest daughter was Sophia, who was born February 21, 1844.[931]

Between cabinetmaker, farmer, and commons trustee, Joe must have had a full schedule. Joe died September 10, 1869. His wife Christina died exactly one month later on October 10, 1869.[932] Joe and Christina are both buried at Garrison Hill Cemetery in Kaskaskia State Park.[933] It is fitting to end this story about the Baranowskis and learn a little more about Kaskaskia with these words from a signpost at Garrison Hill Cemetery State Park.

"Heroes Lie Here"

> The bodies of early Illinois settlers are buried in the cemetery. They were moved here from three cemeteries in Kaskaskia village. When floods began to destroy the village in the late eighteen hundreds, concerned residents acted to transfer the remains to a safer place. According to one account 3800 boxes, some containing entire families were moved. The cemetery was dedicated in 1891.[934]

Joseph Baranowski Jr. has an interesting obituary from the August 2, 1894, *Chester Tribune* newspaper. The newspaper calls him John instead of Joe.

> John Baranowski, the veteran foundry man of Chester, died Wednesday in St. Louis at the Mallanphy Hospital. The funeral was at the Catholic Church and burial was in St. Mary's cemetery. He was about 55 years old and raised in Kaskaskia where his parents resided. While still a boy, he went to Prairie du Rocher and was a clerk in a store. He also clerked in Arkansas in the store of John Sprigg. When the war broke out, he was drafted into the

930 The Genealogy Society of Southern Illinois, John A. Logan College, Carterville, Illinois: [Saga of Southern Illinois, Vol. 16/2 1989] p. 29.

931 Jack D. Westerman, The Church of the Immaculate Conception of the Blessed Virgin, Index of Baptisms: [Located at Randolph County Genealogical Society 1994.] p. 2.

932 Randolph County Genealogical Society, Cemetery Records: p. 219.

933 Randolph County 1800-1850 information binder, [Garrison Hill State Park Cemetery records] p. 219.

934 Kaskaskia State Park.

Confederate army where he served the entire war. After the war, he came back to Kaskaskia and married Miss Emily Hoopenaugh. Several years later, he moved to Chester. He leaves a wife and four children, three boys and one girl.[935]

Otto Kaminski

The 1850 Federal Census shows Otto living in the village of Prairie Du Rocher. Prairie Du Rocher was founded by French settlers in 1722. J. M. Peck wrote in 1832 that Prairie Du Rocher,

> An ancient French village, in Randolph county, on the American bottom, near the Rocky bluffs, and which it derives its name, fourteen miles northwest of Kaskaskia. It is a low, unhealthy situation, along a small creek of the same name, which rises in the bluffs, passes across the American bottom, and enters the Mississippi. The houses are built in the French style, the streets very narrow, and the inhabitants preserve more of the simplicity of character and habits peculiar to early times, than any village in Illinois. It has its village lots, common fields, and commons, the peculiarities of which are noticed under the article "Cahokia." Prairie Du Rocher, in 1766, contained fourteen families; the population at present is estimated at thirty-five families.[936]

History of Randolph, Monroe and Perry Counties, Illinois adds a little more.

> The population of Prairie Du Rocher was about three hundred in 1880. More than one-half of the families are French, the descendants of the early settlers of the vicinity. Some few of the old ladies can speak nothing but the French language, though of late years the English has come into general use. The village wears a thrifty and lately prosperous look, and numerous improvements have lately been made.[937]

---

935 Lola Frazer Crowder, Chester Herald Newspaper Abstracts 1873-1894: [1996] p. 58]

936 J. M. Peck, A. M., A Gazetteer of Illinois, in three parts: [Philadelphia: Grigg & Elliot, 1837.] Facsimile Reprint, Maryland, Heritage Books Inc. 1993. p 276.

937 Combined History of Randolph, Monroe and Perry Counties, Illinois. p. 378.

Prairie Du Rocher has always been a small town. Its present population is 613. I went there hoping to see some reminder of the old French culture but could not find anything. Maybe I missed something, but the town looked like any other American town.

I have not found out a lot about Otto, mostly odds and ends. The 1850 Federal Census is the earliest record I have of Otto in Illinois. On the census, Otto is thirty-seven years old. His occupation is physician, and he lists Poland as his place of birth.[938] Otto married Teresa Pape on May 11, 1852.[939] She was around twenty-three years old at the time. The 1860 census records her place of birth as Poland. Their marriage never produced any children. Otto became a citizen April 29, 1856.[940] I managed to find a record of Otto appraising the value of an eight-year-old sorrel horse in a *Randolph County Estray* book. The horse sold for forty dollars.[941] Otto moved to Kaskaskia by 1859. E. J. Montague lists Otto as a physician in Kaskaskia in the year 1859.[942] On the 1870 census, Otto is living in Chester and has shortened his name to Kamins. Instead of Poland, Otto now lists Prussia as place of birth.[943] Teresa is not listed on the 1870 census, and I suspect she has already died. Otto died March 5, 1873, and was living in the town of Chester at the time. Otto's death certificate say's, "There is no children and no relatives known other than his brother-in-law." Otto's brother-in-law was the executor of his estate.[944]

Charles Szirkowski

Charles lived on a farm near the town of Chester. The Szirkowski name is on page 143 in the "Directory of Randolph County 1859" by E. J. Montague.[945] Chester is located on a bluff along the Mississippi River in the southern part of Randolph County. The town is also at the southern end of the American Bottoms. Samuel Smith was the founder of Chester. He bought land there

---

938 Index to the 1850 Randolph County, Illinois Census: [Yakima, Washington, Yakima Valley Genealogical Society] p. 150.

939 Randolph County Genealogical Society, Marriage Records 1851-1864. p. 24.

940 Randolph County Clerk, Otto Kaminski probate file.

941 Randolph County Estray Book, p. 37.

942 E. J. Montague p.121.

943 Randolph County Genealogical Society, 1870 Randolph County Census: Chester, Illinois: p.116.

944 Randolph County Clerk, Otto Kaminski Probate file.

945 E. J. Montague, p.143.

in 1830 and also built the first house. Smith started and managed a hotel, ran a ferry, and started a mill. His wife was from Chester, England, and the town that grew up there became known as Chester. By 1859, the population was 900.The present population is 5,185.

I wrote earlier about moving the county seat from Kaskaskia to Chester in 1847. Chester and the town of Sparta competed for the county seat, and Chester won by a controversial vote. During the vote, people commented on the "extraordinary increase of the population of Randolph County."[946] The Kaskaskia Republican newspaper reported on July 31, 1847, that there were 135 illegal votes cast in Chester. A fellow named Joe Mattingley made repeated trips across the Mississippi River with his houseboat to bring in voters. Flatboat workers voted repeatedly.

The situation in Sparta was just as bad. Large numbers of "visitors" from other counties showed up. Those who backed Chester were stopped from voting. Chester went on to win the county seat by forty votes and was awarded the county seat by the Illinois circuit court in November 1847. In 1848, the county seat was moved to Chester where it has remained ever since.[947]

Randolph County, Illinois, *Bicentennial* contains a lengthy and informative story about the Szirkowskis. Charles was a government official in Coblentz, Germany, before coming to America. His father-in-law, Heinrich Weber, was an even higher-ranking official in Coblentz and was reputed to be a very competent official there. Charles and his wife Ida spent several years planning to emigrate to America. The Szirkowskis and Webers both left for America on the same ship, landing in Baltimore in June, 1834. The Szirkowski family included Charles, Ida, and their five-year-old son Heinrich. The Weber family contained Heinrich, wife Rosa, and their five children, Theresa, Johann, Heinrich, Gottwalt, and Bertha. The two families were soon on the move and journeyed to St. Louis, Missouri. The Webers were into music and founded a music business right away. Charles and Ida's marriage did not work out, and they divorced in 1837. Divorces were few and far between in those days. Most of the time the husband just abandoned their wives and "left for the long grass of unsettled territory and the women became 'grass widows.'"[948] Charles moved across the river to St. Clair County, Illinois, and married Susan Humphries on December 16,

---

946 Combined History of Randolph, Monroe and Perry Counties, Illinois. p. 120.

947 Combined History of Randolph, Monroe and Perry Counties, Illinois. p. 284, 286, 287.

948 Randolph County, Illinois Bicentennial 1795-1995, p. 360.

1838. Charles and Susan were the parents of Actia, Carl, Charles, Ellen, Mary, and Susan.[949]

After reading the story of the Szirkowski's move to America, you would think they were Germans. According to the 1850 St. Clair County, Illinois, census, the Szirkowskis lived in St. Clair County before moving to Randolph County. The 1850 St. Clair Census shows that Charles is forty years old, occupation trader and born in Poland. Susan is thirty-one years old and born in Illinois. Sons Ferdinand, eleven; Charles, eight; and Albert, one, were all born in Illinois. Daughters Emily, ten; Mary, six; and Arsesha, four, are all born in Illinois.[950] In the 1860 Randolph County census, Charles is a sixty-eight-year-old farmer and born in Poland. Susan is forty years old. Charles's and Susan's ages do not match up on the 1850 or 1860 census. Charles died in 1866, and the 1870 Randolph County Census lists Susan head of household. Her age is fifty, so the 1860 census is the right census concerning age. At the time of his second marriage, Charles would have been forty-six and Susan eighteen, a twenty-eight-year difference. Way to go, Charles. This reminds me of a story in the February 9, 2003, *Chicago Tribune* titled "The Last of the Civil War Widows." Alberta Martin married William Jasper Martin in 1927. She was twenty-one and he was eighty-one. William had been a private in the Confederate army and Alberta was his third wife. According to Alberta, "the old saying is, better to be an old man's darling than a young man's slave."[951]

The 1860 census has a few differences as compared to the Szirkowski story in the Randolph County *Bicentennial.* There are three sons, Ferdinand, twenty-one; Charles, eighteen; and Albert, twelve. The daughters are Mary, fifteen; Actia, thirteen; and Ellen, eight. All were born in Illinois.[952] The 1870 census only mentions Susan, fifty; Albert, twenty; and daughter Susan, seven. Charles would have been seventy-one when Susan was born. Charles has impressed me again.[953]

---

949 Randolph County, Illinois Bicentennial 1795-1995, p. 360.

950 1850 Federal Census of St. Clair County, Illinois: [National Archives, Box 432 Roll 126, Page 443]

951 David Lamb, "The last of the Civil War Widows," Chicago Tribune, 9 Feb. 2003, p. 12.

952 Yakima Valley Genealogical Society, The 1860 Federal Census of Randolph County, Illinois: [Yakima, Washington, 1986] p. 268.

953 Randolph County Genealogical and Historical Society, [1870 Federal Census for Randolph County] p. 73]

Charles's son Heinrich, from his first marriage to Ida Marie, has a small paragraph in the Randolph County *Bicentennial.* "The young German immigrant, Heinrich grew up visiting his father in Randolph County. Here he met and married a lovely Scot immigrant Elizabeth Easton Adams, daughter of James Adams, Jr. of 'Scot Town' Feb. 6, 1858 in Chester."[954]

Charles's son Charles Jr. is also mentioned in the Randolph County *Bicentennial.* Charles changed his name to Charles Warrens.[955] Why he picked the last name Warrens is anybody's guess, but he thought Szirkowski was too difficult to pronounce. Most people of Polish descent in this country are probably used to having their names pronounced wrong. I know I am, and the army was the worst of all.

Charles enlisted in the Union army in 1861. He helped organize a company of the Fourth Missouri Infantry and was elected its first lieutenant. Charles was promoted to major in 1862. Charles got bored in the Fourth Missouri. Most of the time all they did was fight southern guerrillas in Missouri and Charles wanted to be more involved in the war. He got his wish when he was allowed to transfer to the Twenty-ninth Regiment of Missouri Infantry. It looks like transferring to the Twenty-ninth was a bad move. Charles was seriously wounded on December 29, 1862, at the Battle of Chickasaw Bluffs. The battle was a real mess and the army lost contact with many of its soldiers. Charles was listed as AWOL when he was really on a hospital boat. Charles was not able to rejoin his unit because of his wound, so the army made him a recruiter until he regained his health. He worked in this position until the end of the war.

Charles stayed in the army after the war ended and spent the rest of his army career at different western posts. He had a novel way of remembering each post. The middle name of each of his children was named after the post they were born at. Charles's wife died in Colorado from mountain fever on July 30, 1883. Charles retired from the army because of sickness in 1891. He never forgot his hometown of Chester and stayed in touch until his death in 1902.[956]

William Hall

I have only found a very small amount of information about William. On the 1850 Federal Census, he is thirty-two and a farm laborer. His place

954 Randolph County, Illinois Bicentennial 1795-1995. p.360

955 Randolph County, Illinois Bicentennial 1795-1995. p. 172.

956 Randolph County, Illinois Bicentennial 1795-1995. p. 360.

of birth is Poland. He lives and works at the George Harmon Farm. On the same census, George Harmon is fifty years old. He was born in Virginia. His wife Polly is forty and born in South Carolina. The Harmons had ten children. William D. Malone, eighteen, was also working on the farm.[957] William must have changed jobs in 1850 because there is a record of Hall working at James Thompson's farm. Thompson was sixty-two years old, farmer and born in South Carolina. His wife Margaret is fifty-one years old and also born in South Carolina. The Thompsons had six children, all born in Illinois. Logan Greir, thirty-five years old and born in Tennessee was also living with the Thompsons. Hall claims his age is thirty-five on this census.[958]

There is no 1860 census for William. He was not listed on George Harmon's census record either. By the 1870 census, William is back working at the George Harmon farm. His age is 62, but should be 52 according to the 1850 census. His place of birth is now Prussia.[959] William might have been married in 1875. Randolph County Genealogy Society sent me a letter containing the marriage of William Hall to Emeline Harrison February 18, 1875. If this is the same William Hall, then he was married at the age of either fifty-seven or sixty-seven.[960]

The Poles I have just mentioned were the earliest Poles to live in Randolph County but not the most famous. That honor goes to a fellow named Frank "Rocky" Feigle. Rocky was the prototype for a famous comic strip character which I will soon reveal.

Most of the information for this story comes to us from Mrs. Jessie Lee Huffstutler. Mrs. Huffstutler lived in Chester and was a musician and retired teacher. In 1969 and 1970, she started writing down stories about Chester, most from memory. One of those stories was about Elzie Crisler Segar. Mrs. Huffstutler remembered him as a child. Segar would grow up to become world famous for his comic strip *Popeye.*

To develop characters for *Popeye,* he studied the inhabitants of Chester. Besides Popeye, he developed Wimpy and Olive Oyl from Chester residents. Wimpy was Bill Schuchert, who managed the town opera house. Olive Oyl was Mrs. Pascal, whose husband was a local businessman. Our story concerns Rocky Feigle, the prototype for Popeye. According to Mrs. Huffstutler,

957 Yakima Valley Genealogical Society, The 1850 Federal census of Randolph County, Illinois: [Yakima, Washington, 1976] p. 164.

958 Yakima Valley Genealogical Society, p. 71.

959 Randolph County Genealogical and Historical Society, 1870 Federal Census of Randolph County, p.69.

960 Randolph County Genealogical Society, Marriage Records

> "Popeye was Rocky Feigle, a Polish young man who lived with his mother and sister near the Evergreen Cemetery. He was tall, strong, always ready for a fight and always a winner. One day Five Local boys decided to gang up on him and in that way, win the battle, but when they all appeared, and the fight started—in a very short time Rocky had whipped three of them and the other two couldn't be found. They had disappeared. Rocky worked part-time at the George Gozney Saloon on State Street—Now known as Eggemeyer's Tavern. When Rocky had finished his work and a couple of beers in his stomach, he would take a chair out front, seat himself, tilt the chair back, with pipe in his mouth, proceed to take a nap in the sunshine.
>
> Day after day my brothers, Elzie Segar and several other boys would take the long road home from school in order to pass Gozney's place, and if Rocky was still sleeping, they would creep near, yell loudly and run. Of course, Rocky would rouse quickly from his slumber, come out of his chair with arms flying in all directions, ready for a fight, but by that time, the boys would be a block away. Strange to say, he never lost his pipe. As years passed, promoters tried to persuade Rocky to make personal appearance tours, but he wasn't interested. A business man in Chester told me that at one time checks came regularly to Rocky from Segar. This man saw the checks."[961]

Now for one last story about Popeye. While driving around Chester, I came across a statue of Popeye in a park next to the Mississippi River. The following story is from a plaque at Segar Park.

Popeye

> This statue is erected in Tribute to Elzie Crisler Segar. Born in Chester, Illinois 12-8-1894. Died in Santa Monica, Cal. 10-13-1938. Mr. Segar created Popeye from his recollections of Frank "Rocky" Fiegal Jan. 27, 1864-Mar. 24, 1947. Local Scrapper. Popeye first appeared in the cast of thimble theatre 1-17-1929. William "Windy Bill" Schucert 3-8-1857-2-20-1941. Chester

[961] Mrs. Jessie Lee Huffstutler, History of Chester: [At the Randolph County Genealogical and Historical Society, Chester, Illinois] p. 54.

opera house owner and Mr. Segars benefactor, appeared as "Wimpy" the Hamburger fiend.[962]

Other Poles came to Randolph County in the 1850s. I checked the 1860 census and put together this list. Since my book is supposed to end at 1850, I did not do an in-depth look at any of them. I did the best I could with their names.

Peter Merchencosky, age forty-four, farmer, born in Poland. Wife Rosalia, age twenty-seven, born in Poland. Son Rosseaw, age seven, born in Poland. Son Ludovena, age five, born in Illinois.[963] The Merchencoskys lived near Chester. E. J. Montague also lists Pete Merchencosky on page 141 of Directory of Randolph County 1859.[964]

Harmon Norvack, age forty-one, farmer, born in Poland. Wife Julia, age twenty-three, born in Poland. Son John, age six months, born in Illinois. The Norvacks were living near Chester.[965]

Joseph Lousinski, age thirty-eight, Cooper, born in Poland. Wife Julia, age thirty-eight, born in Poland. Daughter Rosage, fifteen, born in Poland. Daughter Lou, age thirteen, born in Poland. Daughter Bol, age three, born in Illinois. Daughters Mary and Agnes, age two, born in Illinois. The Lousinskis lived near Chester.[966]

Jacob Koshma, age thirty-seven, farmer, born in Poland. Wife Pauline, age thirty-seven, born in Poland. Daughter Lena, age eleven, born in Poland. Son Michael, age nine, born in Poland. Son Andrew, age four, born in Illinois. The Koshmas were living near Chester.[967]

Antoine Gninski, age forty, Laborer, born in Poland. Wife Francisca, age forty, born in Poland. Daughter Agatha, age four, born in Illinois. Son inf?, age one, born in Illinois. The Gninskis were living in Chester.[968]

August Wipkiski, age thirty-four, farmer, born in Germany. Wife Sofia, age twenty-eight, born in Germany. Daughter Wilhemina, age five, born in

[962] Segar Park, Chester, Illinois:

[963] Yakima Valley Genealogical Society, The 1860 Federal Census of Randolph County, Illinois: [Yakima, Washington: 1986] p. 183.

[964] E. J. Montague, p. 141.

[965] Yakima Valley Genealogical Society, The 1860 Federal Census of Randolph County, Illinois. [Yakima, Washington] p. 270.

[966] Yakima Valley Genealogical Society, p. 92.

[967] Yakima Valley Genealogical Society, p. 269.

[968] Yakima Valley Genealogical Society, p. 258.

Illinois. Daughter Caroline, four, born in Illinois. Son William, age three, born(?). The Wipkiskis lived near Red Bud.[969]

Frank Spikolski, age twenty-seven, blacksmith, born in Poland. Wife Eva, age twenty-one, born in Poland. Daughter Mary, age six, born in Poland. Daughter Ann, age three, born in Poland.[970]

Michael Schibolski, age thirty, farm laborer on the Jennett Hill farm near Chester. Michael was born in Prussia.[971]

Ferdinand Sigkorowski, age twenty-one, farm laborer on the Robert Douglas farm near Chester. The Douglas farm was next door to the Jennett Hill farm. Place of birth is Illinois, but this is probably a mistake.[972]

Joe Baranowski might still have some descendants living in Randolph County. I tried to contact them but was not successful. Neither Otto Kaminski nor William Hall had any descendants at all. The Szirkowskis are the most written about Polish family in the county. After 1850, these four Poles would have plenty of their fellow compatriots moving into the county. By 1860, the county had forty-seven people who were either Polish or part Polish descendant.

---

969 1860 Federal Census of Randolph County, Illinois: [National Archives Roll 221 page 742 & 743]

970 National Archives, 1860 Randolph County Census: [Box 653, Roll 221, p. 854]

971 Yakima Valley Genealogical Society, p. 269.

972 Yakima Valley Genealogical Society, p. 270.

Sangamon County

Sangamon County had one person of Polish descent named James Reed. Grobicki claims that one of the 234 Polish exiles from Trieste named Karol Komar lived in the town of Rochester.[973] I could not find any records of him living there, so will not write anything more about him. James Reed made a big impact during his stay in the county. He made an even bigger impact after he left the county, and I will get into that later. Edmund L. Kowalczyk wrote an article about James in the Polish Review magazine.[974] He is also written about in two other books that I will list later.

Sangamon County is located in the center of the state. The state capital of Springfield is situated in the county. Springfield is 197 miles southwest of Chicago and 95 miles northeast of St. Louis. Sangamon became a county on January 30, 1821, from parts of Bond and Madison counties. Sangamon County in turn was divided into four new counties. Morgan County was created from Sangamon in 1823 and Menard, Christian, and Logan counties in 1839. Most of Sangamon County was prairie when first settled. The wooded areas were along streams and in groves. Like most of Illinois, the soil is very fertile.

James Reed (Reednoski)

James lived six miles east of Springfield in the present town of Riverton. The Sangamon River flows through the town. Riverton has undergone four name changes during its existence. Its second name "Jamestown or Jimtown," was named after James Reed. James also operated the first factory in town. The house that James lived in is still there too! Riverton's present population is

[973] Aleksander Grobicki, Proba Biografii, Sodalis: [St. Mary's College Library, Orchard Lake, Michigan, Letter K] p. 20

[974] Edmund L. Kowalczyk, James F. Reed-Rydowski California Pioneer: [Polish American Studies, Volume 3-4 July-December 1948]

2,783. *History of Sangamon County, Illinois* 1881 contains a good-size portrait of James Reed. It only touches on what James Reed is most famous for.

According to *History of Sangamon County*, James Reed was born in County Armagh, Ireland, on November 14, 1800. His father was Polish nobility who left Poland because of Russian despotism. He settled in Northern Ireland and at some point changed his last name to Reed. James's mother was of Scottish descent and a member of the Clan Frazier. James and his mother came to America when James was eleven years old and settled in Virginia for nine years. When James turned twenty, he left Virginia for the west. He arrived in Illinois in 1820 and went to work in the lead mines. James staked his own claim near Galena in 1827[975] and mined lead there until 1831. Indian troubles were beginning and the Black Hawk War would start in 1832.

James left Galena and moved to Springfield in Sangamon County. There he enlisted in the Sangamon County militia and fought in the Black Hawk War. George R. Stewart states that Abraham Lincoln and James Reed both served in the same company during the war.[976] James went back to Springfield after the war and went into business for himself. He married Mrs. Margaret W. Backenstoe in 1834. She had one daughter from a previous marriage. He became a very successful businessman and bought a farm outside of town. James must have needed more room to expand his business and moved it seven miles east of Springfield to a location alongside the Sangamon River. There he conducted a "cabinet furniture" factory. His factory employed a substantial workforce. The workers began settling around the factory, and before long, a new town was born. The town was named Jamestown as a tribute to James.[977]

After I read the portrait of James in the county history, I thought the big story was that a town was named after him. I called the Springfield Public Library and asked if the library had much information about him. The first thing the librarian mentioned was the "Reed-Donner party." I had heard the name Donner party before and after thinking a moment, it came to me. Years earlier, I had seen a documentary about a wagon train trapped in the mountains during the winter of 1846. In one of the most notorious stories

975 Robert Hansen & Alfred Mueller, Smith papers, Apply for diggers permit 1977: [At the Galena Public Library] p. 30.

976 George R. Stewart, Ordeal by Hunger: [1936] [Copyright renewed 1988 by Theodosia B. Stewart] p. 13.

977 History of Sangamon County, Illinois; [Chicago: Inter-state Publishing Company, 1881] p. 853.

of the old west, the members of the wagon train had resorted to cannibalism to survive.

George R. Stewart wrote that nine wagons left Springfield on April 14, 1846. James Reed owned three of them. George and Jacob Donner each owned three wagons. Others joined the wagon train along the way until there was a total of twenty wagons. Besides James were his wife Margaret, daughters Virginia and Patty, and sons Jim and Tommy. Margaret's mother Mrs. Keyes also went along. Mrs. Keyes would not make it to California. She died of old age while the wagon train was crossing through Kansas. Margaret was very sickly, but James was optimistic her condition would improve in California.

James Reed and George Donner were already good friends before leaving Springfield. They were both wealthy, James Reed more so. James was forty-six years old while George was sixty-two. Members of the wagon train elected George Donner captain, but James was probably the better choice. He was younger, more energetic, and a sharp businessman. Many on the wagon train, however, disliked James. Their reason being that James was an "aristocrat."

The Reeds stuck out like a sore thumb. Everything they owned was better than anyone else's. One of their wagons was a huge custom-built wagon two stories high. The first floor was used to store food and cloths. The top floor contained beds. Entry to the wagon was by steps on the side, rather then the front or back. A stove heated the wagon with the flue pipe sticking out of the top of the wagon. The seats had springs which where originally made for the finest stagecoaches. The seats proved so popular with the other women of the wagon train that they congregated there to socialize. There was even a girl employed to cook and do laundry while the wagon moved.

The Reeds' oldest daughter Virginia rode about on a pony named "Billy," while the other children rode in wagons or walked. James rode a champion racehorse named "Glaucus." He employed three men to drive his wagons and had an extra man to do odd jobs for him. If you have not figured it out yet, the rest of the members of the wagon train were jealous of the Reeds.

I am going to end the story here. The reason is I am assigning the readers homework. You will have to read the story of the Donner party yourselves. It is an amazing story of human endurance, and after reading it, you will wonder how anyone survived. Read either *Ordeal* by Hunger by George R. Stewart or *Snow Mountain Passage* by James D. Houston. There is also a documentary which I believe is called *The Donner Party.*

St. Clair County

A number of Poles lived in St. Clair County before 1850. Five of them were members of the 234 Polish exiles from Trieste. Dr. Alfonso Xavier Illinski is the most written about of all the Polish settlers in the county. Dr. Illinski was one of the 234 exiles from Trieste and lived in the town of Cahokia. Theophilus Rutkowski, Anton Poniatowski, Joseph Jablonski, and Alexander Matterske were also members of the 234 exiles from Trieste. They all lived on or near the American Bottoms. George Suprunowski was also an exile from Trieste but came here on a different ship than the other five.

Charles Szirkowski lived in the county seat of Belleville. Sometime in the 1850s the Szirkowski family moved south to a farm near the town of Chester in Randolph County. A man with the German-sounding name of Andrew Hohn was born in Poland and lived in the northwest part of the county. The French-sounding name of Louis Annet claimed to be born in Poland. There is also the marriage of John Schmit to Paulina Silcosky on January 26, 1843. Her last name could be Polish.

St. Clair County is the oldest county in the state. It is located across the Mississippi River from St. Louis, Missouri. The county seat of Belleville is only fourteen miles east of St. Louis. The part of the county along the Mississippi River is either steep Bluffs or the American Bottoms. The American Bottoms was a one-hundred-mile-long body of alluvial soil that stretched from Alton to Chester and was from four to fifteen miles wide. Alluvial soil is soil deposited by moving water. It was very fertile but prone to flooding. Most of St. Clair County was rolling prairie. The wooded areas were along streams and on the American Bottoms.

The first European settlers in St. Clair County were the French. Their first settlement was at Cahokia in 1699. In 1762, the treaty of Fountain Bleau ceded everything east of the Mississippi River to Great Britain. In 1772, it became a part of the Virginia territory. In 1784, Virginia ceded Illinois, Wisconsin, Indiana, Michigan, Ohio, and part of Minnesota to the United States. Illinois became a state in 1818.

The first Americans to settle in St. Clair County were mainly from the south. Most were from the states of Kentucky, Tennessee, Virginia, and Maryland. Very few Yankees from New England came to the county in the early days of settlement. The Pennsylvania Dutch were the only northerners to settle in large numbers. The main story of emigration to the county was the German settlers of the 1830s.

A book written by Gottfried Duden inspired the German emigration to St. Louis and Central Illinois. Edward Husar wrote, Gottfried Duden's book, *Journey to the Western States of America*, was published in Germany in 1829. Duden's description of the beauty and richness of Missouri led thousands of Germans to immigrate to Missouri and Illinois.[978]

The *Belleville Germans* by Thomas C. Jewett adds more. From 1815 to 1830, there were only a few German families in St. Clair County. The main German immigrations came in the early 1830s and the late 1840s. The German settlers of the 1830s were known as the "Latin Farmers." They got the name because they could speak Latin better then they could farm. Many were young, wealthy, and educated. Their dream was to go back to nature and live as simple farmers. They were members of the Burschenschaften Movement in Germany. The Burschenschaften Movement promoted liberal ideas and wanted to unite Germany. The movement was responsible for an unsuccessful Prussian revolution in 1830.

Dissatisfied with the Prussian government, they left for America. Once here, the former revolutionists established the Giessen Society. Its goal was to develop a German community within the United States. The German emigrants were very proud of their culture, which they considered superior to American culture. They never intended to assimilate. Their dream "was to establish a separate German colony with German "customs, laws and culture."[979] Quite a bit of hostility developed between the German Latin farmers and American settlers from the south. The German settlers were wealthier and better educated. Some Germans also expressed fault with American culture, raising the ire of the Americans. Jewett writes,

> The clash of cultures between the Latin farmers and the Southerners was immediate. On the groups trip through Belleville to their new farm, they created quite a scene. The Germans were well-dressed, wearing clothes not often seen on the frontier. They rode fine horses and carried double-barreled shot guns. Several of

978 Quincy Herald Whig, October 1985.

979 Thomas C. Jewett, The Belleville Germans: [Belleville, Illinois: 1985] p. 1-8

> the men had chin beards and mustaches, which were not worn at the time by the Americans.[980]

In Prussia, the future Latin farmers had planned to make farming their career in America. A couple years on the farm changed that notion. Most moved to Belleville and went back to the trades they practiced in Prussia. They gained in influence in Belleville and throughout St. Clair County as well. By the next German emigration in the late 1840s, they dominated Belleville "politically, culturally, professionally and eventually in education."[981]

History of St. Clair County 1881 claims the Latin farmers were from wealthy families. The majority of German settlers to America however were poor peasants in Germany. They were the largest group of foreign born in the state, followed by the Irish and English. Many could not pay for the trip here and had to work off the debt as indentured servants to whoever paid for their passage. *History of St. Clair County, Illinois* states,

> Healthy adults get off with three or four years. Youths from ten to fifteen years must serve to their twenty-first year. Many parents are forced to trade off their own children in order to free themselves from the ship's owner, who had furnished transportation on credit. Families are frequently separated in this manner, never to be united again. If any one undertakes to run away from his master because of cruel or inhuman treatment, he will not get far, for the laws in reference to such fugitives are well enforced, and high rewards are paid to the one that captures such fugitives.[982]

Alphonso Xavier Illinski

The most well-known Pole to live in St. Clair County before 1850 was Dr. Alphonso Xavier Illinski. Alphonso was one of the 234 Polish exiles from Trieste.[983] In Lerski's book, his first name is Ksawery, but in America he called himself Alfonso Xavier. *History of St. Clair County, Illinois* 1881 wrote that

---

980 Thomas C. Jewett, p. 6.

981 Thomas C. Jewett, p. 13.

982 History of St. Clair County, Illinois 1881: [Philadelphia: Brink, McDonough & Co.] [Reproduction by the Marissa Historical and Genealogical Society, Marissa, Illinois, Whipporwill Publications, Evansville, Indiana] p. 64.

983 Jerzy Jan Lerski, A Polish Chapter in Jacksonian America: [Madison: The University of Wisconsin Press, 1958] p. 174.

Illinski "reached Castle Garden, New York City, March 28th, 1834."[984] This is the date the 234 Polish exiles landed in New York. He practiced medicine in the American Bottoms, which was a very difficult and dangerous place at the time. All the St. Clair County histories contain a biography of the doctor. He lived in the town of Cahokia. Cahokia is the oldest town in Illinois and located on the American Bottoms. Its present population is about nineteen thousand.

Cahokia was created in 1699 by French Jesuit Missionaries from Canada who sought to convert the Cahokia and Tomoros Indian tribes living in the region. The new settlement was named Notre Dame Des Kahokias but later changed to Cahokia. A trading post soon developed which also traded with the Indian tribes farther north. By 1783, Cahokia and the surrounding area had one hundred families living there. In 1798, Cahokia had a population of about three thousand and was larger than St. Louis. A ferry transported people from St. Louis to purchase supplies from Cahokia's twenty-four stores.

The flood of 1844 almost wiped out Cahokia. The 1844 flood also changed the course of the Mississippi river, moving it almost a mile west. By the time Dr. Illinski lived there, the population was barely three hundred. One-quarter of them black. Most businesses had left town. In fact, the town did not even warrant its own post office.

I mentioned earlier that all the St. Clair County histories contain biographies of Dr. Illinski. My favorite is from Portrait and Biographical record of St. Clair County, Illinois, 1892. Let us see what the doctor wanted us to know about himself.

He was born in Valhejima, "Volhynia," Poland February 3, 1817. His parents were Alexander and Anna Illinski. His father was a landowner and the family was nobility. Dr. Illinski was the second oldest in a family of twelve children. He attended school at the Gymnasium at Kremnitz. Here he studied Mathematics, Science, Greek, Latin, Russian, French, German, and the Polish languages. Illinski attended school five years and was a top student. When the 1830 insurrection broke out, he joined the Polish Army as a lancer at the age of fourteen. He was promoted to first lieutenant by the end of the rebellion.

After the fall of Warsaw, the army that Illinski served in went into Galicia, a Polish province in Austria to escape the Russians. After about a year in Galicia, the Austrians gave him the choice of either returning to Russia or going to America. Illinski was among a group of Poles who were exiled to America. They arrived in the New York City March 28, 1834.

---

984 History of St. Clair County, Illinois 1881, p. 332.

Dr. Illinski always thought the Austrians had arrested him by mistake. He thought his older brother Anthony was who the Austrians were really after. Anthony had been a leader in the rebellion. He managed to evade arrest by going to France and enlisting in the French Army. Later he joined the Turkish army but left to participate in the 1848 Hungarian rebellion. When that rebellion failed, he reenlisted in the Turkish army. In 1856, Anthony was wounded at the battle of Balakava and died a short time later.

After Illinski's arrival in New York, he spent the next year traveling around the country. He ended up working at a hospital in Havana, Cuba. The hospital needed translators and Illinski filled the need. He became interested in medicine while working at the hospital and attended a medical school in Cuba. After graduating, he moved to Louisiana in 1837. Illinski spent one year in Louisiana. In 1840, he enrolled at the McDowell Medical College in St. Louis, Missouri. Illinski graduated two years later in the first class to graduate from that college.[985]

After graduating from college, Dr. Illinski moved across the Mississippi River and settled in Cahokia. Cahokia was a prosperous town at the time but went downhill after the flood of 1844. *East St. Louis Daily Journal* claims that for many years, Dr. Illinski was the only doctor in Cahokia and the American Bottoms. The *Daily Journal* also claimed,

> This service could be performed only by the excellent system of relay horses which he maintained. He had stables at every crossroad, and his horses were thoroughbreds. At one time during an epidemic of cholera, Dr. Illinski had sixteen relays, and old citizens say that he was in the saddle for days at a time. In ordinary years he rode circuits which would astonish a rider of today, but he had a splendid constitution, and an indomitable will. Nor did his fame as a physician dim, as other physicians of note flocked in with the advent of the railroads. Up to the very time of his death he stood in the front rank as a physician, particularly for diseases prevalent on the East Side.[986]

History of St. Clair County 1907 states, Dr. Illinski conducted his medical business on horseback or buggy. He often rode thirty-five or forty miles in a circuit. The doctor rode day or night to check on his patients and his buggy

---

985 Portrait and Biographical Record of St. Clair County, Illinois: [Chicago: Chapman Bros. 1892] [Reproduced by LBS Archival Products 1990] p. 385-386.

986 East St. Louis Journal, April 1, 1928.

served as a bank. He put his patients' payments in a hole in the seat, and at times it contained hundreds of dollars from several days' work.[987]

In August 1843, Dr. Illinski married Mrs. Jane Butler. She was the widow of Dr. Armstead O. Butler. Dr. Butler was a well-known doctor on the east side. Two daughters were born from this marriage. Clementine, born in 1844 and Cora, born around 1847.

In 1849 Dr. Illinski joined the gold rush to California with a group of people from Cahokia and East St. Louis. According to L. H. Zeuch, Dr. Illinski left Cahokia and went to California from 1849 to 1853. While in California, Dr. Illinski continued to practice medicine. He also engaged in merchandising and keeping a public house, "boarding house."[988] Mrs. Illinski died in California in 1852. Maybe her death was the reason he returned to Cahokia in 1853.

L. H. Zeuch also wrote that the American Bottoms were full of swamps, heavily wooded and dangerous. In addition, it was prone to flooding. To find his way around the American Bottom, the doctor cut guideposts on large trees. He was supposed to have had the skill of an Indian following these trails.[989] The *East St. Louis Journal* claims,

> Dr. Illinski had many narrow escapes from death and many other exciting experiences. The high waters of 1844 and 48 and 58, of course, drove the farmers to the high lands. The ridge which connected Cahokia, East St. Louis and Prairie du Pont, was overflowed in many places, and at these points fording was dangerous. The doctor was never daunted, however. He crossed and recrossed, compelling his horse to swim on many occasions. In three instances horse and rider went down, on account of the strong current, the horse being drowned and the doctor reaching shore in safety.[990]

Floods were not the only thing to look out for; bandits also inhabited the American Bottoms. While riding through woods at night, the doctor

---

987 Historical Encyclopedia of Illinois and History of St. Clair County: [Edited by A. S. Wilderman and A. A. Wilderman Volume 1.] [Chicago: Munsell Publishing Company 1907] p. 839.

988 Lucius H. Zeuch, M. D. History of Medical Practice in Illinois: Volume I, [Chicago: The Book Press Inc. 1927] p. 296.

989 Lucius H. Zeuch, M. D. p. 296.

990 East St. Louis Journal, April 1, 1928.

had many close calls with them. He always managed to get away with only minor injuries. Twice during robberies, the bandits recognized the doctor and told him to continue on with his work.

Dr. Illinski was supposed to have had more patients than any doctor in the county. He was known to treat up to sixty patients a day. At times the doctor owned many farms. He was also a big-time beekeeper, owning seventeen hundred hives. I checked St. Clair land records and found the doctor started buying land in 1845. Between 1845 and 1896, there are forty-five land transactions.

Dr. Illinski's house was one of only three buildings in Cahokia built in the old French manner. In the French style the logs are positioned up and down, a few inches apart. In the American style, the logs are horizontal. It was the oldest house in town, built in 1700. The other two buildings were the church and courthouse. Both are still there and are tourist attractions. The doctor's house no longer exists.

I have the 1860, 1870, and 1880 census records for the Illinski family. On the 1860 census, Dr. Illinski is forty-five years old. He is living in the house of Batist Cantin. Batist and his wife were both born in France and their two children were born in Illinois. Three other boarders were also living there. The doctor's two children were living two houses away with John and Julia Butler. Clementine is sixteen and Cora thirteen.[991] Dr. Illinski's wife Jane was the widow of Dr. Armstead Butler. The daughters could have been living with relatives. When I first saw this census, I thought it a strange arrangement. Dr. Illinski was not living with his daughters. Then I thought, his wife is deceased and he is working day and night. Maybe he figured it was the best thing for them.

On the 1870 census, the doctor is head of household and fifty-seven years old. Clemetine must have married and moved out. She is not listed on the census. His daughter, now Cora McCracken, is living there with her two sons, Xavier, six, and Nicolas, two. There are also three boarders living in the house.[992] An article about the Nicholas Jerrot house at the Cahokia Public Library lists the name Illinski as an in-law of Ortance Jerrot. Ortance's first husband was Robert McCracken.[993] Dr. Illinski's daughter Cora was married to their son. Ortance's father was Nicholas Jarrot, an emigrant from France.

991 Kay F. Jetton, 1860 census St. Clair County, Illinois Volume 1: [Decorah, Iowa: The Amundsen Publishing Company, 1981] p. 129-130.

992 St. Clair County Genealogical Society, The 1870 Federal Census, St. Clair County, Illinois: [Published by the St. Clair County Genealogical Society, Belleville, Illinois 1997] p. 390.

993 Nicholas Jarrot House, Cahokia Public Library: p. 8.

Nicholas Jarrot settled in Cahokia in 1794. He started with nothing but made a fortune trading with the Indians. Nicholas had the Jerrot mansion built in 1810, and it is the oldest masonry building in Illinois and is now a popular tourist attraction.

Dr. Illinski was married for a second time to Virginia Black. The wedding took place August 19, 1870. Three children were born from this marriage. On the 1880 census, Dr. Illinski is sixty-four. Virginia is forty-five. Daughters Anielka is seven and Leah is five. Son Alexis is one.[994] Another son was born June 24, 1871, but he died two months later on September 2, 1871.[995] Dr. Illinski received some memorable news on June 28, 1877. The *East St. Louis Gazette* has a record of Dr. Illinski getting a letter from his family in Poland. The first letter from them in forty years.[996] The Russians had forbidden the Polish exiles' use of the postal services for participating in the rebellion.

Adolph B. Suess, author of *The Romantic Story of Cahokia*, wrote a story about Dr. Illinski in his book called *A Distinguished Doctor*. Suess wrote about a couple of Dr. Illinski's calls on sick patients. Suess seems to have known Dr. Illinski good and went with him on some of his calls to patients. On one call, Dr. Illinski braved a snowstorm and high drifts on a Christmas night to go to the cabin of a sick French-Canadian. The grateful family wondered how he made it through all the drifts and Dr. Illinski answered, "Why, by sheer willpower; aided by staunch horsepower."[997] Another call went to a cabin located in a marsh not far from the Mississippi River. It was the home of a sick ex-slave. Dr. Illinski was too late this time and the man was already dead. The cabin was full of the man's grieving family and a number of ex-slaves. The dead man was the first person buried in the new cemetery.

Suess claimed Dr. Illinski was always cheerful and in high spirits. He loved playing cards, sometimes for money. As an old man, he had a large goatee mustache/beard and his hair was snow-white. Suess thought Illinski was from Krakow, Poland, and attended the university there. Suess finished his story about Dr. Illinski by writing,

> This, the faint picture of the life of a pioneer doctor, devoted to study, as his large and well selected library testified; devoted, also, to the culture of flowers and bees-his aviary being taken care of by

994 1880 Federal Census of St. Clair County, Illinois: [National Archives, Box T9, Roll 247, Page 25]

995 East St. Louis Gazette, 6-24-1871 & 9-2-1871.

996 East St. Louis Gazette, 6-28-1877.

997 Adolph B. Suess, The Romantic Story of Cahokia, Illinois: [1949] p. 100.

> slaves, up to the end of the Civil War, and then by trusted employees. Dr. Alexis Illinski lived in St. Clair County long before any of his race and nationality came to this western section of Illinois. He was a noble son of a noble and of a distinguished family.[998]

Slaves! What! I am as surprised as anyone about this revelation. Now it's time for damage control if possible. Slavery was never all that big in Illinois. In 1819, there were only 168 slaves in Illinois. One year later there were 917 slaves, a sizable increase. By 1830, the number had decreased to 746.[999] In 1721, a French businessman tried to mine lead in Galena with 500 slaves he brought with him from Santa Domingo. The venture failed and on the way back he sold some of the slaves to the French settlers living along the Mississippi River in Southern Illinois. The United States government outlawed slavery in the northwest territory in 1784, but St. Clair, the governor of Illinois, let the French settlers keep their slaves. Illinois became a state in 1818, and the legislature started to slowly chip away at slavery in the state. In 1818, it became against the law to bring any more slaves into the state. In addition, those slaves currently in the state became indentured servants. The indentured servants' male children were granted freedom when twenty-one years old and the female children at eighteen years old. All the offspring of indentured servants were freed in 1836. It became illegal to sell an indentured servant in 1841. By 1843, any slaves brought into the state were automatically free. Slavery was finally abolished in Illinois in 1845.

How did Dr. Illinski manage to have any slaves until 1865. All the rest of this paragraph is now speculation. In 1845, there was a court case in Illinois concerning slavery named *Jerrot vs. Jerrot*. This might be the same Jerrots Dr. Illinski would later be related to because of his daughter's marriage. Were the Jerrots and some other die-hard slave owners, including Dr. Illinski, defying the law? Where was the local law enforcement, looking the other way? From what I have read about slavery in the south, the owners did not think they could run their businesses without slaves. Maybe Dr. Illinski thought he could not run his aviary without them. Another possibility is that the doctor's aviary was located across the Mississippi River in Missouri.

Dr. Illinski worked until the age of sixty-five and then his son-in-law Dr. Jennings took over his practice. After retiring, the doctor moved in with his daughter Clementine in East St. Louis. In 1887, Dr. Jennings was killed in

998 Adolph B. Suess, p. 102.

999 Robert P. Howard, Illinois A History of the Prairie State: [Grand Rapids, Michigan: William B. Eerdman's Publishing Company 1972] p. 131.

a buggy accident and Dr. Illinski had to come out of retirement to attend to his former patients. L. H. Zeuch wrote, "Through he was a money-maker, he was a poor saver, and any wild-cat scheme found in the doctor a financial angel to aid its launching; and in consequence he died a poor man."[1000] It looks like Dr. Illinski had money problems and maybe that is the reason he used slave labor for his aviary.

The May 30, 1897, *East St. Louis Daily Journal* contains Dr. Illinski's obituary. I have included some parts of it below. Dr. Illinski died on Saturday morning May 28, 1897. He was ninety years old and died from senile disability. "Doctor Illinski was exiled from the land of his birth." Nothing hindered the doctor from his patients. "No matter what obstacles, often seemingly, insurmountable, came in his way, the doctor never refused to answer a call, so conscientious was he in the practice of his chosen profession. This most admirable trait made him beloved by rich and poor alike." The doctor was always in the forefront of medicine. He "introduced antiseptics, the hypodermic syringe and the fever-thermometer."[1001]

That night the East St. Louis Medical Society met in a special session and created some resolutions which were printed in *The East St. Louis Daily Journal* the next day.

> Whereas, Dr. A. X. Illinski, after a long, active and useful life, has now been laid to rest, be it Resolved, that in his death the medical profession of St. Clair county has suffered the loss of one of its oldest and most esteemed members-a man who at all times upheld the dignity of his profession, who was kind and unselfish in every relation of life, who was quick to discern and adopt all the latest improvements in medicine, who, under all circumstances, answered every call to suffering humanity, and who answered the last great summons as peacefully as "One who wraps his mantle about him and lies down to pleasant dreams."[1002]

George Suprunowski

I will only give a brief summery about George Suprunowski. George lived part of his life in Shelby County as well as St. Clair County. You will find more information about George in my story about Shelby County.

1000 Lucius H. Zeuch, M. D. p. 296.

1001 East St. Louis Daily Journal, 4-1-1928.

1002 East St. Louis Daily Journal, 6-1-1897.

According to Mrs. Isaac D. Rawlings, George was born in Poland in 1810. His family was nobility and George was a count. In 1829, he attended the University in Warsaw. After the rebellion ended, Suprunowski crossed the border into Austria where the Austrians arrested him and threw him in prison. For serving in the Polish Army, the Russians confiscated all his personal property. After a few months in prison, he was exiled to America with forty or fifty Polish exiles. They landed in America on Easter Sunday 1833.[1003] This date has to be wrong. In Lerski's book, the name Jan Suprunowski is on a list of Polish exiles from Trieste who landed in New York in May 1835. The ship was the *Adria* which carried thirty-nine Polish exiles.[1004] Polish American studies published a different list. It is called *Orthography and the Polish Emigrants from Trieste 1834-1835*. In this list, Suprunowski's first name is Grzegarz.[1005] Mrs. Isaac D. Rawlings wrote that George's middle name was Gregory.[1006] Why he changed his name from Jan to George is a mystery, but I think they are the same person.

George learned the skill of hatter in America. He worked as a hatter in New Orleans and St. Louis before moving across the Mississippi River to Cahokia. He also switched occupations, becoming a surveyor. George worked as a surveyor in Shelby County and also bought some land there on March 25, 1839.[1007] George met his future wife in Shelby County too. He married Elizabeth Rogers on March 15, 1842.[1008]

Helen Cox Tregillis writes that after the marriage, the Suprunowskis moved into a big two-story house near the Cahokia Commons Fields in St. Clair County. The Commons were public lands used for grazing, firewood, etc. The idea originated with the early French settlers. The Commons bordered the

---

1003 Mrs. Isaac D. Rawlings, Polish Exiles in Illinois: [Transactions of the Illinois State Historical Society for the year 1927] [Danville, Illinois: Illinois Printing Co. 1927] p. 96.

1004 Jerzy Jan Lerski, p. 180.

1005 Polish American Studies, Volume xxxi No. 2 1974 Autumn: [Orthography and the Polish Emigrants from Trieste 1834-1835] [The Polish American Historical Association of the Polish Institute of arts and sciences in America St. Mary's College, Orchard Lake, Michigan] p. 27-28.

1006 Mrs. Isaac D. Rawlings, p. 95.

1007 Illinois Public Domain Sales, [Produced by the Illinois state Archives] "Shelby County" [At the Shelby County Historical and Genealogical Society, July 1982] p. 408.

1008 Liahona Research, Illinois Marriages 1826 to 1850: [Bountiful, Utah: Heritage Quest 1999] p.801.

Mississippi River. Six children were born to the Suprunowskis there.[1009] George owned thirty-seven improved acres and seventy unimproved acres in 1850. He owned two horses, three milk cows, four other cattle, and six pigs. The farm produced 800 bushels of corn, 400 bushels of oats, and 160 bushels of potatoes. In addition, George sold vegetables in town.[1010] Mrs. Isaac D. Rawlings adds more from an interview George had with Count John Sobiesky.

> I believe in destiny and although mine has been rough, I have had many good things along with the bitter of life. After I came to America earning a rich farm in the Mississippi Bottom, near East St. Louis, twice my possessions were swept away by the floods, now I must die a poor man, but my wife is my greatest comfort and the best women in the world. For fifty years she has been my constant and tender help-mate and has shared my joys and my sorrows.[1011]

The Suprunowskis finally gave up farming on the Mississippi Bottoms and moved back to Holland in Shelby County. George lived until the age of eighty-five. He died May 24, 1895. Elizabeth died exactly one year later on May 24, 1896. They are both buried at Hubbartt Cemetery in Shelby County.[1012]

Jozef Jablonski

Jozef was one of the 234 Polish exiles from Trieste and a second lieutenant in the insurrection.[1013] According to St. Clair land records, Jozef sold land on March 27, 1849, to Alexander Materski.[1014] The land was located on the American Bottoms. There is no record of when Jozef bought the land and no other records about him.

1009 Helen Cox Tregillis, The Shelby County Book: [Decorah, Iowa: The Anundsen publishing co. 1986] p. 15.

1010 1850 Agriculture Census of St. Clair County, Illinois: [Illinois State Archives, Springfield, Illinois, Roll 31-4]

1011 Mrs. Isaac D. Rawlings, p. 96.

1012 Edward Boedecker, [Inscriptions of Shelby County, Illinois Cemeteries Volume viii: 1984] p. 9.

1013 Aleksander Grobicki, Proba Biografii. Sodalis: [St. Mary's College Library, Orchard Lake, Michigan, letter J] p. 28.

1014 St. Clair County Recorder of Deeds, Belleville, Illinois: General Index Book, [Deeds 1790-1908 Roll 7]

Alexander Materski

Alexander Grobicki writes that Alexander Materski was from Lithuania, Poland. He was a second lieutenant in the insurrection and one of the 234 Polish exiles From Trieste.[1015] On the 1850 census his age is fifty-one and his name is spelled Mawthrisk.[1016] Alexander sold his land May 8, 1851.[1017] There are no other records of him after that.

Anton Poniatowski

Anton Poniatowski was a second lieutenant in the 1830 November insurrection and one of the 234 Polish exiles from Trieste.[1018] Anton sold land on the Cahokia Bottoms to Theophilus L. Rutkowski on March 7, 1847.[1019] He then bought land on March 17, 1847, near Mascoutah in the eastern part of St. Clair County.[1020] Anton moved to Prairie Du Chiens, Wisconsin, by 1850 and is on the 1850 census for Crawford County, Wisconsin. His age is thirty-seven and his occupation is silversmith. Anton's wife Sophia is thirty-five years old and born in Canada.[1021]

Teofil L. Rutkowski

Teofil also went by his middle initial L. or by his middle name of Lewis in some of the sources I have about him. Alexander Grobicki states Teofil was from Krolestwa, Poland. He was a second lieutenant in the Uhlans, "Calvary," in the 1830 November insurrection.[1022] Teofil was an expert cavalryman.

1015 Aleksander Grobicki, Letter M. p. 25.

1016 Robert Buecher, St. Clair County, Illinois 1850 Census Index: Volume 1 [Thomson, Illinois: Heritage House] p. 53.

1017 St. Clair County Recorder of Deeds Belleville, Illinois: [General Index Book, Deeds 1790-1908] Roll 7.

1018 Aleksander Grobicki, [letter P] p. 22.

1019 St. Clair County Recorder of Deeds Belleville, Illinois: [General Index Book, Deeds 1790-1908] Roll 8.

1020 St. Clair County Recorder of Deeds, Belleville, Illinois: [Grantee Book R, p 273 Section 20 Township 2n Range 9]

1021 1850 Federal Census of Crawford County, Wisconsin: [National Archives, Box 432, Roll 995, Page 237]

1022 Aleksander Grobicki, [letter R] p. 25.

Edmund L. Kowalczyk wrote, "L. Rutkowski and E. Polkowski, of the Polish Cavalry gave an exhibition of military skills at Peale's Museum in New York on the week of May 26, 1834."[1023]

Teofil was supposed to be one of only a few of the 234 Polish exiles to have made it to the Polish land grant.[1024] The land grant was located on the Rock River in Winnebago County. If he did make it there, he did not stay very long. Rev. L. Siekaniec thinks that Teofil was one of just two Poles in St. Louis in 1834.[1025] Teofil bought land on the Cahokia Bottoms from Anton Poniatowski March 7, 1847.[1026] He sold his land to Ferdinand Klemback on March 21, 1862.[1027] The 1844 St. Louis Directory lists L. Rutkowski as a clerk. The 1844 St. Louis Directory also lists E. Polkowski on it. His occupation was merchant.[1028] It looks like Rutkowski moved back to Illinois by 1860. The 1860 Federal Census for St. Clair County, Illinois, has the name Ls. Routkansky, sixty-two years old and born in Poland. Constance, twenty years old and born in Poland, also lives with him.[1029]

Charles Szirkowski

I am only writing a brief story about the Szirkowskis. The family only spent part of their time in St. Clair County. They moved to Randolph County in the 1850s. The Szirkowskis are the most written about of Polish families in Randolph County, and you will find out more about them there.

Charles, his wife Ida, and son Heinrich emigrated from Germany to Baltimore in 1834. Ida's father, Heinrich Weber, mother, and five brothers and sisters came with them. Charles and his father-in-law Heinrich were both government officials in Coblenz, Germany. Heinrich was supposed to be a real top-notch official. The Szirkowskis and Webers soon moved to St.

1023 Edmund L. Kowalczyk, Polish American studies Vol. V11, No. 3-4 July-December, 1950: [The Polish American Historical Association of the Polish institute of Arts and Sciences in America St. Mary's College, Orchard Lake, Michigan] p. 81.

1024 Aleksander Grobicki, [letter R] p. 25.

1025 Rev. L. Siekaniec, St. Louis, Missouri Hejnal: [May 1982] p. 11.

1026 St. Clair County Recorder of Deeds, Belleville, Illinois: [General Index Book, Deeds 1790-1908] Roll 8.

1027 St. Clair County Recorder of Deeds, Belleville, Illinois: [General Index 1790-1880 O, R, S Box 9 Book K L-3 p. 254.

1028 Rev. L. Siekaniec, St. Louis Hejnal: [Spring 1990] p. 11.

1029 Kay F. Jetton, 1860 Federal Census of St. Clair County, Illinois: p. 159.

Louis, Missouri. The Webers started a music store in St. Louis. Things were not going well with Charles and Ida and they divorced in Jackson County, Illinois, in 1837. Charles stayed in Illinois and was remarried on December 16, 1838, to Susan Humphries. Six children were born to Charles and Susan. Actia, Carl, Charles, Ellen, Mary, and Susan. Charles died in 1866. It almost seems like Charles was a German. His first wife certainly was. Charles claims Poland as place of birth on all his census records.[1030]

There's more to the story but it concerns two of Charles's sons. You will find their story in Randolph County. Charles and Susan were married December 16, 1838, in Franklin County, Illinois.[1031] The 1850 Federal Census of St. Clair County records Charles's age as forty. His occupation is trader and the family lives in Belleville. Charles's place of birth is Poland. Wife Susan is thirty-one and born in Illinois. Their sons are Ferdinand, eleven; Charles, eight; and Albert, one. The daughters are Emily, ten; Mary, six; and Actia, four. All the children were born in St. Clair County.[1032] I have a discrepancy in the ages of Charles and Susan. On the 1860 census, Charles's age is sixty-eight and Susan's forty, a twenty-eight-year difference.[1033]

Also on the 1850 census is Lewis Annet. He is thirty years old and lives in Belleville. Louis was born in Poland.[1034]

Andrew Hohn or Hoen. Andrew is forty-five years old and living in District 5, which is south of Cahokia. His occupation is stonemason and he was born in Poland. His wife Mary is thirty-one and born in Poland. Their daughter Louisa is nine and born in St. Clair County.[1035]

There is also the marriage record of a woman who might be Polish. On January 26, 1843, John Schmit married Paulina Silcosky.[1036] This is the only record I have for them.

1030 Randolph County, Illinois Bicentennial 1795-1995. p. 360.

1031 Liahona Research, Illinois Marriages: 1826 to 1850. [Bountiful, Utah: Heritage Quest 1999] p. 753.

1032 1850 Federal Census of St. Clair County, Illinois: [National Archives, Box 432 Roll 126, Page 443]

1033 Yakima Valley Genealogical Society, The 1860 Federal Census of Randolph County, Illinois: [Yakima, Washington 1986] p. 268.

1034 Robert Buecher, St. Clair County, Illinois 1850 Census Index Volume 2 [Thomson, Illinois: Heritage House 1974] p. 3.

1035 Robert Buecher, [Vol. 1] p. 40.

1036 Liahona Research, Illinois Marriages: 1825 through 1850 [Bountiful, Utah: Heritage Quest] p. 748.

The 1850 Agriculture Census of St. Clair County, Illinois, contains the name Thomas Lapsky. He was living on an eighty-five-acre farm.[1037]

More Poles came in the 1850s. Their names are on the 1860 census.

Joseph Oginski, thirty-eight years old and born in Poland. Joe worked on George Suprunowski's farm on the Cahokia Bottoms.[1038]

Philip Gasperzick, thirty years old and born in Poland. Wife Anna, thirty years old, born in Poland. Their daughter Maria is one year old and born in Poland. The Gasperzicks are thought to be from Poland. There is a question mark after each one's name, so the census is not sure of where the family originated.[1039]

Ignace Depta, twenty-nine years old and born in Poland. His wife Francisca is twenty-three and born in Poland.[1040]

Anthony Brogaski, forty-eight years old and born in Warsaw. Wife Anna is forty-six, born in Warsaw. Their sons are Francis, sixteen, and Jacob, twelve. Their daughters are Anna, ten, and Christina, seven.[1041] Both born in Warsaw.

Andri Ososkey, fifty years old and born in Poland. Wife Rosalie, fifty-two and born in France.[1042]

Anton Tynmanicke, fifty-six years old and born in Poland.[1043]

Francis Czech, forty-one years old and born in Poland. Wife Maria, thirty-seven years old and born in England.[1044]

Ferdinand Tzengolessosky, forty-seven years old and born in Prussia. Wife Wilhemina, forty-five years old, born in Prussia. Their sons are Edward, nineteen; Fred, thirteen, and Charles, six. The daughters are Rosalia, ten; Carolina, eight; and Wilhelmina, four. All the children were born in Prussia except Wilhelmina who was born in Texas.[1045]

William Rudowsky, twenty-seven years old and born in Poland. Wife Caroline, twenty-seven years old and born in Hessia.[1046]

1037 1850 Agriculture Census of St. Clair County, Illinois: [Illinois State Archives, Roll 31-4]

1038 Kay F. Jetton, p. 123.

1039 Kay F. Jetton, p. 67.

1040 Kay F. Jetton, p. 67.

1041 Kay F. Jetton, p. 73.

1042 Kay F. Jetton, p. 130.

1043 Kay F. Jetton, p. 164.

1044 Kay F. Jetton, p. 177.

1045 Kay F. Jetton, p. 71.

1046 Kay F. Jetton, p. 360.

Jordan Elinskey, sixty-five years old and born in Poland. A relative of Dr. Illinski?[1047]

Many people from Poland with German names came to St. Clair County in the 1850s too.

William Ludwick, thirty years old and born in Poland. Wife Maria, twenty-six years old and born in Poland. Their son Paul is two years old and born in Illinois.[1048]

John Schultz, thirty-seven years old and born in Poland. Wife Sophia, thirty-four years old and born in Poland.[1049]

Michail Engleman, sixty-one years old born in Poland. Wife Mary, forty-nine years old and born in Poland. The sons are Anthony, twenty-four; Julius, twenty-one; Constantine, seventeen; and Mack, six. Their daughters are Francis, eighteen; Emily, fifteen; Anna, thirteen; Louisa, eleven; and Eve, nine. All the children were born in Poland.[1050]

Christian Terickers, twenty-one years old and born in Poland.[1051]

John F. Schussler, fifty-six years old and born in Poland.[1052]

The St. Clair County, Illinois, Naturalization Index contains three names which could be Polish.

Joseph Kurtzewski was naturalized in August 1856.[1053]

Gustavus Woydechowsky was naturalized in April 1857.[1054]

Anton Procasky was naturalized in September 1857.[1055]

The Polish settlers in St. Clair County would have noticed a new group of Slavic people arriving in the 1850s. No one on the 1850 census was born in Bohemia. By the 1860 census over 120 people were born in

1047 Kay F. Jetton, p. 241.

1048 Kay F. Jetton, p. 67.

1049 Kay F. Jetton, p. 248.

1050 Kay F. Jetton, p. 284.

1051 Kay F. Jetton, p. 241.

1052 Kay F. Jetton, p. 241.

1053 Robert Buecher, St. Clair County, Illinois Naturalization Index 1816-1905: [Thomson, Illinois: Heritage House 1976] p.23.

1054 Robert Buecher, St. Clair County, Illinois Naturalization Index 1816-1905: [Thomson, Illinois: Heritage House 1976] p.44.

1055 Robert Buecher, [Naturalization Index] p. 30.

Bohemia.[1056] After Chicago, more Poles settled in St. Clair County before 1850 then any other county in Illinois. From 1850 to 1860 it is probably the same story. Dr. Illinski would go through hell to get to his patients and was highly spoken of by just about everyone. Slavery was a black mark on his legacy.

1056 Kay F. Jetton, 1860 census St. Clair County, Illinois [Volume 1]

Tazewell and Peoria

I combined Tazewell and Peoria counties because the combined total of Poles for each county was small. Baron Ludwik Chlopicki lived in both counties for a time before moving to Woodford County. You will find out more about Ludwik in my story of Woodford County. The Probascos were of Polish descent, and a number of them came to Tazewell County before and during the 1840s. The marriage of the Polish-looking name of Nickolas Darsula to Jessica Brooks took place in Tazewell County on October 17, 1832.[1057] There was a family of Sanduskys living in the town of Pekin in Tazewell County in 1850. Edward Polkowski, one of the 235 Polish exiles from Trieste, left a record of himself buying a lot in Peoria in 1846.[1058] He was living in St. Louis at the time and there is no record of him ever living in Peoria. The main Polish emigration to Peoria occurred after 1850, and I will list them later.

Tazewell County was created January 21, 1827, from parts of Fayette and Sangamon counties. It is located in north-central Illinois, close to the middle of the state. Tazewell County's northern boundary runs along the Illinois River. Chicago is about 165 miles northeast of the county. Tazewell County was very large when it first came into being, but was divided to create a part of McLean County in 1830. In 1841, it was divided again to create Mason and a part of Woodford County. Eighty percent of Tazewell County was prairie before the first white settlers came on the scene. The wooded areas were along streams and in groves.

Probasco

I first saw this name while looking through Illinois census records. I thought the name looked similar to some Polish names but not spelled like

[1057] Liahona Research, Illinois Marriages 1826 to 1850: [Bountiful, Utah: Heritage Quest 1999] p. 200.

[1058] Peoria County Recorder's Office, Peoria, Illinois: [Grantee Index T 1825 to 1920] p. 131.

one. While reading the book *Poles in America* by Mocha, I came across a story by Edward Pinkowski. Pinkowski claims Probasco was originally spelled "Probacki."[1059] The 1840 Federal Census has the first record of the Probascos in Tazewell County.[1060] The census contains the name of Jacob Probasco, head of household and living alone. Unfortunately for us, the 1840 census does not show a whole lot, other than head of household. Jacob must have come out to Illinois by himself, or maybe with friends. Jacob married Mary Harris October 20, 1845,[1061] and might have left the state soon after marrying. There are no more records of Jacob after he married. The 1840 Census for Edwards County also lists a Probasco. Peter Probasco is between thirty and forty years old and his wife is between twenty and thirty years old. They have two sons and one daughter under five years old. One son and two daughters between five and ten and one son between ten and fifteen years old.[1062] Edwards County is located on the Illinois-Indiana state line in Southern Illinois.

More Probascos came to Tazewell County in the 1840s. The 1850 Federal Census lists Samuel Probasco, seventy-six years old, occupation farmer and born in New Jersey. His wife Sarah is sixty-six years old, born in Maryland. Daughter Nancy is sixteen years old and born in Virginia. Son William is thirteen years old and born in Illinois. If William's place of birth is correct, Sam was living in Illinois by at least 1837. Also living with the family are Harriet and Kelly Washington. Kelly is seventeen years old, born in Virginia, and his occupation is laborer. Harriet is fourteen years old and born in Virginia.[1063]

Also on the same census page is Rebecca Probasco, maybe Sam's daughter? She is not living with Sam's family but on the farm next door owned by Job Hodges. Rebecca is fourteen years old and born in Virginia. Job is thirty years old, farmer and born in Connecticut. His wife Rachael is twenty-seven years

---

1059 Frank Mocha, Poles in America Bicentennial Essays: [Stevens Point, Wisconsin: Worzalla Publishing Company 1978] p. 304.

1060 1840 Federal Census of Tazewell County: [National Archives, Box 704 Roll 71 Page 34]

1061 David C. Perkins, Tazewell County Illinois Marriage Records Index 1827-October 1859: [Published and copyrighted by Tazewell County Genealogical Society 1982] p. 39.

1062 1840 Federal Census of Edwards County, Illinois: [National Archives, Box 704, Roll 58, page 119]

1063 Bloomington-Normal Genealogical Society, Normal, Illinois, [Tazewell County, Illinois 1850 Census 1978] p. 51.

old and born in Ohio. A seven-year-old boy named George McGinnis also lives with the family.[1064]

It looks like another one of Sam's children was living on the farm next door to Job Hodges farm. Samuel Probasco was living at the farm of Elizabeth Hodgson. Samuel is eighteen years old, occupation farmer and born in Virginia. Elizabeth is fifty-six years old and born in Virginia. Her son Abner Hodgson is twenty-two years old, occupation farmer and born in Ohio. Isaah is eighteen years old, occupation farmer and born in Illinois. Sarah is sixteen years old, born in Illinois. Also living in the house was Jane Caster, twenty-four years old, born in Ohio. William Thomson, twenty-two years old, occupation laborer, born in Ohio.[1065]

The family of another Samuel Probasco is also on the 1850 Federal Census for Tazewell County, Illinois. This Samuel is twenty-four years old, farmer and born in Virginia. His wife Eminence is eighteen years old, born in Illinois. A baby girl Francis is nine months old. There is also a ten-year-old boy living with the family named John.[1066] Samuel has a small write-up in *History of Tazewell County, Illinois.*

> Samuel Probasco was born in Virginia, March 9, 1825. His parents, Francis T. and Margaret [Higgins] Probasco, were natives of the same State. Mr. P. received a common school education and came to this county in October, 1840; settling three miles east of Pekin, in what is known as the Hodson settlement. The subject of this sketch was married in 1849, to Eunice Bennett, a daughter of Michael Bennett, one of the first settlers. He died of the Cholera during the epidemic of 1833. They are the parents of the following children-Francis, born March 7, 1850, he now lives in Colorado; James H., December 15, 1851; Emily J., November 4, 1854, she is the wife of John Trimble; Charles W., May 12, 1857, died September 23, 1858. Mr. P. belongs to the Christian Church.[1067]

The census and sketch do not completely match up, but I personally think the sketch is right.

1064 Bloomington-Normal Genealogical Society, 1850 census, p. 51.

1065 Bloomington-Normal Genealogical Society, 1850 census, p. 52.

1066 Bloomington-Normal Genealogical Society, 1850 census, p. 188 & 189.

1067 History of Tazewell County Illinois: [Chicago: Chas. C. Chapman & Com. 1879] [Reproduction by Unigraphic, Inc. Evansville, Indiana 1975] p. 506 & 507.

Also on the 1850 Federal Census for Tazewell County, Illinois, is Elijah Probasco. Elijah is forty-six years old, occupation plasterer and born in Maine. He married Fidelia Doe in Tazewell County on June 27, 1848.[1068] On the 1850 census, Fidelia is forty years old and born in Maine. Charles Doe is eighteen year old, occupation laborer, and he was born in Maine. Presly, sixteen years old, occupation laborer, born in Maine. Mary Doe, sixteen years old, born in Maine. Jefferson, twelve years old, born in Maine. Allen, ten years old, born in Maine. Wilmar, nine years old, born in Maine. And Emelyn, seven years old and born in Maine.[1069] Looks like Elijah got himself an instant family. They lived in Tremont Township, which is located on the eastern side of Tazewell County. The 1860 Federal Census for Tazewell County lists Elijah's age as sixty, occupation plasterer and born in Virginia. Fidelia is fifty-seven years old and born in Maine.[1070] The census records do not match again. None of the Does are on the 1860 census.

The 1850 Federal Census of Tazewell County shows two members of the well-known Sandusky family living in the home of Dr. Henry Misner in the town of Pekin. Elizabeth Sandusky is sixty years old and born in Virginia. John Sandusky, who must be her son, is thirty-four years old, born in Ohio. All the other Sanduskys I have found in Illinois were from Kentucky. These two seem to be from a much different line from the others. Dr. Misner is thirty-three years old, born in New York. His wife Herriot is thirty-three years old and born in Ohio. Also living with the family is William, six, and Herriot Mark, four years old. Both born in Illinois.[1071]

I have not found any information on when the Probascos first came to America. None of their first names are spelled as if they were recent arrivals, so it looks like they settled in America at a very early date. A John Probasco from Tazewell County served in the Union army during the Civil War. He enlisted September 15, 1862, and was a corporal in Company M, Fourteenth Cavalry. John was discharged July 31, 1865.[1072] The jury is out for Nickolas

1068 David C. Perkins, Tazewell County Illinois Marriage Records Index 1827-October 18859: [published and copyrighted by Tazewell County Genealogical Society, Pekin, Illinois 1982] p. 39.

1069 Bloomington-Normal Genealogical Society, 1850 census, p. 133.

1070 Tazewell County Genealogical Society, Pekin, Illinois [Tazewell County Illinois 1860 Census & Index Eastern Half 1984] p. 97.

1071 1850 Federal census of Tazewell County, Illinois: [National Archives, Box M432, Roll 129, Page 114]

1072 Ben C. Allensworth, History of Tazewell County, Volume 11: [Chicago: Munsell Publishing Company 1905] [Reproduction by Whipporwill Publications, Evansville, Indiana 1986] p. 798 & 799.

Darsula. His name looks Polish, but we will never know for sure. Nicholas moved to Alexander County by 1855.

Peoria County

Peoria County was created January 13, 1825, from Fulton County. Peoria is the county seat. The county is located in north-central Illinois, close to the center of the state. Chicago is 157 miles to the northeast. The city of Peoria sits on bluffs overlooking the Illinois River and its present population is 124,160. Peoria County is located next to and directly north of Tazewell County.

The history of Peoria County starts at a much earlier date than the surrounding counties. The first Europeans arrived there via the Illinois River in 1673. That year, seven French Canadians, including Father Marquette and Louis Joliet, landed near Peoria and spent a short time with the Peoria Indians. The French were on a mission to find the end of the Mississippi River and soon left to complete their goal. After reaching the Gulf of Mexico, the French reversed course and came back up the Mississippi River to the Illinois River. The French made it back to the Peoria Indian tribe on August 1. They stayed until September, and then went on to Green Bay.

Seven more years passed before the next group of French Canadians appeared. On January 1, 1680, nine canoes containing thirty-three people landed at the same Peoria Indian village. This party contained Robert de LaSalle, Father Louis Hennepin, and historian Chevalier de Tonti. Almost right away, trouble arose with the Indians. The French moved to the other side of the river and started building a fort. LaSalle decided to go back to Canada while the fort was still under construction. He split his force and left Father Hennepin in command. Father Hennepin and the remaining force gave up on the venture a few months later and deserted the fort.

The French were back again in 1779. They came to settle for good this time and started a settlement on the shores of Lake Peoria. By this time, the Illinois Territory was a part of the state of Virginia. France had controlled the area from 1682 until 1763. The British ruled it until 1778, and then pulled out. The French settlement was christened "La Ville de Maillet." Before long, the French realized they had chosen a bad spot to build on and decided to move the settlement to the other side of the lake. According to *History of Peoria County*,

> The French erected their cabins near the lake shore, and occupied long narrow lots extending back toward the bluff, the size varying with the industry of the occupant. They were

> almost entirely devoid of education, and lived chiefly by hunting and fishing. About 1781 the inhabitants became alarmed and abandoned the settlement, but returned two years after. At the time Capt. Thomas E. Craig burned the village in the early part of November, 1813, it consisted of not more than twenty-five families, who were without a church or a school, and had less than 200 acres of land under cultivation. Their dwellings were mere hovels.[1073]

The village was burned because Captain Craig suspected the French were allied with the local Indians. The War of 1812 was underway at the time, and the Indians in the region were allied with the British. The French left for good after their village was burned. All French attempts to colonize this part of Illinois resulted in failure. Only Indians inhabited the area until the first Americans came in 1819.

In 1832, the settlement of Peoria contained about fifteen to twenty log cabins. Two frame houses were also located there and five more built in 1833. Peoria became a refuge for Illinois pioneers during the Black Hawk War in 1832. By 1845, Peoria had a population of 1,619. Ludwik Chlopicki is on the 1850 Federal Census for Peoria County so was living in Peoria on or before then.[1074]

Besides Ludwik Chlopicki, Edward Polkowski is the only Pole to leave any record of himself in the city of Peoria or Peoria County before 1850. Edward bought a lot in the city of Peoria on August 7, 1846.[1075] He was living in St. Louis at the time and does not appear to have ever lived in Peoria. Edward was one of the 234 Polish exiles from Trieste and a second lieutenant in the uprising.[1076] Edmund L. Kowalczyk wrote, "L. Rutkowski and E. Polkowski of the Polish Cavalry gave an exhibition of military skills at Peale's Museum in New York on the week of May 26, 1834."[1077]

1073 The History of Peoria County, Illinois: [Chicago: Johnson & Company. 1880] [Reprinted 1981, auspices of the Peoria County Genealogical Society, the Print shop, Dixon, Illinois] p. 450.

1074 Patricia Combs O'Dell, 1850 Peoria County, Illinois: [October, 1972] p. 2.

1075 Peoria County Recorder's Office, Peoria, Illinois: Grantee Index 1825-1920 p. 131.

1076 Aleksander Grobicki, Proba Biogrfii, Sodalis: The Polish American Historical Association of the Polish Institute of Arts and Sciences in America St. Mary's College, Orchard Lake, Michigan: [Letter P] p. 22.

1077 Edmund L. Kowalczyk, Polish-American Studies, [Jottings from the Polish American Past] [Volume V11, No. 3-4 July-December, 1950] [The Polish

The 1850s saw the first real Polish emigration to Peoria County. My book is supposed to end on 1850. Since there is not much to write about before 1850, I will write about the Poles who came later. The information I have ends in 1880. Poles recorded on the 1860 Federal Census for Peoria County are listed below. I never checked the 1870 census.

Thomas Stowitsky, twenty-eight years old, occupation shoemaker, and born in Poland. Wife Barbara, nineteen years old and born in? Daughter Emily, one year old, born in Illinois. They lived in the First Ward of the city of Peoria.[1078]

Hiemer Showiski, thirty-five years old, occupation cigar maker and born in Poland. Hiemer was living at the boarding house of Henry Rheimenschnider, also a cigar maker. They lived in the First Ward of the city of Peoria.[1079]

Dominick Minkosiewiez, thirty-nine years old, occupation laborer, and born in Poland. Wife Susan, twenty-nine years old, born in? Daughters Susan, two, and Anna one, both born in Illinois. The Minkosiewiezes lived in the Third Ward of the city of Peoria.[1080]

Christian Kowalski, twenty-two years old, occupation shoemaker, and born in Prussia. Wife Catherine, twenty years old and born in? Daughter Paulina, five months old, born in Illinois. John Kowalski, probably Christian's brother, was also living there. John is twenty-six years old, occupation brickmason, and born in Prussia.[1081] Christian married Catharine Slitt on March 31, 1859. Paster Neuber officiated.[1082] The 1880 Peoria City Directory lists Christian's occupation as a saloon keeper, and his address is at the corner of Bridge and Water streets.[1083]

A few marriage licenses were issued to two people with Polish-looking names.

American Historical Association of the Polish Institute of Arts and Sciences in America, St. Mary's College, Orchard Lake, Michigan]

1078 1860 Peoria County, Illinois Census: [Published by The Peoria Genealogical Society. Peoria, Illinois 1983] p. 48.

1079 1860 Census, p. 20

1080 1860 Census, p. 20

1081 1860 Census, p. 111.

1082 Marriage Licenses issued in Peoria County 1825-1860: [At Peoria Historical Society, Peoria, Illinois] p. 322.

1083 The History of Peoria County, Illinois 1880, p. 666.

On August 12, 1856, Anna Cecelia Commysky married James Byrnes. Commysky looks like a Polish name but could be Irish. I have seen Irish names spelled similar to this name. Father James Fitzgerald married them in a Catholic church.[1084]

On February 29, 1859, Julia Stepcienski married Anton Gordzilch. Father J. Neubery married them in a Catholic church.[1085]

On the 1880 Peoria City Directory are these Polish-looking names.

John Prohaski, occupation collar maker, 113 S. Washington Street.[1086]
F. Swinbasky, occupation farmer and living in Kickapoo Township.[1087]
John Penski, occupation farmer and living in Peoria County.[1088]
J. Notzka, occupation farmer and living in Kickapoo Township.[1089]
Theodore Kroleskey, occupation farmer and living in Peoria Township.[1090]

There were also some Polish Jews around in 1880. On the Peoria City Directory, the following people are listed.

A. Schradski, occupation clothing and address, 108 Adams Street.[1091] Mr. Schradski was a trustee of the Progress Lodge No. 113.[1092] Mrs. Schradski was secretary of the Peoria Hebrew Relief Association.[1093]

J. Schradski, occupation clothing and address, 217 Main.[1094] J. Schradski was a trustee of the Standard Literary and Social Association.[1095]

John Korsoski held various offices in the Moses Montifiore Lodge No. 155, including President, Conductor and Monitor.[1096] John was also a Trustee in the Jewish Congregation Anshai Emeth.[1097]

1084 The History of Peoria County, Illinois 1880, p. 23.
1085 The History of Peoria County, Illinois 1880, p. 31.
1086 The History of Peoria County, Illinois 1880, p. 684.
1087 The History of Peoria County, Illinois 1880, p. 790.
1088 The History of Peoria County, Illinois 1880, p. 779.
1089 The History of Peoria County, Illinois 1880, p. 769.
1090 The History of Peoria County, Illinois 1880, p. 775.
1091 The History of Peoria County, Illinois 1880, p. 689.
1092 The History of Peoria County, Illinois 1880, p. 510.
1093 The History of Peoria County, Illinois 1880, p. 513.
1094 The History of Peoria County, Illinois 1880, p. 689.
1095 The History of Peoria County, Illinois 1880, p. 510.
1096 The History of Peoria County, Illinois 1880, p. 510.
1097 The History of Peoria County, Illinois 1880, p. 467.

Two Polish Jews have good-sized write-ups in the Peoria City Directory.

> Samuel Lidwinosky, dealer in dry goods, notions, boots and shoes, clothing, etc., 535 S. Adams street, was born in Poland, in May, 1851, and is the son of Jacob Lidwinosky. He came to America in 1869, and landing at New York in August of that year, headed straight for Peoria, and during the next four years peddled notions, etc, through Peoria and adjoining counties. Six years ago he started a permanent place of business and has since continued it. When seventeen years old he married, in his native country, Rachael Brin, by whom he has had five children—Jacob, Erris, Annie, Rachel and Hannah. He conducts a prosperous business, and carries a stock of about $5,000.[1098]
>
> Jacob Conigisky, of Conigisky Bro., 108, 110 N. Adams street, was born in Poland, May 19, 1840, and emigrated to the United States in 1856, and located in New York, where he remained until 1864,when he came to Peoria and engaged in the dry goods business, which he has followed since. Married Miss Bertha Pearl in 1870. She was a native of London, England, and came to this country in 1868. They have three sons. They employ eighteen hands in their business. The Conigisky's are doing a fine trade, have a fine store building fronting on Adams street, and do a wholesale and retail business of $100.OOO to $125,000 per annum. Mr. C. is a member of the I. O. O. F. Silas, senior partner and an elder brother, came to the United States the same time; have been together in business since they came to the country.[1099]

Polish settlement in Peoria started a bit late. After 1850, Polish settlers had some impact there, especially the Polish Jews. Most of my history of Poles in Illinois ends by 1850. I threw this Polish history in Peoria together after 1850 without delving too deeply on the subject. It is entirely possible more could have lived there.

[1098] The History of Peoria County, Illinois 1880, p. 668.

[1099] The History of Peoria County, Illinois 1880, p. 636.

Wabash County

Wabash County had one Pole named Gabriel Goldburgh before 1850. He settled in the small town of Lancaster. Gabriel lived in Wabash County at least sixteen years and was involved in Lancaster's affairs for much of that time. With a name like Goldburgh, it is not too far-fetched to say that Gabriel might be a Polish Jew.

Wabash became a county December 27, 1827, from part of Edwards County. The county is in the southeastern part of the state. Its eastern boundary is the Wabash River, which is where it got its name. The Wabash River also divides Illinois from Indiana. About two-thirds of the county is considered uplands. The other third is bottomland along the Wabash River and Bonpas Creek. The uplands were sparsely wooded when first settled, while the wooded areas were mainly in the bottomland. Wabash County had a large variety of wild animals well into the 1850s. It was home to wolves, panthers, deer, and rattlesnakes. The last bear was killed there in 1850.

The first settlers to the area were from Kentucky. In 1816, about a dozen families arrived from Alleghany County, New York. Starting in the 1830s, a large number of Pennsylvania Dutch settled in the county. Many settled around the town of Lancaster. If you did not know, the Pennsylvania Dutch were not of Dutch but German descent. Most of the Pennsylvania Dutch came from the area around Lancaster, Pennsylvania, which is how the town got its name. Lancaster was located in a prairie about a mile and a half in diameter known as Round Prairie. The population in 1883 was 250. It went down to only 120 people in 1911. The present population is unknown. I drove through Lancaster and never saw any signs as to the number of people living there. There is a couple of churches, a school, and a few businesses. I counted about fifty houses and trailers spread out for a least a half mile on both sides of the highway.

Gabriel Goldburgh

The 1850 Federal Census for Wabash County lists Gabriel's age as thirty-eight. He was born in Poland and his occupation is merchant. His wife Nancy is twenty-six years old and born in Kentucky. Son Albert is two, born in Illinois. Also living with the Goldburghs were two young boys. Marion, ten years old, and Ezra Moore, seven. Both were born in Illinois.[1100] Nancy died June 13, 1852.[1101] Gabriel married Phebe Knight by 1855.[1102] He was appointed postmaster of Lancaster on March 20, 1854.[1103] Gabriel was also Lancaster's election clerk a number of times in the early 1850s.[1104] He was involved in some type of Lancaster bond issue during the same period. I cannot figure out what it is about and would need a village attorney to explain it to me.[1105] Gabriel also owned five lots in Lancaster.[1106]

The 1860 federal census for Wabash County lists Gabriel's age as forty-eight and still a merchant. His second wife Phebe is thirty-five years old and born in Wabash County. Phebe was a charter member of the Lancaster Church of Christ. Lear claims that most of the charter members were converted at the Church of Christ's parent church at Barney's grove. They were supposed to be religious fanatics and not well liked by the other churches in the area. According to Lear, "the brethren gave the more diligent study of the word, often taking their bibles to the fields with them, where, while the teams rested, these zealous souls would study to show themselves approved unto God, workmen that needeth not to be ashamed, rightly dividing the word of Truth."[1107] Phebe left the church when she married Gabriel and became a Methodist.[1108] The 1860 census shows Gabriel and Phebe parents of Albert, twelve; Benjamin, nine; and Charles, three years old. Daughter Nancy is four years old.[1109] The Goldburghs lived in Lancaster until at least 1866.[1110] There is no mention of them after that.

1100 Mrs. Bernice C. Richard, 1850 Federal Census of Wabash County, Illinois: [1974] p. 90.

1101 Cemetery Book, Wabash Friendsville Lancaster Precinct, Lancaster Precinct: [At the Mount Carmel Library] p127.

1102 Bill P. Currie, Early Marriages, Death Notices, Obituaries and Divorce & Estate, Land & Tax etc. Notices from Mount Carmel Newspapers 1830's-1857: p.62.

1103 Beulah Lear, A History of Lancaster Area: [At the Mt. Carmel Public Library November 11, 1981] p. 23.

1104 Proceedings of the Wabash County Commissions 1844-1857: Volume 11 [At the Mt. Carmel Public Library Genealogy 977.378]

1105 Proceedings of the Wabash County Commissions 1844-1857:

1106 Lorraine Garner, 1859 Tax List for Lancaster, Wabash County: [Mt. Carmel Public Library Genealogy Collection, 929.3773] p. 18.

1107 Beulah Lear, p. 52.

1108 Some Wabash County Illinois Church Records. [Early] [At the Mt. Carmel Public Library: Mt. Carmel, Illinois] 11.

1109 Mrs. Geraldine Satterthwaite, 1860 Federal Census of Wabash County, Illinois: [1981] p. 82.

1110 Wabash County Recorder of Deeds, Mount Carmel, Illinois: [Deed Book H] p. 114.

WILL COUNTY

Will County had one Pole by 1850, S. Poniatowski. I have not found much about this guy, not even his first name. The only information I have about him is on the 1850 census of Will County. Poniatowski was living at the home of John Gregory in the boomtown of Lockport. Poniatowski is thirty-nine years old, male, occupation shoemaker, and born in Poland. John Gregory was also a shoemaker, twenty-eight years old, and born in Ireland. His wife Ann E. is twenty-five years old, born in Canada. Son James is six years old, born in New York, and daughter Ellen is one year old, born in Illinois.

John almost seems to have been running a shoemaker's boarding house. Also living at the Gregory house.

Michael Flaherty, thirty-eight years old, occupation shoemaker, and born in Ireland.

John Hunt, twenty-five years old, occupation shoemaker, and born in England.

Joseph Donnelly, twenty-two years old, occupation shoemaker, and born in Ireland.

William Clark, twenty years old, occupation laborer, and born in New York.

William Alsaver, twenty-two years old, occupation cooper, and born in New York.

Ella Mahoney, seventeen years of age, no occupation listed, and born in Ireland.

Thomas Robinson, twenty-seven years old, occupation shoemaker, and born in New Jersey.[1111]

I do not have any more information about Poniatowski, so will write a little about Will County. Will was part of Cook and Iroquois counties

[1111] 1850 Federal Census of Will County, Illinois: [National Archives, Box M432, Roll133, Page 7]

until it was formed January 12, 1836. Joliet is the county seat. Most of Will County was prairie with very little wooded areas. Some townships had no woods at all. A number of large rivers flow through Will County. The largest is the Kankakee, followed by the Des Plaines and Du page. Just outside Will County in Grundy County the Des Plaines and Kankakee rivers meet to form the Illinois River. The Illinois and Michigan Canal also runs through Will County with the first lock located in the town of Lockport. The canal was the biggest employer in town and Lockport grew up around it.

Lockport is thirty-three miles southwest of Chicago and situated on the banks of the Des Plaines River. The first settlers came in 1830, and most were Yankees from the east. Lockport's population in 1830 was 25 to 30 people. During the 1830s and 1840s, many Irish and German emigrants came to town looking for jobs building the canal. By 1850 it had grown to 1,648. Its current population is around 9,000 but will probably grow much more in the future. In 2007 a major new highway was built making it much easier to drive to Lockport.

The major story about Lockport is the Illinois and Michigan Canal, which linked Lake Michigan to the Illinois River. Work on the canal started in the mostly Irish Bridgeport neighborhood of Chicago on July 4, 1836. Construction began after a large ceremony by the city of Chicago in which three cannons were fired. A recession in 1837 temporarily stopped the project. Work stopped again in the summer of 1838 when many of the workers got sick. Andreas writes,

> During the summer months, from June to September, the work on the canal, the most considerable source of revenue to the paralyzed town, was nearly suspended for a time by a most mysterious disease which broke out among the laborers. It was in its symptoms sufficiently like the Asiatic cholera to give the community an added dread of it. It seized its victims suddenly, and carried them off, if it did not abate, in a few hours. Many of the dead were brought from where they died to the vicinity of Chicago, and dead bodies lay along the road near Bridgeport, unburied for days, so fearful were the inhabitants that the infection might be conveyed to the city.[1112]

[1112] A. T. Andreas, History of Cook County, Illinois: [Chicago: A. T. Andreas 1884] [A reproduction by Unigraphic, Inc. Evansville, Indiana 1973] p. 384.

Work resumed again in September, 1843, but once again sickness slowed down the project. The year 1846 saw another outbreak of disease, and in 1847, a strike stopped work. The canal was finally completed on April 16, 1848, and was ninety miles long, sixty feet wide, and thirty-six feet deep. A number of Irish laborers settled alongside the length of the canal and became farmers. *History of the City of Chicago* wrote, "It opened amidst gala celebrations on April 16, 1848. Sixteen boats set out on the first day, loaded with prominent Canal officials and civic leaders from Chicago and with sugar and other goods from New Orleans."[1113] The canal saw heavy use until 1882, then saw business drop dramatically. The canal was not deep enough for large ships and could not compete with the railroad.

There is no other information about Poniatowski. I checked state census records but found nothing else about him. He must have moved out of state.

[1113] Historic City, The Settlement of Chicago: [Department of Development and Planning 1976] p. 18.

Winnebago County

Winnebago County was the site of the Polish land grant. A few Polish exiles were supposed to have come to Winnebago County because of the land grant. Only Baron Ludwik Chlopicki, Francis Easinski, and Stanislaus Bielansky left any records of themselves in the county. Mrs. Isaac Rawlings claims that Ludwik Turowski and a handful of other Polish exiles settled on the Polish land grant during the winter of 1835.[1114] I researched Turowski in Winnebago County but found no records of him ever living there. It is possible. Turowski could have come out with Francis Easinski who did come out at an early date. If Turowski did settle on the land grant, he did not stay for long. Turowski moved south and became a farmer in Arkansas. Grobicki thought Teofil L. Rutkowski also made it out to the Polish land grant, but there is no evidence in Winnebago County that he ever did.[1115] I write more about Rutkowski in my story about St. Clair County. I have already written about Baron Ludwik Chlopicki in the Woodford County story so will not write a great deal about him now. The same goes for Francis Easinske. You will find his story in DeKalb County. That leaves only Stanislaus Bielansky. Stanislaus only left a very small amount of records, and he does not appear to have stayed in the area very long. Most of the story will be about the Polish tract and Winnebago County history.

Winnebago County is located in the center of the state, in far northern Illinois. The county's northern border is the Wisconsin state line. Winnebago County was created from Jo Daviess County on January 16, 1836. Boone County was formed from Winnebago County on January 4, 1837, and Stephenson County created shortly afterwards on March 4, 1837. At one time, it was the hunting grounds of the Winnebago Indian tribe. The county

---

1114 Mrs. Isaac D. Rawlings, Polish Exiles in Illinois: [Transactions of the Illinois State Historical Society for the year 1927] [Danville, Illinois: Illinois Printing Co. 1927] p. 91.

1115 Aleksander Grobicki, Proba Biografii, Sodalis, [St. Mary's College Library, Orchard Lake, Michigan] letter R, p. 25.

took its name from the same Indian tribe. The Rock, Pecatonica, Sugar, and Kishwaukee rivers all flow through Winnebago County. The banks of these rivers were all wooded, which supplied the first settlers with plenty of lumber to build their homesteads. The rest of Winnebago County was Prairie, interspersed with groves of trees.

The first white settler to Winnebago County was Stephen Mack. Kett wrote that he settled in the northern part of the county in 1829. Mack settled with the Winnebago Indians and married the daughter of one of their chiefs. Mack supposedly married her because she saved him from death by the Winnebagos, or he knew she would inherit land from her father. Kett claims, "That it was not a love match is beyond doubt."[1116] The marriage produced eight children. Mack was supposed to have lived like a hermit. On August 24, 1834, four more settlers showed up, Germanicus Kent, Thatcher Blake, a Mr. Evans, and an unidentified man. The unidentified man was probably Germanicus Kent's slave, Lewis Lemon. They all settled on the west side of the Rock River. Germanicus Kent and Thatcher Blake are considered the founders of the city of Rockford. The first settler on the east side of the river was Daniel S. Haight, who first came to Winnebago County on April 9, 1835. Francis Easinski bought a lot from Haight on the east side.[1117]

Haight's wife was the first white woman in the county. Thurston wrote about an interesting experience she had in Winnebago County. Apparently, some Indians were still living in the county when Mrs. Haight arrived. One day she was washing clothes in the river. She left for a while and went back to the cabin. Mrs. Haight returned a short time later only to find an Indian running away with her laundry. She ran after him and caught up with him in the Indian camp. The camp was about a half mile up river. Once in camp, Mrs. Haight entered his tepee and recovered her laundry. The other Indians in camp ridiculed her the whole time by shouting, "Squaw, squaw, squaw."[1118]

The fall of 1835 saw a large surge in settlers to the county. The newly arriving settlers noticed the sparsely settled Winnebago County. They saw no cabins or farms for miles but when inquiring about the vacant land were told

1116 The History of Winnebago County, Illinois, Its Past and Present: [Chicago: H.F. Kett & Co. 1877] [Facsimile Reprint by Heritage Books, Inc. Bowie, Maryland, 1990] p. 223.

1117 Winnebago County Recorder of Deeds, Rockford, Illinois: Roll F. page 57.

1118 John H. Thurston, Reminiscences, sporting and otherwise, of the Early Days in Rockford, Illinois: [Rockford, Illinois: Press of the Daily Republican 1891] Reprinted by The North Central Illinois Genealogical Society of Rockford, Illinois, [Dixon, Illinois: The Print Shop] p. 9.

that it was already claimed. Most of it probably was too, but because of the Polish tract, no one knew if they owned it or not. The Galena District Land Office finely put the land up for sale in 1839. Those living on the east and west side of the Rock River in Rockford and Rockton townships had to wait until 1843 to buy their land. According to Thurston, "the first few settlers felt uneasy about their claims, and some wanted to unload, provided they could get their price, which was more than the land would bring for years after. A great many claim-holders hung around seeking whom they might devour."[1119] The east and west sides of Rockford incorporated in 1839. The combined population was 235. The current population of Rockford is 139,712.

The Polish Land Grant

The 234 Polish exiles from Trieste landed in New York March 28, 1834. They hoped to remain together and petitioned Congress for a land grant to build a Polish settlement. On June 30, 1834, President Andrew Jackson signed a bill known as "Donation of Lands to Polish Patriots."[1120] A site for the settlement was to be chosen in either the territory of Michigan or the state of Illinois. Baron Ludwik Chlopicki and John E. Prehal were chosen by the Polish Committee to select a site in Illinois.

Baron Ludwik Chlopicki arrived in Chicago on September 20, 1834.[1121] He found the perfect location for the Land Grant by the end of November. Ludwik chose an eighteen-mile-long-by-two-mile-wide tract of land on the west side of the Rock River in Winnebago County. The site was eighty miles northwest of Chicago. There were a few American settlers living there under squatter title, and a few half-breed Indians living on "Floating Land." Floating Land was sections of land (640 acres), given to any half-breed Indian wishing to stay in Winnebago County. The half-breeds belonged to the Winnebago Indian tribe, which had recently moved west. While he was in Winnebago County, Ludwik stayed in the cabin of one of the squatters, Germanicus Kent.

Germanicus and the other squatters started to worry that Ludwik intended to choose the land they were already settled on. Ludwik told them they had nothing to worry about and after finishing his work left to make a report to the land office. Ludwik's reply was not to their liking, and

1119 John H. Thurston, p. 24.

1120 Jerzy Jan Lerski, A Polish Chapter in Jacksonian America: [Madison: The University of Wisconsin Press 1958] p. 135.

1121 The Sangamo Journal Newspaper, [September 20, 1834]

Germanicus was sent to Washington to defend their claims. In Washington, Germanicus was told by the land commission that "every settler in the county was a trespasser, and that he had no legal right to a foot of the land which he had so unceremoniously taken."[1122] Germanicus and the other squatters were not ready to give up so easily, however. They went to their representatives in Congress for help, and the once-friendly citizens of Illinois sided with the squatters over the matter.

The Winnebago settlers were not about to let anyone take their land, whether Poles or otherwise. Boies wrote that numerous little stockade forts were built with loopholes for muskets, and a determination was expressed to drive the Polish emigrants out of the country, and they were entirely successful. They never occupied their grant."[1123] The settlers fought with each other as well. Claim jumping was a problem. They increased their land holdings by moving or burning their neighbors' fences at night. They pulled down each other's cabins and burned them. Other times claim jumpers would build a shanty, haul it by wagon at night, and deposit it on someone else's land. Another method was to plant someone's field at night and then claim it as your own. I cannot see how this would have worked. Eventually, settler courts were formed to settle disputes.

Frontier regions are many times lawless areas. Winnebago County was no exception. The nearby counties of Ogle, Lee, and DeKalb were bad too. Horse theft was the number one crime. Robberies and counterfeiting were common too. The settlers reacted by forming Vigilante societies to drive lawbreakers out of the county. The vigilante societies generally worked, but a number of innocent settlers were always driven out as well. Most of the settlers were very poor. According to Thurston,

> In the early forties the people of this county were so poor they "couldn't cast a shadow," to use a most appropriate expression of "Judge" E.S. Blackstone. I venture to say that in 1841-2 there were not twenty farmers in the county who possessed a suit of clothes suitable to wear to church or to court, which they had purchased with the avails of labor on their farms. Alas for those among the settlers who had passed their prime physically. Too old to withstand

[1122] Charles A. Church, History of Rockford and Winnebago County, Illinois: [W. P. Lamb, Book and Job Printer 1900] [Published by the New England Society of Rockford, Illinois] p. 211.

[1123] Henry L. Boies, History of DeKalb County, Illinois: [Chicago: O. P. Bassett 1868] [A Reproduction by Unigraphic, Inc. Evansville, Indiana 1973] p. 384.

> the hardships of pioneer life, they sickened, and in some instances they straggled back to the old homes at the east to die. Among the latter were my own parents, leaving me in 1842 to fight the battle of life alone.[1124]

Before getting back to the Polish claim, I have to write one more story about the settlers. It is one of my favorite stories about the Winnebago County settlers and concerns their creativity. Thurston wrote about a charivari, which took place in Rockford. A charivari occurred to a couple on their wedding night. Their friends would gather and serenade them with any musical instruments they could find. Making as much noise as possible seems to have been the goal. The musicians at the charivari were too tired to play anymore, so a carpenter named Nick Smith devised a new instrument called a "swinette."

> Followed by the regiment, he appeared on the scene, each man carrying under his arm as large a shoat "pig" as he could well handle-there were lots of "em sleeping around every manure pile in town—while grasping the muzzle of the animal in his hand, when he produced a high or a low note by opening or shutting its mouth. When the pig became partially exhausted they'd carry him into the bar-room and "tune up the Swinette," as Nick said, "with a glass of whisky. If pandemonium reigned before, it was doubly intensified now with each pig squealing in all the notes of the gamut. When the supply of small hogs gave out they caught the large ones, dragging them by the hind legs as long as they could utter a sound, and so ended the most noted charivari party of northern Illinois.[1125]

One problem after another prevented the Polish exiles from claiming the land. They could not settle on the land until it was surveyed, but the survey took all the year 1835. At the same time, new squatters were coming into the county. Ludwik saw what was happening and tried to redraw the land grant. D. A. Spaulding, a big shot at the St. Louis Regional Land Office vilified Ludwik and the Polish exiles. He also tried to convince Illinois Congressman William L. May that the citizens of Illinois were completely against the Polish land grant. The results of the survey made it to Washington in the spring of

---

1124 John H. Thurston, p. 35.

1125 John H. Thurston, p. 101 & 102.

1836, but politics got the survey results tied up in the House of Representatives for the whole of that year. The year 1837 brought new troubles. Two of the half-breed tracts were found to be on the land grant. Ludwik was told to redraw the tract. He went back to work and picked out different land. The commissioner of the land office turned down the new proposal claiming it "inadmissible on account of the description being defective, and their not conforming to the legal subdivisions."[1126]

This was the end of the line for Ludwik, and the Polish Committee fired him April 15, 1837. John Rychlicki replaced Ludwik. Rychlicki ran into the same type of problems Ludwik had encountered, mainly state politics and trouble with the half-breed Floating Lands. In the fall of 1839, the Galena District Land Office put all land in Winnebago County for sale, with the exception of Rockford and Rockton townships. The now-many-times-redrawn Polish tract was located in these two townships. The Polish Committee sent Congress another plan in 1840, but to no avail. The end came on June 14, 1842, when President Tyler agreed with Congress that the Polish exiles had not lived up to their end of the contract. On November 3, 1843, The Polish grant was sold at public sale. Congress cited three reasons for their decision.

1. The lack of the second agents (John Prehal's) signature
2. The fact that thirty-eight, and not thirty-six, sections, as explicitly provided by the act, were taken for Polish locations
3. That the selections might interfere with the rights of individuals under the preemption laws.[1127]

Stanislaus Bielansky

I have only found a very small amount of information about Stanislaus. He was not one of the Polish exiles from Trieste. The July 3, 1841, *Galena and Northwestern Gazette* notified Stanislaus that there was a letter for him. They spell his name Stainiat Birbauski, but I believe it is the same person.[1128] Winnebago County marriages have a record of Stanislaus Bielansdy marrying

1126 Jerzy Jan Lerski, p. 149.

1127 Mieczyslaw Haiman, Z Preszlosci Polskiej W Ameryce: Szkice Historyczne. [Buffalo: 1927] p. 211.

1128 Wisconsin State Historical Society, Extracts from the Galena Advertiser & Northwestern Gazette 1834-1845: [Madison, Wisconsin: microfilm collection]

Mary Ann Mariah James on August 23, 1841.[1129] The 1850 Federal Census for Winnebago County only contains the name Mary Ann Balansky, thirty-one years old and born in Connecticut. She was living in the small town of New Milford, located a little south of Rockford. She has a nine-year-old son named Charles.[1130] What happened to Stanislaus after he married Mary Ann is a mystery at this time. Maybe I will find new information about him in the future.

Baron Ludwik Chlopicki never spent a lot of time in Winnebago County. He is on the 1840 census for Tazewell County.[1131] Ludwik was living in Peoria County in 1850,[1132] However, most of his life in America was spent in Woodford County, were he died in 1869.[1133] There is more about Ludwik in my story about Woodford County. Francis Easinski lived in the east side of Rockford until 1846, and then moved to DeKalb County.[1134] There is more information about Francis in the story about DeKalb County.

1129 Liahona Research, Illinois Marriages, 1826 to 1850: [Bountiful, Utah: Heritage Quest 1999] p. 63.

1130 1850 Federal Census of Winnebago County, Illinois: [Copied by Mrs. Bernice C. Richard] [Chicago, Illinois: Chicago Genealogical Society 1972] p. 110.

1131 1840 Federal Census of Tazewell County, Illinois: [At the National Archives, Roll 71 p. 20]

1132 Patricia Combs O'Dell, 1850 Peoria County, Illinois Census [October 1972] p. 2.

1133 El Paso Story: [The Centennial Book of El Paso, Illinois: Sponsored by The El Paso, Illinois Library Board 1954] p. 63.

1134 DeKalb County Probate records, Sycamore, Illinois: [Francis Easinski file]

WLODECKI

Now we get to my ancestor, Franciszek. Before we go any farther, let me just say that although I am writing this story, three people did the research for it. Zbigniew Wlodecki of Krakow, Poland; my cousin Joe Lodesky; and myself spent years collecting the information for this story. Zbigniew in particular was most helpful. He found information for us in libraries in Poland and Ukraine. Nice of him since we are not even sure if we are related, other than we have the same uncommon last name of Wlodecki. Our name went through many different spellings before we settled on Lodesky. The WL beginning of our name is pronounced more like a WV sound and there is no pronunciation for it in English. The closest spelling for Wlodecki from Polish to English would be Wodetzky.

Franciszek was born on September 17, 1794, in Raszkow, the province of Podolia. He was the son of Josef and Domicella Wlodecki. His father Jozef was an official in the District of Baltsk.[1135] Podolia was divided between Upper and Lower Podilia (Bratslav). Raszkow was located in Lower Podolia. Upper Podolia became a part of Poland in 1366 and was under Polish control for most of its history until the second partition of Poland in 1793. Lower Podolia was ruled by Lithuania until 1569, then became a part of Poland. It was also lost to Russia in the second partition. The Cossacks and Turks ruled over Lower Podolia for a time from 1649 to 1699. Franciszek was a lieutenant[1136] in the Cavalry[1137] during the 1830 Polish uprising and was one of the 234 Polish exiles from Trieste.[1138] He first bought land in Warren Township, Lake County, Illinois in the fall of 1843 and moved to Illinois with his family in the fall of 1844.[1139]

1135 Genealogia y Dowdy o Szlachectwie, Wlodeckiego: [Archives at Kamyanets-Podilskyy, Ukraine]

1136 Mieczyslaw Haiman, Slady Polskie W Ameryce: [Chicago, Illinois: Drukiem Dziennika Zjednoczenia, 1938] p. 123.

1137 Josef Bialynia Cholodecki, General Kolyszko and his subordinates in the area of Galicia: [Lwow: Polonia Printing-House, Ossolinskich 16, 1912] p. 1.

1138 Jerzy Jan Lerski, A Polish Chapter in Jacksonian America: [Madison, Wisconsin: The University of Wisconsin Press 1958] p.178.

1139 Lake County Museum Association: [Volume 24, No. 1 Spring 1996] p. 2.

We had one thing going for us when we started to research our family history, a signet ring that Franciszek wore on a chain around his neck. It was his only possession from Poland. The firstborn son in the family always inherits the ring. My Great-grandfather was the youngest son, so the ring passed to his oldest brother Joseph. Our family and Joseph's family lost contact in the 1930s, but Joe and I contacted them in the late 1990s. Franciszek's grandfather Antoni told him that his grandfather did not know how old the ring was. The coat of arms on the ring or in Polish herb (clan) is the symbol (SAS). SAS has a gold crescent moon pointing upwards at the bottom of the ring's shield. Each end of the moon has a six-pointed gold star above it. There is a silver arrow in the middle of the moon, which points straight up, all on a blue or red shield. Ours is red! The crown at the top has either a peacock's tail or ostrich feathers, with a silver arrow running through the feathers. The arrow always points left.[1140] It is supposed to be one of the oldest coat of arms from the eastern region of Poland or the present western Ukraine.[1141] Finding out that we were SAS enabled us to concentrate our family search to mainly the country of Ukraine. Polish clan members were not always blood relatives like the west. The warrior band that became the Clan SAS had many different families using the same coat of arms. They all considered themselves equals. Each clan usually fought as a unit and had its own battle cry as well.

Herb Sas—Coat of Arms

From Wikipedia Commons

[1140] Slawomir Gorzynaski, Jerzy Kochanowski and Adam Jonca, Herby Szlachty Polskiej: [Warsaw: Wydawnictwa Uniwersytetu Warszawskiego I Wydawnictwa Alfa 1990] p. 140 & 141.

[1141] Polska Encyklopedja Szlachecka, [Warsaw: Wydawnictwo Instytutu Kultury Historycznej 1935] Vol. 3 p. 391.

There is disagreement over the origins of SAS. SAS means Saxon in Polish and one theory claims that the Clan SAS were Saxons (Germans) from Transylvania.[1142] Janusz Bieniak wrote that there were two groups from Transylvania, one German and the other Walachian, (Romanians).[1143] Henryk Lowmianski writes that in 1340, Walachians began settling in the area south of the city of Lwow, Ukraine, and all the way down to the right and left banks of the Dniester River. The Clan SAS defended Poland's southern border from the Tartars and Hungarians.[1144] Hipolit Stupnicki has a different take on the story. He says Saxons from Transylvania joined the army of a Ukrainian prince named Lew (Leo). Leo's army then united with an army from Lithuania that was campaigning in Mazowsze (Mazovia). Warsaw, the capital of Poland, is located in the province of Mazovia. Leo (1264-1301) was the ruler of the Ukrainian state of Galicia-Volhynia and was always hostile to Poland. He managed to get his brother proclaimed ruler of Lithuania in 1267-68 and might have invaded Mazovia at this time. After the campaign, the Saxons settled in Ukraine and became the Clan SAS.[1145] Dlugosz, a famous fifteenth-century Polish historian, has a completely different theory. Dlugosz lived a hundred years after the Clan SAS came into being and said the clan was originally from Wolosk. Wolosk was in the northern part of the present country of Belarus, along with a small area in southern Lithuania. Until recently, the country of Belarus was known as "White Russia," so the Clan SAS would have been White Russians. Modern science agrees with Dlugosz's theory. If Dlugosz's theory is correct, SAS was probably allied with Lithuania until some point in the 1300s, then went over to Poland. In 1349, Poland took over Galicia. The Clan SAS ancestral homeland is located in Galicia, south of the city of Lviv.[1146]

Franciszek's father Josef must have been a very important man. He was the plenipotentiary for all the businesses belonging to Prince Alexander

---

1142 Norman Davies, God's Playground A History of Poland: [New York: Columbia University Press 1982] p. 209.

1143 Karol Modzelewski, Comites, Principes, Nobiles. The Structure of the Ruling class as Reflected in the Terminology Used by Gallus Anonymous: [In The Polish Nobility in the Middle Ages] [Wroclaw, Poland: Zaklad Narodowy im. Ossolinskich 1984] p. 133.

1144 Henryk Lowmianski, The Rank Nobility in Medieval Poland: [In The Polish Nobility in the Middle Ages] p. 30.

1145 Hipolit Stupnicki, Herbarz Polski I Imionospis: [Lwow: Drukiem Kornefa Biffera Volume 1, 1855] p.43 & 44.

1146 Slawomir Gorzynaski, Jerzy Kochanowski and Adam Jonca, p. 140 &141.

Lubomirski, Prince Kalext Poninski, and Antoni Wislocki.[1147] The *Oxford English Dictionary* describes *plenipotentiary* as "invested in full power, esp. as the deputy, representative, or envoy of a sovereign ruler; exercising absolute power or authority."[1148] In Poland, plenipotentiary was usually given to close friends or relatives. I assume Josef was the representative for the three people just mentioned in the district of Baltsk. One story told to us by relatives was that the Wlodeckis were one of the richest families in Poland. I investigated this story but never found our name anywhere, let alone among the magnates who were the wealthiest Poles. It is possible Franciszek's interpretation to his descendants was misunderstood. The relatives were actually close. The Lubomirski family was one of the richest families in Poland. Alexander Lubomirskis father Stanislaw (1704-1793) owned 31 towns and 728 villages situated on twenty-five thousand square kilometers, most of it in Podolia.[1149] Teresa Zielinska writes that Stanislaw Lubomirski owned more estates than any one person in Polish history. He is supposed to have been mentally unstable and lost most of his estates playing cards. In 1768, three of his cousins had to intervene in his affairs to save the rest of the estates for his sons. Stanislaw agreed to sign over his estates to his sons in 1770. Stanislaw's son Alexander Lubomirski was either a general or major in the French Army. He married Rozalia Chodkiewiczowna. They were the parents of one daughter, Rozalia. She went on to marry Waclaw Rzewuski, better known as the "Emir." We will hear more about the Emir later. Alexander died in 1808.[1150]

The Lubomirskis owned the town of Raszkow when Jozef lived there. In the old Polish Commonwealth, Raszkow was located on Poland's southwestern border with Turkey and situated on the east bank of the Dniester River. The Dniester originates in the Carpathian Mountains and flows to the Black Sea. It is the second largest river in Ukraine, and many streams and rivers flow into it. The Dniester has always been a tough river to navigate. The northern part of the river is a swift-flowing mountain stream. After leaving the mountains, the river snakes around through gorges and rapids. It is usually deep but not very wide and contains many rocks along the whole length of the river. The

1147 Genealogia y Dowdy o Szlachectwie, Wlodeckiego:

1148 The Oxford English Dictionary: [Prepared by J. A. Sampson and E. S. C. Weiner Volume X1] [Oxford: Clarendon Press 1989] p. 1040.

1149 Rodziny, The Journal of the Polish Genealogical Society of America: [Chicago, Illinois: November 1993] p. 23.

1150 Teresa Zielinska, Poczet Polskich rodow arystokratycznych : [Warsaw: Wydawnictwa Szkolne I Pedagogiczne 1997] p. 146 & 147.

river freezes for six or seven weeks a year. The Dniester River has always been the border between Ukraine and Moldavia.

World War II changed all that. After the war, Stalin gave Moldavia a long, thin strip of Ukrainian land situated on the east side of the river. When the Soviet Union broke up in 1991, the east side of the river declared their independence from Moldavia. The population of the east side of the river is mainly Slavic Ukrainians and Russians, while the west bank is of Romanian origin. Raszkow still has some Poles there. With some help from the Russian Army and three thousand Cossacks, the east bank Slavs seceded from Moldavia and formed the country of Prednostovia or in English the Trans-Dniester Republic. I have been to Raszkow and found the surrounding region beautiful but poor. The Trans-Dniester's population is six hundred thousand. The country is in a political limbo right now and not recognized as a state by hardly any country in the world.[1151] I think Russia recently recognized Trans-Dniester.

There were settlements in the Raszkow area as early as the AD fifth century, but the Zamoyskis get credit for establishing the town in the late 1600s. In 1682, the region of Raszkow included the town and ten surrounding villages. Raszkow was part of Barbara Zamoyska's dowry, and the town came under the rule of the Koniecpolskis until 1703. First Cossacks and then Turks destroyed Raszkow during the Koniecpolskis' administration. The Lubomirski family gained control of Raszkow sometime after 1703. In 1775, the town of Raszkow had 65 houses, and the surrounding 255 houses but the town still had not recovered from the Cossack-Turkish wars. Alexander Lubomirski inherited Raszkow and the surrounding 15 villages in 1776. He appointed Josef Wlodecki plenipotentiary on March 15, 1788.[1152] Catherine the Great of Russia bought Raszkow in 1793. Raszkow has always had a variety of different ethnic groups living there. Besides Poles and Ukrainians, there were Wolochs (Romanians), Greeks, Armenians, and Jewish traders and merchants. Gypsies were very numerous in the surrounding areas, and Tartars lived in villages on the north shore of the Black Sea. For some reason the Armenians were kicked out of town in the 1800s. The area around Raszkow has many caves, and the local shepherds keep their sheep in them during the winter.[1153]

Prince Kalext Poninski (1753-1817) was not as wealthy as the Lubomirskis but managed to make himself well-known for the times. He was a cadet in Knight School from 1766 to 1770. Kalext was granted the title of prince in

---

[1151] McClean's magazine, July 27, 1992: p. 20 & 21.

[1152] Genealogia y Dowdy o Sklachectwie Wlodeckiego:

[1153] Encyklopedyja Powszechna: [Warsaw: 1865] p.952.

May 1774. He became a member of the Polish Parliament at twenty-five years of age in 1778. In parliament, he was on committee's responsible for hospitals and mediating land disputes. He also voted to return the power to mediate land disputes to the king. He married Barbara Lubomirski in 1780 and acquired her estates in Volhynia.[1154]

An important event occurred in Ukraine in 1774: the Turks were on the losing end of a war with Russia. The Turks had closed all ports on the Black Sea to Poland and Russia for hundreds of years. Now all the ports on the north end of the Black Sea were open. Before this time, Podolian products were shipped to either Danzig (Gdansk) on the Baltic Sea or over the mountains into Austria. The new ports on the Black Sea were much closer, lowering transportation costs considerably. In 1785, Kalext became the first Pole to transport lumber by barge down the Slucz River to the port of Kherson on the Black Sea.[1155] In 1786, he built rafts to haul lumber down the Slucz, as well as the Pripet and Dnieper rivers. It was very difficult navigating these new river routes at first. Both the Dniester and Dnieper were full of rocks. New roads were needed. The river dams dismantled. Work on canals linking the rivers together soon commenced. From the beginning, Kalext took an active role in establishing the river trade routes. He spent his own money cleaning up rivers when necessary. He also tried to persuade others to help out, as well as urging them to haul their cargos to the new Black Sea ports. Kalext appointed Josef his plenipotentiary on May 22, 1778.

Kalext's marriage to Barbara Lubomirski was his first and her second marriage. Barbara's daughter from her first marriage, Marrianna Lubomirski, married the governor of Kiev, Prot Potocki. A dispute arose between Kalext and Prot over one of Barbara Lubomirski's estates. In 1792, the dispute escalated when Prot challenged Kalext to a duel. Kalext was confident a court would settle the case in his favor and wanted no part of a duel. Kalext lost the case in court and had to turn over the estate to Prot and give Prot an apology. The whole episode bankrupted him. At the same time, Barbara was having an affair with his brother Adam. Barbara divorced Kalext in

1154 Polski Slownik Biograficzny: [Krakow, Poland: Zaklad Narodowy Imienia Ossolinskich Wydawnictwo Polskiej Akademii Nauk 1982] Volume 17 p. 539 & 540.

1155 Henryk Klimesz, Poland's trade through the Black Sea in the eighteenth century: [The Polish Review Volume, XV, No. 2 Spring, 1970] [A Quarterly Published by The Polish Institute of Arts and Sciences in America, Inc. New York, N. Y. 1970] p. 79.

1793 and married Alexander Winnicki. To add insult to injury, Hilarego Zalaski portrayed Kalext as an envious brute bent on stealing his neighbor's estate in the book *Poland*. I am not sure exactly when this book was printed. Kalext must have thought the world had just ended.

I cannot let the story end like this. Kalext did many good things too. He donated money to the Knight School when the school was in need. In 1789, Adam Poninski, Kalext's brother, was arrested and imprisoned in Warsaw. Kalext paid Adam a visit and gave him enough money to improve his conditions in prison. He bailed Adam out of prison in 1790. Three years later, the grateful Adam carried on an affair with his wife Barbara. Kalext let a Polish Army use one of his estates to help keep the army's expenses down. He was awarded the "White Eagle" Army Metal in 1781. In 1792, Kalext gave 2 cannons and 120 hats to the army. Even when bankrupt, Kalext managed to find money to donate to Kosciuszko during the uprising in 1794. He was always concerned about the high degree of poverty the peasants in Volhynia endured and hoped the new ports on the Black Sea might improve their condition. He tried to develop the Black Sea trade using his own money. Kalext attained the highest level in the Masons. He was an avid hunter and organized large hunting expeditions. Kalext's second marriage was to Ludwika Chrzszczonowska. Do not ask me how to pronounce that name. Neither marriage produced any children.[1156]

I was not able to find much information about the Wislockis. Josef was designated the plenipotentiary for Antoni Wislocki on November 9, 1778.[1157] The Wislockis might be Lemkos. Their estates are listed in the book *Lemkowie Zapomniani Polacy*.[1158] The Lemko people live in the far southeast corner of Poland in the Carpathian Mountains. There is a debate over whether they are a separate ethnic group or Ukrainians. Their language is close to Ukrainian, and they are Eastern Orthodox in religion.[1159] The Wislockis were also members of the Clan SAS.[1160] The Lemko territory was near the SAS ancestral homeland in Galicia.

[1156] Polski Slownik Biograficzny, p. 539 &540.

[1157] Genealogia y Dowdy o Sklachectwie Wlodeckiego:

[1158] Lemkowie Zapomniani Polacy, Polskie Osadnictwo Historyczne: [Warsaw: 1939]

[1159] Matthew Bielawa, Stratford, Connecticut, What are Ruthenians? [Pathways & Passages, Volume 18, No. 2 Spring 2002] p. 6.

[1160] Kaspra Niesieckiego S. J. Herbarz Polski: [W Lipsku Nakladem I Drukiem Breitkopfa I hertela 1841] Volume 8, p. 283.

Map of Podolia

Podolia in the 18th century

From *New Encyclopedia Britanica*

After I found out we were from Podolia, I decided to find out more about the place. The region once known as Podolia is now located in southwestern Ukraine and the name of Podolia has not been in use since World War II. Ukraine means frontier or borderlands. Podolia's western borders were the Dniester and Zbruch rivers. The Dniester River is the border with the country of Moldavia, while the Zbruch divides upper Podolia from lower Podolia. The province of Volhynia was to the north. The eastern border is the Southern Bug River. The Kodyma and Jahorlyk Rivers are its southern borders. Below the southern border is the Black Sea Lowlands. Podolia's soil is black, and it has always been a very rich agricultural region famous for its cattle. The upper part of Podolia came under Polish rule in 1366 while Lower Podolia became a part of Poland in 1569. The Polish provinces of Kiev, Cherihiv, and Lower Podolia were lost to the Cossacks in 1649. Turkey invaded Podolia in 1672 and ruled there until 1699, when Poland regained control. Russia took all of Podolia during the second partition of Poland in 1793. A French diplomat named Hugon wrote in the late 1700s,

> The Ukraine and Podolia are perhaps the most fertile lands under the sun. The soil, even when not ploughed deeply, yields the most abundant crops. The forests are full of excellent timber. Other wood can be used for Potash manufacturing. Hemp grows

> in large quantities. The steppes feed numerous herds of strong and fat cattle. The hives supply honey in abundance.[1161]

The first book I read about Podolia is called *Remembrances of a Polish Exile* by August A. Jakubowski. August was one of the 234 Polish exiles from Trieste. He was born alongside the Dniester River in Podolia in 1815. First published in 1835, *Remembrances of a Polish Exile* is one of the first Polish books written in America. August never got over leaving Poland and committed suicide two years after publishing *Remembrances*. He wrote a great description of Podolia.

> Of Podolia, I will yet speak. It was the cradle of my childhood, the spot where the first flowers of my youthful thoughts expanded.
>
> It is a lovely, beautiful, fertile and romantic country; and in ancient times, it was called the granary of Poland. But a happy fate was not for Podolia. Lying on the frontiers of Turkey, it has always been the theatre of cruel scenes, from the ravages of the Turks, Tartars and Cossacks. In the 17th century, a great part of it, together with its capital, Kamienniec, was subdued by the Turks, and neither the sword of John Sobieski, nor the valour of its inhabitants could deliver it. At last the King, Augustus the second, regained it by treaty. Kamienniec has yet some relics of the Turks, which give it a foreign and oriental cast. The old castle of Kamienniec, now in ruins, speaks with its dark stones of yet darker times, and stands as a specter amid the green trees that surround it.
>
> The misfortunes of Podolia have imprinted their traces on its inhabitants. The people have a fantastic, romantic and poetic character. It may be said, with truth, that Podolia is to Poland, as Scotland to England. No people are so prejudiced as the peasantry of Podolia. The church-yards are full of ghosts and vampires; every grave in the field and every cross, is consecrated by some legend: If you ask the Podolian peasant of the plague, he will tell you that a woman has passed there in a white dress with one hand waving the habiliments of the grave, with the other holding a black handkerchief-and she is the plague. None of them die without the prophecy of the owl's cry or the dog's groan.[1162]

1161 Henryk Klimesz, p. 67.

1162 August A. Jakubowski, The Remembrances of a Polish Exile: [Albany: Packard and Van Benthuysen 1835] p. 65 & 66.

Count Henry Krasinski published a book about his experiences in Podolia in 1843. He was born alongside the Boh River in Podolia near the Turkish border. The count lived in Podolia about the same time as August Jakubowski and has some interesting things to say about it. The flag of Podolia was white with a golden sun in the center. Speaking about the music, "Podolian airs, at once so tender, so sad, so wild, the tones of which, blended with the thrilling music of the harp, are so strikingly imitative of the whizzing bullets and the neighing of the steed."[1163] Leslie wrote, "It was only natural that the Poles living south of the Pripet marshes in Volhynia, Podolia and the Ukraine should similarly seek to express their own past in prose and poetry. The southeastern regions were the land of the Cossacks, of the wars against the Tartars and of the struggle against Turkey in the defense of Christendom."[1164] The *Remembrances of a Polish Exile* contains some Podolian poems. I am not much of a fan of poetry, but one poem called "The Insurrection" caught my attention. One stanza goes like this,

Leave those that round ye weep
Leave home and friends once more
That sword though dimmed with tears,
Shall glow with Turkish gore.[1165]

The count claimed that the women of Podolia and Lithuania were the most beautiful.[1166] Herring thought Polish women were the most beautiful women he had ever seen.[1167] As they say, beauty is in the eyes of the beholder. Wherever I went in Poland or Ukraine, I saw beautiful women. The people of Podolia live at the bottom of ravines and valleys to protect themselves from the east wind and grow their crops on the plains above. The old capital of Podolia was Kamyanets-Podolsky. Kamyanets-Podolsky is some city. It sits like an island surrounded by a two-hundred-yard-wide and fifty-yard-deep ravine created by nature. Many of the local Ukrainians live on small farms in the ravine. Their houses, barns, etc., are all painted different colors making for a very picturesque scene. The Smotych River also flows though the ravine.

1163 Henry Krasinski, The Poles in the Seventeenth Century, [London: T. C. Newby 1843] p. 34.

1164 R. F. Leslie, Polish Politics and the Revolution of November 1830: [Westwood Connecticut: Greenwood Press 1969] p. 102 & 103.

1165 August A. Jakubowski, p.67.

1166 Henry Krasinski, p. 241.

1167 Harro-Herring, P. Poland under Russian Dominion: [London: 1831] p. 185.

The old part of town was divided into Polish, Ukrainian, Armenian, and Jewish quarters and contains a large fortress. The newer town is located east of the ravine. Podolia contained five major religions for much of its history. Besides Roman Catholics, there were Orthodox, Protestant, Jewish, and Islam faiths. Podolia even had its own Robin Hood. The leader of a group of peasants named Ustym Karmaliuk used to assail and rob Podolian nobility in the 1820s and 1830s. He gave everything he stole to the poorest peasants until he was murdered in 1835.[1168]

The Tartars were still a problem well into the late 1700s. At thirteen years of age, Count Henry Krasinski accompanied his father in a surprize attack on a nearby band of Tartars. The Tartars were professional slavers, and I will explain more about them later. The Poles killed the Tartar Khan and many of his men. They also freed all of the Tartars' captives. Although only thirteen, Henry killed a few Tartars. His father, a retired soldier of thirty years, was so proud of his son he actually cried when he told his family about Henry's bravery. Training for knighthood began at an early age for the Polish nobility of Eastern Poland, and Henry was already an accomplished swordsman at thirteen years of age. The eastern nobility carried on the old Polish customs much longer then in Poland. Polish nobility traditionally carried swords at all times and sword-fighting contests were common at all the fairs and get-togethers. Franciszek used to take on all four of his kids at the same time in swordfights and easily wipe them out. They used sticks instead of swords of course. His oldest son Joe claimed they really tried to beat Franciszek. Polish nobility were also expert horsemen and considered themselves the best lancers in the world.[1169]

Henry's next encounter with the Tartars did not go as well. One of the family servants had a grievance against Henry's father. The servant was secretly corresponding with the Tartars and one night he let the Tartars in the house while everyone was asleep. Henry awoke to screams of "the Tartars" and found the house on fire. He grabbed his sword and ran out of his room only to find his sisters, brother-in-laws, and their children all hacked to death. The Tartars were trying to kill his father while others were dragging his mother away by her hair. Henry himself was captured by the Tartars and then sold to the Turks. The Turks nursed his wounds, and then sold him to an Arabian merchant. He spent the next two years as a slave for the Arab and traveled around Arabia, Egypt, and Asia Minor. Henry claims the Arab treated him

1168 Ukraine, A Concise Encyclopedia: [Halyna Petrenko, editor] [South Bound Brook, N. J. Ukrainian Orthodox Church of the U. S. A. 1987] p. 669.

1169 Henry Krasinski, p. 302.

well. Two years later, his master died and Henry became the property of one of the Arabs relatives. This relative was not as nice as his first owner and tried to convert Henry to Islam. Henry steadfastly refused. His new master was determined to win a new convert for Islam and threw Henry in the dungeon. There they tried to convert him by torture. He thought about committing suicide many times but one night his luck changed. The Arab's wife took pity on him and released him. She explained that her grandmother was from the same region as he was and had also been carried off into slavery. She loved her grandmother very much and admired his stubbornness to remain a Christian. She also made him promise not to take revenge on her husband.

Henry wanted to go back to Poland but did not think it was possible to go through Turkey. Instead, he went east to Persia (Iran) and enlisted in the army. Persia was at war with Russia at the time. Soon after that war ended, Persia went to war with Turkey. Mulay Hassan, the grand vizier's cousin, captured Henry in the second battle of the war. Mulay admired Henry's ability with a bow and took a liking to him. This turned out to be a good thing for both of them. On the way back from Persia they got lost in the desert and then attacked by Bedouins. Henry shot the Bedouin leader in the heart and saved Mulay's life. Mulay was so grateful he not only gave Henry his freedom but offered his daughter to Henry as a wife. Henry just wanted to go back to Poland so declined Mulay's offer of a wife. Mulay was determined to show his gratitude and gave Henry his best horse, a brave dog, and an escort to Poland. He also asked Henry if he would take an old Christian slave woman along with him. Henry tells what happened next.

> A female advanced in years, now presented herself before me: grief had traced its lines upon her care-worn face. At beholding her, I experienced a feeling far stronger than compassion. She spoke a few words to me in broken Polish,-I shuddered-some unearthly influence seemed to attract me to her. She suddenly fixed her eyes upon me, a livid paleness settled on her cheeks, she extended her arms to me, and exclaimed; "Stanislaus ! My son!" She then fell into a deep swoon. It was indeed, my mother![1170]

I do not know why she called him Stanislaus when his name is Henry, but she can call him anything she wants. The astonishment of seeing her son again was too much for his mother. She was bedridden for eight days. It looked like she was going to recover and told him what happened to her

1170 Henry Krasinski, p.34.

after the Tartars captured her but died in his arms two days later. Henry was gone for thirteen years when he finally made it back to Podolia.

Poland and Russia were semifeudal societies until March 3, 1861, when Russia freed the serfs. The Polish nobility in western Ukraine owned 90 percent of the land on the right bank of the Dnieper River but were only 10 percent of the population. The vast majority of the people were landless Ukrainian peasants, most owing a set number of days of work to their lord. As would be expected, the Polish nobility and the peasants had their differences over the years. I am now going to explain how the Polish nobility came to own most of the land on the right bank of the Dnieper River. The Tartars get most of the credit.

The Tartars were the remnants of Genghis Khan's Mongol army. They were not Mongols, however, but were a Turkish people. Originally, three different ethnic groups inhabited Mongolia. The Mongols lived in the center of Mongolia; Turkish tribes lived in the west and the Tungus, in the east. The Turkish tribes moved west, while the Tungus moved east and became the Manchurians. Genghis Khan conquered the Tartars a number of times and incorporated them in his army but they always rebelled. Genghis had enough of it and came up with a solution in AD 1204. He killed every Tartar taller than the axle of a cart and brainwashed those left into thinking they were Mongols. It worked for a time and the remaining Tartars grew up to be his best troops. Genghis died in AD 1227 and his son Ogodei took over. Ogotei attacked Eastern Europe with a Mongol/Tartar army in AD 1240. The Mongol branch of the army invaded Hungary, Serbia, and Bulgaria while the Tartar branch invaded Russia, Ukraine, and Poland. Genghis's grandson Batu set up a Mongol capital named Sarai on the Volga River in southern Russia. Soon they broke away from Mongolia and called themselves the Golden Horde. They converted to Islam in the early 1400s. The Tartars were able administrators and ruled over a great part of Russia and Ukraine exacting tribute. They were masters of the area for over one hundred years until the Lithuanian army was victorious over them in AD 1363. The Golden Horde held on in parts of Russia until the 1400s, and then splintered into separate groups because of infighting. The various Tartar bands then settled along the north shore of the Black Sea from the Dniester to the Kuban Rivers and proceeded to cause a lot of trouble. Genghis Khan's problem was now Eastern Europe's problem.

The Tartars no longer received tribute and the only occupation on the steppes was herding livestock. The Tartars were accustomed to a more luxurious lifestyle then livestock production could provide and embarked on the more lucrative enterprise of kidnapping. They began kidnapping eastern Europeans by the thousands and selling them as slaves to the Turks. The

Tartars became masters at their trade. Most of their slave raids took place in the provinces of Kiev and Bratslav (Lower Podolia), but the western part of Ukraine and Poland were frequent targets too. They usually came at night or early morning and in groups of up to 30,000 strong. The largest Tartar raid in Polish History occurred in 1575 when a 100,000-man horde of Tartars captured about the same number of people. Over a third of the total 35,340 were nobility.[1171] Eighty-six raids took place in Ukraine from 1450 to 1586, and seventy more raids from 1600 to 1647. The average number kidnapped was supposed to be about 3,000. One out of three villages in Podolia were destroyed or deserted between the years 1578 to 1583. Subtelny writes, "Year after year, their swift raiding parties swept down on the towns and villages to pillage, kill the old and frail, and drive away thousands of captives to be sold as slaves in the Crimean port of Kaffa, a city often referred to by Ukrainians as "the vampire that drinks the blood of the Rus."[1172] The Tartars hauled their captives to the Crimea in baskets and sold them to the Ottoman Turks, who then used them as galley slaves, servants, concubines, etc. A Polish Army commander wrote about a Tartar raid in 1654, "I estimate that the number of infants alone who were found dead along the roads and in the castles reached 10,000. I ordered them to be buried in the fields and one grave along contained over 270 bodies. All the infants were less than a year old since the older ones were driven off into captivity."[1173] Ten thousand infants seem like a high estimate but you get the picture of what it was like to have the Tartars for neighbors. Stalin exiled the Tartars from the Crimea to Central Asia and Siberia in 1943. This has to be the only case in Russian history that Stalin actually went too easy on some group. I would have banished them to an iceberg in the Bering Sea.

The result of all this was that the lower half of the Ukraine was soon depopulated and was compared to a desert or no-man's-land. Those not kidnapped by the Tartars fled to the safer areas north of the cities of Kiev, Vinnytsia, and Kamianets. Europe's most productive and fertile land sat empty and uncultivated. The Lithuanians ruled over the most devastated regions and were unable to stop the raids. It took the Poles and Cossacks some time but eventually they got control of the situation and Ukraine was resettled. The Tartar raids lasted about two hundred years, but they continued to be a nuisance for some time. The Russians conquered them in 1783. There are

---

1171 Norman Davies, p. 423.

1172 Orest Subtelny, Ukraine: a history: [Toronto: University of Toronto Press 1988] p. 106.

1173 Orest Subtelny, p. 136.

still a few Tartar villages in Poland, and they served in the Polish armies up until World War II.

The Union of Lublin occurred in 1569 and change was about to occur in Ukraine. Poland and Lithuania united to form one republic. The two countries had been united since 1385, but now they were both ruled by the same king. At the same time, all the Ukrainian lands ruled by Lithuania were transferred over to Polish control. Tartars or no Tartars, the Polish King and nobility had their eyes on the fertile but depopulated no-man's-land. The wealthiest Polish and Ukrainian nobility or magnates soon embarked on a campaign to recolonize the area. It was a scene right out of our old west. The magnates personal armies advanced into Ukraine in wagon trains. They circled the wagons to form an armed camp whenever the Tartars appeared and could hold off thousands of them at a time. Next, they refortified many of the former towns destroyed by the Tartars. The magnates carved up Ukraine into large mega estates. The Wisniowiecki estate alone contained 230,000 serfs and 38,000 households. The Polish king had little or no control over any of them. The magnates had their own armies and defended their estates from Tartars and Cossacks. When there were no Cossacks or Tartars to fight, they engaged in feuds amongst themselves. Some estates were as large as small countries. The owners became known as "kinglets "and ran their estates as they saw fit. Peasants from northern Ukraine were recruited to work on the large estates. The newly recruited peasants were free of labor requirements on their lord's estates for up to forty years in some cases. After forty years, the serfs were obliged to work a set number of days a week on the estate.

Further in the east, a different type of colonizing occurred. The Cossacks were carrying on the fight against the Tartars along the Southern Dnieper River. Cossack is a Turkish word for "free men who lived by war or banditry on the edge of society." The first Cossacks were actually Tartar mercenaries staffing Lithuanian forts along the Dnieper River. Before long, Ukrainian peasants and outlaws were joining up with the Tartar mercenaries. At the same time, other Ukrainians were leaving their homes in the safer cities in the north and going down into the no-man's-land. Leaving in the spring, they spent most of the year hunting, fishing, and gathering wild honey, then returned home for the winter. They lived their lives similar to how our own fur trappers did in the old west, but instead of Indians, they were on the lookout for Tartars. By 1492, Ukrainians had become the dominant majority of Cossacks. After much trial and error, the Ukrainian Cossacks soon learned how to fight the Tartars and began attacking and robbing bands of Tartars of their loot and captives. The number of Cossacks swelled with the arrival of runaway serfs from Polish estates, burghers from the cities and the lower class of Ukrainian nobility. Membership was open to anyone. Adventurers from Poland, Russia, Moldavia, White Russia, and even Tartars joined them. Prince Dmytro Vyshnevetsky united the different bands of Cossacks along the Dnieper River in the 1540s. Vyshnevetsky then built a fortress on the lower Dnieper on the island of Khortytsia known as the "Sich."

In their early years, the Cossacks fought mainly the Turks and Tartars. The Cossacks took the fight right too the Tartars and Turks and started raiding Tartar settlements in Crimea and Turkish cities on the coasts of the Black Sea. Thousands of slaves were freed in 1616 when the Cossacks captured the town of Kaffa, the Turks' main slave market. Once they burned the harbor at Istanbul in front of the sultan. Victories on land became more successful too. In 1629, the Cossacks captured eighty thousand Tartars, one prisoner being the Khan's brother. Despite Polish and Cossack victories, Tartar raids continued. The Polish Army used Cossack units, as did the Polish kinglets in the east. Poland had dominion over Cossack territory but had little control over them. In the late 1580s, Cossack raids on Turkish areas started causing diplomatic problems between Poland and Turkey. The Cossacks were Polish subjects and something had to be done. The Poles forced the Cossacks to recognize Polish Army officers as their commanders, but the plan backfired. The lure of plunder must have been too much for the Polish captains, and they were soon leading the Cossacks on raids. In addition, the Cossacks were able to learn Polish Army tactics and training from their Polish captains.[1174]

The Cossacks themselves were classified into a number of different categories. The Cossacks along the Dnieper River were Ukrainians, while the Cossacks along the Don River were Russians. There were registered Cossacks in the Polish Army, town Cossacks, Sich Cossacks, and helper Cossacks who could not afford to buy their own weapons. The Cossacks also had their own nobility who were the remnants of the lower class of the old Ukrainian nobility not Polonized. I will explain more about Polonization later. The Cossacks continued to grow stronger and soon attacked Poland. The Polish-Cossack wars are famous in books and film. Alliances were always changing too. At times, Poles and Cossacks fought Russians or Cossacks and Tartars fought Poland. The Polish provinces of Kiev, Cherihiv, and Lower Podolia were lost to the Cossacks in 1649. Catherine the Great of Russia destroyed the Cossack Sich in 1775. The Sich Cossacks were then dispersed into different bands and were settled farther east along the Kuban River or near the Sea of Azov.

The Polish Commonwealth had five social classes during this time, clergy, nobility, burghers, Jews, and peasants. The nobility, or, in Polish,

---

[1174] Norman Davies, p. 446.

"Szlachta," were all considered equal and divided into three classes. The magnates were the first class. They were small in number but were the most powerful and prosperous class of nobility. They controlled the senate and the most important positions in government. The magnates also owned most of the land in the country. Some made their fortunes by acquiring and settling large tracts of land in Ukraine. Others amassed their wealth serving the king. Earlier, I referred to the magnates living in Ukraine as kinglets. Their estates were the size of small countries and the magnates had total control. Most had their own private armies as well. Over time, the magnates managed to take away most of the king's power. About one hundred magnate families controlled the Polish Commonwealth. The second class or middle nobility were the Szlachta Zamozna or "nobility with means." From one-third to two-fifths of the nobility were in this category. They owned small estates containing a few serfs. The middle nobility also served as army officers and administrators on magnates estates. We were probably in this category. There was quite a bit of tension between the middle nobility and the magnates. The third and largest class was the Holota, (rabble). Most did not own any land or serfs. They became soldiers, tenant farmers, or laborers on the estates. Some lived in private villages restricted to nobility and were not any better off than the peasants.

One more item of note about the Polish nobility in Ukraine, many of the nobility there were actually Polonized Ukrainians. When the Union of Lublin united Poland and Lithuania in 1569, all of Ukraine ruled by the Lithuanians came under Polish rule. The Ukrainian nobility was now eligible for all the rights of the Polish nobility if they converted to Catholicism. Poland was the farthest extension of western culture in Europe and was going through a Renaissance at the time. Their Jesuit schools were the best. It was also the place to be if you were nobility. Before 1569, the Ukrainian nobility was more duty bound to their rulers than the Polish nobility. In addition, their ruler could confiscate their estates almost at will. Poland was completely different. The nobility had not paid any taxes on their estates since 1374. By the early 1400s, a noble could not have his estate confiscated or even be arrested without a court trial. They controlled Poland's legislature from the 1500s onward and used it to gain even more power over the rest of the country. According to Norman Davies, "the entire economic life of society was organized in their interest."[1175] From 1573 onwards, the nobility elected the king. Most of the Ukrainian upper and middle nobility became Polonized after the Union of Lublin in 1569. They became Catholic,

[1175] Norman Davies, 212.

spelled their names in Polish and began speaking Polish as well. Some of Poland's greatest magnates were Polonized Ukrainians. The lower Ukrainian nobility remained Orthodox, continued to speak Ukrainian, and became the Cossack nobility. The peasants also retained their Orthodox faith and spoke Ukrainian. The opposite occurred to the Polish peasants who came to Ukraine with the nobility. They became Orthodox and started speaking Ukrainian. I mentioned earlier that the Clan SAS became Polonized in the 1340s. Starting in 1386, the Lithuanian nobility slowly became Polonized. The White Russian nobility soon followed the Lithuanians. These Polonized nobility intermarried amongst themselves and with the Polish nobility, so were an ethnic mixture, but Polish in culture. Leslie writes, "The adoption of the Polish language emphasized still further the distinction between the upper and lower ranks of society in the east, but it would perhaps be unwise to stress factors of language before 1848, because the Polish nobles of Lithuania, White Russia and Ruthenia were proud of their local affinities, much as the Protestant landowners of Ireland came to be proud of being Irish."[1176] Ruthenia is another name for the Ukraine.

Sixty percent of the population was serfs or peasants. The practice of serfdom got underway in Eastern Europe while it was dying out in Western Europe. Some peasants managed to remain free but most were powerless to stop it. Just as the nobility had different classes, the peasants had different categories as well. The main cause of serfdom in Poland was the beginning of the Polish grain trade in the fourteenth century. Until then, the peasants paid cash rents to their lords but increasing amounts of grain production now required more labor. The nobility was soon ordering the peasants to work in their fields instead of paying cash rents. At first, the peasants only worked in their lords fields for eight to twelve days a year. As time went on, life got progressively worse for the peasants. Leaving their villages without the noble's permission was forbidden in 1496. They were expected to work one day a week by 1520. By the eighteenth century, many worked on their lord's estate six days a week and were basically slaves. The peasants in central Poland had it the worst. Farther away in Ukraine the situation was a little different. When Polish landowners first settled on Ukrainian territory, peasants were in short supply. Peasants from the northern Ukrainian regions were recruited and in many cases not obligated to work for their lord for up to forty years. If you treated your peasants too harshly in Ukraine, they were liable to run away and join the Cossacks. By the eighteenth century, the peasants in Ukraine were also suffering.

[1176] R. F. Leslie, p. 4.

The arrangement was not as one-sided as it looks. The lord protected his peasants during war and fed them during famines. He replaced the peasants' livestock or buildings when they were struck by lightning. The peasants had a bad habit of acting dumb and doing the least amount of work possible. There was also an annual rite before the crops were harvested called "przednowek." The peasants' stockpile of food always ran short then and the lord was compelled to supply them with more. They used this opportunity to stick it to the lord and squandered what was given to them. The average person in the United States works from New Year's Day well into May to pay their own taxes, so in a sense we all work a number of days for the government. Most peasants lived in dire poverty, and their lord had complete control over their lives. He could beat them or throw them into the dungeon. He could even kill them up until 1786. The serfs in Russia and the Polish/Ukraine were freed on March 3, 1861. Of course, us Wlodeckis never did anything bad to our serfs. Actually, we do not know. My relatives never knew anything about it. The situation reminds me of the antebellum south where some masters beat their slaves while others did not, and everyone else was somewhere in between.

Now that we know something about Podolia, I will get back to family history. In 1830, a small group of conspirators concocted a plan to kill or capture the Russian tsar's brother, Grand Duke Constantine. Grand Duke Constantine was commander in chief of the Polish Army and lived in the Belvidere Palace in Warsaw. He was known for his cruel treatment of his troops and was universally hated by the Poles. The leaders of the conspiracy were Peter Wysocki, a teacher at the Infantry Cadet School and Colonel Josef Zaliwski. In addition, a group of civilian conspirators led by Ludwik Nabielak joined them. On November 29, 1830, Nabielak and seventeen others attacked the Belvidere Palace intending to kill or capture Grand Duke Constantine. Wysocki and his cadets were supposed to disarm the Russian troops in town, and then capture the arsenal. Nothing worked to plan, however, and Grand Duke Constantine escaped out of town with his Russian troops. After the Russians left, everything was confusion. At first, the moderate faction decided to negotiate with the tsar for more freedom, etc. The tsar was not in any mood for negotiations and used the opportunity to show the Poles who was boss. A Russian Army was sent into Poland in January. The Russian Army waited until February before fighting any battles, probably because it was winter. Meanwhile, several different Polish factions jockeyed for control of the government, each one more extreme than the last.

The Polish Army was well trained, but the country lacked any weapons manufacturers. They had little money with which to buy weapons or supplies. The troops were enthusiastic and brave but their generals were not always up to par. Despite these problems, the Polish Army won a number of battles at first. The Poles lost a battle at Grochow on February 25, but inflicted ten thousand casualties on a one-hundred-thousand-man Russian Army. The Poles failed to capitalize on their victories, and the Russians used the time to recover. The Poles decided to take the war to the Russians in Lithuania and Ukraine. General Gielgud was ordered to Lithuania while General Dwernicki, with a force of 1,500 cavalry and 6 cannons, was sent to invade Ukraine. Dwernicki was also expected to recruit the local Polish nobility in Ukraine. Dwernicki had to stop for a time at the Ukrainian city of Zamosc because of muddy roads. While there, a Major Chrosciechowski paid him a visit. Try pronouncing that name. Chrosciechowski had been sent by the Lithuanian magnet Radziwill to find out how prepared the nobility in the Ukrainian region actually were. Chrosciechowski exaggerated the readiness of the nobility to Dwernicki. Dwernicki then sent Chrosciechowski back to order the nobility to prepare for war. Most of the Polish nobility in the region were not ready for war. This is surprising because the whole of Poland and western Russia was full of secret societies conspiring against the Russians for years. The Patriotic Society had sent agents to the Ukraine since 1821.[1177] Dwernicki crossed the Bug River on April 3, expecting help from the nobility, as well as supplies. About 2,000 nobility showed up. A large Russian Army showed up too and the two armies fought at Boromel on April 18. Dwernicki's army was too small and had to withdraw from battle. They were probably out of supplies as well. Dwernicki's army of 3,500 men[1178] headed for the Austrian border and crossed into Austria on April 27. The Austrians arrested Dwernicki and were supposed to of let the rest of his army go back to Poland. Casimir Gzowski, one of Dwernicki's officers, claims that he was arrested and imprisoned for the next two years.[1179]

According to Tokarz, after Chrosciechowski left Dwernicki's camp, he went to Kamieniec Podolski, the capital city of Podolia. There he met with the chief conspirators of the Ukraine and Podolia on April 24 and told them to start the revolt on April 28. The insurgents from Podolia had already been making plans for an uprising before Chrosciechowski arrived and were waiting for news from Poland. According to Tokarz, the next day they got an

---

[1177] R. F. Leslie, p. 111.

[1178] Florian Stasik, Polish Political Emigres in the United States of America, 1831-1864: [New York: Columbia University Press, Copyright by Polish American Historical Association 2002] p.19.

[1179] Ludwik Kos-Rabczwicz-Zubkowski, Sir Casimer Stanislaus Gzowski a biography: [Toronto, Canada: Thorn Press 1959] p.12 & 13.

unwelcome surprise when the Russian Fifth Infantry Regiment marched into Kamieniec Podolski. Until this time, the Russians only had a small number of troops in Podolia. Chrosciechowski postponed the order to rebel until May 7.The appearance of the Russian Fifth Regiment ruined all the insurgents' plans. The conspirators living along the Dniester River had been planning surprise attacks on all the district towns (county seats) along the Dniester River. Franciszek lived alongside the Dniester River and might have been one of these conspirators. Then with the help of the Wereszcynski regiment from Galicia, the insurgents would march on Kamieniec Podolski and take the town. The insurgents from Northern Podolia decided to forget about the plan and left with Chrosciechowski to join Dwernicki's army. The insurgents from Lower Podolia were in a state of confusion over what to do next.[1180]

Alexander and Izydor Sobanski of Olhopol knew what to do next. Alexander Sobanski (1797-1861) was a member of the Patriotic Society, one of the most radical groups of conspirators. He had been conspiring against the Russians since the 1820s. His name was on a list of the most dangerous people in Podolia and the Russians police were already watching him. When the rebellion started in Poland on November 29, Alexander began organizing the insurrection in Lower Podolia with great vigor. The Russians had assigned a police officer to report on Alexander's every move, but Alexander had him thrown in prison. Now he had no choice but to rebel. The Russians ordered a trial for Alexander but before they could arrest him,[1181] he started his own rebellion on April 20.[1182] Alexander Jelowiecki claims the Russians almost caught Alexander before he could start his rebellion and the Sobanski family was scared to death over the incident.[1183] Alexander got some help from the Jelowickis of Hajsyn who ran cover for him. Hajsyn is about forty-five miles north of Olhopol and about one hundred miles southwest of Kiev. The Jelowicki brothers were in charge of the czar's investigations in the region. The czar sent Edward Jelowicki a dispatch saying Alexander Sobanski was under a major investigation and ordered him to look into it as soon as possible. The Jelowickis stalled the investigation instead and sent all the witnesses out of the area.[1184] According to Gnorowski, the other Polish rebels "likened

[1180] Waclaw Tokarz, Wojna Polako-Rosyjska 1830-1831: [Warsaw, Poland: 1959] p.298.

[1181] Polski Slownik Biograficzny, Volume 39, p.418 & 419.

[1182] Aleksander Jelowicki, Moje Wspomnienia: [First published in 1839] [Warsaw, Poland: 1970] p.219.

[1183] Aleksander Jelowicki, 225.

[1184] Aleksander Jelowicki, 219.

Alexander Sobanski to another Achilles."[1185] The Sobanskis had promised Wincenty Tyszkiewicz to wait for his orders before doing anything, but because of the situation, had to act sooner.[1186] Tyszkiewicz was the leader of the conspirators in the province of Kiev.

Izydor Sobanski (1791-1847) was Alexander's older brother. Izydor inherited a number of estates containing a total of 1,642 serfs and a partnership in a trade company in Odessa. He set out to modernize his estates and brought in sugar beets, a new crop to the area. Izydor also constructed the first sugar factory in Podolia. The Sobanski estate at Piatkowka, in the district of Olhopol, was the primary residence of Alexander and Izydor. Izydor was educated at the famous Polish School of Kamieniec. He married Seweryna Potocka in 1816. The Potocki family was a rich and well-known magnate family in Podolia. After his marriage, the new couple spent a few years traveling around Europe. Izydor was also active in starting the rebellion in Podolia and formed a company of men from his serfs.[1187]

Before we go further, I have to explain how Franciszek fits into all this. Josef Bialynia Cholodecki lists Franciszek as an "outstanding conspirator" in the rebellion in Podolia.[1188] We lived at or near the town of Raszkow which is located on the Dniester River were the insurrection in Podolia was supposed to begin. The Sobanskis were the major conspirators of the area and their estate at Piatkowka is about forty miles east of Raszkow. Western Russia was full of secret societies in the 1830s and Franciszek could have known the Sobanskis well. The main Polish secret societies in the area were the Patriotic Society and the Masons. The Ukrainians and Russians had their own secret societies as well. One society called the United Slavs was composed of Poles, Ukrainians, and Russians. Most of the societies were in contact with each other.[1189]

Franciszek might also have known the Sobanskis from the town of Odessa. Franciszek spoke to his sons about Odessa. The translation came down to us as either Franciszek owned a house there or loved the city. Odessa is located on a plateau on the north shore of the Black Sea. Various

---

1185 S. B. Gnorowski, Insurrection of Poland in 1830-31, and the Russian rule preceding it since 1815: [London, 1839] p.294.

1186 Polski Slownik Biograficzny, Volume 39, p. 418 & 419.

1187 Polski Slownik Biograficzny, Volume 39, p. 418 & 419.

1188 Josef Bialynia Cholodecki, p. 3.

1189 William L. Blackwell, Russian Decembrist Views of Poland: [The Polish Review Vol. 111. No. 4 Autumn, 1958] [A Quarterly published by the Polish Institute of Arts and Sciences in America: New York, N. Y. 1958] p. 51.

people have lived on the site since prehistoric times. The Turks ruled the town from 1480 to 1774. Russia took control after the Russo-Turkish War of 1774. I mentioned earlier in the story what an important event this was for the region. Soon after taking over, the Russians restored the town's fortifications and harbor. Odessa was the destination for most of the cargo coming down the Dniester, Boh, and Dnieper rivers. The population grew from 2,300 in 1795, to 53,000 in 1829. By the 1830s, it was the largest and most sophisticated city in Southern Ukraine. Wheat was the number one commodity and most of it came from the Polish estates in Ukraine and Podolia. The Sobanskis and Potockis both had palaces there. I could not make the connection between Poland and Odessa when I first started to research our family history. Odessa is a long way from Poland, and I thought we lived in the present country of Poland. It was only after I learned we were from Podolia did the connection with Odessa make sense. Arthur Prudden Coleman wrote that the Sobanskis and Rzewuskis made annual trips to Odessa every fall.[1190] More about the Rzewuskis later. Coleman also claimed that the Polish nobility living near the Turkish border were known as "Border Gentry."[1191] and that, "Odessa was full of earnest, idealistic young men in 1825, and these were, moreover, friendly at the time to Polish hopes of liberation."[1192]

The Sobanskis left Piatkowka with their forces on May 1, 1831, and were joined by Waclaw Rzewuski. Rzewuski was a real character who went by the name of "Emir Rzewuski." August A. Jakubowski claims the Emir was fascinated with Arab culture and went to Arabia and enlisted in the army. There he won much fame and was given the name of the Emir. After spending time there, he came back to Poland fitted out in Arab garb.[1193] According to Bielecki, the Emir was born in Lviv on December 15, 1784. He went to school in Vienna and then enlisted in the Austrian Cavalry in 1808. He sustained a leg wound in battle and resigned from the army in November 1811. His father died the same year and Waclaw returned to the Ukraine. He went to Istanbul, Turkey, in 1817. Two years later, he was living in Aleppo, Syria, and studying Arabic customs. The Emir also purchased some fine Arabian horses there and took them back to Poland. After he came back from the Middle East, he joined the Patriotic Society and was

1190 Arthur Prudden Coleman, Slavic Studies: [Ithaca, New York: Cornell University Press 1943] p. 25.

1191 Arthur Prudden Coleman, p. 13.

1192 Arthur Prudden Coleman, p. 12.

1193 August A. Jakubowski, p. 19.

the subject of an investigation in 1826.[1194] Alexander Jelowicki adds more, the Emir was great friends with the Jelowicki family. The Emir talked to his horses in Arabic and dressed like an Arab, always wearing a red coat. He liked talking about his adventures in Arabia and describing what the desert and oasis looked like. He frequently ate Arab food so spicy that no one else could stand it. When the Emir came to visit, he always lived in a tent he put up in the middle of the garden across from Jelowicki's house. The Emir's own house was totally disorganized and you could barely find a comfortable spot to sit. It was packed full of souvenirs and expensive weapons from the Arab world. His farm was as disorganized as the house. He liked looking for buried treasure. Some old woman once told him there was a treasure buried in the walls of a castle and the Emir almost tore down all the walls looking for it. The Emir was a brave soldier, a poet, musician, and painter and wrote operas. He had a great imagination but never accomplished anything of real importance in any field. The Emir also spent a lot of time training teenagers how to ride horses and use weapons, hoping they would someday fight for Poland's independence.[1195] *Encyclopedia of Ukraine* claims that in the 1820s, the Emir conducted a training camp for young men on his estate based on the methods of the Zaporozhian Cossack Sich.[1196] No wonder the Russians investigated him in 1826. I thought the Emir was unusual for dressing like an Arab, but the middle nobility had been dressing like Asians up until the end of the 1700s. They also shaved their heads like Asians wearing the scalplock.[1197] The Emir did not shave his head, however. King John Sobieski had his troops wear a special badge on their hats to tell them apart from the Turks when Poland came to the rescue of Vienna in 1683.[1198]

On May 3, insurgents from the district of Hajsyn started gathering at Waclaw Jelowicki's estate. Benedykt Kolyszo, the future commanding general of the uprising being one of them. They decided to meet the Sobanskis at an estate in the small village of Krasnosiolka. Krasnosiolka is located south of Hajsyn on the Boh River at the boundary of the district of Olhopol.[1199] I

1194 Robert Bielecki, Slownik Biograficzny Oficerow Powstania Listopadowego: [Warsaw, Poland: Wydawnictwo Neriton Volume 3, 1998] p. 430.

1195 Aleksander Jelowicki, p. 171, 172 & 173.

1196 Encyclopedia of Ukraine, Edited by Danylo Husar Struk: [Toronto, Canada: University of Toronto Volume 4, 1993] p. 89.

1197 R. F. Leslie, p. 14.

1198 Adam Zamoyski, The Polish Way: [New York: Hippocrene Books 2004] p.197.

1199 Aleksander Jelowicki, p. 219-227.

think the Potocki family owned the estate but do not quote me. The insurgents appropriated the estates mansion and turned it into their headquarters. The mansion is still there, but is now abandoned. The local boys in town use the ballroom for a basketball court now. Waclaw Jelowicki and his three sons, Alexander, Edward, and Eustachy, left Hajsyn for Krasnosiolka on May 3, with 680 cavalry and 120 infantry and combined their forces on May 5 with the Sobanskis' 290 cavalry and 30 infantry. They were joined by 190 cavalry and 40 infantry from the district of Baltsk, 130 cavalry from the district of Braclaw, and 130 cavalry from the district of Jampol. The districts of Baltsk and Jampol are situated along the east banks of the Dniester River, while Braclaw was a little east of Baltsk. Franciszek might have arrived with the forces from the district of Baltsk.[1200] The now combined force was 1,420 cavalry and 190 infantry.

The first thing needed was a commander. Major Josef Orlikowski was the first choice, but he did not want the job. He thought that Edward Jelowicki should be the commanding officer. Edward was a veteran of the Polish Congress Army, but only twenty-seven years old and not experienced enough. Besides, the thinking was that no one would listen to such a young commander. Guess what! They would not listen to an old commander either. According to Tokarz, Kolyszko was not able, even for one moment take control of the gathered Szlacta (nobility).[1201] General Kolyszko was elected commander in chief because of his experience. Orlikowski was elected second in command.[1202] Bielicki writes that Kolyszko was not from Podolia, but born in Volhynia in 1749, which made him eighty-one years old in 1830. It seems anyone who could walk could join the rebellion. Soldiers were as young as twelve, and as old as when you were dead or disabled. Most of the army was cavalry and Kolyszko had a lot of experience in the cavalry. He enlisted in the Polish Cavalry in 1778, and promoted to warrant officer in the Sanguszki Regiment in 1784. Kolyszko was promoted to lieutenant in the Mokronowski Eighth Brigade in 1792, then to major the same year. Kolyszko also earned the Golden Cross for bravery in battle. He participated in the Kosciuszko uprising and was personally given a ring by Kosciuszko in June 1794, which said, "From the Homeland to its defender."[1203] Kolyszko left Poland after

[1200] Aleksander Jelowicki, p. 256.

[1201] Waclaw Tokarz, p. 298.

[1202] Aleksander Jelowicki, p. 226.

[1203] Robert Bielecki, Slownik Biograficzny Oficerow Powstania Listopadowego: [Warsaw, Poland: Wydawnictwo Neriton Volume 2] [Warszawa: 1996] p. 302.

the Kosciuszko uprising failed and moved to Italy. He came back to Poland when the uprising started in 1830.[1204]

Orlikowski immediately began to organize the army into companies at Krasnosiolka. The blessing of the banners occurred on May 7. The army first marched past General Kolyszko and then formed up in a half-moon around the altar. Then a priest blessed all their banners and said mass. After mass, everyone held up their weapons and took an oath of allegiance to be faithful to the cause. The rebels considered the blessing of the banners to be one of the most important events of the rebellion.[1205] The insurgents next made plans to march to the Czartoryski estate in Granow, with the hope of enlisting the help of the peasants. The peasants there had always been devoted to the Czartoryskis. During the Polish partitions in the late 1700s, the peasants had furnished a regiment for the Polish Army. After Granow, they would march to Wlodzimierz Potocki's estate in Dashov and recruit his peasants. Wlodzimierz was on very good terms with his peasants too. After Dashov, it was on to the Branicki estate in Byelaya Tserkov. Here they were going to appropriate three million rubles from the Russian widow of a Polish magnate named Branicki. In layman's terms, it sounds like they were going to rob her.

The insurgents also tried to recruit the local peasants from their own districts, but without success. Promises of freedom from working for their lord did not work because the peasants would not believe them. The peasants were all under the control of the local Orthodox priests, and the priests were usually on bad terms with the nobility. On the road to Granow, the peasants in the various villages along the way greeted the insurgents with bread and salt, but most of the peasants were loyal to the tsar and wanted nothing to do with the rebellion. The priests rarely bothered to come out of their houses when the Poles came through town.[1206] According to the book *Ukraine*, **a concise encyclopedia**, "The Russian government called upon the peasants on the right bank of the Dnieper River to arrest their Polish lords who took part in the war against Russia and hand them over to the authorities; in return, they were promised freedom from subjection to the lords. The peasants responded enthusiastically."[1207] Mykola Venger wrote a story about the peasants lynching

---

[1204] Robert Bielecki, Volume 2, p. 302.

[1205] Antoni Urbanski, 2 czarnego szlau, Tamtych Rlibiezy Zabski Polskie Przepadee Na Podolu, Wolynim, Ukraine: [Warsaw, Poland: Drukarnia St. Niemiry Syn 1927] p. 48.

[1206] R. F. Leslie, p. 200 & 201.

[1207] Ukraine: A Concise Encyclopedia: [Halyna Petrenko, editor] [South Bound Brook, N. J. Ukrainian Orthodox Church of the U. S. A. 1987] p.672.

their Polish lord to stop him from joining the rebellion.[1208] After the war, the Russian government went back on their word and forced the peasants back to the remaining Polish estates.[1209]

Tokarz wrote a description of the army, "We looked-tells one of the participants—because of the selection of horses and people very impressive. But unfortunately we have discovered from the beginning the weakness in the lack of the military discipline and the impossibility of keeping subordination between the new soldiers, who in the people in charge have seen only equal citizens and neighbors."[1210] The supply wagons moved at a snail's pace when the army left for Granow on May 11. On the way, they met up with bands of insurgents from the Kievian districts of Lipowiec and Uman. Lipowiec brought 240 cavalry and 100 infantry, while Uman brought 70 cavalry. Tyszkiewicz and the insurgents from the other districts of Kiev showed up at Granow with 400 cavalry and 60 infantry. The total strength of the army was now 2,130 cavalry and 350 infantry[1211] and 1 cannon.[1212] Most of the provinces of Ukraine stayed out of the rebellion because the Polish magnates there coerced the rest of the nobility not to participate. The insurgents' original plan calculated that an army of roughly 20,000 men could be raised from the Dniester area alone, so the force now assembled at Granow was very disheartening. The province of Kiev guaranteed 6,000, but only 870 came.

When the insurgents arrived at Granow, they found out the manager of the estate had no intention of ever helping them. The insurgents still hoped to get the peasants on board anyway. Jelowicki writes that the priests at Granow were Greek-Orthodox, not Russian Orthodox. Alexander Jelowicki decided to call all the priests and peasants to the local church to speak to them. Once again, the peasants were promised their freedom. Jelowicki blamed the tsar for their condition and claimed the Poles were trying to give them freedom. The tsar was compared to the devil and that he had already been overthrown. Their lord Czartoryski was now the king of Poland and you will not see any more Russian soldiers again. God will bless you if you will fight for your freedom. Jelowicki gave the peasants a line of BS. It almost worked. The peasants were actually receptive to the idea, but only after the insurgents

1208 Serhiy Bilenky, The Clash of Mental Geographies: Poles on Ukraine, Ukrainians on Poland in the time of Romanticism: [The Polish Review Volume LIII 2008 No. 1] p. 89.

1209 Ukraine: A Concise Encyclopedia, p. 672.

1210 Waclaw Tokarz, p. 298.

1211 Aleksander Jelowicki, p. 256.

1212 S. B. Gnorowski, p. 294.

won their first battle. The priests were receptive too, after learning that their "ecclesiastical profits would be increased."[1213] The insurgents left Granow with one hundred new volunteers who were mainly from the lower class of Polish nobility. If they won their first battle, the peasants would join them. The priests blessed the army and off they went.[1214]

The Potocki estate at Daszow was next. Gnorowski claims, "The following day they marched towards Daszow hoping to surprise a detachment of Russians stationed in Biala Cerkiew. But so entirely had they neglected every military precaution that they did not even conjecture that General Rott was close behind them."[1215] Tokarz said on May 14, the insurgents were slowly marching with their supply wagons and driving a herd of horses they had acquired in Granow. The disorganized columns of rebels were thrown into a state of confusion at the appearance of the Russians. The attacking Russian Army consisted of fourteen cavalry squadrons and four cannons. About four miles from Daszow, the Russian Army opened fire and charged. Tokarz claims three squadrons of Poles from the end of the column turned around and charged the Russians. They broke through the Russian infantry and engaged the cavalry, but were driven back by artillery. Orlikowski charged with three more squadrons but at the last moment decided to halt the charge, thinking it better to rejoin Kolyszko's main army for one grand charge. Orlikowski ordered a retreat. The retreating squadrons rode back in such disarray that the rest of the army thought they were running from the battle. The sight of them caused everyone else to panic and soon everyone was running off the battlefield. The officers tried to rally the men, but fear and panic had already set in. The Russians' cavalry continued to advance and a slaughter might have occurred if not for a group of fifty Polish cavalrymen who protected the retreat. The Russians sustained a high number of casualties in the cavalry battle that followed and called off the attack.[1216] Izydor Sobanski commanded two squadrons at Daszow and was cited for bravery.[1217] Most of the insurrectionists' army had evaporated after the battle and by the following day only about five hundred to six hundred men remained.[1218]

1213 S. B. Gnorowski, p. 295-297.

1214 S. B. Gnorowski, p. 297.

1215 S. B. Gnorowski, p. 297.

1216 Waclaw Tokarz, p. 298.

1217 Polski Stownik Biograficzny, Volume 39, p. 418.

1218 Waclaw Tokarz, p. 298.

Gnorowski has a little different take on the battle. He claims that when the Russians first attacked, one squadron of Poles rode out to meet them. The Poles drove back two Russian Cavalry charges but the Polish commander was killed in the second charge. The squadron then retreated in a very disorganized way. Orlikowski rode in with two more squadrons. The Russians responded with cannon fire. The Russian gunners were not very accurate and only a few Poles were actually hit. The men wanted Orlikowski to lead them on but Orlikowski changed his mind. He thought General Kolyszko was ready to charge and ordered a retreat. Orlikowski had to repeat the order three times before anyone responded. Orlikowski wanted to fall back, but his men misunderstood the order and thought he meant retreat from the battlefield. Orlikowski's men took off headlong in every direction, many fleeing straight into the now-panic-stricken General Kolyszko's squadron. They in turn ran into the second squadron, and on and on it went. The whole situation became an uncontrollable mess. Kolyszko and his officers tried to regroup the men but to no avail. The Russian Cavalry were still advancing and the panic-stricken soldiers running from the battlefield might soon be cut to pieces. A group of about fifty Polish cavalrymen realized the danger, formed up, and galloped off at full speed towards the Russian Cavalry. They fought their way right through the cavalry and took the Russian cannons, but then found themselves surrounded. They had to cut their way back through the Russian Cavalry to escape. The Polish attack killed many Russian soldiers and the Russian commander called off his army. Many of the Poles who ran from the battlefield were later captured and sent to Siberia. About four hundred men regrouped and headed west towards Poland. Orlikowski never forgave himself for not attacking that day. The Russians lost around two hundred men in the battle,[1219] while the Poles lost forty men.[1220]

The remaining four hundred men headed west where they spotted two squadrons of Russians at Tyvrow on May 17. Kolyszko wanted to steer clear of them, but Edward Jelowicki thought it would be better for the men's morale to attack. Jelowicki took two hundred men, crossed the Boh River, and attacked the Russians. The Russians were annihilated and those not killed drowned in the river trying to escape. Their situation was still dismal because they were surrounded on all sides. On May 17, the rebels seized a message stating that Russian General Szczucki planned to block their retreat at Obodne with three squadrons and two cannons. The message was intercepted too late. Szczucki was already at Obodne and soon opened fire with his cannons. The Poles

1219 S. B. Gnorowski, p. 297, 298 and 299.

1220 R. F. Leslie, p. 202.

immediately charged and reached the cannons before a second volley could be fired.[1221] They captured General Szczucki, 17 of his officers, and 290 of his men. In addition, 60 Russian soldiers were killed in the battle.[1222] The captured Russians were nothing more than a hindrance to the Poles. They decided to let them all go the following day after giving the Russian soldiers a speech about freedom.

Leaving Obodne, Kolyszko's army continued west and hooked up with another band of insurgents from the city of Bar. This group of rebels had occupied Bar for a time, but vacated the town at the approach of a large Russian Army. Ludwik Chlopicki was one of the organizers of this band. I wrote about Ludwik in my story about Woodford County. The countryside was full of Russian forces by now and before long, they caught up with the Poles at Majdan on the May 23. Russian General Szariemietjew, with six to eight squadrons and two cannons, attacked the Poles in terrain not suitable for cavalry. The Poles were all cavalry and needed space to maneuver, but the bad location made it impossible to attain battle formation. Nevertheless, a long and savage battle ensued in which both forces sustained high casualty rates. After a time, the more numerous Russians had recaptured the two cannons from Obodne and were pressing forward. Kolyszko ordered retreat and headed for the Russo-Austrian border. About six hundred to seven hundred Polish rebels crossed into Austria at Satanow and Woloczyska on May 26 and were disarmed and arrested by the Austrians.

What an inglorious end for the Podolians. They had fought Turks, Tartars, and Cossacks for hundreds of years but the rebellion was over in 12 days. The appearance of the Russian Fifth Regiment at Kamieniec Podolski had messed up everything, but there is more to the story. Few magnates supported the rebellion openly. Some secretly gave money. Henryk Klimesz claims that after the Black Sea ports opened, the old southeastern provinces of Poland began to thrive.[1223] Leslie wrote, "When its economy was beginning to be concentrated upon the eastern market, war against Russia meant commercial disaster. The substantial gentry on the whole accepted the Russian connection and had little wish to overthrow it. The improvement of the country, though slight, was noticeable and a source of satisfaction."[1224] Much of the lower nobility did not support the rebellion either. They had something to lose too, immunity from taxation. That leaves only the middle nobility left to do all

[1221] S. B. Gnorowski, p. 299.

[1222] Waclaw Tokarz, p. 298.

[1223] Henryk Klimesz, p. 66.

[1224] R. S. Leslie, p. 95.

the fighting. Their aim was to unite the eastern (Ukrainian) provinces with Poland again. They also saw themselves as patriots. I am a conservative guy and have to confess that it would be a real tough choice risking everything I owned to fight a country the size of Russia. My advice would be to go to Poland and fight the Russians there. If Poland wins, they will retake the eastern provinces when they are strong enough. Most of the insurgents must have been either super patriots or radical extremists.

The war in Lower Podolia started on May 14 and was over on May 26, lasting but twelve days. The whole episode was short, but the consequences for the insurrection were long term or death for many. Waclaw Jelowicki and his son Eustachy were killed at Majdan.[1225] Waclaw's other two sons, Alexander and Edward, were arrested by the Austrians but escaped. Alexander made his way to Warsaw and enlisted as a private of artillery in the still at war Polish Army. He was awarded a Gold Cross but refused to accept it because he thought others deserved it more. After the rebellion was over, he went to Paris, France, with the famous Polish poet Mickiewicz. Alexander joined the Polish committees in Paris and started a bookstore with Janusz Kiewiczem. He also published many books. I used one of his books for this story. Alexander became a priest in December 1841 and went to Italy in 1842 to speak with the pope about the condition of the Polish church. Starting in 1844, he was in charge of the Polish mission in Paris. Alexander went to Rome in 1877 because of an eye problem where he died on April 15, 1877. The Polish church in Paris built a monument to him soon after.[1226]

Edward Jelowicki was a lieutenant in the uprising and was arrested by the Austrians after Majdan. The Austrians sent him to a prison in Lviv, but he escaped and went to Warsaw. He soon left Warsaw and removed to Galicia but was captured by the Austrians again. This time they imprisoned him in Brno, a city in the current Czech Republic. All the future exiles from Trieste were imprisoned in Brno. Edwards's mother knew the right people and managed to get him out of prison. Edward traveled to Switzerland in 1833 and then France in 1835. He attended a military school in Paris and then enlisted in the French Army and served in Algeria in 1841. Edward was living in Rome in 1846. While in Rome, he also met the pope. He moved to Vienna in 1848. A new Polish uprising occurred in 1848 and Edward enlisted in General Bemen's army. That rebellion was a failure too. Edward was imprisoned after the rebellion ended and then executed

[1225] S. B. Gnorowski, p. 300-301.

[1226] Robert Bielecki, Volume 2, p. 217.

by firing squad on November 10, 1848. Gaszynski wrote a poem in honor of Edward.[1227]

After Majdan, Alexander Sobanski escaped from the Austrians, went to Poland, and enlisted in General Skrzynecki's army. He was promoted to captain in June 1831 and awarded the Golden Cross. After the war, the Russians confiscated his two large estates in Podolia and the three thousand serfs who worked on them. He married Melania Uruska in 1832. The Russians confiscated her estate for marrying Alexander, but the senate gave it back to her in 1858. After the insurrection ended, Alexander and his wife moved to Switzerland and became citizens there. The Swiss either gave him or sold him Kyburg castle at Vevey. Alexander kept in touch with the other Polish exiles in Switzerland and sometimes helped them out financially. Alexander's marriage to Melania produced two sons, Alexander and Izydor. Alexander died on November 27, 1861, and is buried in Kyburg Castle.[1228]

Izydor Sobanski escaped through the forest after Majdam and joined the Fifth Zamoyski Ulans (cavalry) squadron in June 1831 as a lieutenant. The Zamoyski squadron was part of an army commanded by General Ramorino. Izydor was awarded Poland's highest medal for bravery at the battle of Lublin. After the rebellion ended, he went first to Lviv and then to Switzerland. The Russians confiscated all his estates after the war. Izydor's only son Arthur died of apoplexy on December 31, 1831. After his son's death, Izydor went to France and hooked up with Prince Adam Czartoryski at the Hotel Lambert in Paris. Czartoryski persuaded him to go to Rome on a political mission, but Izydor excused himself from the mission at some point by claiming he was a bad Catholic. He went to Great Britain instead to visit a friend and then traveled around the country. Afterwards, Izydor went back to France where he became a director of the Polish Club and involved with the Polish Literary Society. He also became good friends with some of Poland's most famous people including Adam Mickiewicz and Frederick Chopin. Izydor was not a big fan of the Catholic Church and became involved with a mystic church organization known as the Resurectionists. He had some type of falling out with them. None of the Resurectionists attended his funeral when he died of a heart attack on January 28, 1847. Stanislaw Kozmian was one of the few people who spoke at his funeral and stated that Izydor was quiet and had a good heart but was a mystic.[1229]

[1227] Robert Bielecki, Volume 2, p. 217.

[1228] Polski Stownik Biograficzny, Volume 39, p. 418.

[1229] Polski Stownik Biograficzny, Volume 39, p. 418 & 419.

The Emir never made it past Daszow. Rumor has it that he went back to Arabia after the battle. Most likely a Cossack killed him for his money belt during the battle.[1230] Major Josef Orlikowski blamed himself for the defeat at Daszow. He was blinded when a cannon blew up in his face at the battle of Majdan. Orlikowski committed suicide with his pistol at Majdan, preferring death to capture. He left a wife and four children.[1231] General Kolyszko was arrested by the Austrians and sent to Lviv. He was under surveillance until his death on April 16, 1834. He is buried in the famous Lyczakowski Cemetery in Lviv. I saw his grave at the cemetery.[1232] Pavel Sobelewski, whose story I write about in Boone County was from Hajsyn and would have come to Krasnosiolka with the Jelowickis. Pavel is also mentioned as an outstanding conspirator in the rebellion.[1233] Alexander Bilinski and possibly Theodor Dombski, who both settled in Lake County, were also in Kolyszko's army. Ludwik Chlopicki would have participated in the battle of Majdan.[1234] He settled in Woodford County, Illinois.

The Polish rebels were guilty of high treason and all their property was eligible for confiscation. Captured Polish nobility were court-martialed and shot on the spot by their Russian captors. An estimated forty-five thousand noble families were deported to Siberia and the Caucasus. Ten thousand more Poles chose to emigrate. According to Boswell, "The Polish army retreated to the south-west, and with it went a melancholy procession of all the leading Poles, destined to perpetual exile. They passed through Leipzig, when the young Wagner saw them and was inspired to write his 'Polonia' as they passed through Germany and settled in Western Europe, chiefly in Paris."[1235] One thousand one hundred forty-six Poles were condemned to death in absentia.[1236] Some of the rebels were drafted into the Russian Army. Norman Davies states, "It took years before the endless lines of convict wagons, with their clanking chains and groaning inmates, winded their way to their final destinations four and five thousand miles away in distant Siberia."[1237] The Russians initiated a

---

1230 Robert Bielecki, Volume 3, p. 430.

1231 Robert Bielecki, Volume 3, p. 237.

1232 Robert Bielecki, Volume 2, p. 302.

1233 Josef Bialynia Cholodecki, p. 3.

1234 Robert Bielecki, Slownik Biograficzny Oficerow Powstania Listopadowego: [Warsaw, Poland: Wydanictwo Trio 1995] p. 289.

1235 Bruce A. Boswell, M.A. Poland and the Poles: [New York: Dodd, Mead and Company 1919] p. 82.

1236 R. S. Leslie, p. 260.

1237 Norman Davies, 331.

policy of intense Russification in Poland after the rebellion. In addition, the Russians revoked the nobility of 340,000 Holota or the lower class of Polish nobility during the next twenty years.[1238]

We do not know what happened to Franciszek's family after the rebellion. Franciszek was single, but whatever happened to his parents? His father Josef would have been seventy-eight years old at the start of the insurrection, so he was most likely deceased by then. Was his mother Domicella still alive, we do not know. He did have some relatives left in Podolia at the start of the rebellion. Franciszek told his sons that his brother was killed in one of the battles and his own horse shot. We know he had a brother named Pavel. He might have had another brother or relative participate in the rebellion as well. Franciszek wrote a letter to Prince Adam Czartoryski in Paris, France (date unknown)

> Dear Prince, I am asking for your help,
>
> If it is possible to inquire among the emigrants in France about any information regarding Konstanty Wlodecki, if he will be found to ask him to contact by letter Franciszek Wlodecki in New York.[1239]

The Russians would not let the exiles send letters to their families for a long time. Dr. Illinski, another exile residing in St. Clair County, Illinois, did not get a letter from his family in Poland until June 28, 1877.[1240] Franciszek, along with another exile named Franciszek Petrynowski, sent a letter on May 12, 1842, to Prince Czartoryski inquiring about their families.

> Sir Prince!
>
> Please to forgive us, your landsmen, that we dare to occupy you with our request, to send our letters, if it will be possible, to Russia, to the District of Kijow and Podole. Because of our misery and lack of comforts, we often dream of our country's nest, and we would like to let our family know about us. We would like to

1238 Encyclopedia of Ukraine, Edited by Danylo Husar Struk: [Toronto: University of Toronto Press, Volume 3 1993] p. 607.

1239 Czartoryski Library, Krakow, Poland: [Archive of the Manuscripts, 5500 1V, 5479 1V vol. 1]

1240 East St. Louis Gazette, June 28, 1877.

humbly repeat our requests and remaining forever with the deepest regards of your Sir Prince,

Lowermost servants,
Franciszek Wlodecki
Franciszek Petrynowski[1241]

Franciszek obviously had great respect for his superiors. I am sure all the other nobility did too. He told his descendants that the Russians confiscated the family estate. He also told the Austrians during an interview in 1833 that he was a landowner.[1242] The book *Les Confiscations des biens des Polonis Sovs le Regne de L' Empereur Nickolas Ier L. Lubliner* is a register of the names of Poles whose estates were confiscated in Podolia. Part B is an "Alphabetical chart by name of Poles whose possessions and properties were confiscated but are not included in the official public documents either by the number of serfs or by sums of money." The Wlodecki property, no first name, is recorded as having the value at seven male serfs.[1243] One male serf is worth 175 silver rubles. The Historical Archives in Krakow found a notice published in the Warsaw Gazette on December 16, 1852. List 2 of the notice contains "Wlodecki, first name unknown" and is a record "of the persons whose estates possible for sequestration and confiscation have not been discovered." Alexander Bilinski from Lake County, Illinois, is also recorded there.[1244] This might indicate that he did not even own any land. It looks like they found something. One story that came down to us is about an incident that happened after Franciszek settled in Illinois. Franciszek found out some Russians were looking for him and ran off, coming back when they were gone. My relatives thought the Russians had come to pay us for our estate in Poland and it was just our luck to have missed out on a fortune. Pavel Sobelewski's daughter wrote that a letter from the tsar appeared in the *Atlantic Monthly* magazine, which stated that the estates of the Polish exiles would soon be returned to them if they returned to Russia.[1245] Alexander II

1241 Czartoryski Library, Krakow, Poland: [Archive of the Manuscripts, 5479 vol. 1, p. 241, 244]

1242 Osterreichisches Staatsarchiv Kriegsarchiv, Vienna, Austria: [August 1833]

1243 Les Confiscations des biens des Polonis Sovs Le Regne de L' Empereur Nicholas Ier L, Lubliner: [Brussels-Leipzig 1861] p. 48.

1244 Warsaw Gazette, December 16, 1852.

1245 Paul Sobelewski file, Illinois State Historical Library, Springfield, Illinois: [Biography copied from handwritten biography sent by Mrs. Shane to Mrs. Rawlings] p. 2.

became the Russian tsar in 1855 and pardoned the Poles who participated in the 1830 uprising in 1856.[1246]

After Kolyszko's army was arrested, the Austrians began to gather information about the ringleaders. The Austrians turned a blind eye to the common soldiers who were escaping in droves, partly because of the cost of maintaining them. The Austrian government was also uncomfortable about the large numbers of Polish rebels already in Austria. The Poles still under guard were taken to a large castle in Czortkow, Ukraine. It was still relatively easy to escape from the castle and the number of captives got smaller daily. The ringleaders, however, were watched closely. The castle at Czortkow is still there and is currently used to store propane gas. A decision was made to move the Podolian insurgents, as well as the rebels from Dwernicki's army, to the prison at Siedmiogrod on July 1, 1831. According to Cholodecki,

> The road was taking them throughout Tluste, Uscieczko, Horodenka, Sniatyn, Dubowce, Storozyniec, Czudyn, Wikow dolny, Mardziana, Solka, Gurahumora, Wama, Kimpolung, Valeputzna, Pojanastampi and further throughout the high peak of the huge Mogura, on the charming way to Tyhuzzy, Jaad, Borgoprund, Bystrzyca and inside of the flat area of the steppe country.[1247]

Most of these towns are still there. Tluste, Horodenka, Sniatyn, and Storozyniec are all located in the present country of Ukraine. Solka, Gurahumora, Kimpolung, Watradorna, and Bystrzyca are in the mountains of Romania. The steppe country must have been Hungary. Siedmiogrod might be Brno, in the current Czech Republic, but I am not completely sure. The prisoners were moved around to different prisons during the next two years and their last stop in prison was at Brno.

In order to keep a closer watch, the prisoners were divided into two companies before leaving Czortkow. Those two companies were in turn divided again. The first group of each company was reserved for "the most dangerous revolutionaries."[1248] Each company was guarded by one company of infantry and twelve hussars (cavalrymen). The most dangerous revolutionaries were under much tighter control. The first company left Czortkow on July 15, while the second left the next day. Supply wagons brought bread, but

---

[1246] Norman Davies, p. 348.

[1247] Josef Bialynia Cholodecki, p. 2.

[1248] Josef Bialynia Cholodecki, p. 2.

the prisoners also relied on the charity of the people they met along the way. The donated food had to pass through the commissioner first, and they were not allowed to eat in anyone's home. The prisoners slept in isolated fields far from populated areas. They traveled for three days and rested one day, then repeated it all over again. The Austrians must have loosened up a little during the march. They started allowing anyone who could afford a horse and wagon to use one. No riding horses though. Towards the end of the trip, the wealthy prisoners were ordering food and straw to sleep on. Cholodecki wrote, "Uncertain about their future, not knowing what was going to happen to them, saying good bye with their painful heart to their native land, listening if by any chance the breeze of wind would bring them a good news of rescue from Wisla and Bug Rivers, from the heart of the Lithuanian forests, or the steppe of the far away Ukraine."[1249] Franciszek was one of the 71 most dangerous revolutionists in the first group of the second company. The second group had a total of 171 people. Pavel Sobelewski of Boone County is also a member of the first group.[1250]

There were two different sources of exiles sent to Brno. The first group was imprisoned for two years. Kazimierz Gzowski, one of the exiles who served in Dwernicki's army, claims he was moved around to several different prisons. Over the next two years, he spent time in prisons at Steiermark, Grostow, Czernowitz, and Sanok.[1251] This first group were members of General Kolyszko's and General Dwernicki's armies.[1252] Pavel Sobelewski told his daughter that he was imprisoned for two years.[1253] Alexander Bilinski also claimed that he was imprisoned for a length of two years.[1254] Franciszek served with Sobelewski and Bilinski so was certainly imprisoned for two years as well.

The other source of exiles were arrested as a result of the Zaliwski rebellion. They only spent three or four months in prison before the Austrians decided to exile them. Zaliwski had been one of the leaders of the November 1830 uprising in Warsaw. He was at it again in March 1833, when he attempted to start a rebellion in the Russian controlled area of Poland. This one was a complete fiasco. Twenty-seven people were killed and a number of other Poles sent to Siberia. The Austrians arrested those Poles suspected of

---

1249 Josef Bialynia Cholodecki, p. 2.

1250 Josef Bialynia Cholodecki, p. 2 & 3.

1251 Ludwik Kos-Rabczwicz-Zubkowski, p.12 & 13.

1252 Ludwik Kos-Rabczwicz-Zubkowski, p. 13.

1253 Polish Genealogical Society Newsletter: Spring, 1992] p. 15.

1254 Carlson Family History Manuscript:

being members of the Zaliwski rebellion or of helping the rebellion in May 1833, and taken to Brno. The Austrians initially told them that they were getting passports to France where most of the Poles wanted to go anyways. The Austrians were conducting talks with the Prussians at the same time and both countries decided to deport all the Poles in their prisons. Prussia had a large number of prisoners from the uprising in its prisons too.

Gzowski wrote about his bleak life in prison. He did not know what the Austrians planned to do with him. Zubkawski wrote, "He was completely cut off from his family and his friends and might never see his native land again. His whole future seemed dark and uncertain."[1255] All the other Poles probably felt the same way. The prospect of being sent back to Russia must have also been on their minds. Vincent Dziewanowski, another Polish exile, claimed that he persuaded Prince Ferdinand of Austria not to send the Poles back to Russia. Dziewanowski had been to the Austrian court before the rebellion. He knew either the grand duke or the emperor and convinced the guards to arrange a meeting for him.[1256]

On August 1, 1833, a committee of Austrian officials summoned each prisoner before them. The committee gave them the option of either going back to Russia or deportation to the United States. Going back to Russia meant certain death in Siberia. They did not want to go to America either because it was too far. The Poles wanted to continue with the rebellion in Europe and preferred to go to either England or France. No countries in Europe would take them, so they all consented to go to America.

The Austrians began marching about three hundred Poles to the port of Trieste, Italy, on August 14. Trieste was a part of Austria at the time. The Austrians also threw in a few criminals with the now-departing Poles. Dziewanowski kept a diary of the trip to Trieste, but some of it is missing. The diary begins on August 23, as the exiles were crossing a 1,200-foot-long bridge over the Danube River in Austria. Dziewanowski recorded the names of the towns they marched through and described the countryside. They walked through the forested mountains and saw a number of old castles along the way. In Austria, they traveled through the towns of Pelten, Wilhemburg, Hayfeld, Altmart, Wiener, Grats, and Wildonanurt. Few of the residents of the town of Bruex, Austria, came out to see the procession because of a rumor that the Poles whistle at the girls. Dziewanowski also claimed that most of the people in the southern part of Austria were fat and the farmhands in the

[1255] Luudwik Kos-Rabczwicz-Zobkowski, p. 13.

[1256] Mrs. William F. Allen, A Polish Pioneer's Story: [Dziewanowski File at the Wisconsin State Historical Society, Madison, Wisconsin. p. 378.

area could throw knives with great accuracy at fifty paces. He also claimed the people of Austria were always amiable towards the Poles. The party crossed into Slovenia, also under Austrian rule and went through the cities of Marburg, Cilli, and Laybach, before arriving in Trieste, Italy. This part of Italy was ruled by Austria at the time.

In Slovenia, the Poles were confined for three days in some barracks in the beautiful town of Laybach and were permitted to tour the city in small bands. One night the police came and took away one of the Poles named Bentkowski. He was never seen again. They visited a famous grotto in one of the nearby towns and crossed over bridges high in the mountains. The Poles found the fields close to Trieste full of rocks. They came down from the mountains into Trieste on October 22 and were immediately imprisoned under heavy guard. The Austrians kept them under permanent confinement for almost a month; then the pot boiled over. The Poles thought their confinement was too harsh and kept petitioning the Austrians to relent.[1257] Stasik claims the Poles rioted for the right to leave the barracks for short periods. Both Poles and Police were hurt in the melee that followed and the army was called out to stop it.[1258] The Austrians finely relented and small groups of Poles were allowed to tour the city under guard. Dziewanowski described Triest as a beautiful city and its people attractive. He also added that the people were also very spiteful.

The first two shiploads of Polish exiles left Trieste at 8:00 p.m. on November 22, 1833. The *Guerriera* carried 93 exiles and the *Hebe* 141 exiles for a total of 234 prisoners. Some of my sources claim that there was 235 exiles. Later ships brought more exiles. Lerski estimates that the total number of Polish exiles reaching America at this time was about 424 people.[1259] The majority were from twenty-six to forty years old. Franciszek was almost forty years old when they reached New York. At least three were in their late teens. One of the exiles named Kwiatkowski brought his wife along. Descendants of Antoni Gajkowski think Antoni's son was smuggled aboard.[1260] One of the exiles named Ludwik Jerzykiewicz was a priest. Half the exiles were officers and major was the top rank. The Polish exiles from Germany never did make it to America. Bad weather caused them to dock in England and they never left.

1257 Dziewanski Diary, Dziewanski File, at the Wisconsin Historical State Historical Society, [Madison, Wisconsin]

1258 Florian Stasik, p. 42.

1259 Jerzy Jan Lerski, p. 97.

1260 Francis Casimir Kajencki, Poles in the 19th Century Southwest: [El Paso, Texas: Southwest Polonia Press, 1990] p. 3.

The 234 exiles ate the same food as the ship's crew. Breakfast was at 9:00 a.m. and rotated between biscuits, cheese, and rum or biscuits, cheese, and cocoa. At 3:00 p.m., it was biscuits, rice or macaroni, and pork. They ate beans and fish twice a week. Dziewanowski said they got used to it. The crew also gave them some clothes to wear. Dziewanowski described a few cities along the Italian coast, the main one being Venice. The diary stops on November 23 and does not continue until they reach the rock of Gibralter on February 12.[1261] Lerski claims the drinking water was tainted five days into their journey.[1262] Stasik wrote that it took seventy days to reach Gibraltar from Trieste. They docked at Gibraltar around February 1 to make repairs and to resupply the ships.[1263] After two weeks, the trip continued. As they were leaving port, Dziewnowski said the crew of the *Guerriera* fired a twenty-one-gun salute. The Spanish soldiers in the fort responded in turn with their own twenty-one-gun salute. The exiles said farewell as the shores of Europe and Africa passed by.

They reached the island of Madeira after five days sailing on February 20 but did not stop.[1264] The trip took place during the middle of winter, and everyone was freezing their asses off. According to Lerski, there was a small fire on board the *Hebe* during the trip from Gibraltar to America.[1265] The exiles were probably just trying to keep warm. Dziewnowski claims that on March 26, they sailed into a bad storm about 200 miles off the coast of America, which lasted for two days. The wind broke the masks and cracked the decks.[1266] There was no way to steer the ships during the storm and they were blown about 160 miles that night. The storm ended the next day and they found themselves near the shores of America. They sailed in to the port of New York on March 28, forty-two days after leaving Gibraltar. Dziewnowski also said the *Guerriera* fired off a twenty-one-gun salute when they arrived to New York and the castle there fired a twenty-one-gun salute back. Castle Rock was the predecessor of Ellis Island and I am not sure if there were any cannons there. The Rev. W. Kruszka of Milwaukee, Wisconsin, translated Dziewnowsli's diary and could have accidentally mixed up the twenty-one-gun salute at Gibraltar with the landing at New York. Two parts of the diary are missing.

1261 Dziewanski Diary:

1262 Jerzy Jan Lerski, p. 95.

1263 Florian Stasik, p. 44.

1264 Dziewanski Diary:

1265 Jerzy Jan Lerski, p. 95.

1266 Konarzewski, Kronika Emigracji Polskiej, 11, p. 152-53.

It was supposed to be real hairy entering the port of New York because of all the sandbars and guideposts in the water. A representative from the harbor had to sail out to the ships to guide them in. There was also a great deal of friction between the Poles and the Italian crew. The Poles were confined to the ships for the first three days after docking. The Italians almost kicked the Poles off the ships on the second day. The third day, they did kick them off. Some Americans found the Poles wondering around the shore and took them to Castle Rock. The next day American officials and members of the Austrian consulate went out to the ships to get some money the ships had carried over from Austria. They also asked the ship's captain why he did not notify the Americans before he had ejected the Poles. Later that day the Americans sent out an official to the ships with an arrest warrant.[1267]

The Poles all wished to stay together as one group in America. Only two of the exiles could speak English, so it made sense to stick together. During the wait in New York's harbor, the Poles organized the first Polish Committee in America. At the same time, the New York newspapers found out that two boatloads of Polish exiles would soon be landing and wrote a column about them. The column caused quit a stir and a host of New Yorkers hiked down to the docks to see the exiles. The Americans were fascinated by the Poles' colorful garments and long mustaches. On April 1, the exiles went back to the ships to each collect $33 the Austrian government had put aside for each one of them. None of the exiles had any money and the $33 was supposed to help support them for a time. Crowds of Americans were waiting to see the Poles disembark from the ships. Archacki claims, "The Poles, sensing the drama of the moment, instinctively straightened up and with firm military step marched off the dock to many cheers and some mixed jeers coming from the street urchins."[1268] Some Americans tried talking to the exiles, but it was impossible to understand each other. Frank Golder claims that Russian spies were also there.[1269] The next incident might well get me in some hot water with Poles living now, but I carefully thought it over and decided to use it anyways. After marching off the ships, the Poles marched right into the first bar they found and proceeded to get stinking drunk. Before long, and probably after many toasts to Poland, there were drunken Poles passed out

---

1267 Dziewanski Diary:

1268 Henry Archacki, America's Polish gifts to Canada: [Polish American Studies: Volume XXV, No. 2 July-December, 1968] [The Polish American Historical Association, St. Mary's College, Orchard Lake, Michigan] p. 73.

1269 Frank A. Golder, Guide to Materials for American History in Russian Archives: [Washington: Carnegie Institution of Washington, 1917]

all along the street. Dziewnowski said the Americans had to carry them all back to Castle Rock and were greatly disappointed in them.[1270] What a sight that must have been. Don't get too down on the exiles for their transgression. They had just been through long, tough, and uncertain times. I say let them blow off some steam. Besides, your author did the very same thing when he got out of the army. They were only drunk for one night while I was drunk almost every night of the following year, managing to squander five different jobs in the process.

Speaking of jobs, it was now time for the exiles to find one. They were told in Austria that the American government would take care of them, which was BS, of course. American charities did find boarding houses for them to live in and gave them financial help for a time. A few of the exiles found low-paying jobs right away. Most had a very hard time adjusting to their new life in America. They were not used to doing any type of physical work. In Poland, the peasants or serfs did the hard work and all the trades. The burghers handled all the trading. The nobility served in the military, government posts, and administration. Any type of physical work was considered below their dignity. It was like this in much of Europe.

Franciszek said he did not know how to do anything when he came here. Anything meaning no type of skill or trade. I think he did know how to farm. Most of the exiles were educated and many had educations comparable to college. Most also spoke several languages; unfortunately, only two spoke English. Not knowing English was a great disadvantage for them and all they could get were the most menial and low-paying jobs. The English and Irish emigrants were paid more for the same jobs because they knew English. Making the problem worse, the exiles usually hung around with each other and were not learning English fast enough. Some of the exiles thought they were here temporarily and would soon go back to Poland. Others thought they would soon move out to the Polish land grant in Illinois. More about the land grant shortly. A large number of exiles could not find jobs at all and the money raised by the charities was starting to run low. The Poles had wanted to stay together but now it was time to look for work elsewhere. Franciszek was one of thirty exiles sent to Albany and upstate New York. Twenty-five went to Philadelphia and over thirty to Boston.[1271] Most of the others stayed in New York. They each formed their own committees and with the help of sympathetic Americans, found jobs. The mayor of Albany, Erastus Corning,

1270 Dziewanski Diary:

1271 James S. Pula, Polish Americans an Ethnic Community: [New York: Simon & Schuster Masmillan, 1995] p. 5.

and the Rev. William B. Sprague were particularly helpful to the exiles in Albany. Franciszek found work as a waiter and porter at the City Hotel in Albany.[1272] August A. Jakobowski was also a member of the Albany group, as was Napoleon Koscialowski, who settled in Morgan County, Illinois. Lerski has an interesting comment about the jobs the exiles took. "Sons of aristocratic families worked as express riders, lumberjacks, and road builders, or took to grubbing, woodcutting, and ditch-digging."[1273] Others worked on farms or in factories. Most had managed to reduce themselves to the level of their former peasants and serfs for taking part in the insurrection. I wonder what was going through their minds. Thirty-seven exiles from Trieste enlisted in the army at one point or another. This number includes all the exiles from Trieste, not just the first two ships.[1274] Bogdan Grzelonski printed a letter written by one of the exiles during this tough time.

> The feeling of deep despair is mixed with an irresistible urge to laugh when I think of Olszanski, who is kept busy by the Negro house servants, now being told to polish some boots, now being told to empty the chamberpots; or to see old Morawski carrying rubble into the street and loading it on those wheelbarrows, while taunted by children. Or Komar carrying an enormous pipe through town, with several hundred boys trailing after him shouting 'Pole, Pole!' Purowski performed the most menial of tasks in the house and stable. And the portly Fakuwicz, while digging a ditch for the town's mayor, became so bogged down in marsh that he was barely retrieved with ropes. I got a job in a tannery and worked for a bit to begin with, although my hands became blistered. But that is nothing compared to when I was told to climb from roof to roof to stretch the stinking hides eventually fell to the ground, I was so Miserable that I quit and am now like a madman without roof over my head or a bite to eat. Were it not for the belief that I may still be of use to my homeland someday, I might put an end to such a miserable life. In this town there are several of us in a similar situation, and we are all suffering. When we meet each other

1272 House of Representatives, First Session, The thirty-Fourth Congress, 1855-56: [Washington: Cornelius Wendell printers, 1856] p. 5.

1273 Jerzy Jan Lerski, p. 121.

1274 Maria J. E. Copson-Niecko, The Poles in America from the 1830's to 1870's: [Located in Poles in America Bicentennial Essays, Frank Mocha, Editor. Worzalla Publishing Company, Stevens Point, Wisconsin. 1978] p. 172.

> our normal greeting is: Have you eaten today? We weep over our fate-here you have the constant picture of our misery.[1275]

The newly formed Polish Committee was attending to an entirely different situation. I wrote extensively about the Polish land grant in my stories about Woodford and Winnebago counties, so I will not spend too much time on the subject now. The Polish Committee's first undertaking was to ask the United States government for a grant of land. The exiles wished to create a new Poland and wanted to stay together. On April 13, 1834, the Polish Committee sent three delegates to Congress with a letter explaining how and why the Poles came to be here and their petition for land. On April 27, the letter and petition were introduced to the House of Representatives. President Andrew Jackson signed the bill called "Donation of lands to Polish Patriots" on June 30, 1834.[1276] The exiles were giving the option of choosing land in either the territory of Michigan or the state of Illinois.

The Polish Committee next sent delegations to the territory of Michigan and state of Illinois. It did not take long before the Michigan delegation concluded that all the decent land in Michigan was already taken. Ludwik Chlopicki was in charge of locating land in Illinois. By the end of November, he had selected a site eighty miles northwest of Chicago. The site was eighteen miles long, two miles wide, and bordered the Rock River. It encompassed parts of Rockford, Owen, and Rockton townships in Winnebago County. There were also some American settlers living under squatter title and a few half-breed Indians settled on what was known as the "Floating Land." After checking the Winnebago County histories, I counted eleven American squatters residing in the whole area when Ludwik first arrived in the fall of 1834. Ludwik stayed at the cabin of Germanicus Kent while he picked out the site. Germanicus was one of the squatters and was soon beginning to have doubts about Ludwik's intentions. The other squatters felt the same way, but Ludwik assured them all that they had nothing to worry about and left for the land office. Germanicus and the other squatters were still not convinced of Ludwik's trustworthiness and they decided to send Germanicus to Washington to defend their claims. Germanicus made the long trip to Washington only to be told by the land commission that "every settler in the county was a trespasser, and that he had no legal right to a foot of the

[1275] Bogdan Grzelonski, Poles in the United States of America 1776-1865: [Warsaw, Poland: Interpress Publishers 1976] p. 121.

[1276] Jerzy Jan Lerski, p. 136.

land which he had so unceremoniously taken."[1277] That was all Germanicus needed to hear. He went back to Illinois as fast as possible and contacted his state and federal representatives.

Surveying the grant proved to be a long-drawn-out affair and took nearly all of the year 1835 because of bad weather and sickness. The fall of 1835 saw a big increase of squatters to the area. One thing or another stopped the exiles from claiming the land grant over the next few years. Meanwhile the squatters continued to grow in number and had the state politicians on their side as well. After almost eight years of uncertainty, the United States Congress came down on the side of the squatters. I wrote more about Ludwik Chlopicki in my story about Woodford County. I do not think he ever intended to take any of the squatters land, but planned to work around them instead. He redrew the boundaries of the tract to avoid them, which only helped to void the original bill. Franciszek is the only exile who ever managed to get any land out of the bill. He appealed to Congress in 1856 for his share of the Polish land grant of 1834. Congress reviewed Franciszek's petition and awarded him 120 acres. President Buchanan signed the bill on April 21, 1858.[1278] We never have found out where the land was located. Franciszek already owned his farm in Warren Township when he appealed to Congress.

The squatters were not sure if they owned their land for eight years. They were actually building small stockades to defend their land from the Poles.[1279] I would have advised the exiles to keep away for their own safety until everything was resolved. After President Jackson signed the Polish land grant, about seventy exiles left New York and Philadelphia for Illinois. Most had not been able to find jobs. They did not all leave together but rather in small groups and intended to walk the whole distance. It was a rough trip. They had little money for food or lodging and had to sleep outside in all kinds of weather. Some turned back. Wojciech Rostkowski, the oldest exile, found the trip so difficult he committed suicide.[1280] Others stopped along the way in Louisville, Kentucky, Cincinnati, Ohio, Vandalia, Illinois, or St.

1277 Charles A. Church, History of Rockford and Winnebago County, Illinois: [Rockford, Illinois: W. F. Lame, Book and job printers 1900] p. 211

1278 Jerzy Jan Lerski, p. 153 & 154.

1279 Henry L. Boies, History of De Kalb County, Illinois: [Chicago: O. P. Bassett 1868] [A Reproduction by Unigraphic, Inc. Evansville, Indiana 1973] p. 383 & 384.

1280 Kronika Emigracji Polskiej, 1835, 11, 272; The New York Daily Advertiser, December 25, 1835.

Louis, Missouri.[1281] Nevertheless, a few exiles did make it out to Winnebago County. Only two Poles left any records of themselves in the county and you can read more about them in my story about Winnebago County. Franciszek Easinske lived in the town of Rockford for a time, and then moved to De Kalb County. Stanislaus Bielansky was the other. Stanislaus left a very small amount of information about himself. He was not one of the 234 Polish exiles from Trieste, however, and I am not sure how he got here.

Franciszek worked at the Union Hotel in Albany for two years and then moved back to New York. I am particularly proud of the letter of recommendation written for Franciszek by the owner of the City Hotel.

City Hotel, Albany, May 26, 1836.

> The bearer of this paper, Francis Wlodecki, one of the exiled Poles, came to live with me as a waiter and porter in the early part of the summer of 1834, and has remained with me in that capacity up to the present time. His conduct has been during that time such as to entitle him to the character of an honest, sober, and industrious man. He is at all times willing to work, and I cheerfully recommend him to any person who may wish to employ him. I should be pleased still to keep him in my employ; but it is his own wish to leave.
>
> Sidney Chapin.[1282]

Twelve boarders of the hotel also signed the letter and "fully concur in every part of the above recommendation."[1283] Three days later on May 29, Franciszek married Ellen O'Sullivan in Albany. Sometimes the name is just spelled Sullivan. G. B. Pandow officiated at their wedding and Joseph and Mary Levern were witnesses.[1284] Franciszek and Ellen were staunch Catholics and are among the earliest members of St. Mary's (Immaculate Conception) Catholic Church in Waukegan.[1285] G. B. Pandow does not even sign his name as reverend. I have to wonder if they were even married in a Catholic church.[1286]

1281 Florian Stasik, p. 67.

1282 House of Representatives, p.5.

1283 House of Representatives, p. 5.

1284 Marriage Certificate of Francis Wlodecki and Ellen Sullivan, [Albany New York, May 29, 1836: Personal property of James Lodesky]

1285 Immaculate Conception, Baptisms, marriages and Deaths 1847-1915: [F.H.L. 1571961 Item 1]

1286 Marriage Certificate of Francis Wlodecki and Ellen Sullivan.

Franciszek and Ellen moved to New York in June and their trail gets cold after that. We do not know what type of work Franciszek engaged in or where they lived in New York. Franciszek became a citizen April 11, 1842.[1287] Franciszek and Ellen did not waste any time starting a family and their first son Joseph, was born April 16, 1837. Uncle Jimmy Sullivan was one of the sponsors at Joseph's baptism. Jimmy shows up later in the story. Daughter Maria Teresa was born October 8, 1839. Her sponsors were Barbara Jablonska and Charles Turzanski. Son Anzlem (Ansel) was born on April 21, 1844. His sponsors were John Kucharski and Helena Niedzwiecka. Father Ludwik Jerzykiewicz,[1288] who was also one of the 234 exiles from Trieste, baptized all three. Father Jerzykiewicz was the first treasurer of the Polish Committee. The committee selected him because of "his high moral integrity."[1289] A second Polish Committee called the "Association of Poles in America" was formed in March 1842, and Father Jerzykiewicz was elected its president.[1290] My great-grandfather Francis was their youngest child and born in Lake County, Illinois, on January 14, 1845. I was surprised to see that they waited until May 4, 1851, to baptize Francis at Immaculate Conception Catholic Church in Waukegan.[1291]

Franciszek bought the farm near Gurnee in Warren Township, Lake County, Illinois, on October 1, 1843, and paid $750 for 136 acres of land.[1292] The farm is still in the Lodesky family and is a centennial farm. A centennial farm is a farm owned by the same family for over one hundred years. It is also the oldest farm in the county owned continuously by the same family.[1293] It is also one of the only farms left in the county. Lake County is full of housing developments now. Franciszek managed to buy one of the best farms in the county, and I will explain more about that later. To get to Lake County from New York Franciszek would have taken a train from New York to Albany. In Albany, he would have taken the Erie Canal to Buffalo, New York, and a steamship from Buffalo to Chicago. Benjamin F. Shepard, an early settler of Warren Township wrote that it took him sixteen days to travel from Boston

1287 House of Representatives, p. 2.

1288 Baptism Certificate of Wlodecki Children, August 31, 1844 in New York. [Personal property of James Lodesky]

1289 Jerzy Jan Lerski, p.99.

1290 Jerzy Jan Lerski, p. 156.

1291 Baptism Certificate of Wlodecki Children:

1292 General Index Lake County, Illinois 1800-1935: [Francis Wlodecki, book 20]

1293 Centennial farms: [State of Illinois Department of Agriculture: Springfield, Illinois 2001]

to Chicago in 1842.[1294] The cost of the steamboat from Buffalo to Chicago was fifteen dollars in 1842.[1295] Franciszek bought the farm in 1843, but did not move out there with his family until the fall of 1844. Ellen was either pregnant with Ansel or raising him during most of the year 1844. They left for Lake County sometime after August 31, 1844, which is the date on Ansel's baptism in New York.[1296]

This reminds me of another story passed down to us by Franciszek. My grandfather thought that Franciszek did not intend to settle in Illinois but was on his way to settle in Wisconsin or had a friend who lived in Wisconsin. There were three Polish exiles in Wisconsin at the time. Vincent Dziewnowski settled in Iowa County and Thaddeus Pienkowski and Pavel Sobelewski in Kenosha County. Neither Dziewnowski or Pienkowski were in the same army as Franciszek. I also know their stories good and do not think they would have had much contact with Franciszek after they arrived here. That leaves only Pavel Sobelewski. They were both out here in the fall of 1844. Sobelewski was buying[1297] and selling land in Kenosha County, Wisconsin, on October 18, 1844.[1298] Franciszek and Pavel served in the same army and spent two years together in Austrian prisons. I write more about Pavel Sobelewski in the story of Boone County.

We never heard anything about the other Polish exiles in the county. I found all of them in the census records. In fact, I am not sure just how much contact they actually had with each other in Lake County. When I first learned there were other Polish exiles living here, I imagined all of them meeting at St. Mary's Catholic Church in Waukegan every Sunday. It looks like it never happened. Both Stanislaus Lisiecki and Stefan Gasiorowski lived in Waukegan and there is no record of them ever attending a single mass at St. Mary's. A friend told me they saw Stanislaus's son Phillip recorded as a member of a Protestant church in Waukegan. I have not found this document so cannot say with any certainly if this is true. Alexander Bilinski was a charter member of the Diamond Lake

---

1294 Louise Osling, Historical Highlights of the Waukegan Area: [Waukegan, Illinois: North Shore Printers, Inc. 1976] p. 14.

1295 William V. Pooley, The Settlement of Illinois from 1830 to 1850: [Madison, Wisconsin: May, 1908] [Ann Arbor, Michigan: University Microfilms 1968] p. 74.

1296 Baptism Certificate of Wlodecki Children:

1297 Racine County, Wisconsin, Mortgages, [Racine County Register of Deeds Office, Racine, Wisconsin Book D p. 325 &326]

1298 Racine County, Wisconsin Deeds, [Racine County Register of Deeds Office Book K p. 215.

Free Church.[1299] Theodor Dombski's descendants all went to the Congregational Church's in Grayslake or Waukegan.[1300], [1301] Thaddeus Pienkowski's family all attended a Baptist church across the state line in Illinois.[1302] Besides our family, only the Basil Jaroshinski family stayed Catholic. The church records contain a number of mentions of the Jaroshinski family, so I thought that at least they saw each other every Sunday. Then I found out that St. Mary's Church in Waukegan had a satellite church in Old Mill Creek, about a half mile north of Jaroshinski's house. So I guess they never saw each other on Sundays but went to the nearest church instead. How often they visited each other is a mystery. Nothing ever came down to us about any of them and we thought that Franciszek was the first Pole to settle in the county. The exiles' sons might have known each other from the Lake County Fair.

I now have to mention that we have to be one of the luckiest families to have ever researched their family history. Franciszek bought 137 acres in Warren Township from Julia McClure on October 1, 1843. Her husband, James McClure, homesteaded the farm in August 1837. Their daughter Annie McClure-Hitchcock just happens to write a small book about their experiences homesteading the very farm we bought from them. Could a genealogist ask for more! Annie was only four years old when they moved away, so everything she wrote about was second-hand information. The title is *Some Recollections of Early Life in Illinois, Lake County in 1840.*[1303] It is really more like an article (eleven pages) then a book and contains many notes she or someone else added to it after the book was printed. The notes mention us twice. Two of James McClure's brothers, William and Thomas, were early settlers of Warren Township. They had already picked out the farm for James before he came out to the county. Their descendants became a very well-known family in Gurnee and the surrounding area for years. I grew up next door to McClure's garage and farm and even dated a descendant of one of the McClure brothers for a time.

1299 Memories of Mundelein 1909-1984: [Mundelein Community Days Committee] p. 5.

1300 Waukegan Daily Sun [Mary A. Thompson Obituary May 11, 1918]

1301 The Waukegan Daily Sun, [Find women dead on floor of home] July 15, 1919

1302 Mrs. Sarah Norton Lockhart Young and Mrs. Minnie Eliza Pienkowski Buckley, A Brief Sketch of the Life History of our Father and Mother: [Donated to me from Robert Pienkowski of Blacksburg, Virginia] p. 13.

1303 Annie McClure-Hitchcock, Some Recollections of Early Life in Illinois, Lake County in 1840: [At Warren Township Historical Society.]

James and Julia McClure and their three children came out to Lake County by way of the Erie Canal and steamship to Chicago in 1837. James was of Scotch-Irish descent. The family had been living in Philadelphia where James was an architect and builder. He had worked on some important buildings there but was starting to have trouble with his health. James and Julia decided to move out west, with the hope that a better climate would be good for his health. James's brothers must have told him there were no schools in Warren Township, so he packed up all their books to take with them. They planned to home school their children when they reached Illinois. The McClures brought much of their household with them to Illinois. James needed all his tools to build a house, etc., and Julia could not part with her favorite household items, some being wedding presents.

Annie describes how Lake County looked when the family arrived. The prairie was covered with wild flowers and the forests contained valuable mixed hardwood trees. The whole county abounded in wildlife. I mentioned earlier that Lake County was a favorite hunting ground of the Indians. Annie claims that Indians returning home from selling their furs in Chicago would sometimes ask to sleep by their Kitchen fire. Run-ins with bears were common and they listened to the wolves howl every night. There were no roads, just trails. The farm had numerous springs on it. Sometime in the early 1900s, the farm was tiled and the springs are all gone now. She mentions how the Des Plaines River is almost two miles wide in the spring but very narrow and shallow in the fall. I am not sure if it ever gets two miles wide, but there is a major flood there about every twenty years or so. In a dry summer, the river is barely ten to fifteen feet wide and less than a foot deep. Nearby Gurnee is located on the floodplain. When I grew up in Gurnee, our basement and backyard flooded every year like clockwork.

James was supposed to have built the first or one of the first frame houses in the county. The house was built on a hill about one-half mile west of the Des Plaines River. It was a two-story building separated in the middle by a large, wide foyer or entranceway. The rooms were on each side of the entranceway. The inside was built out of black walnut and the outside of oak and it sat on the edge of the woods where the prairie began. The house also served as the local library. The neighbors found out that the McClures owned a lot of books and were soon asking to borrow them. Most of their neighbors were of English descent, except for "a very cultivated Polish family."[1304] That would be us. The McClures called it the "Hill Farm."[1305]

[1304] Annie McClure-Hitchcock, p.6.

[1305] Annie McClure-Hitchcock, p. 8.

James built a small chapel in the corner of the farm and Annie claims that Franciszek helped him build it. According to Annie, two English families helped her father build the chapel with the help of "a Polish exile, of most courtly manners, was a congenial friend."[1306] Someone wrote between the lines of her book that he "later bought the farm."[1307] Franciszek was supposed to be living in New York at the time. We are not sure what Franciszek was doing from 1836 to 1844, so maybe he was in the county earlier than we thought and already knew the McClures. Somehow, he managed to buy the farm but not because he did not have the money. He only had to save $1.65 a week for nine years to come up with $750. Usually a local insider buys a large, valuable piece of property before anyone else knows it is even for sale. Maybe none of the other pioneers had the money to buy it or they were satisfied with the land they already owned. One of the other exiles could have written to Franciszek in New York and told him that a good farm was for sale. It has always been one of the top farms in the county.

Moving west only made James's health worse. He was so occupied with building the house and farm that he barely knew any of his neighbors. He might have contracted the ague as well. Ague was malaria, and those settlers living close to the river were most affected by it.[1308] Four years of pioneer life was too much for James and he died on May 12, 1841, leaving a wife and five children. James had only begun to farm the land and had just ten acres of corn under cultivation.[1309] Julia rented the farm out on shares for the next two years. You supply the land and someone else supplies the labor. You both split the profit. Julia wanted to educate the children in the city and she put the farm up for sale two years after James died. Annie wrote, "We fled away from the tangible and intangible terrors of western frontier life, to try those of a frontier town."[1310]

Franciszek's farm is located about one and a half miles southwest of Gurnee in Warren Township, Illinois. Your author grew up in Gurnee. It was much smaller when I lived there, about 1,500 to 1,800 people. Now it is around 17,000. Originally, Warren Township was named Franklin Township. Two early pioneers from Warren Township, Herkimer County, New York, liked Warren Township better than Franklin Township and succeeded in getting the name changed. The Warren Township in New York is named after

1306 Annie McClure-Hitchcock, p. 7.

1307 Annie McClure-Hitchcock, p. 7.

1308 Annie McClure-Hitchcock, p. 7.

1309 Land Patent Records: [National Archives, Washington, D. C.]

1310 Annie McClure-Hitchcock, p. 4.

Joseph Warren, a Revolutionary War general killed at Bunker Hill.[1311] Warren Township is in the northeast part of Lake County. Its eastern border is about four miles west of Lake Michigan and its northern border about six miles south of the Illinois-Wisconsin state line. The first settlers came up the Des Plaines River from Chicago in 1835. The Milwaukee Road ran north from Chicago on the west side of the Des Plaines River, crossed the river at the future site of Gurnee, and then headed east. Most of the first settlers claimed land alongside the river. The terrain east of the river was wooded while the land west of the river was mainly small prairies surrounded by forest. Mill Creek also runs though the township. The first settler in Gurnee was a free black named Amos Bennett. He claimed to be "the first white man that ever planted corn upon the O'Plain River."[1312] The River has gone through three name changes. To simplify matters, I will only refer to it as the Des Plaines. Most of the first settlers in Warren Township were New England Yankees and most were Protestant. The Catholics all lived south of town along the plank road, now Illinois Route 120.[1313] The name Gurnee did not come into use until 1874. Simplifying matters again, I will only use Gurnee.

The woods along the Des Plaines River were overrun with wolves for years, and it took almost one hundred years to get ride of them all. Two types of wolves inhabited the area, grey or timber and prairie. Prairie wolves are known today as coyotes. Large-scale wolf hunts were held during the 1870s, but they were largely unsuccessful. There was usually a bounty on wolves and individual hunters met with the most success. There were also wild pigs living in the woods along the river just south of Gurnee. This is near Franciszek's farm. The pigs had all escaped from nearby farms and had turned wild. You had to watch your step around them or they were liable to run you up a tree.

Larry Lawson wrote a portrait of Franciszek in his book about Gurnee's first settlers. He got some of it wrong or mixed up, including Franciszek's name, but nonetheless, we appreciate that he included us in his book. We do not know where he got most of his information from, but Lawson wrote that Franciszek's first job in Illinois was building a fence for a deer park on

[1311] Dianna Dretske, What's in a Name? The Origin of Place Names in Lake County, Illinois: [Published by the Lake County Discovery Museum: Wauconda, Illinois] Letter W.

[1312] Elijah M. Haines, Historical and Sketches, of Lake County, Illinois: [Waukegan, Illinois: E. G. Howe, 1852] p. 100.

[1313] Edward S. Lawson, A History of Warren Township [Lake County, Illinois: [Published by the Warren-Newport Public Library, Gurnee, Illinois 1974] p. 50.

John Gage's farm.[1314] Gage owned a lot of land (1,600 acres)[1315] a couple miles southwest of Franciszek's farm. Theodor Dombski's farm was a little west of Gages farm. Located on Gages former property was a large lake, which is called "Gages Lake" to this day. Gage moved to Lake County in December 1847 and was one of the developers of the plank road from Waukegan to Mc Henry County.[1316] Franciszek moved to Lake County in 1844, if not sooner, so maybe Lawson meant that building a fence for Gage was Franciszek's first job off the farm. With only 10 acres out of 136 under cultivation, Franciszek would have had far then enough work to do on his own farm.

Franciszek was fifty years old when he became a pioneer, old for the times. Franciszek was starting when everyone else was winding down. John H. Thurston, an early Winnebago settler wrote, "Alas for those among the settlers who had passed their prime physically. Too old to withstand the hardships of pioneer life, they sickened, and in some instances they straggled back to the old homes at the east to die. Among the latter were my own parents, leaving me in 1842 in fight the battle of life alone."[1317] Franciszek does not seem like the type of person to come out west as a greenhorn farmer with a family to support. He must have known what he was doing. We know he was tall, and I think he was probably sturdy as well to be able to withstand the rigors of pioneer life at his age. Franciszek got some help in the 1850s from Ellen's brother Jimmy O'Sullivan. The 1860 census for Warren Township shows Jimmy living with Franciszek and Ellen. His occupation is listed as a farm laborer. Jimmy was no spring chicken himself being sixty-three years old in 1860.[1318]

It looks like the Wlodecki farm got off to a slow start. The Agriculture Census for Warren Township shows that they were living on a real bare bones farm in 1850. Only thirty acres were under cultivation. Fifty more acres were unimproved and probably used for pasture and hay. The rest must have been forest. They lived in a nice house, but it looks like they were living kind of a Spartan existence. They had two pigs but no horses. The value of their farm

1314 Edward S. Larson, p. 112.

1315 Edward S. Larson, p. 21.

1316 The Waukegan News-Sun, Waukegan, Illinois: November 5, 1955.

1317 John H. Thurston, Reminisences, sporting and otherwise, of the Early Days in Rockford, Illinois. [Rockford, Illinois: Press of the Daily Republican 1891[Reprinted by the North Centrall Illinois Genealogical Society of Rockford, Illinois. [Dixon, Illinois: The Print Shop] p. 35.

1318 1860 Federal Census of Lake County, Illinois: [National Archives, Box 653, Roll 193, Page 591]

equipment was forty dollars. They had three milk cows, three calves, and two working oxen.[1319] Oxen were stronger than horses and all the pioneers used them to plow up the prairies. I think Franciszek was probably raising his own oxen and was concentrating all his resources on turning over the prairie to grow wheat and corn. Franciszek might have scraped together every penny he could find just to buy the farm and did not have much left over to start farming.

We have only found three mentions of Franciszek in the local papers. Al Westerman found one, and I found the other two. An ad in the September 6, 1856, *Waukegan Gazette* writes, "For Sale, Two Mares, six years old, good for any use. Enquire of Francis Wlodeski." Underneath his name are the words "The Old Polander."[1320] Everyone must have known him as the Old Polander. On July 2, 1858, Franciszek found a briefcase full of important papers lying on a Waukegan Street and put a notice in the *Gazette.*[1321] Sidney Chapin, owner of the City Hotel, said Franciszek was honest.[1322] The last mention took place in October 1863 when someone filed "disturbing the peace" charges against Franciszek. The circuit court dismissed the case and ordered the "complaining witness" to pay court costs.[1323] Franciszek was old at this time. We heard he was sick the last few years of his life. He died on August 28, 1864, after having lived one very exciting life.

I wonder if he kept up the chapel built by James McClure. I'll bet he did, and I will also bet he prayed there every single day for the rest of his life. Franciszek had much to be grateful for. True he lost everything in Podolia and went through some tough times but at least the Austrians did not send him back to Russia, to a certain death in a Siberian mine. Instead, he got a second chance in America, plus a wife and four children to boot. He died owning his own land, and I cannot help but think that the farm's black soil would have reminded him of Podolia every day. The farm had steadily grown since the 1850 Agriculture Census was taken. Franciszek's will shows one team of work horses, one team of oxen, one two year old bull, five cows, three steers, and fifty-seven sheep. Also a much larger line of equipment.[1324] Ellen died on March 27, 1891. I have to confess that we know next to nothing about her.

1319 1850 Agriculture Census, Lake County, Illinois: Illinois State Archives, Springfield, Illinois Roll 31-2]

1320 The Waukegan Gazette, Waukegan, Illinois: September 6, 1856.

1321 The Waukegan Gazette, July 3, 1858.

1322 House of Representatives, p. 5.

1323 The Waukegan Gazette, October 17, 1863.

1324 Index to Probate Files, Lake County, Illinois: [at Waukegan, Illinois, File 729 Book 1 1843-1963]

Joseph, Franciszek's oldest son, left the farm sometime in the 1850s. He moved to Chicago and took up the trade of guilder, applying gold leaf to churches, etc. He married an Irish emigrant named Bridget Hughes and they had three children, Frank, Jim, and Nellie. Our families lost touch in the 1930s, and I have only met this side of the family twice. They have our family ring. I do not know much more about them except that they seem to be more into education than our side of the family.

Daughter Maria Teresa married an ambitious but uneducated Irishman named Robert Dady on April 6, 1861. Uneducated meaning he never learned to read or write. Robert was orphaned at seventeen years of age but he was not about to let a few disadvantages hold him back. Starting with nothing, he became the richest man in the county. Robert and Mary had three children, Frank, Nellie, and Lorena. Robert accumulated mainly farmland all his life and rarely sold any of it. When he died in 1919, he owned farms all over the county and in at least three other states. He also owned twenty or thirty houses on the south side of Waukegan. Robert bought and fed out fifteen thousand sheep a year when raising a few hundred sheep was considered a big operation. He had problems with people though, especially his own offspring. He severed all connections with his son Frank and daughter Nellie for years.[1325] Son Frank had a falling out with his dad when Robert foreclosed on the mortgage of Frank's bakery in Waukegan. Frank left town and did not see his father again until the year 1918. Robert was very sick that year, and Frank came down from Milwaukee to see him. The first they saw each other in fifteen years.[1326] After his bakery was closed, Frank went to Milwaukee, started a roofing business,[1327] and became a millionaire on his own. His marriage never produced any children.[1328]

Nellie married a prominent Waukegan businessman named John Conrad. John died when he was fifty years old of pernicious anemia.[1329] They never had any children either, and she never remarried. Her trouble with her father started after her husband and father got into a disagreement when their partnership in a hotel went sour. Frank and Nellie were both cut out of Robert's will and everything was left to Lorena. Lorena never married and died of an infection of the jaw in 1919.[1330] Robert was sick at the time and

[1325] The Waukegan Daily Sun, Waukegan, Illinois. June 10, 1919.

[1326] The Waukegan Daily Sun, June 17, 1919.

[1327] The Waukegan Daily Sun, June 28, 1919.

[1328] The Waukegan Daily Sun, June 17, 1919.

[1329] The Waukegan Daily Sun, December 2, 1918.

[1330] The Waukegan Daily Sun, March 29, 1919.

died two and a half months later without ever changing his will. Frank and Nellie were the closet relatives and got the inheritance anyways.[1331] Nellie went on to become a noted businesswoman in Waukegan. She founded the town's roller rink, the Valencia Ballroom, and the Times Theatre, besides owning a lot of real estate around town.[1332] My grandfather used to play the organ at Nellie's roller rink. My dad and uncle used to go to the roller rink when they were kids and claimed Nellie was so cheap that they always had to pay the full admission price to enter.

I have not mentioned a thing about Franciszek's daughter Mary Wlodecki-Dady, who was supposed to be the subject of this story. There are quite a few records of Mary and Robert in the Immaculate Conception Church records. She died suddenly in 1914. According to her obituary, Mary "was a very unassuming and quite a home-woman, having helped greatly in her husbands career which has been marked by acquisition of extensive farm property in Lake County."[1333] Looks like Aunt Mary was overshadowed by the rest of the family. She probably stayed in the background while the rest of the family fought it out with each other.

Anzlem (Ansel) was real close to my great-grandfather Frank. They were partners on two farms, a grain threshing business, and buying real estate. Even their burial plots are next to each other. I will explain more about their partnership when I write about Frank. Ansel married Celia Raftree June 9, 1884. Four children were born from the marriage, Frank, Florence, Mary, and Celia. Ansel's wife Celia died when the children were young. Ansel's second marriage was to a schoolteacher named Maggie Gannon. Ansel was twenty-seven years her senior. Way to go, Uncle Ansel. Their marriage produced one son, Joseph, born in 1896. Son Frank died in 1936 at fifty-one years of age.[1334] He was married but no children were born to the marriage. He was supposed to have lived next door to Jack Benny's mother in Waukegan. Florence went to Northern Illinois University[1335] and then became a teacher at the Wilson School in Warrentown. She married someone named Specht and moved to Chicago.[1336] Daughter Mary married someone by the name of Timmell and also moved to Chicago.[1337] Celia taught at Wilson School for a

1331 The Waukegan Daily Sun, May 23, 1929.

1332 The Waukegan News Sun, July 29, 1949.

1333 The Waukegan Daily Sun, December 14, 1914.

1334 The Waukegan News Sun, October 15, 1936.

1335 The Waukegan Daily Sun, June 26, 1908.

1336 The Waukegan News Sun, November 20, 1923.

1337 The Waukegan News Sun, November 20, 1923.

time and married Frank Guber. Celia died from a heart attack May 30, 1925, leaving a husband and three children.[1338] Ansel sold his farm in 1915 and moved to Waukegan.[1339] Most farmers from the county seem to have moved to Waukegan when they retired. Ansel died November 19, 1923.[1340]

Franciszek and Ellen were lucky in the respect that none of their children died young, as opposed to the Dombskis or Jaroshinskis, who lost a number of offspring. All our bad luck came later. Ansel's son Joseph came to a bad ending. Joe went to high school at Notre Dame University and looked to have a bright future. Notre Dame had a high school in those days. Joe also went to the university and played on the football team. On October 28, 1916, the *Waukegan Daily Sun* claims that "Joe had been playing one of the important positions on the University eleven since the season opened, and he was making good when he met injury."[1341] Jesse Harper was the head coach then. Knute Rockne was Harper's assistant at the time and became head coach in 1918. The famous George Gipp ([the Gipper) was one class behind Joe. In the end of October, Joe was playing a pickup football game with the other freshman. While running with the football, Joe stepped in a hole and broke his leg in two places. Both breaks were below the knee of the right leg and the large artery of his leg was torn in half.[1342] Gangrene set in a week later and part of Joe's leg was amputated before informing Ansel and Maggie.[1343] A week later, they had to amputate more of his leg.[1344] The February 19, 1917, *Daily Sun* reported that "Joe hovered between life and death for the last several weeks. Death was due to blood poison and Gangrene which resulted from an accident which the young man suffered while playing football on the Notre Dame College football team last fall."[1345] The Notre Dame Scholastic reported that "the accident on the football field, that finally resulted in his death, is the first one that has ended fatally in the many years that the game has been played at Notre Dame."[1346] The scholastic also wrote, "From his first

1338 The Waukegan Daily Sun, June 3, 1925.

1339 The Waukegan Gazette, June 12, 1915.

1340 Certificate of Death, Lake County, Illinois County Clerk # 210. [Waukegan, Illinois]

1341 The Waukegan Daily Sun, October 28, 1916.

1342 The Waukegan Daily Sun, October 28, 1916.

1343 The Waukegan Daily Sun, November 6, 1916.

1344 The Waukegan Daily Sun, November 14, 1916.

1345 The Waukegan Daily Sun, February 19, 1917.

1346 The Notre Dame Scholastic. [Published by The University of Notre Dame, Indiana: February 24, 1917 Volume 1] p. 320.

day with us several years ago, Joe endeared himself to everyone by his heart and gentle manliness."[1347] We have lost touch with all of Ansel's descendants and do not know where any of them live now.

My great-grandfather Frank was a real go-getter and seems to have had his fingers into everything. The 1870 census shows Frank, Ansel, and Ellen living on the farm.[1348] The *Waukegan Gazette* wrote in 1870 that Frank entered a "handsome bay Stallion" in the Lake County fair.[1349] Frank took first for best-matched three-year-old colts and second for best three-year-old gelding in the 1873 Lake County Fair in Libertyville.[1350] The year 1873 saw the creation of the Lake County Agricultural and Horse Growers Association Fair in Waukegan. Frank got second in Waukegan for best working mare between three and four years old and first in carriage horses for the best pair of three-year-old colts.[1351] On October 10, 1874, The *Waukegan Gazette* wrote, "Some six or eight work teams were shown and after much consideration on the part of the committee the blue ribbon was given to a pair of young gray horses belonging to Frank Wlodeskie of Warren."[1352] This was at the Waukegan Fair and grays were draft horses of the Percheron breed. The same year, Frank found the time to judge a mowing match. The contest was between the Williams and Superior combines and "Good judges of machine work are expected to be in attendance."[1353] It seems that another combine named the Johnston was admitted later to the contest. The July 4, 1874, *Gazette* carried the results of the mowing match. "Deducting the difference in width of cut the Johnston would make the draft 228 pounds; and also that the Johnston runs much smoother and steadier." The Johnston won and Frank is one of the three judges that picked the winner.[1354] The last record of Frank exhibiting horses was at the 1876 Lake County Fair in Libertyville where he won first for best pair "horses at work."[1355]

Frank and Ansel started a grain-threshing business sometime in the 1870s.[1356] Threshing grain made for a hot, tough, and long day. On the positive

---

1347 The Notre Dame Scholastic, p. 320.

1348 Lake County, Illinois Genealogical Society, 1870 Census of Lake County, Illinois: [Mundelein, Illinois: Copy Systems] p. 123.

1349 The Waukegan Gazette, October 1, 1870.

1350 The Waukegan Gazette, September 27, 1873.

1351 The Waukegan Gazette, October 11, 1873.

1352 The Waukegan Gazette, October 10, 1874.

1353 The Waukegan Gazette, June 27, 1874.

1354 The Waukegan Gazette, July 4, 1874.

1355 The Waukegan Gazette, September 30, 1876.

1356 Edward S. Larson, p. 54.

side, the wife of the farmer getting his grain threshed provided large meals for the threshing crew. You also got to know your neighbors a lot better. Threshers were large steam-powered machines that took a crew of men to operate. Moving threshers from farm to farm became such a problem that laws for moving them were enacted in the 1880s. The sight of a thresher must have spooked a lot of horses. One of the thresher crew members was required to walk up to two hundred yards ahead of the thresher to warn everyone and to help control their livestock if necessary. It was also required to turn off the thresher's engine when a team was one hundred yards away. Crossing bridges was another problem. The thresher had to carry four, twelve feet long 2 × 12's with them. Two of the twelve footers had to be under the thresher wheels at all times when crossing a bridge. The other two 2 × 12's were moved ahead of the other two on longer bridges.[1357] I wonder how many bridges gave out before this law was enacted.

Ansel bought his own farm sometime in the 1870s. Frank and Ansel were partners and ran both farms as one. In 1880, the Wlodeskie Brothers had 167 acres under cultivation, 80 acres of pasture, and 60 acres of woods. They grew 20 acres of corn, 20 acres of oats, 3 acres of potatoes, and 65 acres of hay. There was also a sixty-tree apple orchard on three acres. The farm produced 175 pounds of butter every year. For livestock they had 4 horses, 2 milk cows, 2 calves, 30 steers, 275 sheep, 4 pigs, and 35 chickens.[1358] I found a couple mentions of Frank in the *Gazette* during this time. In 1878, Frank and Ansel sent a train-car full of sheep to market but, after arriving, found out the price of sheep was very low that day. They took all the sheep back to the farm rather then sell them so cheap.[1359] In 1886, Frank bought thirty-two head of cattle from his brother-in-law Robert Dady for $3.70 per hundredweight.[1360] One of my relatives said that Frank used to ship his grain by barge on Lake Michigan to Chicago. My cousin Joe heard that Frank would put a bundle of cornstalks over his shoulder and the cattle would follow him all the way to the train station.

Frank and Ansel bought and sold land in Lake County on a continual basis for most of their lives. Sometimes as partners, other times individually. Frank's or Ansel's names our recorded as buying land or lots about sixty times from 1870 until close to their deaths in 1923. They sold land or lots around fifty times during the same period. Frank bought a feed mill in 1884, but I

1357 The Waukegan Gazette, August 8, 1885.
1358 1880 Agricultural Census for Lake County, Illinois: [T1133 #43]
1359 The Waukegan Gazette, October 26, 1878.
1360 The Waukegan Gazette, June 19, 1886.

have never found any evidence of him ever selling feed.[1361] Most of Frank's lots were located on the south side of Waukegan. He hired contractors to build houses on many of his lots in Waukegan, and then rented them out to mainly foreign emigrants. Most of his renters were Croatians, Slovenians, or Armenians. Dad thought Frank owned at least seventeen houses. Another relative thought he owned more than seventeen. He also owned a building on Oak Street that two Armenians used for a distillery.[1362]

Ansel married Celia Raftree on June 9, 1884, while Frank married Bridget McCarthy on November 25, 1885. Each was forty-one years old when they married. Frank and Bridget were the parents of Mary (October 12, 1886-June 30, 1981), Kitty (February 25, 1888-1967), Frank "Dan" (July 18, 1889-February 15, 1971), George (December 25, 1893-October 29, 1928), Bessie (March 30, 1898-July 8, 1988) Gene (July 6,1901-1984), and Joseph (1903-1980). Joe's grandfather is Dan, while my grandfather is Gene. Frank was fifty-six years old when my grandfather was born and fifty-eight when Uncle Joe was born. Uncle Joe always said he turned out pretty good for being in the bottom of the bag.

Great-grandmother Bridget McCarthy was born in Wilson, Illinois, on August 15, 1860. She was twenty-five years old when she married Frank. Bridget was from a large family and her parents were Irish emigrants from County Kerry. He father, Dan, was a farmer and one of the organizers of the Warrenton School.[1363] Bridget taught there for a time herself.[1364] Her future nieces, Florence and Celia Wlodeski, taught at the same school later. Bridget was always involved with Catholic organizations at the Immaculate Conception Church. She was elected a trustee in the Women's Catholic Order of Foresters in 1897.[1365] Bridget worked in the "Frappe and Fruit Booth" at the annual Catholic Bazaar held at the Waukegan Armory in 1912.[1366] What is Frappe? Ansel's wife worked in the "Lunch Booth" at the same time. She was elected sentinel by the Women's Catholic Order of Foresters in 1915[1367] and chairperson of the Lady Foresters in 1920.[1368] Bridget died when I was five years old, but I remember visiting her once in the nursing home. All my older relatives spoke of

---

1361 General Index Grantees, Lake County, Illinois: [1800-1935 Book 12]

1362 The Waukegan Daily Sun, June 11, 1898.

1363 Dedicated to the Memory of Four Pioneers: [At the Warren Township Historical Society, Gurnee, Illinois] p. 2.

1364 The Waukegan News Sun, p. April 11, 1956.

1365 The Waukegan Daily Sun, December 22, 1897.

1366 The Waukegan Daily Sun, October 22, 1912.

1367 The Waukegan Daily Sun, December 14, 1915.

1368 The Waukegan Daily Sun, February 21, 1920.

her in the most glowing of terms. They claimed she not only helped her adult children's families out but all the neighbors and their families as well. Bridget stayed active all her life and took care of the rental houses almost to the very end. The family suggested she retire but she always said that she "did not want to rust." The *Waukegan Daily Sun* thought that she was the last person in the county to use a spinning wheel.[1369] Bridget died April 11, 1956.[1370]

By the mid-1880s, Frank and Ansel were doing well. Ansel built a new house on his farm and Frank built one of the largest barns in the county on his farm.[1371] The house purchased by Franciszek in 1843 burned down at some point. A new house was built but at the other end of the farm on Grange Hall Road, now Washington Street. The only reminder of the old house is a large lilac bush on top of the hill. Joe's grandfather said never plow it under. Frank and Ansel's partnership dissolved in 1895 when Frank moved his family to Waukegan.[1372] Frank hired someone to manage the farm and concentrated on his rental houses. He claimed to be retired on the 1899-1900 Waukegan City Directory.[1373] Frank must of considered taking care of rental houses retirement. A disastrous event occurred at the farm on April 5, 1900, and it was not until 1913 that Frank would claim to be retired again.[1374]

> All buildings burned-one of the best farms in the county is laid to ruin, great loss to owner
>
> The fire at the Frank Lodeskey farm just east of Grange Hall yesterday morning was the worst that has occurred in the county in a long time. While it was known here in the afternoon that the blaze was a disastrous one, the damage was much greater than was reported.
>
> Every building on the Lodeskey farm was totally destroyed and roughly estimated the damage to buildings, material, household goods, etc. would not be much less than eight thousand dollars. Mr. Lodeskey said this morning "Six thousand wouldn't replace the loss to me along."

1369 The Waukegan Daily Sun, February 25, 1911.
1370 The Waukegan News Sun, April 11, 1956.
1371 The Waukegan Gazette, December 18, 1886.
1372 Waukegan City Directory, [1895-1896] p. 103.
1373 Waukegan City Directory, [1899-1900] p. 120.
1374 Waukegan City Directory, [1913-1914] p. 208.

Where It Started

It was about ten o'clock when Mrs. Mat Shumer, whose husband conducts the farm for Mr. Lodeskey, looked towards the barn and saw smoke issuing from the roof. She ran out and sounded an alarm and soon the farm hands were on the scene. The smoke seemed first to issue from the northwest corner of the building, so it is presumed the blaze started in a large bin of corn on the second floor of the building.

In the meantime the flames had spread rapidly but the help had liberated several horses and cows, though being unable to remove machinery, etc.

A strong wind was blowing from the southwest, the other buildings on the place being east of the burning farm. The flames were fanned until, although the neighbors endeavored to save the houses etc. the immediate danger of all the buildings was apparent.

Fire Spread Rapidly

From the barn, which by the way is one of the largest in the county, being 100 by 50 ft. with a high basement and worth over $2,000, flames leaped to the dwelling place occupied by Mr. Shumer, about ninety feet away. This building and contents were soon burned. The flames then spreading to the house of Nick Brosier, about 200 feet away, this building was also consumed. Other buildings on the place entirely destroyed were a large chicken house, granaries, large milk house, 45ft. wind mill, pig pens, corn cribs and a large tool shop. In these various buildings were all kinds of farming implements, a better and more complete supply perhaps being hard to find in the county.

The furniture in neither of the houses mentioned was saved and as the owners carried no insurance the loss to them is considerable.

Ten young calves, about three or four weeks old which were stalled in the east side of the basement in the barn were burned,

> the flames having surrounded them before assistance could get there.
>
> The insurance carried by Mr. Lodeskey in the Millburn Insurance Co. amounts to $3,000.
>
> Mr. Lodeskey is as yet undecided as to whether he will rebuild immediately. He will hold an auction Tuesday afternoon at one o'clock when he will dispose of 35 head of cattle.[1375]

Frank rebuilt the farm and it seems to me the new barn was larger then the one that burned down. If you did not notice, Frank was underinsured. By the way, Al Westerman of Zion, Illinois, found this story and the next one. Every now and then, I have come across other stories of fires in Frank's rental homes, but nothing like what happened at the farm. Another freak accident happened in 1906. A Mrs. Cudworth was struck by lightning twice in the kitchen of the farm and killed.[1376]

Frank was a Waukegan election judge in the First Ward, Second Precinct in 1899.[1377] He was on three school board committees in 1906.[1378] He retired from the board in 1907.[1379] Frank was a juror in what has to be one of the most unusual court cases of 1903. *John Strand vs. Mrs. Anna Isaacson.*

> Strand charged that Mrs. Isaacson came into his store and used very strong language, emphasizing her remarks by striking her fist upon the counter.
>
> He said that he could not, like mayor Pearce, stand for such language, and consequently he asked that the court ease his feelings by fining the defendant.[1380]

Four juror's voted to acquit Mrs. Isaacson and two wanted her fined. I do not know how Frank voted. How does a case like this even get to court? The foreman of the jury was Frank Milhizer, who became a relative about

1375 The Waukegan Daily Sun, April 5, 1900.
1376 The Waukegan Daily Sun, June 4, 1906.
1377 The Waukegan Daily Sun, March 29, 1899.
1378 The Waukegan Daily Sun, June 1, 1906.
1379 The Waukegan Daily Sun, May 9, 1907.
1380 The Waukegan Daily Sun, May 14, 1903.

twenty years later when my grandfather married his niece. Frank was in other juries over the years but none like this one.

Frank had some real excitement in 1908. He was hauling a wagonload of dirt on Washington Street and somehow his team backed over a culvert alongside a seventy-five-foot ravine. The wagon started rolling backwards down the ravine and Frank had to jump for his life. The wagon must have unhooked from the horses because his team was all right. The wagon however was "smashed into twenty different pieces."[1381]

He was also a member of the Waukegan Industrial Association. The association had about two hundred members who each contributed money for the construction of factories in Waukegan and North Chicago. North Chicago is the town directly south of Waukegan, not the north side of Chicago. The association bought land, built factories, and sold them to businesses. The aim was to increase the population and prosperity of Waukegan and North Chicago. An annual dividend of 6 percent was paid to the stockholders. Meyer Kubelsky, father of the late comedian Jack Benny, was also a member.[1382]

A surprising event occurred in 1913 when an arrest warrant was sworn out against Frank. This has to be his first brush with the law. According to the *Waukegan Daily Sun*, "This afternoon Health Officer Hicks swore out a warrant against Frank Lodeski, a prominent West Side resident, charging him with committing a nuisance when he dumped the contents of an outbuilding on a vacant lot which he is said to have leased near his home. The officer was looking for him but had not found him."[1383] There is nothing in the paper after that, so Frank must have cleaned up the mess in a hurry. A run-in with the police did seem to diminish anyone's belief in Frank's competence. Later in the same year, he was recommended to sit on a committee to select a company to provide streetcar service to Waukegan.[1384]

Frank was sick for the last few years of his life. It sounds like he might have had Alzheimer's disease. He kept wondering off from home and they would find him in different parts of town. I asked my grandmother about Frank once. He was bedridden when she was dating my grandfather, and all she could remember was that he was an "Old Polack." Frank died January 10, 1923.[1385]

1381 The Waukegan Daily Sun, January 28, 1908.

1382 The Waukegan Daily Sun, February 2, 1912.

1383 The Waukegan Daily Sun, July 17, 1913.

1384 The Waukegan Daily Sun, November 13, 1913.

1385 Certificate of Death, Lake County, Illinois County Clerk #6. [Waukegan, Illinois]

Woodford County

Woodford County had one very famous Pole, Baron Ludwik Chlopicki. He was a Captain in the 1830 uprising and one of the 234 Polish exiles from Trieste. His uncle, General Josef Chlopicki, was Polish dictator at the start of the 1830 Polish uprising. Ludwik was chosen by the Polish Committee to select a site for the Polish land grant in Illinois. According to Edmund L. Kowalczyk, Ludwik was nobility and had a good education. In school, he studied mathematics and drawing (drafting?). Besides Polish, Ludwik could speak French, German, and English.[1386] He lived for a time in Tazewell and Peoria Counties, but most of his time was spent in the town of El Paso in Woodford County. Chicago is about 125 miles to the northeast of El Paso. The present population of El Paso is 2,676.

Woodford County was created from Tazewell and McLean counties on February 27, 1841. Woodford County is located in north-central Illinois, in the center of the state. Hanover is the county seat. The western boundary of Woodford County is the Illinois River. Most of the county was rolling prairie. The wooded areas were either along streams or in small groves. The soil is black or dark brown and up to four feet deep.

The first settler in Woodford County was William Blaylock who came in 1819. At the time, the area was a part of Sangamon County. The earliest settlers claimed he lived like an Indian. Blaylock lived by hunting and fishing and never built a cabin or did any farming. Most of the first settlers were from the states of Virginia, Kentucky, or Indiana. Yankees from New England came soon after them. European-born settlers were from England, Scotland, Ireland, France, and Germany. El Paso Township, where Ludwik lived, had a large number of settlers from Ohio.

El Paso Township was settled later then the rest of the county. The first pioneers always settled in or near the woods, and El Paso Township was almost all prairies. The town of El Paso also had a late start and did not

---

1386 El Paso, Illinois Story: [The Centennial Book of El Paso, Illinois: Sponsored by The El Paso Public Library Board 1954] p. 64.

come into existence until 1856. El Paso grew up around the junction of the Illinois Central, and Peoria and Oquawka Railroads. According to Ethel Eft, the town was laid out before the railroad was finished and the streets already named. The last rail track of the Peoria and Oquawka Railroad was laid out at the junction of the Illinois Central Railroad on April 1, 1856. The first train brought a load of lumber which the Jenkins brothers used to build the first store. At the time, there was one house belonging to Ben Hazlett and a small building where the rail workers lived. The Jenkins brothers would become good friends of Ludwik, and frequently dined at his restaurant. A name for the new town could not be agreed on so the matter was decided by drawing straws.[1387]

Ludwik Chlopicki

Ludwik is still well remembered in El Paso. An entire chapter was devoted to him in the *El Paso, Illinois, Story*. Much of the information for the following story came from chapter 5 of the *El Paso Story*. County histories in both Woodford and Winnebago counties have also written about Ludwik. Each county has a different take on him. In Winnebago County, he is not written about in glowing terms because of the Polish land tract debacle. In contrast, Woodford County histories consider him a colorful figure in the early days of El Paso's history.

According to Bielecki, Ludwik was born October 17, 1789, in Krosno, the province of Braclaw. The region had been a part of the Russian empire since the second partition of Poland in 1793. Braclaw was also known as Lower Podolia. It was located in the southwestern region of the present country of Ukraine. Under Russian rule, Lower and Upper Podolia were combined into one province of Podolia. My ancestors were also from Lower Podolia.

Ludwik enlisted in an Engineering Battalion in 1815. I am not sure if he enlisted in the Russian or the Congress Kingdom of Poland's army. The Congress of Vienna created the Congress Kingdom in 1815. The Russian tsar was the Kingdom's king. Its population was only 3.3 million and its territory encompassed mainly the area around Warsaw. Ludwik left the Army in February 1820, for family reasons. He held the rank of captain.

The Polish rebellion against Russia began in Warsaw on November 29, 1830. Ludwik, along with two others named Kurowski and Olszewski, organized a cavalry and infantry battalion in Podolia. In May 1831, they

1387 Ethel Eft, The Woodford County History: [Bloomington, Illinois: Pantagraph Printing and Stationery Company 1968] p. 52 & 53.

combined their forces with Nagorniczewski's battalion. The combined force then captured the town of Bar, in Upper Podolia. Bar was only held a short time when a large Russian Army appeared and Bar was abandoned. The combined battalions joined up with General Kolyszko's forces and crossed over into Austria. My ancestor Franciszek was in Kolyszko's army.[1388]

My ancestor and many of the officers in Kolyszko's army were arrested. Ludwik, however, managed to get away. He turned up in Warsaw in July and enlisted in General Ramorino's army. By September, the rebellion was about over. General Ramorino's army crossed into Austria on September 16, 1831. This time the Austrian's arrested Ludwik and through him in prison. The rebellion had lasted for a total of 325 days. Ludwik was exiled to America on November 22, 1833, with 233 other Polish exiles. They landed in New York City March 28, 1834.[1389]

The Polish exiles formed a committee on board the ship *Hebe* on April 1, 1834. They decided to petition Congress for a land grant. The exiles hoped to stay together and build a Polish settlement. The committee sent three delegates to Congress with a letter on April 13. The letter explained how and why the exiles came to be here, and their petition for land. On April 27, the letter and petition was introduced to the House of Representatives. President Andrew Jackson signed the bill, known as "Donation of Lands to Polish Patriots" on June 30, 1834.[1390] The exiles were given the option of choosing land in either the territory of Michigan or the state of Illinois.

The Polish Committee selected Ludwik and John E. Prehal to find a site in Illinois for the land grant. Prehal was not one of the Polish exiles, but was probably picked because he could speak good English. Prehal turned out to be a bad choice. He left Ludwig in Illinois and went throughout the country raising donations for the "Fund of the Polish settlement, without the permission or knowledge of the committee's headquarters in New York."[1391] Prehal then took all the money he raised, and went back to Europe.

The *Sangamo Journal* wrote on September 20, 1834, that,

> Three of the exiled Poles, to whom Congress at its last session granted a township of land, arrived at Chicago on the 7th inst. on

1388 Robert Bielecki, Slownik Biograficzny Oficerow Powstania Listopadowego A-D: [Warszawa: Naczelna Dyrekcja Archiwow Panstwowych 1995] p. 289.

1389 Jerzy Jan Lerski, A Polish Chapter in Jacksonian America: [Madison: The University of Wisconsin Press 1958] p. 94 & 95.

1390 Jerzy Jan Lerski, p. 135.

1391 Jerzy Jan Lerski, p. 141.

> an excursion in quest of a location. A public meeting was held in Chicago immediately on their arrival, at which it was resolved "that the hospitality of the town of Chicago, be respectfully tendered through the president of the board of Trustees, to the Polish exiles now in said town." Committees were appointed to receive donations for the benefit of the Poles, to invite those remaining in New York to visit Chicago, and to address a circular to the citizens of this state, soliciting for the unfortunate exiles, their civilities and attentions.[1392]

Ludwik received a similar welcome in Vandalia, the state capitol. The residents of Vandalia had sent a letter to the exiles in May 1834, inviting them to settle in Illinois. Stasik claims the letter contained language like, "Noble descendents of a brave nation come to us. Heroes of freedom come to us, etc.[1393] The citizens of Vandalia also formed a committee to help the Poles. They solicited and received donations of money, grain, livestock, and farming equipment. Ludwik thanked the Vandalia Committee on December 6, 1834.[1394] All support for the exiles stopped when the unfortunate situation of American settlers on the Polish land grant became known.

By the end of November, Ludwik had picked out a site about eighty miles northwest of Chicago in Winnebago County. The site was eighteen miles long and two miles wide and bordered the west side of the Rock River. It was located in Rockford, Owen, and Rockton townships. The site also had some American settlers on squatter title, and a few half-breed Indians on what was known as "Floating Land." According to History of Rockford and Winnebago County, Ludwik stayed at the cabin of Germanicus Kent while he was checking out the site. Germanicus and the other squatters on the Polish site began to have some anxiety about their claims. Ludwik assured the squatters they had nothing to worry about and left to make a report to the land office. Germanicus and the others still had their doubts and the settlers decided to send Germanicus to Washington to defend their claims. Germanicus went before the land commission in Washington but was told, "Every settler in the county was a trespasser, and that he had no legal right to a

---

1392 The Sangamo Journal Newspaper, [September 20, 1834]

1393 Florian Stasik, Polish Political Emigres in the United States of America, 1831-1864: [Distributed by Columbia University Press, New York 2002] p. 65.

1394 The Sangamo Journal Newspaper, [January 10, 1835]

foot of the land which he had so unceremoniously taken."[1395] This would start a struggle over the Polish claim that would not be resolved until 1843.

Lerski writes that about thirty families were living on the site of the Polish tract when Ludwik showed up.[1396] After checking the various Winnebago County histories, it looks like the total number of settlers might have been much less then that. Church claims, the first white settler to Winnebago County was Stephen Mack. He settled in Rockton Township and might have been living on the north end of the Polish tract. Mack was described as a hermit who was married to the daughter of an Indian chief. On August 24, 1834, four more settlers arrived to the county. They were Germanicus Kent, Thatcher Blake, a Mr. Evens, and an unidentified man. This last person could have been Germanicus Kent's slave, Lewis Lemon.[1397] They all settled on the west side of the Rock River.

We the people of Winnebago County adds more. These four immediately went to work and built a twelve by twenty-four-foot cabin for Germanicus. After that cabin was finished, work started on Thatcher Blake's cabin. Jefferson Garner, Squier Garner, and Joseph Garner were next on the scene. They all went to work for Germanicus building a sawmill. Before Germanicus was done building, he would also own a general store, blacksmith shop, ferry, and "primitive hotel, a crude system of banking, and mail facilities of a sort."[1398] A few half-breeds were living on Floating Land in the western part of Rockford Township. Floating land was sections of land (640 acres) given to any half-breed who chose to stay in the county. The half-breeds were members of the Winnebago tribe, which had moved west a few years earlier. Thirty-six half-breeds took advantage of the offer. Only a few were living on the Polish tract however.

These are the only records of anyone living in Winnebago County when Ludwik arrived in 1834. More could have come in the two months prior to Ludwik's appearance. If this was it, Ludwik probably thought he could easily work around the few squatter's claims. Kett claims only eleven people lived in

---

1395 Charles A. Church, History of Rockford and Winnebago County, Illinois: [Rockford, Illinois: W. P. Lamb, Book and Job Printer 1900] [Published by the New England Society of Rockford, Illinois] p. 211.

1396 Jerzy Jan Lerski, p. 141.

1397 Charles A. Church, Past and Present of the City of Rockford and Winnebago County, Illinois: [Chicago: The S. J. Clarke Publishing Co. 1905] [A Reproduction by Unigraphic, Inc. Evansville, Indiana 1972.] p. 6, 7, and 48.

1398 C. Hal Nelson, We The People... of Winnebago County: [Mendota, Illinois: Wayside Press 1975] p. 16.

Rockford before June 1835. Most on the west side of the river. Settlement of Winnebago County did not begin in large numbers until the fall 1835.[1399]

The land tract had to be surveyed before any exiles could settle on it and the surveying took almost all of the year 1835. Stasik claims a hot summer and some type of sickness in the fall slowed down the survey.[1400] The squatters also put up a fight. They had been securing allies in state and federal government. D. A. Spaulding of the St. Louis regional land office did everything possible for the squatters. He hindered the survey and wrote letters to Illinois Congressman William L. May, claiming the citizens of Illinois were completely against the Polish tract. One of Spaulding's letters called the Polish exiles "a gang of morally degraded vagabonds without any qualifications for becoming respectable American citizens." He also claimed that Ludwik ran a brothel.[1401]

Despite all the setbacks, the survey was sent to Washington in the spring of 1836. Secretary of the treasury, Levi Woodbury, had some problems with the survey. He worked them out, though, and the matter went to Congress May 31, 1836. The squatters and their allies managed to drag out the proceedings in the House of Representatives for the rest of the year. All the while, more settlers were converging on Winnebago County. Ludwik knew the county's population was growing fast and tried to make some changes to the land grant. The settlers in Winnebago County were not about to give up their land without a fight. Boies wrote that "numerous little stockade forts were built with loop holes for muskets and a determination was expressed to drive the Polish emigrants out of the country, and they were entirely successful. They never occupied their grant."[1402]

In January 1837, a new problem arose. Two of the half-breed Floating Lands were found to be on the Polish land grant. C. H. Harris, the commissioner of Indian affairs, now got involved. The matter was taken to President Jackson on February 20, 1837. The president sided with the commissioner of Indian affairs. The General Land Office told the Polish Committee they could not select a site with any Floating Lands on it.

[1399] H. F. Kett & Co. The History of Winnebago County, Illinois, Its Past and Present: [Chicago: H. F. Kett & Co. 1877] [Facsimile Reprint, Heritage Books, Inc. Bowie, Maryland 1990] p.235.

[1400] Florian Stasik, p. 78.

[1401] Mieczyslaw Haiman, Z Preszlosci Polskiej W Ameryce: Szkice Historyczne. [Buffalo: 1927] p. 205 & 206.

[1402] Henry L. Boies, History of DeKalb County, Illinois: [Chicago: O. P. Bassett 1868] [A Reproduction by Unigraphic, Inc. Evansville, Indiana 1973] p.84 & 383.

Ludwik had to change the grant again. He made the changes and brought it to the commissioner of the St. Louis regional land office. The commissioner turned down the new proposal claiming it "inadmissible on account of the description being defective, and their not conforming to the legal subdivisions."[1403] The Polish Committee gave up on Ludwik and fired him April 15, 1837. John Rychlicki replaced him. As we will see later, Ludwik must have taken his firing and failure to establish a Polish land grant very hard.

Rychlicki was also one of the 234 Polish exiles from Trieste and was one of the three delegates sent to look for a land grant in Michigan. He made St. Louis, Missouri, his permanent home after leaving Michigan. Rychlicki picked all new land but ran into state politics right away. His new proposal was not sent to Washington until February 1, 1838. Once in Washington, the House Committee on Public Lands never submitted it to Congress for consideration. Meanwhile, the American settlers on the Winnebago County Polish tract were increasing their political influence. New problems also arose in August 1838 on the half-breed Floating Lands. More time was lost waiting for Congress to make a decision.

In the fall of 1839, the Galena District Land Office put all land near the Polish tract for sale. The disputed Rockford and Rockton townships were not included. Rychlicki must have already given up claiming Owen, the middle township. On December 12, 1839, Illinois Senator Richard M. Young proposed to Congress that the Poles had not met the conditions of the land grant and the grant should be forfeited. The Poles still had some influence in secretary of the treasury, Levi Woodbury. Levi Woodbury wrote, "The failure to take possession was more the fault of Congress than of the Poles."[1404]

In 1840, the Polish Committee sent a new proposal to Congress. Nothing became of it. In 1842, Congress finally put an end to the issue and sided with the American settlers. President Tyler signed the act on June 14, 1842. On November 3, 1843, the Polish grant was sold at public sale for one dollar and twenty-five cents an acre. Congress cited three reasons in siding against the Poles.

1. The lack of the second agents (John Prehal's) signature
2. The fact that thirty-eight, and not thirty-six, sections as explicitly provided by the act, were taken for Polish locations
3. That the selections might interfere with the rights of individuals under the preemption laws[1405]

[1403] Jerzy Jan Lerski, p. 149.

[1404] Jerzy Jan Lerski, p. 152.

[1405] Mieczyslaw Haiman, p. 211.

Stasik writes that Ludwik settled in Pretoria, Illinois, after he was fired[1406] The *El Paso, Illinois, Story* wrote that Ludwik applied to become a citizen in St. Louis on April 11, 1835. Ludwik is also on the 1836-37 St. Louis Directory. His occupation is tavern keeper.[1407] Ludwik did not stay in St. Louis for long. His name is listed on the 1840 Tazewell County, Illinois Census.[1408] Tazewell County was a much-larger county when Ludwik lived there. In 1839, three of Tazewell's southern townships were given to Logan County, and in 1841, Mason County was created from Tazewell County. Also in 1841, part of Woodford County was established from Tazewell County. In 1840, Ludwik was living somewhere in Tazewell County, but I cannot say where. Ludwik moved again by 1850, this time to Peoria County. The census lists his age as fifty-five, and occupation victualer ([cook).[1409]

Now we get to Woodford County. According to *El Paso Story*, Ludwik came to El Paso soon after the railroad was built in 1856. George Bestor, the president of the Peoria and Oquawka Railroad, is supposed to be responsible for bringing Ludwik to town. Bestor owned the first restaurant in town, but Ben Hazlett ran it. Bestor hired Ludwik to run the restaurant in 1856. Bestor was supposed to have known Ludwik from Peoria. The 1860 Federal Census of Woodford County shows that Ben Hazlett and his family continued to work and live at the restaurant. Ludwik lived there as well. It was only supposed to be a small one-story building but a nineteen-year-old laborer from Prussia named Anthony Sheitz was also living there in the spare room.[1410] Where did Ludwik sleep, the bathtub?

In El Paso, no one ever called Ludwik by his real name, but only referred to him as the "count." Ludwik was really a baron but somehow got the name of count in El Paso. Supposedly, no one in town even knew his name was Ludwik. They were also skeptical that he was really nobility. In fact, no one knew anything about him or his past. Ludwik never talked about his past and seemed to give everyone the impression that it was better not to ask him about it either! Chapter five of *El Paso Story* is titled for obvious reasons *A Mysterious Old World Stranger.*

The residents of El Paso described Ludwik as quiet, polite, polished, and having perfect manners. Ludwik also refused to call the new town El

---

1406 Florian Stasik, p. 77.

1407 El Paso, Illinois Story, p. 67.

1408 1840 Federal Census of Tazewell County: [At the National Archives, Roll 71 p. 20]

1409 Patricia Combs O'Dell, 1850 Peoria County, Illinois Census: [October, 1972] p. 2.

1410 1860 Federal Census of Woodford County Volume 3: [The McLean County Genealogical Society Normal, Illinois 1994] p. 49.

Paso. There had been disagreement over what to name the town and he preferred to call it "Illinois Junction." Ludwik and his restaurant stuck out like a sore thumb in El Paso. The restaurant was high class, serving "stylish type European dinners, where the table service, food and formal manners confounded some of the less tutored frontiersman."[1411] Despite his ways, Ludwik was friends with most people in town.

Ludwik's restaurant had some very distinguished customers. Richard Cobden, a famous member of the British Parliament, ate there twice. He wrote in his diary, had "breakfast at a little hotel at the station kept by an old Polish refugee called the Count."[1412] William Henry Osborn, president of the Illinois Central Railroad, dined there. George Brinton McClellan, the chief engineer at the Illinois Central Railroad, ate there many times. McClellan is better known as a general in the Union army during the Civil War. The most famous person to dine there was Abraham Lincoln. He stopped there August 28, 1858, two years before he became president.

During the Civil War, Ludwik's restaurant did a good business. Business went downhill after the Civil War when the business section of town moved a block north. The rail depot moved along with it. Three hotels and more restaurants were soon under construction in the new business section. Ludwik's restaurant was now in a bad location. Even though his restaurant was failing, Ludwik refused to move from his old location. He struggled with money problems for the next few years but kept it to himself.

Ludwik died in 1869, and was eighty years old. A friend found him lying dead on the floor of the restaurant. It looks like he died in poverty; no money was found on him, or in the restaurant. There had been a customer earlier in the day, but there was no sign that any struggle had occurred. That customer was never seen in town again.

Ludwik was buried in the family plot of William M. Jenkins in an unmarked grave. Jenkins and his brother were among the first settlers in El Paso and were old friends of Ludwik. The Jenkins brothers built the first store in El Paso. Those attending the funeral wondered if anyone there knew anything about the Count, but all any of them knew was that "he had been a leader of some exiled Poles, and that he must have been in some kind of trouble about which he would never talk, and beyond that they could only wonder what the Count's story might be."[1413] To them, the count was definitely *A Mysterious Old World Stranger.*

1411 El Paso, Illinois Story, p. 58.

1412 El Paso, Illinois Story, p. 59.

1413 El Paso, Illinois Story, p. 64.

This might have been the end of the story. Lucky for us a man named Cassell C. Kingdom took an interest in Ludwik's story in 1952. According to an El Paso newspaper called the *Advertiser*, Cassell was a cashier at the Woodford County National Bank. He was also president of the El Paso Kiwanis Club as well as a history buff. Cassell was with a group of El Paso citizens researching the town's history and came across the count's story. Cassell took an interest in the count's story and decided to find out more about him. He conducted his own research as well as contacting Polish historian's Edmund L. Kowalczyk and Arthur L. Waldo. Kowalczyk had written a small article about Ludwik in Polish-American studies the same year.[1414] Both Mr. Kowalczyk and Mr. Waldo sent what information they had to Cassell.

Cassell was also involved in something else of interest. The count was buried in an unmarked grave. Cassell convinced the Kiwanis Club that the count needed his own headstone. The Kiwanis Club raised enough money to erect a monument to the count. The Kiwanis put up the monument during a celebration at Evergreen Cemetery in 1952. I drove out to El Paso to see the monument and wrote down the words.

Erected by El Paso Kiwanis Club 1952.

In Memory of Ludwik Chlopicki 1789-1869. Baron and Major who sacrificing all in Polands lost struggle for independence in 1830. Was exiled to the United States and became a pioneer El Paso businessman in 1856.

Freedom is not Free.

Ludwik was obviously upset about the outcome of the Polish land grant. He never talked about it to anyone in El Paso. I doubt if anyone could have found a site for the Polish land tract in Illinois. There was too much politics involved, and American pioneers settled faster then the tract could be surveyed. It might have been possible in a state or territory further west or north, but the government only designated a site in Michigan or Illinois

Things did not work out for Ludwik's rival Germanicus Kent either. Germanicus and his partner, Thatcher Blake, are considered the founders of the city of Rockford in Winnebago County. For a time Rockford was called

[1414] Edmund L. Kowalczyk, Jottings from the Polish American Past, Polish-American Studies: [The Polish American Historical Association of the Polish Institute of arts and sciences in America St. Mary's College, Orchard Lake, Michigan Volume ix Number 3 & 4 July-December 1952] p. 88.

Kentville. With all of Germanicus's business interests, you would think he had a great future as a wealthy and influential man in town. It did not work out that way. Germanicus sold too many items to pioneers on credit. A depression occurred in 1837, and they could not pay Germanicus back in cash. Germanicus lost all his business interests and had to move back to Virginia in 1844. He was originally from Virginia. Germanicus died March 1, 1862, in Virginia.[1415]

Only Lewis Lemon, Germanicus's slave, saw his luck change for the better. Germanicus bought Lewis in 1829 in Virginia. Lewis was seventeen years old and Germanicus paid $450 for him. Rather than be sold again, Lewis asked Germanicus to take him north with him. On the way north, Germanicus agreed to set Lewis free in six years and seven months. At that time, Lewis would pay Germanicus eight hundred dollars with 10 percent interest. Lewis, however, managed to pay the amount in four years and four months. Lewis became a free man in September 1839. He bought land in Rockford and made a living by raising vegetables. Lewis died in Rockford in September 1877.[1416]

We have to thank my assistant, Mike Kozuch, of Chicago, for his help in finding the *El Paso Story* for me.

[1415] C. Hal Nelson, p. 16.

[1416] Charles A. Church, Past And Present of the City Of Rockford and Winnebago County, Illinois [1905] p. 48.

Epilogue

The Poles are definitely the first Slavic people in Illinois. They lived in the state since the very beginning and were spread out around the state by the 1850s. Illinois has a little more Polish influence in its early history and genes than previously thought, but it is still small. Many of Illinois's early settlers might have known a Polander. Abraham Lincoln certainly knew a few. Thirty-five Polish exiles from Trieste made it out to Illinois. Almost all their descendants in Illinois do not use a Polish last name because the women descendants are married or the male descendants left the state. It looks like my family are the only descendants of Polish exiles left in Illinois still using a Polish last name, making us the "last of the Mohicans." We're barely hanging on ourselves. There are still a good number of descendants from the first Polish emigrants or families of Polish descent, particularly the Sanduskys and Wodetzkys.

Bibliography

Zabriskie

George Olin Zabriskie, The Zabriskie Family:

Sandusky and Baum

Indianola History Book Committee, The History of Carroll Township 1836-1986: [Danville, Illinois: The Interstate Printers and Publishers, Inc. 1986]

The Past and Present of Vermilion County, Illinois: [Chicago: The S. J. Clark Publishing Co. 1903]

Portrait and Biographical Album of Vermilion County, Illinois: [Chicago: Chapman Brothers, 1889] [Reprinted by Illiana Genealogical and Historical Society, McDowell Publications, Owensboro, Kentucky 1981]

H. A. Coffeen, Vermilion County, Historical, Statisical, and Descriptive: Danville, Illinois:

Katherine Stapp and W. I. Bowman, History Under our Feet, The Story of Vermilion County, Illinois: [Interstate Printers and Publishers, Inc. 1968]

The History of Menard and Mason Counties, Illinois: [Chicago: O. L. Baskin & Co. 1879] [Reprinted by Mason County Historical Society, Havana, Illinois, Whipperwill Publications: Evansville, Indiana 1985]

H. W. Beckwith, History of Vermilion County: [Chicago: H. H. Hill and Company 1879]

H. M. Aiken, Franklin County History: [Evansville, Indiana: Unigraphic, Inc. 1975]

Sue E. Watkins, The Sandusky Story: [At the Polish Museum and Library, Chicago, Illinois 1983]

The Heritage of Vermilion County, Quarterly by the Vermilion County, Illinois Museum Society: [Vol. 33. No. 2 Spring 1997]

Obituary Records from the Scrapbooks kept by Rev. Frank Gilroy of Sidell, Illinois:

Hejnal, Polish American Cultural Society of St. Louis: [Summer 2001]

Orval W. Baylor, Pioneer History of Washington County, Kentucky: [Owensboro, Kentucky: McDowell Publications 1980]

Marsoen Moore Akin, Springs Settlement: [Browning Township] Franklin County, Illinois: [Spokane, Ca.: United Litho 1998]

Joseph Cochrane, Centennial History of Mason County: [Springfield, Illinois: Rokker's Stream Printing House 1876] [Reprinted in 1986 by Havana, Illinois, members of the Church of Jesus Christ of Latter-day Saints]

Joe Jurich, This is Franklin County: [Benton Evening News Print, 1954]

Facts and Findings: [Published Quarterly by Frankfort Area Genealogical Society, West Frankfort, Illinois]

Portrait Biografical Record of Shelby and Moultrie Counties, Illinois: [Chicago: Biographical Publishing Co. 1891] [Reprinted by Shelby County Historical and Genealogical Society, Utica, Kentucky: McDowell Publications]

History of Morgan County, Illinois: [Chicago: Donnelley, Loyd & Co. 1878] [Reproduction by Unigraphic, Inc. Evansville, Indiana 1975]

The Illiana Genealogist: [Published by, Illiana Genealogical and Historical Society, Danville, Illinois]

Adam's County

Carl A. Landrum, Historical Sketches of Quincy, Illinois: [The Historical Society of Quincy and Adams County, 1886]

The History of Adams County, Illinois: [Chicago: Murry, Williamson and Phelps, 1879] [Windmill Publications, Inc. Mt. Vernon, Indiana 1995] [Sponsorship by the Great River Genealogical Society, Quincy, Illinois]

Rev. Landry C. Genosky, The Story of Quincy, Illinois 1819-1860: [Washington, D.C., The Catholic University of America 1949]

People's History of Quincy and Adams County, Illinois: [Editor: Rev. Landry Genosky, O.F.M.] [Quincy, Illinois: Jost & Kiefer Printing Co.]

Alexander County

John M. Lansden, A History of the City of Cairo, Illinois: [Carbondale, Illinois: Southern Illinois University Press
1910] [Reproduced by Duopage Process, Cleveland, Ohio: Bell & Howell]

History of Alexander, Union and Pulaski Counties, Illinois: Editor William Henry Perrin. [Chicago, Illinois: O. L.
Baskin & Co. 1883] [Reprinted bu Unigraphic, Inc. Evansville, Indiana 1969]

Boone County

History of Boone County, Illinois: [Chicago: Munsell Publishing Company 1909]
Jerzy Jan Lerski, A Polish Chapter in Jacksonian America: [Madison: The University of Wisconsin Press 1958]
Past and Present of Boone County, Illinois: [Chicago: H. F. Kett & Co. 1877] [A Reproduction by Unigraphic, Inc. Evansville, Indiana 1973.]

Magazines

The Polish Review, The Polish American Historical Association of the Polish Institute of Arts and Sciences, St. Mary's College, Orchard Lake, Michigan: [Volume xix 1974]
Polish-American Studies, The Polish American Historical Association of the Polish Institute of Arts and Sciences in America St. Mary's College, Orchard Lake, Michigan [Volume iv January-June 1947]

Chicago

Ulrich Danckers and Jane Meredith, A Compendium of the Early History of Chicago in the year 1835 when the Indians left: [Published by Early Chicago, Incorporated, River Forest, Illinois 2000] [Printed by Inland Press, Menomonee Falls, Wisconsin 1999]
Ethnic Chicago A Multicultural Portrait: [Edited by Melvin G. Holli and Peter d' A. Jones] [Grand Rapids, Michigan: William B. Eerdmans Publishing Company 1995]
H. L. Meites, History of the Jews in Chicago: [Chicago, Illinois: Chicago Jewish Historical Society: Wellington Publishing 1990]
A. T. Andreas, History of Cook County, Illinois: [Chicago: A. T. Andreas, Publisher 1884] [The Reproduction of this book has been made possible through the sponsorship of the South Suburban Genealogical and Historical Society, South Holland, Illinois] [A Reproduction by Unigrafic, Inc. Evansville, Indiana 1976]
The People of Chicago, who we are and who we have been: [City of Chicago Department and Planning 1976]
Historic City, The Settlement of Chicago: [Department of Development and Planning 1976]

Howard B. Furer, Chicago: A Chronological and Documentary History 1784-1970: [Dobbs Ferry, New York: Oceana Publications 1974]
Joseph John Perot, Polish Catholics in Chicago, 1850-1920: [DeKalb, Illinois: Northern Illinois Press 1981]
Miecislaus Haiman, Poles of Chicago 1837-1937: [Chicago, Illinois: Polish Pagent, Inc. 1937]

DeKalb County

Lewis M. Gross, Past and Present of De Kalb County, Illinois: [Chicago: Pioneer Publishing Company 1907]
Henry L. Boies, History of De Kalb County, Illinois: [Chicago: O. P. Bassett 1868] [Reproduction by Unigraphic, Inc. Evansville, Indiana 1973]
Jerzy Jan Lerski, A Polish Chapter in Jacksonian America: [Madisn, Wisconsin: The University of Wisconsin Press 1958]
Otto John Tinzmann, Selected aspects of early social history of De Kalb County, Illinois: [Loyola University of Chicago, Illinois Copyright by Otto John Tinzmann 1986]
Helen Bingham, My Scrapbook of Collections and Recollections: [Copyright 1972 by Helen Bingham]

Effingham and Shelby Counties

Effingham County Biographical, [Chicago: Munsell Publishing Company 1910] [Reproduction by St. Clair Chapter DAR. Unigraphic, Inc. Evansville, Indiana 1977]
History of Effingham County, Illinois: [Chicago: O.L. Baskin & Com. 1883] [Reproduction by Ann Crooker St. Claire Chapter Daughters of the American Revolution, Effinghan, Illinois Unigraphic, Inc. Evansville, Indiana 1972]
Portrait and Biographical Record of Shelby and Moultrie Counties, Illinois: [Chicago: Biographical Publishing Co. 1891] [Reprinted by Shelby County Historical and Genealogical Society, Utica, KY: McDowell Publications]
Combined History of Shelby and Moultrie Counties, Illinois: [Philadelphia: Brink, McDonough & Co. 1881] [Reproduction by Unigraphic, Inc. Evansville, Indiana 1974]
Mrs. Isaac D. Rawlings, Polish Exiles in Illinois: [Transactions of the Illinois State Historical Society for the year 1927, number 34] [Danville, Illinois: Danville Printing Co. 1927]

Fayette County

Francis Casimir Kajencki, Poles in the 19th Century Southwest: [El Paso, Texas: Southwest Polonia Press 1990]
Documentary History of Vandalia, Illinois, October 1954:
Historical Encyclopedia of Illinois and History of Fayette County Vol. 1: [Chicago: Munsell Publishing Company 1910] [A Reproduction by Unigraphic, Inc. Evansville, Indiana 1972]

Greene and Jersey Counties

History of Greene County, Illinois: [Chicago: Donnelley, Gassette & Loyd, Publishers 1879] [Reproduced under the sponsorship of The Greene County Historical Society of Illinois by Unigraphic, Inc. Evansville, Indiana 1974]
History of Greene and Jersey Counties, Illinois: [Springfield, Illinois: Continental Historical Co. 1885] [The reproduction of this book has been made possible through the sponsorship of the Greene County Historical and Genealogical Society, Carrollton, Illinois. A Reproduction by Unigraphic, Inc. Evansville, Indiana 1980.
History of Jersey County, Illinois: [Chicago: Munsell Publishing Company 1919] [Facsimile reprint by Higginson Book Company, Salem, Massachusetts 1984]

Hancock County

Thomas Gregg, History of Hancock County, Illinois: [Chicago: Chas. C. Chapman & Co. 1880] [Reprinted by The Anundsen Publishing Co. Decorah, Iowa 1984]
Board of Supervisors of Hancock County, Illinois, History of Hancock County, Illinois 1818-1968: [Carthage, Illinois: Journal 1968]
Theodore Calvin Pease, The Frontier State: [Chicago: A. C. McClure & Co. 1922]

Julian Hulanicki

The History of Lee County, Iowa: [Chicago: Western Historical Company 1879] [Reprinted by Higginson Book Company, Salem, Massachusetts]

Jackson County

Newsome, History Sketches of Jackson County, Illinois: [1894] [Reproduction by Jackson County Historical Society, Murphysboro, Illinois 1987]
Woodson W. Fishback, A History of Murphysboro, Illinois 1843-1882: [Brandon, Mississippi: Quail Ridge Press, Inc. 1982]
J. M. Peck, A. M. A Gazetteer of Illinois: [Philadelphia, Greg & Elliot 1837] [Reprinted by Heritage Books Inc. Bowie, M.D. 1993]
John W. D. Wright, Jackson County, Illinois Residents in 1850: [Carbondale, Illinois: 1972]

Thomas Jaworski

A. T. Andreas, Chicago: [A. T. Andreas, Publisher 1884] [Reproduction by South Suburban Genealogical and Historical Society, South Holland, Illinois Evansville, Indiana: Unigrafic, Inc. 1976]

Jo Daviess County

Philip Williams, Galena, Illinois A Footnote to History: [1941]
A Polish Pioneer's Story: [The Wisconsin Magazine of History, Volume V1 1922-1923] Published by the State Historical Society of Wisconsin, Madison, Wisconsin.
The History of Joe Daviess County, Illinois: [Chicago: H. F. Kett & Co., 1878] [Reproduction by Unigraphic, Inc. Evansville, Indiana 1973]

Lake County

John J. Halsey, A History of Lake County Illinois: [Chicago: Harmegnies & Howell Copyright, 1912, by Roy S. Bates] [Reprinted by Higginson Book Company Salem, Massachusetts]
The Past and Present of Lake County, Illinois: [Chicago: Wm. Le Baron & Co. 1877] [Reprinted by Higginson Book Company Salem, Massachusetts]
Elijah M. Haines, Historical and Statistical Sketches of Lake County, State of Illinois: [Waukegan, Illinois: E. G. Howe, 1852]
Hon. Charles A. Partridge, Historical Encyclopedia of Illinois and History of Lake County: [Chicago: Munsell Publishing Company 1902] [Reproduction by Unigraphic, Inc. Evansville, Indiana 1975]
Jane Snodgrass Johnson, History of Lake County with Biographies: [1939]

Louise A. Osling, Historical Highlights of the Waukegan Area: [Waukegan, Illinois: North Shore Printers 1976]
League of Women Voters of Waukegan and The City of Waukegan Lake County Museum, Waukegan Illinois its past, its present: [Waukegan, Illinois: North Shore Printers, Inc. 1967]
Memories of Mundelein 1909-1984: [Village of Mundelein] [At the Lake County, Illinois Discovery Museum and Library, Wauconda, Illinois]
Village of Hainesville Bi-centennial Commission, Reflections of Hainesville Past and Present: [1976]
Grayslake Historical Society, Grayslake A Historical Portrait: [1994]
Ruth Drummond Mogg, Glimpses of the Old Grayslake Area: [1976]
Bridge to the Past: Wadsworth, Illinois Bicentennial Book: [At the Lake County Discovery Museum and Library: Wauconda, Illinois]
William and Mildred Corris, Russell Illinois 100 years of Memories 1873-1973:
Stephen L. Ragno, Winthrop Harbor and Environs: [Part two Early History 1835-1900]

LaSalle County

La Salle County Lore: [Marilyn Rasmusen, Editor] [Henry, Illinois: M. & D. Printing Co., Inc. 1992]
History of La Salle County, Illinois, Volume 1. [Chicago: Inter-state Publishing Co. 1886] [Reprint by Brookhaven Press, La Crosse, Wisconsin 2000]
The Past and Present of La Salle County, Illinois: [Chicago: H. F. Kett & Co., 1877] [A reproduction by Unigraphic, Inc. Evansville, Indiana 1978]
Elmer Baldwin, History of La Salle County, Illinois: [Chicago: Rand, Mc Nally & Co. 1877] [Reprinted by Higginson Book, Salem, Massachusetts]

Lee County

Memories, Paw Paw 1882-1982: [Paw Paw, Illinois Centennial July 20 25, 1982]
1904 History of Lee County, Illinois: [Edited by Mr. A. C. Bardwell] [Chicago: Munsell Publishing Company 1904]
Frank E. Stevens, History of Lee County, Illinois, Volume 1: [Chicago: The S. J. Clarke Publishing Company 1914]
History of Lee County: [Chicago: H. H. Hill and Company, Publishers 1881]

Logan County

Cecil Calvert Pryor, The Smith-Clark and Seick-Wodetzki-Davis Families: [Kewanee Public Library, 1979]
History of Logan County, Illinois: [Chicago: Inter-state Publishing Co. 1886]
The Namesake Town, A Centennial History of Lincoln, Illinois: [Lincoln, Illinois: Feldman's Print Shop 1953]
Lawrence B. Stringer, History of Logan County Illinois: [Chicago: Pioneer Publishing Company Volume 1 1911][Reproduced under the sponsorship of the Lincoln Public Library, Lincoln, Illinois, by Unigraphic, Inc. Evansville, Indiana 1978]
Theodore Calvin Pease, The Frontier State 1818-1848: [Urbana and Chicago: University of Illinois Press 1918] [Reprinted by the Board of Trustees of the University of Illinois, 1987]

Madison County

History of Madison County, Illinois: [Edwardsville, Illinois: W. R. Brink and Company, 1882] [A reproduction by Unigrafhic, Inc. Evansville, Indiana 1973]

Marion County

History of Salem, Illinois and surrounding Territory: [By the Continental Historical Bureau of Mt. Vernon, Illinois]
History of Marion and Clinton Counties, Illinois: [Philadelphia: Brink, McDonough & Com. 1881] [Reproduction by Unigraphic, Inc. Evansville, Indiana 1974]
J. E. G. Brinkerholl, Brinkerhoff's History of Marion County, Illinois: [Indianapolis, Indiana: B. F. Bowen & Company 1909] [Republished by Marion County Genealogical and Historical Society: McDowell Publications Hartford, Kentucky 1979]
Biographical and Reminiscent History of Richland, Clay and Marion Counties, Illinois: [Indianapolis, Indiana: B. F. Bowen & Company 1909] [A reproduction by The Richland County Genealogical and Historical Society 1987]

Monroe County

History of Columbia Precinct Monroe County, Illinois 1859-1959 and Centennial Celebration Columbia, Illinois July 3-4-5, 1959.

Combined History of Randolph, Monroe and Perry Counties, Illinois: [Philadelphia, J. L. McDonough & Co. 1883]

Morgan County

Poles in the 19th Century Southwest by Francis Casimir Kajencki: [El Paso, Texas: Southwest Polonia Press]
History of Morgan County, Illinois: [Chicago: Donnelly, Loyd & Co. Publishers 1878] [A Reproduction by Unigraphic, Inc. Evansville, Indiana 1975]
A Polish American Letter by Adolph Pazik: [Polish American Studies: Volume iii No. 3-4 July-December 1946]
Morgan County's First Railroad by Virginia Chamberlain: [At Jacksonville Public Library]
Battle of Buena Vista by James Henry Carlton: [New York: Harper and Brothers, 1848]
The Mexican War by Bertha Mason: [At Jacksonville Public Library, Jacksonville, Illinois]
A Polish Chapter in Jacksonian America by Jerzy Jan Lerski: [Madison: The University of Wisconsin Press, 1958]

Montgomery County

Workers of the Writers Program, Hillsboro Guide: The Montgomery News 1940.
History of the City of Hillsboro, [compiled by the Hillsboro Public Library]

Randolph County

Combined History of Randolph, Monroe and Perry Counties, Illinois: [Philadelphia: J. L. McDonough & Co. 1883]
Randolph County Genealogical Society, Randolph County, Illinois Bicentennial 1795-1995: [Paducah, Kentucky: Turner Publishing Company, 1995]

Sangamon County

History of Sangamon County, Illinois: [Chicago: Inter-state Publishing Company, 1881] [Reproduction by the Sangamon County Genealogical Society, Springfield, Illinois: Unigraphic, Inc. Evansville, Indiana 1977]

George R. Stewart, Ordeal by Hunger: [1936] [Copyright renewed by Theodosia B. Stewart]
Mrs. Edna Peddie, 125th Anniversary Riverton, Illinois: 1972
Bruce Alexander Campbell, 200 years, An Illustrated Bicentennial History of Sangamon County: [Springfield, Illinois: Phillips Brothers Inc. 1976]

St. Clair County

Historical Encyclopedia of Illinois and History of St. Clair County Volume 1: [Chicago: Munsell Publishing Company, 1907]
History of St. Clair County, Illinois. [Philadelphia: Brink, McDonough & Co. 1881] [Reproduction by Marissa Historical and Genealogical Society, Marissa, Illinois. [Evansville, Indiana: Whipporwill Publications]
Mrs. Isaac D. Rawlings, Polish Exiles in Illinois: [Transactions of the Illinois State Historical Society for the year 1927] [Danville, Illinois: Illinois Printing Co. 1927]
Portrait and Biographical Record of St. Clair County, Illinois: [Chicago: Chapman Bros. 1892][Reproduced by LBS Archival 1990]
Adolph B. Suess, The Romantic Story of Cahokia, Illinois: [1949]
10. Historical Encyclopedia of Illinois and History of St. Clair County: [Chicago: Munsell Publishing Company 1907] p. 839.

Tazewell & Peoria

History of Tazewell County, Illinois: [Chicago: Chas. C. Chapman & Co. 1879] [Reproduction by Unigraphic, Inc. Evansville, Indiana 1975]
Ben C. Allensworth, History of Tazewell County Volume ii. [Chicago: Munsell Publishing Company 1905] [Reproduction by Whipporwill Publications, Evansville, Indiana 1986]
The History of Peoria County, Illinois: [Chicago: Johnson & Company 1880] [Reprinted by the Print shop, Dixon, Illinois 1981]

Wabash County

Combined History of Edwards, Lawrence and Wabash Counties, Illinois: [Philadelphia: J. L. McDonough & Co. 1883] [Reproduction by Unigraphic, Inc. Evansville, Indiana 1966]
Beulah Lear, A History of Lancaster Area: [1981]

Will County

Lockport Legacy, Themes in the Historical Geography of an Illinois Canal town: [Edited by Michael P. Conzen and Adam R. Daniel] [Chicago: Committee on Geographical Studies, The University of Chicago 1990]

The History of Will County, Illinois: [Chicago: Wm. Le Baron, Jr. & Co. 1878] [Reproduction by Unigraphic, Inc. Evansville, Indiana 1973] [Sponsored by The South Suburban Genealogical and Historical Society, South Holland, Illinois]

Historic City, The Settlement of Chicago: [Department of Development and Planning 1976]

A. T. Andreas, History of Cook County, Illinois: [Chicago: A. T. Andreas 1884] [A reproduction by Unigraphic, Inc. Evansville, Indiana 1973]

Theodore Calvin Pease, The Frontier State: [Urbana and Chicago: University of Illinois Press 1918] [Reproduction by the Board of Trustees of the University of Illinois 1987]

Harold M. Mayer, Richard C. Wade and Glen E. Holt, Chicago: Growth of a Metropolis: [Chicago: The University of Chicago Press]

Winnebago County

The History of Winnebago County, Illinois, It's Past and Present: [Chicago: H. F. Kett & Co. 1877] [Reprinted by Heritage Books, Inc. Bowie, Maryland 1990]

Charles A. Church, Historical Encyclopedia of Illinois and History of Winnebago County Volume 1: [Chicago: Munsell Publishing Company 1916]

Charles A. Church, History of Rockford and Winnebago County, Illinois: [Rockford, Illinois: W. F. Lamb, 1900] [Published by the New England Society of Rockford]

We, the people . . . of Winnebago County: [Edited by C. Hal Nelson and published by the Winnebago County Bicentennial Commission 1975]

Jerzy Jan Lerski, A Polish Chapter in Jacksonian America: [Madison: The University of Wisconsin Press 1958]

Florian Stasik, Polish Political Emigres in the United States of America, 1831-1864: [New York: Columbia University Press 2002] [Copyright by Polish American Historical Association 2002]

Wlodecki

John J. Halsey, A History of Lake County Illinois: [Chicago: Harmegnies & Howell, Copyright 1912 by Roy S. Bates] [Reprinted by Higginson Book Company, Salem, Massachusetts]

Hon. Charles A. Partridge, Historical Encyclopedia of Illinois and History of Lake County: [Chicago: Munsell Publishing Company 1902] [Reproduced by the Libertyville-Mundelein Historical Society, Libertyville, Illinois 1975] [Reproduced by Unigraphic, Inc. Evansville, Indiana 1975]

Jane Snodgrass Johnson, History of Lake County with biographies: [1939]

The Past and Present of Lake County, Illinois: [Chicago: Wm. Le Baron & Co. 1877] [Reprinted by Higginson Book Company Salem, Massachusetts]

Warren Township, A Little History, Past and Present: [Published by Breakfast Exchange Club of Gurnee & Warren Township Historical Society, Printed by Otar Printers, Ltd.]

Edward S. Lawson, A History of Warren Township [Lake County, Illinois] [Published by Warren-Newport Public Library, Gurnee, Illinois 1974]

Annie McClure Hitchcock, Some Recollections of Early Life in Illinois, Lake County in 1840: [at the Warren Township Historical Society] [Hitchcock Papers]

William V. Pooley, The Settlement of Illinois from 1830 to 1850: [Madison, Wisconsin: May, 1908] [Bulletin of the University of Wisconsin # 220] [University Microfilms: Ann Arbor, Michigan 1968]

Louise A. Osling, Historical Highlights of the Waukegan Area: [Waukegan, Illinois: North Shore Printers, Inc. 1976]

Jerzy Jan Lerski, A Polish Chapter in Jacksonian America: [Madison: The University of Wisconsin Press 1958]

Florian Stasik, Polish Political Emigres in the United States of America 1831-1864: [New York, Columbia University Press 2002] [Copyright 2002 by Polish American Historical Association]

Bogdan Grzelonski, Poles in the United States of America 1776-1865: [Warsaw, Poland: 1976]

James S. Pula, Polish Americans, an Ethnic Community: [New York: Twayne Publishers 1995.

Aleksander Jelowicki, Moje Wspomnienia: [Wydanie Czwarte Spolka Wydawnicza Polska W Krakowie 1903]

Waclaw Tokarz, Wojna Polsko-Rosyjska 1830-1831: [Warsaw, Poland: 1959]

S. B. Gnorowski, Insurrection of Poland in 1830-31 and the Russian Rule Preceding it since 1815: [London, 1839]

R. F. Leslie, Polish Politics and the Revolution of November 1830: [Westport, Connecticut: Greenwood Press 1969]

Norman Davies, God's Playground A History of Poland: [New York: Columbia University Press 1982]

Ludwik Kos-Rabcewicz-Zubkowski, Sir Casimir Stanislaus Gzowski: [Toronto. Cananda: Thorn Press 1959]

Henry Krasinski, The Poles of the Seventeenth Century: [London: T. C. Newby 1843]

Encyclopedia of Ukraine, Edited by Danylo Husar Struk: [Toronto: University of Toronto Press]

Ukraine: a Concise Encyclopedia: [Halyna Petrenko, editor] [South Bound Brook, N. J. Ukrainian Orthodox Church of the U.S.A. 1987]

Orest Subtelny, Ukraine: a History: [Toronto: University of Toronto Press 1988]

Encyklopeyja Powszechna: [Warsaw, Poland: 1865]

Magazines

Edward Zalewski, Polish Emigres in the United States in 1835: [Polish American Studies, [Published by The Polish American Historical Association of the Polish Institute of Arts and Sciences in America, St. Mary's College, Orchard Lake, Michigan] Volume 1X, No. 3-4 July-December 1952.

Joseph Wieczerzak, Pre—and Proto-Ethnics: Poles in the United States before the Immigration "after bread." [The Polish Review, Volume XX1, No. 3 1976]

Fr. Ladislas I. Siekaniec OFM, Polish American Teachers 1830-1870: [Polish American Studies] Volume X1X, No. 2 July-December, 1962.

Woodford County

The Past and Present of Woodford County, Illinois: [Chicago: W.M. Le Baron, Jr. & Co. 1878][reprinted by W. H. Perrin and H. H. Hill, Culver, Page, Hoyne & Co.,]

The Woodford County History: [Compiled by the Woodford County Sesquicentennial History Committee] [Bloomington, Illinois: Pantagraph Printing and Stationary Company]

El Paso Story: [The Centennial Book of El Paso, Illinois: Sponsored by The El Paso Public Library Board 1954]

Jerzy Jan Lerski, A Polish Chapter in Jacksonian America: [Madison: The University of Wisconsin Press 1958]

Florian Stasik, Polish Political Emigres in the United States of America, 1831-1864: [New York: Columbia University Press 2002] [Copyright by Polish American Historical Association 2002]